# Essays on Religion, Science, and Society

T0311319

Herman Bavinck (1854–1921)
Graphite Sketch by Erik G. Lubbers

# ESSAYS ON RELIGION, SCIENCE, AND SOCIETY

HERMAN BAVINCK

JOHN BOLT, GENERAL EDITOR

HARRY BOONSTRA AND GERRIT SHEERES,
TRANSLATORS

Baker Academic
a division of Baker Publishing Group
Grand Rapids, Michigan

© 2008 by the Dutch Reformed Translation Society
P.O. Box 7083, Grand Rapids, MI 49510

Published by Baker Academic
a division of Baker Publishing Group
P.O. Box 6287, Grand Rapids, MI 49516-6287
www.bakeracademic.com

Paperback edition published 2011
ISBN 978-0-8010-4867-8

Printed in the United States of America

The Library of Congress has cataloged the hardcover edition as follows:
Bavinck, Herman, 1854–1921.
    [Verzamelde opstellen. English]
    Essays on religion, science, and society / Herman Bavinck ; John Bolt, general editor ;
Harry Boonstra and Gerrit Sheeres, translators.
       p.  cm.
    Includes bibliographical references and indexes.
    ISBN 978-0-8010-3241-7 (cloth)
    1. Christianity. I. Bolt, John, 1947– II. Title.
BR123.B34513 2008
230—dc22                                          2007040631

# CONTENTS

# Editor's Introduction

Like his sixteenth-century spiritual forefather John Calvin, Herman Bavinck (1854–1921)[1] was first and foremost a son and servant of the church, dedicating his energy, his genius, and his remarkable intellect to knowing God better and helping God's people to witness more effectively to their world. But, also like Calvin, Bavinck believed that Christian renewal was not restricted to the church; the whole person in the totality of human experience, including life in society, was called to obedience before God (*coram deo*). As this English translation of a collection[2] of Bavinck's occasional writings on religion, science, and society goes out into the world, it is worth recalling Bavinck's first visit to North America, to the Fifth General Council of the Alliance of Reformed Churches holding the Presbyterian System meeting in Toronto, Ontario, Canada, on September 21–30, 1892. At this assembly Bavinck gave a keynote address with this far-reaching title: "The Influence of the Protestant Reformation on the Moral and Religious Condition of Communities and Nations."[3] Less than a year earlier at the First Social Congress held in Amsterdam, November 9–11, Bavinck had provided a discussion paper on what at that time was referred to as "the social question" with this all-encompassing

1. This introduction is not a full biographical commentary on Herman Bavinck, only an introduction to the significance of this volume. For a more comprehensive treatment, see the introductory essay in this volume by Bavinck's childhood friend, Henry Dosker, and my Editor's Introduction in any one of the four English volumes of *Reformed Dogmatics* (Grand Rapids: Baker Academic, 2003–8).

2. Aside from the Editor's Introduction and Henry Dosker's biographical sketch of Bavinck, this volume is a complete translation of the Dutch collection *Verzamelde opstellen op het gebied van godsdienst en wetenschap* (Kampen: Kok, 1921). The original foreword by Bavinck's brother, the Rev. C. B. Bavinck, is provided in appendix A, pp. 279–80.

3. The speech is recorded in the Proceedings of the Fifth General Council of the Alliance of Reformed Churches holding the Presbyterian System (London: Publication Committee of the Presbyterian Church of England, 1892), 48–55.

visionary title: "According to the Holy Scriptures, what general principles govern the solution of the social question, and what pointers are provided for the solution in the concrete application of these principles that is given for the people of Israel in Mosaic law?"[4] These two titles tell us much about the man, his faith, and his profoundly catholic, Reformed, Christian vision.[5]

The Dutch Reformed Translation society was established in 1994 by people who believed that the Dutch Reformed confessional and theological tradition contained a treasury of material that would bless the worldwide church if it could only be made available in the dominant language of modern world communication. Our first project was to translate the major work of the greatest Dutch Reformed theologian, Bavinck's four-volume *Reformed Dogmatics*, into English with the hope that the work of translation would be carried on further by the worldwide church. That has come to pass: the *Reformed Dogmatics* is now being translated into Korean, Portuguese, Indonesian, and Italian. Bavinck's extraordinary gift as a theologian is reflected in the fact that one hundred years after it was written, the *Reformed Dogmatics* remains timely and speaks directly to issues the church faces at the beginning of the twenty-first century.

This volume of essays demonstrates that good theology is not restricted to private matters of personal piety and faith but has an essential public dimension. The Triune God, who saves us through the work of Christ and incorporates us into the body of Christ, the new people of God, by the powerful work of the Holy Spirit, is the same God who is Creator of heaven and earth. We are able to distinguish different works in the economy of the Triune God, but we may never separate them. Salvation does not take us out of creation or elevate us above it but heals and restores creation's brokenness. In theological terms, grace opposes sin, not nature; grace does not abolish nature but restores it.[6]

It is the insistence on taking creation seriously as God's revelation without in any way diminishing the necessity of biblical revelation as the key to understanding it that is the hallmark of Bavinck's writing on matters of religion, education, science, and society. In the remainder of this introduction,

4. "Welke algemeene beginselen beheerschen, volgens de H. Schrift, de oplossing der sociale quaestie, en welke vingerwijzing voor de oplossing ligt in de concrete toepassing, welke deze beginselen voor Israel in Mozaïsch recht gevonden hebben?" in *Proces-verbaal van het Sociaal Congress, Amsterdam, November 9–12, 1891* (Amsterdam: Höveker en Zoon, 1892), 149–57. This was the same congress in which Abraham Kuyper delivered his famous address later published as *The Problem of Poverty* (Grand Rapids: Baker Academic, 1991), and the same year Pope Leo XIII issued his encyclical *Rerum novarum*.

5. The fullest expression of Bavinck's vision in a single essay is likely his "The Catholicity of Christianity and the Church," trans. J. Bolt, *Calvin Theological Journal* 27 (1992): 220–51.

6. For an excellent summary of Bavinck's distinctive Reformed understanding of the relation between nature and grace, see Jan Veenhof, "Nature and Grace in Bavinck," trans. Al Wolters, *Pro Rege* (June 2006): 10–31.

I shall briefly highlight four closely related themes that recur in the fifteen essays of this volume: biblical faith, revelation, and religion; Christianity and the natural sciences; Christianity and the human sciences; Christianity and politics/social ethics.

Unlike Karl Barth in the twentieth century, for example, Bavinck had no qualms about considering Christianity as a *religion* that on a formal level shares characteristics with all religions. In particular, the phenomena of revelation and faith are common to the religious life of all people (chap. 1). In the center of the human person, integrating all our faculties and diverse expressions, is what the Bible calls the *heart*, the locus of a seed of religion (*semen religionis*) or sense of divinity (*sensus divinitatis*). In his works, God is present to all people; the world is the theater of his glory; the human heart responds in faith activated by grace or in rebellious, inexcusable unbelief, but it cannot avoid responding. We humans are inescapably and incurably religious.

What is distinctive about the Christian religion is that it comes to us as a message of grace in Jesus Christ. A Christian is not just someone who knows something about God in general, but also one who believes everything promised in the gospel. The Christian faith is not a matter of subjective feeling or moral doing, but a confident trust that in biblical revelation we have been given the saving *knowledge* of the one true God in the person and work of Jesus Christ.

From this it follows that the essence of Christianity (chap. 2) cannot be found in religious experience, even if sought in the experience of the historical Jesus (Schleiermacher, Harnack), or in the reduction of the historical Jesus to an idea (Strauss, Hegel), or in Christlike moral practice (Kant, Ritschl). No, only when the believer acknowledges that Jesus Christ in his person and work is the way, the truth, and the life; only when we know him to be the subject and object of our faith, the center and core of the gospel message itself—only then are we Christians. That is the essence of the matter.

Two additional things flow from this: religious studies, including the philosophy of religion (chap. 1) and the psychology of religion (chaps. 4, 9, 10, and 11), provide useful and important insights for Christian theology, but Christian theology must be clearly distinguished from and never folded into religious studies (chap. 3). In these essays, Bavinck shows himself to be extraordinarily well-informed about the latest scholarship in these matters and also very politically and culturally aware of what was happening in his nation and in Europe more broadly. Bavinck's observations and insights into such matters as the relation between will and understanding (chap. 11), the unconscious (chap. 10), and matters of education and pedagogy (chaps. 12 and 13) remain invaluable introductions to important issues that still vex us today.

Not only the human sciences (*Geisteswissenschaften*) of psychology and pedagogy—not to mention beauty and aesthetics (chap. 14), subjects on which one might at least expect a theologian to be minimally knowledgeable—but also the natural sciences receive profound treatment in Bavinck's capable hands. In addition to the straightforward treatment of evolution and development (chap. 6), which provides useful pointers to how Christians should still frame the debate today, Bavinck gives us a remarkable treatment of the topic of Christianity and the natural sciences from the political side of matters in colonial education of all things (chap. 5). That this thoughtful and thorough treatment of a very complex scientific and political matter reflects Bavinck's own public career as a member of the First Chamber in the Dutch Parliament makes this all the more remarkable. It is hardly the sort of careful and informative speech that we are accustomed to as part of our political and scientific rhetoric. More is the pity for us.

The most challenging for us, and perhaps the potentially most rewarding essays, in my judgment, are the three sociopolitical essays in chapters 7, 8, and 15. The treatment of the two Genevan reformers named Jean (Calvin and Rousseau) is fascinating, informative, and profoundly challenging to many of our contemporary commonplaces, especially the notion of equality. Be prepared to be provoked in these chapters; pay careful attention to the biblical thoughtfulness and sound reasoning. Here too, the issues Bavinck dealt with then are still with us. What we lack is the kind of biblical wisdom and historical awareness that Bavinck enjoyed in great measure. We are blessed to be able now to share them also in the English language.

English readers can be grateful to the D. R. T. S. and Baker Academic for this enriched portrait of Bavinck as a social philosopher, someone knowledgeable in the latest developments in psychology and pedagogy and culturally attuned to the spirit and spirits of his age. He was indeed the master theologian of the *Reformed Dogmatics* and is rightfully renowned for that. However, he was also more, much more as these essays show. Gratitude is also due to the competent work of translators Harry Boonstra and Gerrit Sheeres, whose fluency in French and German as well as Dutch and English was required for this volume. Boonstra is the translator of chapters 1–3 and 11–15, Sheeres of chapters 4–10. Both men also checked each other's work for accuracy and consistency. The original foreword by C. B. Bavinck, Herman's younger brother, was translated by the editor. The editor was also responsible for updating the footnotes to twenty-first-century standards and for, wherever possible, correcting errors. In some instances it was not possible to trace and fully check a reference to an obscure journal; these were left as originally given and marked with an asterisk (*). In addition to Bavinck's own notes, additional explanatory notes by the editor are clearly marked. Page numbers to the original Dutch edition are set in square brackets within the text.

Bavinck's thought has been my companion in the academy and the church for thirty years. That has been a rare privilege. With gratitude and joy I join those whose work has made it possible for these essays to reach a wider audience and bless many more.

Grand Rapids
Anno Domini 2007

# HERMAN BAVINCK

## A EULOGY BY HENRY ELIAS DOSKER

In these latter days the great leaders of Calvinism have all been swept away
in a comparatively short space of time. Gone is that dour Scotsman, Doctor
James Orr, who struck such mighty blows in defense of the Scriptures. Gone
is Doctor Kuyper, that matchless leader of men, a genius of the first rank,
recognized as such the world over, and yet in his faith as simple as a little
child. Gone is our own unique leader, Doctor B. B. Warfield, incomparable
as a teacher, tireless as a student and author, consistent in his sturdy faith,
the greatest of all leaders of American Calvinism. And gone last of all, but
not least, is a man who was buried at Amsterdam on August 2, 1921, Doctor Herman Bavinck, whose deep researches, tireless industry, boundless
horizon, wide variety of interests, and stirring eloquence made him the pride
of the Reformed Churches of the Netherlands and a leader of worldwide
Calvinism.

Of all these great scholars and leaders, Bavinck's scholarship was perhaps
the broadest and technically the most perfect. But it is impossible, at least at
this distance in time, to make a comparison, in any way adequate or reliable,
between Kuyper and Bavinck or Bavinck and Warfield. The law of perspective forbids it. Each had his own peculiar points of excellence and also his
own peculiar limitations; none of them could have occupied the place of the
other. We might be surer of our ground had Kuyper left a well-worked-out

From *Princeton Theological Review* 20, no. 3 (1922): 448–64, with minor style changes. This article
can be found online at http://scdc.library.ptsem.edu/mets/mets.aspx?src=BR1922203&div=5&img=1
(accessed August 11, 2007).

magnum opus on theology. It was in his mind to do so, but he never accomplished the task. The same is true of Doctor Warfield, and therefore the real data for comparison (*data comparationis*) are lacking.

What Luther and Melanchthon were in the German Reformation, Kuyper and Bavinck were in the Neo-Calvinist period in the Netherlands. Each supplied what the other lacked. And both will shine with added luster as the distance that separates them from us increases.

Herman Bavinck was my lifelong friend, and I have written this brief sketch with the thought that it may serve as a friend's tribute to his memory. We studied together in the gymnasium of Zwolle and have been separated since 1873, but the tie of friendship remained unbroken; during all these well-nigh fifty years, almost to the time of his death, we corresponded, and our repeated visits, on either side of the Atlantic, deepened our friendship. Besides this, I have been a constant reader of his writings and gladly admit that he was my preceptor as well as my friend. As I set myself to the task of writing this sketch of the life of a truly great man, it seems best to etch his life with a few strokes of the pen and then make an attempt at analyzing his character as a theologian: his personality, methods of work, and variety of interests.

In this life no one stands by himself. Seething and struggling in our veins are innumerable physical and intellectual traits, as bequeathed to us by preceding generations. I admit at once that in some respects, viewed from the standpoint of his parentage, Doctor Bavinck is a conundrum. He was so like and yet so absolutely unlike his parents. His father, Reverend Jan Bavinck, was born at Bentheim, in Hanover, in 1826; his mother was Gesina Magdalena Holland of Vrieseveen, in the province of Drenthe. The older Bavinck was one of the epigoni, if not one of the founders, of the Free Church of Holland, which separated itself from the State Church in 1834. Sent by the few persecuted and hounded Separatists of Bentheim to Holland for his theological education, he must have been a phenomenal student, and must also have enjoyed considerable earlier advantages, for in the small theological seminary at Hoogeveen, where he went, he took over the classes in Latin, Greek, and Hebrew. And he must have been a considerable Latinist, for Doctor Bavinck years later committed to him the final revision of the *Synopsis purioris* (1880); as the son testified, his father "made many corrections."

Wherever he went, the elder Bavinck always remained a teacher. He had a perfect love of teaching (*amor docendi*) and proved to be a most acceptable teacher. When he went to Hoogeveen, he assisted Rev. W. A. Kok, the head of the small theological school from which he had graduated, as second docent; and when in 1854 the educational interests of the Free Church were unified and a more pretentious institution was established, the elder Bavinck was the first to be nominated by the General Synod as one of the professors. Was it his innate modesty, his underestimate of his own powers, that pessimistic view of things, which ever sees lions in the way, of which his illustrious son also had a share? Who can tell us? He made the lot settle the matter and declined the call.

I knew both the parents of Doctor Bavinck intimately. They were typical of their environment and cherished all the puritanical and often provincial ideas and ideals of the early Church of the Separation. Simple, almost austere in their mode of life, exhibiting something of what the Germans call *Kultur-feindlichkeit* (hostility to culture), they were pious to the core, teaching their children more by example than by precept. The mother was uncommonly clear-visioned in her ideas and never afraid to express them; the father was diffident, aroused only with difficulty, but then evincing rare power. Such were the parents of Doctor Herman Bavinck. The pulpit was his father's throne, and there he displayed what his son once, in my hearing, described as a "healthy mysticism." He knew how to "speak comfortably" to Zion. Many of the qualities of mind and heart and intellect, which later distinguished the great son, were therefore evidently inherited from his parents. But, as I have said, in many respects he differed from them.

Herman Bavinck received his early training in the Hasselman Institute, a private training school of great celebrity. In 1870, with my brother and myself, he entered the gymnasium of Zwolle, of which Doctor E. Mehler, a converted Jew and celebrated Graecist, was the rector. After his graduation he spent a single year at the seminary of Kampen, and then, obeying an ir-resistible impulse, despite universal and bitter opposition, he sought regular university training. It was a daring move. Of all places, he went to Leiden, where the celebrated Doctor Kuenen, one of the most influential of the Higher Critics of the nineteenth century, was then the leading professor. Doctor J. H. Scholten was still there, the founder of that new system of Reformed theology, of which reason, determinism, and monism were the main pillars. But Scholten was beyond his prime and no longer swayed the hearts of the students as of yore; his was a setting sun. Prins was there, the archenemy of the Separation, and [L. W. E.] Rauwenhoff, one of the fathers of modernism; Tiele and Oort, de Goeje and de Vries, Pluygers the Latinist and Cobet the marvelous Greek scholar.

What an environment for a son of the Churches of the Separation! And Bavinck had been so thoroughly grounded in the old simple faith of the Reformed doctrine! But he came to seek after truth and in God's wise plan it was just this environment and this training that was to fit him for his life task. But he had many a bitter struggle at Leiden. Kuenen especially, with his "heart of gold," was his idol among his professors. I remember his let-ters of that period, his description of serious doubts and questionings and battles; but all these struggles only tested and purified his faith. Beloved of all his teachers, he left the university with the degree of Doctor of Theology, June 10, 1880, after writing a thesis on *The Ethics of Zwingli*. The absolute fairness and objectivity of this work explains many things in his later life. It is certain that nowhere else in his later writings is the subconscious influence of Kuenen—not, of course, his uncompromising antisupernaturalism, but his scientific method—so palpably felt as here, both in the method of approach and in the treatment of his subject.

Most valued of all the gains that came to him in Leiden was the lifelong friendship of his fellow student Snouck Hurgronje, who later became a distinguished Semitic scholar, succeeded de Goeje as professor of Arabic in the University of Leiden in 1906, and is widely known as one of the very few Christians, who, in disguise, have succeeded in penetrating the holy precincts of Mecca and lived to tell the tale. The two supplemented each other; through all their student days, they were like David and Jonathan, and the tie between them was broken only by Bavinck's recent [1921] death.

Returned to Kampen, Doctor Bavinck at once presented himself for examination by the seminary authorities. Because of his university training, this naturally was more carefully conducted than in ordinary cases, but he passed with the highest honors. And wherever he went, till his death, he remained a loyal son of the Church of the Separation of 1834.

For a brief interval of two years he became pastor of the Church of Franeker, a mere episode in his life. Twice in succession he declined the call to the recently founded Free University of Amsterdam, because he had decided to identify himself fully with the hated "Seceders." The two years spent at Franeker were golden. He there acquired a full mastery of the art of preaching, and he learned to understand the viewpoint of the common people and to appreciate the practical side of the ministry. The church was always crowded to the doors, for people came from great distances to hear him. Small wonder, for he was indeed a princely preacher; with wonderful depth of analysis and the profoundest reverence for God's holy Word, he spoke with rare simplicity and a thrilling eloquence all his own.

In 1882, the General Synod called Doctor Bavinck to the vacant chair of dogmatics in the seminary at Kampen. He accepted and began his work on January 10, 1883, with an oration on *The Science of Sacred Theology*, defining its principle, content, and aim. This address was heard with breathless attention. It struck a new note in the history of the seminary and of the church. It heralded the dawn of a new day. And every eye was fixed on him as the coming man. Said Doctor Kuyper in *De Heraut* (January 21, 1883): "Now this is really scientific Reformed Theology. Here the first principles are again correctly set forth; here a road is staked out which may lead to an excellent development. . . . I have hardly ever read a treatise with such undivided attention, from start to finish, as this inaugural." And the great leader did not exaggerate nor miscalculate the future. For the next twenty years Doctor Bavinck was the soul of the seminary. Kuenen once said of Leiden, "Leiden is Scholten," and for these two decades, "Bavinck was Kampen," its pulsing heart, its irresistible dynamic, lifting the whole plane of teaching from the mediocre and ultrapractical into the academic sphere of scientific idealism. Every teacher felt this influence, all later-comers modeled as much as possible after the new pattern, and the whole school was lifted on the shoulders of this Atlas. What Kampen is today it owes, under God, to Bavinck's presence and influence.

Bavinck was naturally the hero of the students. As I write, before me lies a sheaf of testimonies, too long to quote, to his rare ability and inspiring power as a teacher, all written by students who sat under him in these glorious days. He was only thirty-five years old when he began his work at Kampen, but he carried an old head on young shoulders. He had read deeply and widely to an astonishing degree, as all his published works testify. In those fruitful Kampen years he wrote and published the first edition of his magnum opus, *Reformed Dogmatics*, in four volumes, later expanded and republished in the Amsterdam period of his labors. His life knew no wasted moments. He wrote a steady stream of brochures on various subjects as he staggered along under an almost insupportable burden of occupations. One does not wonder that at last he sank under the load, but rather that he held out so long.

His university training had lifted him out of the narrow groove in which nearly the entire ministry of his church, as well as the mass of its members, was moving. Their *Weltanschauung* was practically that of the old Dutch Anabaptists, who sought their strength in separation from the world, in its cultural, social, and philosophical aspects. And Doctor Bavinck was a white raven among them. He dressed differently, spoke differently, taught differently—he was a man apart. And that very thing attracted his students and made him so mighty a factor in the cultural advance of the church that he loved and for which he labored so assiduously for the next two decades.

Bavinck had a thoroughly disciplined mind, yet with the heart of a child. God's holiness on the one side, human sin on the other, and between these forever the mystery of the cross. All his teaching, all his preaching, all his writing was shot through and through with the richness of divine grace as revealed in Christ. Says one of his disciples: "He never preached a sermon in which Christ was not glorified." As a preacher he was a constant pattern for his students, as to both form and substance. Doctor W. H. Gispen, one of the foremost preachers of the Church of the Secession and one of its choicest spirits, has said of the preaching of Doctor Bavinck: "That which unspeakably enthralls and attracts in Bavinck's preaching is the simplicity, the clearness, the sharp definition of ideas, and the logical progress of his reasoning. . . . His thorough apprehension of his subject in its fundamental aspects and content enables him to speak about it so easily and intelligibly to others."

At Kampen he lectured on dogmatics, ethics, the history of philosophy, encyclopedia, psychology, rhetoric, logic, and aesthetics. The undermanned condition of the seminary was responsible for this multiplicity of labors and variety of subjects. One marvels how he found time in this period of his life to prosecute his studies and to write as voluminously as he did. Meanwhile God had given him a wife and helpmeet in Johanna A. Schippers, daughter of a typical representative of the Dutch higher middle class, well educated and fully able to stand by his side, who shared his triumphs and trials to the end. He was now in the full flush of mature manhood, an acknowledged authority in his chosen field, known far and wide through his writings and, with the single exception of Doctor Kuyper, the most widely recognized leader of the Free Churches of the Netherlands. And now came the greatest crisis of his life.

Under the leadership of Doctor Kuyper, in 1886 a new secession from the State Church had occurred. They called themselves *Doleerenden*—a Church under the Cross—and they sought rapprochement with the Free Churches of 1834. The training for the ministry proved to be the crux of the whole question. Was that training to be free, or was it to be under the control of the church? To us the answer seems easy; not so for university-trained Dutchmen. Bavinck's position on this question was predetermined by his own experience. He loved the freedom of scientific study and doubted the right of the churches to make a demand, of which the founders of the church in the days of the Reformation had never dreamed; but he also loved his own church and thus was placed in a most difficult position. I have neither time nor space to enter into a full discussion of this crisis. Suffice it to say that it was decisive for his later career. Together with his colleague and bosom friend Petrus Biesterveld, he was called to the Free University of Amsterdam, and both accepted. Thus he left the Kampen seminary, where he had passed the best years of his life, to begin his labors in an entirely new field.

During these twenty years he had been ceaselessly at work. His doctoral thesis on *The Ethics of Zwingli* (1880) had been followed the next year by the sixth edition of *Synopsis purioris theologiae*, which he managed. In 1883 appeared his *Science of Sacred Theology*; in 1884 *The Theology of Doctor Chantepie de la Saussaye*; in 1888 *The Catholicity of Christianity and of the Church*; in 1889 *Eloquence*, a treatise on the art of speaking; in 1894 *Common Grace*; in 1895 his *Reformed Dogmatics* (now in its third edition); in 1897 *Principles of Psychology*; in 1901 *The Sacrifice of Prayer*, a practical and experimental treatise on the Christian life; and in 1901 *Creation or Evolution*.[1] Besides this he had written a mass of ephemeral literature, had for a time edited *de Bazuin* (*The Clarion*), the denominational paper, and had with Doctor Kuyper and Doctor Rutgers prepared a revised edition of the Bible, which purified and modernized its diction. As he removed from Kampen,

---

1. Ed. note: The English translation is *Creation or Development*, trans. J. Hendrik de Vries (1901).

he carried with him the sweetest memories of what had been, as one of his friends describes it, "the glory period of his life."

In the Free University he succeeded Doctor Kuyper, and great as Doctor Bavinck was, he was able to hold his own only by reason of the total dissimilarity of his talents from those of his great predecessor. Again, let me say, it is practically impossible to compare these two great leaders. It may be done later, or it may forever be out of the question. Only this may be said, though with great hesitation: I have read the writings of both for years, I admire them equally, and I feel deeply indebted to both of them in many ways. But it seems to me that in breadth of accurate scholarship, Doctor Bavinck may have excelled Doctor Kuyper, while Doctor Kuyper excelled Doctor Bavinck in giving definite conclusions and daring utterances. The one gently tries to untie Gordian knots; the other cuts them through with mighty blows of his keen sword. Says one competent to judge, "Bavinck was an Aristotelean, Kuyper a Platonic spirit. Bavinck the man of clear conception, Kuyper the man of the glittering idea. Bavinck built on historical data; Kuyper speculated with intuitively conceived ideas. Bavinck was in his thinking principally inductive, Kuyper deductive."

What a wonderful pair they were! Rarely has God given to an institution two such men to teach sacred theology. But so much is certain—the task of Doctor Bavinck, in entering the Free University of Amsterdam in 1902, was a far greater test of his capabilities than his entrance into the Kampen Seminary in 1882; and with it the second great period of his life begins.

Do I imagine that after 1902 a different note was sounded in his letters? Did he ever regret the change? In leaving Kampen, he had to rend in twain bonds of love that had been growing ever stronger with the passing years. In one way he gained much by the change; in another he lost something. At Kampen he had stood forth as preeminent; at Amsterdam he was one of many unquestionably erudite teachers, all of whom had enjoyed the same advantages that he had. But at Amsterdam his position was more commanding, his sphere of influence wider, his words carried farther. "Give me a fulcrum," said Archimedes, "and I will move the world." How true it is!

On Wednesday, December 17, 1902, he began his work at Amsterdam with an oration on *Religion and Theology*, a model of its kind, which gives the reader some conception of the vastness of his learning. Yet he was deeply conscious that he was to sit in a chair, as he said on that occasion, "which these many years had been filled by the most richly talented and most many-sided man, whom God in the last half century has given to the professors of his name in these lands." It was a heavy task that was laid on his shoulders.

At Amsterdam Doctor Bavinck taught dogmatics, philosophy, and ethics. His mind had now attained its full maturity. The experience of Kampen was repeated here in the deep impression he made on his students and colleagues. He was greatly respected by an increasingly growing circle of men

of standing in the community and in the whole country, and his ripe scholarship was recognized on all hands. And as he grew in power, he also grew
in modesty—at least his letters seem to indicate that; and what is more, his
faith grew ever more simple. Perhaps the greatest thing he ever said was the
simple statement, made at the close of an address of congratulation in his
own home, on the occasion of his silver jubilee as professor of theology: "*I
have kept the faith.*" That was great! To have drunk deeply at every fountain,
to have weighed all the evidence to a degree possible only to a mind as acutely
trained as was his, to have scanned the whole horizon of philosophical and
theological debate, and then at the end of years, to be able to say these simple
words! And thus he remained to the end. About this time he wrote me, "As
I grow older my mind turns more and more away from dogmatic to philosophical studies, and from these to their application to the practical needs
of the world about me."

In the same year in which he began teaching at the university, his *Heden-
daagsche moraal*, a study in contemporary ethics, appeared; two years
later came his *Christian View of the World*, and his *Science from the Christian Standpoint*. In this period also his interest in Christian education,
always one of the foundation stones of the Free Church movement, began
to deepen. In 1904 he published his *Pedagogic Principles*, and soon he
gained the front rank among the promoters of this cause and became an
unquestioned authority on pedagogy. In 1907 his dispassionate discussion
of evolution—*Pro et contra*—attracted wide attention. Besides all these
smaller works, in 1907 he published his second major work *Magnalia
Dei*, and a year later his Stone lectures on the *Philosophy of Revelation*.
His interest in educational matters continued unbroken to the last, as
witnessed by his *Manual for Training in the Christian Religion* (1913),
*Training of the Teacher* (1914), *Education of Adolescents* (1916), and *New
Education* (1917). And in the last year of his active life, he published a
volume on *Biblical and Religious Psychology* (1920). Thus he was engaged
in the Master's business till the end.

The war sorely tried him. In 1918 he wrote a letter which reads like a
sob. Said he, "Our modern civilization is dead. It will take a century before
it regains its poise." New problems arose on every hand. In the face of the
strongest opposition, he had the courage to publish a volume on *Woman in
the Modern World* (1918), in which he unequivocally defended woman suf-
frage. He was forever at work teaching, writing, lecturing, preaching, in all
parts of the country. Wherever an educational convention met, he was sure
to be among the leaders; at the General Synod his advice carried the utmost
weight. And at one of these meetings came the beginning of the end. At the
Synod in Leeuwarden in 1920, at the close of a masterly address, he sank
down in his chair and was compelled to leave the meeting. His work was
finished. It was the touch of death.

For months he struggled against the deadly heart attack, but neither love nor medical skill was able to avert the inevitable. He fell asleep in Christ July 29, 1921. When questioned whether he feared to die, he said, "My dogmatics avails me nothing, nor my knowledge, but I have my faith, and in this I have all." And another time, "I have one wish, but it cannot be fulfilled; and it is this: that when I have entered the heavenly glory, I might be permitted for a moment to return to this world to testify before all God's people and even before the world to that glory." He died as he had lived, a simple child of God. Now he rests from his long and arduous labors, and many of the riddles that staggered him here below are clear and illumined by the light of the throne of God.

Physically Doctor Bavinck was an imposing figure. As I remember him as a youth, he was tall and slender with wavy light hair and clear friendly gray-blue eyes. Even then there was something aristocratic in his appearance, wholly apart from what his parentage and early training could have suggested. As he grew older, he grew portly, which gave him a still more impressive appearance. Physically, mentally, and temperamentally, he stood in a class by himself. One of his friends, I think, expressed things correctly when he said: "Doctor Kuyper was the man of the common folks [de kleine luiden], who from day to day, in his Standaard articles and asterisked paragraphs, quickened the interest of the common people. Bavinck was the aristocrat of the spirit, who from time to time, in masterly orations, alike chaste in form and rich in content, threw his searchlight on the big things of life. Kuyper was always at the head of his hosts; Bavinck fought an independent battle."

The outstanding characteristic of Doctor Bavinck was his modesty. He utterly forgot himself. He hated fulsome praise. All the silly mouthings, so often bestowed on popular favorites, were abhorrent to him. He was modest, as all truly great men are, because he knew full well that with all his attainments, he had only lifted the tip of the veil of the great truth he was searching out. His was the glory of infinite pains. He was a tenacious friend. Once let a man enter his heart, and he would never show him the door. Yet his temperament forbade him to be too lavish with his gifts, so he had many friends and but few intimates. The greatest among the latter undoubtedly were Snouck Hurgronje and Petrus Biesterveld, whose early death he bitterly lamented. He was retiring by nature, almost to shyness. His fund of small talk was limited and drawing-room repartee easily bored him. Though his pulpit or platform vocabulary was limitless, he seemed to be lacking in words on trivial occasions. His true life was that of the study: his books were his best friends.

And yet as modest and retiring and self-contained as he was, fires were burning underneath the outward calm, which at times burst into bright flame. Take what happened on the day when he had successfully passed his candidate's examination. Under the new law of April 28, 1876, the old "grades" were abolished so that the successful student received a simple certificate.

But the theological faculty was still permitted, in exceptional cases, to give a "cum laude." Snouck Hurgronje was examined the day before Bavinck and received his certificate; Bavinck's brilliant examination, the next day, brought the exceptional "cum laude." Believing an injustice had been done his friend, Bavinck, when the diploma was handed him, threw it on the table and asked the professors either to strike out the "cum laude" or to tear up the whole paper, after which he left the room abruptly. Fortunately the professors, who loved and admired him, saw what was wrong and advised him to take a long rest before he resumed his work. But the "cum laude" remained, one of the few cases in which a Leiden student has been so honored.

His mentality was marvelous. Few men have a mind as adaptable as his. He might have excelled in almost any branch of study. A wonderful linguist, a leading star in the field of dogmatics, great as a philosopher, an authority in pedagogy, wonderfully human in his contact with everyday life, and tenderly moving when he touched the Christian experience—he was indeed gifted above ten thousands.

His absolute fairness to an opponent sometimes created the impression of indecision, but those who accused him of this weakness were utterly mistaken. Read his *Reformed Dogmatics*, and you stand amazed at the wealth of information here displayed and at the breadth of horizon of the author. It is a history of dogmatics as well as a dogmatics itself. Every tendency and every error that has appeared in the long history of the church is put to the touchstone of the truth. If there is a ray of light, an atom of truth, it is gladly recognized; Bavinck becomes dogmatic only when he has penetrated to the very foundations of a truth and speaks from the standpoint of a clear vision. He never makes the mistake of placing an exclamation point where he sees, however faintly, a question mark. That made him sometimes hesitate where others were enthusiastically confident, but it was the hallmark of his true greatness. Those who criticized this apparent indecision did not know him. He was honest with the truth as he was honest with himself; and because he loved it so, he searched for it so diligently and expounded it insofar as he had clearly apprehended it.

In his later years, as has been indicated, Doctor Bavinck paid marked attention to philosophical studies, to educational matters, and to social questions; it seemed to some as if the new love was crowding out the old one. But he lived and will live preeminently in the field of dogmatics. Calvinism, or rather Neo-Calvinism, has lost in him one of its greatest leaders; as it looks today, no one can fill his place. He was a Calvinist by both training and deepest conviction and taught its fundamental principles with incomparable clearness and power. The formal principle of the Reformation, the absolute authority of the Holy Scriptures, was the cornerstone of all his theology. How wonderful is that chapter in his *Dogmatics* on the "principium externum," how sharp his distinction between religion and revealed religion: "In the one, human seeks God; in the other, God seeks human. And it is that seeking which makes revelation necessary."

Doctor Bavinck strenuously upholds the central and organic conception of revelation. It occupies a definitely teleological position; it reveals to us the coming of God to humanity, forever to dwell with humankind. How sharp are his definitions, how keen his antitheses! Frequently his style is epigrammatic, vivid, and picturesque. As has been said he places himself foursquare on the doctrine of inspiration. But he is unafraid of all critical attacks on the Scriptures. These are to be expected "because the writings of prophets and apostles originated in, not *outside*, the sphere of history. . . . In entering into a human, the Holy Spirit entered into his style and language and intellectual equipment." Hence the diversity but also the organic oneness of the Scriptures. Striking in Bavinck's theology is the comparison between the incarnation of the Logos in the flesh and that of the Holy Spirit in the word.

How Bavinck makes all doctrine to live! In reading his *Dogmatics*, one can easily see how his students must have been carried away by his lectures. Theology was to Bavinck more than a science, more than a full concept of the teachings of the Scriptures, systematically arranged and philosophically expounded. The grace of God, a living faith in the Scriptures as principium, a hearty assent to their truth—all this was a prerequisite to its teaching and exploration. And every page of the *Reformed Dogmatics* indicates how true the great teacher was to his own principles. Of him as of Paul, it might well be said, he brought every thought into captivity to the obedience of Christ. This explains his uncompromising attitude toward rationalism. The latter, we are told, "must inevitably end in the bankruptcy of theology." In these days of rationalistic exploitation of the truth, we hear a great deal of "a static theology," and we are looked on as examples of arrested development. How Doctor Bavinck lashes that idea! He views theology as an organism always expanding, so long as the fullness of the Word is not exhausted. *God*, not *religion*, is the object of theology. Forgetting this, men have lost themselves in mazes of what is called the science of comparative religion, and they have cut themselves loose from Christian theology. And this theology has for its only object to learn more and ever more of God, whom theology possesses by faith. The service of God, both with heart and intellect, is the aim of all true Christian theology.

In these days we are frequently told that science is exact and built on facts, while the theologian builds his science on faith. Doctor Bavinck admits that God belongs to the invisible world and as such may be unknowable to science, but he warns the scientist against the maxim "All the invisible is unknown." Accept this maxim, and what remains of ethics, psychology, philosophy, even of natural science itself? Every science ultimately rests on and demands faith. The claim that Christian theology is unscientific is therefore absolutely denied.

I wish I had time and space to follow Doctor Bavinck through his *Reformed Dogmatics*. He is always the man of highest culture and sweetest spirit, always recognizing what is good in an opponent, lucid in treatment of doctrine, careful in definition, sparing of denunciation, clear in conclusions. As I said before, he never rants: in his system are no vehement explosions, no bitter attacks. He is ever the man of endless erudition, new and old, and he uses his information in the most judicious way.

Conservative? Absolutely so. But how? Listen:

> Theology is truly conservative; it accepts the inheritance of past generations, yet not to scatter it but to hand it over, if possible increased and still more "reformed," to the generations that follow. Theology receives these acquired treasures, not to cast them again and again into the melting pot of criticism, but to hand them over to us to see whether we also, as mightily as in former days, may experience their truth and beauty in our own souls. It is a mere illusion always to try to find something new in the field of theology. The glittering results of nature studies may have led many theologians to try to find novelties in the theological field, but disappointment has always punished such curiosity. But at the same time theology is a progressive science. Reverencing the past, theology builds upward on the foundations that are laid, till theology itself is complete and has attained its final object. Theology does not rest at Chalcedon or Dordt. Theology holds the conviction that it will please God to cast ever more light on the Holy Scriptures in days to come, on what till now was dark or nebulous in them. Till then theology has not completed its task or attained its object.

Such was the theology of Doctor Bavinck! It is to be deeply regretted that his *Dogmatics* was not translated into English,[2] but the task is Herculean: very few men have the idiomatic knowledge of both tongues to make it a success, and *no translation is far better than a poor one.*

Great honors were heaped on Bavinck. The queen of Holland knighted him with the Order of the Dutch Lion; he was made a member of the First Chamber of the States General, was a member of several scientific societies, and was sought after everywhere and always as a public speaker.

He appeared where no member of his church or faculty would have been invited. Thus he addressed the "Scientific Society," on July 7, 1915, on the "Doctrine of the Unconscious," and again delivered an oration before the eighth "Dutch Philological Congress" on "The Conquest of the Soul." Some timid souls saw in this universality of interest a sign of weakness, an attempt to hold out a hand to the common foe. In reality it was a mark of his true greatness. His was a Johannine soul. When he died, he left no enemies. Friend and foe alike mourned him when he was taken home.

Presbyterian Seminary of Kentucky, 1922

---

2. Ed. note: It took nearly a century, but Dosker's lament is now answered. All four volumes of Bavinck's *Reformed Dogmatics* have been translated into English, published by Baker Academic (2003–8).

# 1

# Philosophy of Religion (Faith)

[9] The title of the subject briefly discussed here requires further explanation in order to avoid misunderstanding. One can understand the genitive ("of religion/faith") in such a way that it is subjective, in which case "philosophy of religion/faith" is a philosophical view that finds its origin in religious faith, and is governed by it from beginning to end. But "of religion/faith" can also be an objective genitive, and then the reference is to a philosophical view about religion/faith itself—in the first place, about the essence and nature of religious faith [*fides qua creditur*]; and second, about the object or content of religious faith [*fides quae creditur*]. In this essay the title has the second meaning; the intent is to consider briefly the essence and object of religious faith.

Such a consideration of religion/faith has become especially necessary because the Reformation gave a different meaning to faith than was customary before that time. In Roman Catholic theology the view of faith was and is very simple: it generally is the acceptance of a witness on the basis of the trustworthiness of the spokesman, and it retains this meaning also in the religious arena. It is true that an operation of the Spirit is necessary to illumine the mind and to bend the will. Still, faith is and remains an

Ed. note: Originally published in 1918 in *Annuarium* of the Societas Studiosorum Reformatorum (Rotterdam: Donner, 1906), 62–72. The original title of Bavinck's essay is "Philosophie des geloofs [Philosophy of Faith]." For the sake of clarity and consistency of usage (also see the source note to chap. 3), the term is translated as "philosophy of religion," which, as the conclusion of the essay shows, is Bavinck's proper subject. In order to retain as much of the original as possible, we will at given points use a double term such as "religion/faith" or "religious faith."

activity of the mind. It exists in the acceptance of and agreement with God's truth as contained in Scripture and tradition, on the basis of the inerrant authority of the church. That is why faith is not sufficient for salvation, for the reception of saving grace. Faith is only one of the preparations for baptism, in which grace is conveyed, and it must be completed by love and good works.

The Reformation, however, presented a completely different view of faith. [10] Even though faith could properly be called knowledge, it was, as Calvin said, still more a matter of the heart than of the mind. According to the Heidelberg Catechism, faith is not only a certain knowledge by which I hold everything that God has revealed to us in his Word to be true, but also a firm trust that not only others, but that I too have been given forgiveness of sins, eternal justification, and salvation, granted by God out of grace.[1] Faith thus received from the Reformers a unique, independent, *religious* meaning. It was distinguished *essentially* from the faith of which we speak in daily life, and also from historical and temporal faith, or faith in miracles. It was not just an acceptance of divine truth, but it also became the bond of the soul with Christ, the means of fellowship with the living God.

However, this view gave rise to various very difficult questions. What is the nature of this knowing that is mentioned first as an element of faith, and what is its content? What is the nature of the trust that, second, describes the essence of faith? Does this trust really and from the beginning include the assurance that God has granted me personal forgiveness of sins, eternal justification, and salvation? How can we make it clear to ourselves and to others that faith is knowing as well as trusting, that it is at the same time a matter of the head and of the heart? And what is the relationship between these two—do they just stand next to each other, or are they intrinsically connected? Do they both come from the same source and foundation? If so, what do they have in common? Which is the higher, or rather, the deeper synthesis that incorporates both of them? All these questions have been discussed at length in both scholarly and popular writings, but up to the present day the views about the essence of faith remain widely divergent in both scholarly and pious circles.

In everyday life a lack of a solution to these questions was even more sad. When the struggle of the Reformation was past and the enthusiasm had cooled, the two elements of faith were pulled apart more and more. On the one hand, a cold orthodoxy emerged that interpreted faith only in terms of doctrine, and on the other hand, a Pietism that valued devoutness above truth. This dualism in religion, church, and theology was strengthened by the twofold orientation of the newer philosophy that, after Descartes and Bacon, eventually ended up in dogmatism and empiricism.

1. Ed. note: Lord's Day 7, Q & A 21.

[11] It was Immanuel Kant's goal to reconcile this philosophic dualism. Although he was an adherent of the Enlightenment, he did undergo a remarkable change, especially under British influence. During his study of the natural sciences, he came under the allure of mechanical explanation of natural phenomena, especially as this was held as the ideal of science by Isaac Newton. In epistemology, Kant was especially influenced by the criticism in Britain, notably by David Hume, so that he turned his back on dogmatism and became convinced that rationalism in theology and metaphysics was untenable. From now on, according to Kant, genuine scholarship/science was possible only in the world of phenomena. The transcendental and supernatural world are inaccessible to the human mind; all proofs adduced for the supernatural end up in an antinomy.

However, Kant was too religious, or at least too moral, to be satisfied with the results of his theory. He could not surrender faith in himself: faith in the moral worth of each human person that transcends the whole world. If this faith was not to be a chimera, then it had to rest on another, firmer foundation than the cogent reasons and proofs of rationalism. Kant discovered such a better foundation for faith in the writings of Rousseau. Also a son of the Enlightenment, Rousseau for a time was friendly with the Encyclopedists. However, in 1749 a tremendous change took place in his life.

The Academy at Lyon had announced a writing contest with this question: Has scientific and artistic progress contributed to the impoverishment or the improvement of morality? During a walk, Rousseau learned about this contest in the *Mercure de France*, and suddenly a new light dawned on him. He saw another world, and he became another person. Suddenly he became conscious of the deep and sharp contrast between nature and culture that was evident in his time. From that point on he became the enthusiastic preacher of the gospel of nature and a living protest against the Enlightenment, as the father of Romanticism. In his teaching about society and state, education and religion, he turned from the corrupt culture of his time to the truth and simplicity of nature. In all areas, the historical had to make room for what was originally given, [12] [abandoning] decaying society for innocent nature, positive Christianity for natural religion, the false reasons of the mind for the impulse of feeling. Certainty about the truths of religion was also to be found in feeling. Rousseau does make use of rational arguments to prove the existence of God, the freedom of the will, and the immortality of the soul. However, for him these arguments are subordinate and of incidental worth. For him the final certainty of these truths of the faith are not to be found in the theoretical but in the practical sphere, in the original and immediate witness of feeling that is deeper and much more reliable than the reasoning mind. Each person is assured in his heart about a supersensory world.

Rousseau's influence on his contemporaries and their descendants was overwhelming. Lifestyle and clothing were reshaped according to his example.

His thoughts about inequality among people became the material from which communist and socialist systems were built. Without Rousseau, France would not have had a revolution. Modern teachings about religion, morality, and education are permeated by his spirit. The philosophy of Kant, Fichte, and Jacobi; the Romanticism of Schlegel and Tieck; the theology of feeling of Schleiermacher—all these have been influenced by his ideas. The practical orientation of Kant's religious philosophy is especially reminiscent of the teaching about feeling on which Rousseau had built religion.

But Kant was not a person of emotions and therefore could not identify positively with Rousseau's thoughts. He did, however, learn one thing from Rousseau, that religious truths possess a different certainty for people than truths of the mind or reason, of science or philosophy. For Kant this insight provided spiritual liberation, the freeing from an oppressive restraint. If religion and morality really contain their own certainty, then metaphysics does not need to provide all kinds of proofs for God's existence, the freedom of the will, and the immortality of the soul. Moreover, science could then freely go its own way and be bound only by its own character and laws. Criticism also would have freedom to investigate the most sensitive topics, without having to fear negative results. Morality and religion would then have their own foundation and would be safe and secure from all attacks of science.

For Kant this foundation was not feeling (as with Rousseau), [13] but practical reason, the moral nature of man. In his conscience, man feels himself bound to a categorical, unconditional, absolute imperative. The "thou shalt" of the moral law supersedes all considerations and excuses, and demands the whole person for itself, always and in all circumstances. Here a power arises in man himself that is far above all other powers in nature. As a moral creature, man is therefore a citizen of another, higher order than nature; he belongs to a kingdom of invisible elements that exceeds all earthly treasures. If this moral world order is to be true reality and not an illusion, and if it is to triumph one day over all that is great and strong and mighty in this world, then man must be free in his actions and his soul must be immortal to receive his reward in the hereafter, and God must exist in order to reconcile in eternal harmony the terrible opposites between virtue and luck that exist on earth. These are not conclusions legitimately deduced from preceding scientific premises, but they are postulates put forth by man according to his moral nature. He cannot prove, he cannot demonstrate, that it is all true, but he is subjectively certain of it; he believes and acts as if it were true; he does not *know*, but he *believes*, and he has moral grounds for his belief. Kant therefore gladly relinquished knowledge about religious and moral matters, because he had found another, safer place for faith.

All those who join Kant in this transition from theoretical to practical reason go, as a matter of principle, in the direction that is usually called "ethical"[2] in religion and theology, in metaphysics and philosophy. First, they limit knowledge to what the senses can observe, and last, they see the only basis for faith to be in a supernatural order. However, "ethical" includes many differences of insight and views among the followers of this orientation. In his negative views, Kant agreed with Rousseau, but in his positive views he went in a totally different direction. In the same way Schleiermacher mainly agreed with Kant in epistemology, deducing that man cannot know the absolute psychologically because of the limitation of human knowledge, but with Fichte he also deduced this lack philosophically from the infinity of the absolute. Schleiermacher, in distinction from Kant, held that willing and acting and knowing do not disclose the supersensible world, because this willing also moves in opposites and never reaches unity. [14] This unity, this oneness, of thinking and being in the absolute can be experienced and enjoyed only in feeling, which precedes thinking and willing and is completely independent of absolute power. But whether one goes in Kant's moral (ethical) direction or in Schleiermacher's mystical direction, in both cases one is in direct opposition to Hegel. Elevating reason to a cosmic principle, Hegel recognized the essence of things in self-moving thought and considered religion, just like art and philosophy, to be a developmental stage in the movement of absolute spirit.

However, all these orientations, the ethical and mystical as well as the speculative, suffer from a significant one-sidedness. By limiting religion to one human faculty, they diminish man's universal character. They divide man in two and separate what belongs together. They create a gulf between religion and culture, and they run the danger of reducing religion to moral duty or aesthetic emotion or a philosophic view. But according to the Christian, confession religion is other than and higher than all those views; religion must not just be *something* in one's life, but *everything*. Jesus demands that we love God with all our heart, all our soul, and all our strength. In our thinking and living, there can be no division between God and the world, between religion and culture; no one can serve two masters.

Therefore, if we want to do full justice to religion, we must return to the central unity in man that is the basis for differentiating his faculties and which in Holy Scripture is often designated the heart, from which proceed all expressions of life in mind, feeling, and will. Reformed theologians sought that central point for religion in (as Calvin called it) the seed of religion [*semen religionis*] or sense of divinity [*sensus divinitatis*], and in the Christian

---

2. Ed. note: The Dutch word *ethisch* not only refers to the moral/ethical realm but also applies to an entire school of nineteenth-century Dutch Reformed theology (founders: Daniel Chantepie de la Saussaye [1818–74]; Johannes Hermanus Gunning [1829–1905]) that accented the personal, existential relationship with Jesus over that of doctrine and confession. In that context *ethisch* has the weight of "existential." When referring to Kant later in this paragraph, Bavinck uses *ethisch* in a more restricted *moral* sense and there has distinguished it from the mystical sense.

religion theologians went behind faith and conversion to regeneration, which in principle is a renewal of the whole man. When they took a position in this center of man, they saw opportunity to avoid all one-sidedness of rationalism, mysticism, and ethicism, and to maintain that religion is the animating principle of all of life.

In due time, under the operation of word and Spirit, conversion comes from this new life that is planted in regeneration. Conversion affects the will and emotions, and faith comes to the level of consciousness. [15] With this point of view, all reasons to rob faith of its genuine character and to change it into a mood or inclination disappear. One can then, without danger of error, describe faith as a habit or act of consciousness because it arises out of regeneration [and] is always a loving faith in principle distinguished from what is [popularly] called "faith." Faith is the light that comes to one's life, because it is born from this life. It is not a blind faith forced by authority, but a free deed from the new life that is born from God and reaches out to have fellowship with God.

The advantage of this view, which teaches that faith maintains its own character, is not trivial. It is noteworthy that the Christian religion, as taught by Holy Scripture, has called this action of regenerated consciousness "faith," not feeling or experience. There must be a reason why the word "faith" is chosen for this activity of the Christian and is kept in all the confessions. That reason must be that the Christian faith is not a mood, inclination, or sensation, but binds us to an object and thus protects us from dangerous subjectivism.

That object to which the faith of the Christian is bound is, generally speaking, the revelation that God gives us of himself, the witness that proceeds from all his works, and the Word through which he speaks to us. Faith and revelation, revelation and faith belong together. Just as light and eye, sound and ear, the known object and the knowing subject correspond to each other—in the same way faith in our soul responds to God's revelation in his works. They are made for and intended for each other.

This revelation of God to which faith responds is detected most fully in all the works of his hands, in all of nature, in all of history, in the totality of the universe. If we could see properly, we would be able to see God's revelation everywhere, because he is and works everywhere; God is not absent anywhere. In him we live and move and have our being. The pious person sees God everywhere—within and outside of himself, in his heart and consciousness, in the leading of his life, in the blessings and catastrophes that come to him. There is nothing that is apart from God in our small and large worlds, nothing that does not ultimately carry the stamp of his glory.

However, this view does not deny that there are a variety of differences in the revelation of these all-encompassing works of God; the unity includes great and rich diversity. Centrally and finally this revelation comes to us in the person of Christ, and in the Word that testifies about him. Revelation then becomes a revelation of grace. In the Christian religion we do not just find revelation and faith in general, but grace and faith in a special sense that correspond to each other. [16] The Christian must believe everything promised in the gospel. Revelation, grace, and promise are the content of the gospel, and it is only a childlike faith that can gratefully accept and appropriate these benefits from God.

Thus the Christian faith has not only its own origin but also its own object: a word, a witness, a benefit, a gift, a promise from God to which it cleaves, by which it is encouraged, and to which it abandons itself with complete trust, in need and in death. This faith is not only a subjective mood or experience; it includes knowledge—knowledge of the one true God in the face of Jesus Christ, whom he sent. Such knowledge is life and light, grace and truth at the same time.

# 2

# THE ESSENCE OF CHRISTIANITY

[17] The question about the essence of Christianity first arose in rather recent times. Until about the eighteenth century, no one felt the need to instigate a special search into the essence of the Christian religion. People enjoyed the possession of Christianity and felt completely at home in the singular view in which the church to which they belonged had formed itself within that Christianity. For everyone, Christianity was identical with the dogma, the worship, and the governance that was found in one's own religious denomination. Whatever departed from that was impure and mixed with smaller or greater errors.

However, during and after the Reformation various confessions, churches, and sects continually increased, launching a different view about Christianity. Reformed and Lutheran orthodoxy soon made a distinction between fundamental and nonfundamental articles of faith. The theologians from Helmstad returned to the Apostles' Creed. Biblical scholars claimed to find true Christianity in New Testament teaching which, according to their idea, was obtained by an exegesis independent of church doctrine. Deists and rationalists judged that the essence of Christianity was to be found only in the doctrines proclaimed by Jesus that corresponded to reason and were also discovered by reason, or at least could be discovered by reason.

In all these views, the essence of Christianity was sought especially or exclusively in doctrine. A change in this came through Schleiermacher. In

Ed. note: Originally published in 1906 in *Almanak* of the Free University of Amsterdam Student Body (NDDD), 251–77.

accordance with his thought that religion is seated not in the mind and the will but in the emotions and in a feeling of complete dependence, he taught that Christianity was not knowledge or action but that its distinguishing mark was to be found in a singular relationship with Christ as Redeemer. Christ was our Redeemer, not through what he taught or did, but through what he was, through this complete and unremitting God-consciousness. [18] Christ felt complete dependence on God, the full fellowship with God was continually present, and thus the essence of religion was completely fulfilled. From this, Christ derived strength to create and strengthen in us that feeling of dependence, those religious feelings: by taking us up into his communion, he leads us to communion with God. In Schleiermacher's construction of the essence of Christianity, one finds at least this positive element: the person of Christ again came to the foreground.

Actually, Kant had already perceived in the person of Christ the example, the symbol, the representative of the idea of a humanity pleasing to God. It is true that Kant held that faith in the historical appearance of this idea about Christ had no significance for salvation, but he did propose it and posited a certain connection between this idea and the person of Christ, although it was only a historical connection.

The historical appearance of Christ was of more significance in the philosophy of Schelling and Hegel. For Schelling, Christ was the one in whom the incarnation of God, begun in creation, came to its highest revelation and realization. And since Christ embodied the unity of divine and human, when he became the head of a congregation, all the members of the congregation had to embody this unity in the same manner. But while Schelling incorporated this unity in the process of development, Hegel let it become more complete in the area of consciousness. Christ was the God-man, because he was most conscious of this unity and expressed it most clearly.

In the first half of the nineteenth century, under the influence of all these men, the essence of Christianity was sought primarily in the person of Christ. Christ possessed this oneness of God and man either as the first one conscious of it and proclaiming it or as the first one to realize it in himself. The difference between these two approaches came to light especially in 1835, when Strauss, drawing the consequence from Hegel's philosophy, pronounced that the idea "does not like" to pour out its total fullness into one individual.

[19] Thus Strauss consciously and deliberately raised the problem of the relationship between the idea of a God-humanity union and the historical person of Christ. But the significance of Strauss was even greater in another area. Until then only philosophy had dealt with the question, but now, because of Strauss, historical criticism entered the discussion. Who Jesus was became a purely historical question and must be answered by a study of sources, especially of the Gospels. Strauss himself held that a sharp distinc-

tion must be made between the historical person of Jesus and the Christ of the congregation.

Jesus alone was the occasion through which the idea of God-humanity entered the consciousness of the congregation. Inspired by this idea, the religious fantasy of the congregation—aided by subconscious, symbolic inventions and messianic predictions—clothed the historical person of Jesus as the Christ of faith. The Christ figure is a creation of the congregation.

The arguments with which Strauss defended this interpretation of the original Christ soon proved to be untenable, but the thought that the Christ figure is a product of the congregation continued to dominate in many theological circles up to this day. However, if Jesus was not personally and in truth the Christ, then the Christ figure (which the congregation had in sight from its beginning) must of course be explained in a different manner and from other influences. Exceptional effort has been expended in the search for the origin and composition, the affinity and difference among the Gospels. All kinds of factors were called on to make the origin of the Christ figure in the congregation comprehensible. In turn scholars proposed influences from the Old Testament, Judaism, the Essenes, the Talmud, Hellenism, Persia, India. Recently the Babylonian-Assyrian interpretation of Christianity is in fashion. Not only scenes from the book of Revelation and elements in the theology of Paul and John but also all events in the life of Jesus, his preexistence, birth, baptism, temptation, exaltation, miracles, resurrection, ascension—all these are drawn from mythological views. A single feature of correspondence, a brief expression, an innocent word—all these are often sufficient for the proponents of the history-of-religions [*religionsgeschichtliche*] method to imagine historical dependence.

Some went so far as to deny that Jesus can be known from the sources, [20] or they even cast doubt on Jesus's existence. Even those who do not go so far are still far apart in how they picture him. One counts Jesus as a moral reformer, a preacher of humanity, who resisted all externals in religion and founded a purely internal and spiritual religion. Another sees in him a forerunner of socialism, who protected the poor against the violence of the wealthy and mighty. For a third, Jesus is the preacher of Buddhist individual redemption, who counts all culture as evil and wants to lead people back to the truth and simplicity of nature. Each has his own view about the person of Jesus. There is much truth in Kalthoff's mockery of the Professor-Christ, who appears very differently at one university than in another, and yet this image is presented to the common people as the ideal example, as the way, the truth, and the life.

Among those who recently have spoken about the essence of Christianity, no one has been more prominent than the well-known professor from Berlin, Adolf Harnack. In the winter of 1899/1900, his lectures on this subject were heard by a great number of students from all disciplines; these lectures created great interest in many circles and called forth enormous response when they were published.[1] On the one hand, there was great agreement among Harnack's sympathizers, many Jewish scholars, and some Roman Catholics, such as A. Loisy. This group lauded the book about the essence of Christianity as a deed of great courage, as a personal confession, as a ripe fruit of theological scholarship, as a provision for the needs of the present time, as the most fortuitous reconciliation of modern science and the Christian faith. But the moderate and strong orthodox asserted that in this work Harnack simply revealed himself as a proponent of liberal theology and as an opponent of ecclesiastical Christology. Christianity as advocated by him was robbed of its very core; it was a Christianity without the Trinity, without Christ, without reconciliation, without church and sacrament. In his view, the spirit of the times, religion as a private affair, and natural religion of the eighteenth century celebrated their triumph.

Whoever knows Harnack's lectures is not surprised by these different judgments, because according to him the essence of Christianity consists in deriving the experience [*Erlebnis*] that God is their Father and they are his children from the appearance, teachings, and life of Christ. For the [21] moral person, there is a deep conflict between the visible and the invisible, the external and the internal, the body and the spirit, this world and the afterlife, between God and the world. But the Christian religion lifts the person above these painful opposites. It places him on God's side, provides him eternal life in this life, and creates a relationship and communion between God and the soul. The Christian religion does this because it always proclaims the fatherhood of God and the nobility of the human soul, and in these two truths the Christian religion declares itself completely. Therefore, not the Son but the Father belongs in the original gospel as proclaimed by Jesus. Jesus did not proclaim himself, he did not demand faith in his person, he did not have a Christology. The poor publican, the woman putting her mite in the treasury, and the prodigal son all show this sufficiently.

However, this does not take away that for others Jesus, through his completely unique knowledge of God, through his person and word and deeds, truly is the leader to God and the way to the Father. Thousands have come to God through Jesus. He was the personal realization and the power of the gospel, and he remains such until today. The personal life in us derives its being only from his personal powers. Harnack does not explain how Jesus received this completely unique knowledge of God by which he obtained such an eminent place. He appeals only to the mystery of personality. But we come to such communion with God, to peace of soul, to conquest of the world solely in the way of faith in the gospel of Jesus. However, this faith consists not in the acceptance of doctrine, because the gospel is not a doctrine but a joyful

1. Ed. note: A. von Harnack, *What Is Christianity?* trans. Thomas Bailey Saunders (New York: Harper & Brothers, 1957).

message; it consists in moral experience, in doing the will of the Father, in a life in keeping with the gospel of Jesus, in a personal experience of the soul, which is created in us through his appearance, his word, and his life.

Whoever begins research into the essence of Christianity must first understand the task he undertakes. We noted above that the question about the essence of Christianity first arose in modern times. Indeed, the question was first considered when a breach was created between church dogma and personal faith, when the subject could no longer agree with that view of Christianity that was honored in the confession and worship of the church. This fact sheds surprising light on the intent with which a search [22] for the essence of Christianity was initially begun. Those who insisted on such a search were those who could not agree with the church's view of Christianity. They were of the opinion that the church had assumed features in its confession and worship that supposedly did not belong to the essence of Christianity. Under the influence of Greek philosophy, pagan superstition, political thirst for power, and all kinds of other factors, the churches had imported many doctrines and ceremonies that had nothing to do with real Christianity. That is why it was necessary to free Christianity from all those strange additions and to conceive it in its original purity.

Thus the search for the essence of Christianity was originally prompted by a protest against various, supposedly false, interpretations that had been produced by the official churches in their confessions. And these searchers had no other objective than to place beside and over against the incorrect view of Christianity in the churches another, purer view that did more justice to Christianity. The search for the essence of Christianity is thus simplified and clarified, because it really comes down to this question: What is the true, genuine, inerrant, that is, original Christianity?

If the intent of the search for the essence of Christianity is thus correctly interpreted, then a special light is cast on the results of that search from the beginning. All the churches and confessions represent certain views of Christianity. Nosgen said correctly, "What characterizes the confessions is the unique understanding of Christianity in each one of them." If there are persons who cannot agree with the church's view of Christianity and want to provide their own, new interpretation, then they are fully entitled to do so, but then one can possibly deduce that they are right and that all the churches throughout the ages have been wrong. But one cannot approve such searchers who provide their own individual view of Christianity, place themselves high above the churches, and propose that their view is the only true one, over against the confessional errors. However, such a proud tone is sometimes assumed about the essence of Christianity, for example, in the small volume of Bruch.

Just as unbelief, time and again identifying itself with science, deserves disapproval, so also it is presumptuous if those who interpret the gospel differently than in the churches immediately establish their view as the true gospel over against [23] the dogmatic, one-sided, and false view of the official confessions. Or to put it still more clearly, a doctrinal interpretation of the gospel in the confessions and a critical-historical interpretation such as Harnack gives do not stand over against each other. Even less does the latter outrank the former; they simply stand next to each other as different views of the gospel. The churches also, in their confessions and liturgies, in their worship and governance, have wanted to give the purest view of the gospel. And men such as Harnack, who reject this view and offer their own interpretation, get no further than that they also give a view of the original gospel, which in their eyes deserves preference above all others. They therefore do not put the gospel in place of church dogma, but they place another view of the gospel next to the one honored by the churches. At the most, they only multiply the number of interpretations that, through the ages, have been given of the original gospel.

I say "at the most" because the human spirit is not so original and ingenious that it can unshackle itself completely from the past and turn in a new direction that has never been trodden by anyone else. Even the most independent thinker had his forerunners and pioneers. When we consider the individual views that have been proposed about the essence of Christianity by Anabaptism and Socinianism, by rationalism and pietism, by Kant and Schleiermacher, by Hegel and Schelling, by Strauss and Feuerbach, by Ullmann and Bruch and Harnack, then it appears that all these views are not brand new but were proposed already in the first centuries and then consciously rejected and opposed by the church for good reasons, after careful research.

Neither is it true that the churches never concerned themselves with the question about the essence of Christianity and only or primarily paid attention to issues that actually had nothing to do with Christianity. It is true that the churches have always been on guard against the opposition between the essence and the incidentals in Christianity that was often asserted later; but in their confession and worship they always tried to do justice to the genuine, original, and at the same time complete, full Christianity. Whether they succeeded is another question. The Reformation contends that the Roman Catholic Church in many instances blended original Christianity with many strange components; however, the Reformation itself does not profess an abstract "essence" of [24] Christianity but has attempted to restore complete, full Christianity to honor. If one, appropriately, makes a distinction between the gospel itself and dogma as our interpretation, then the situation is simply that Harnack and his followers do not place the gospel over against church dogma, but they set forth their own dogma of the gospel next to the dogma of the church. And then the question is, Who is right? Who does most justice to the genuine and full gospel—the dogma of the church or the dogma of others, such as the individual views of Schleiermacher or Kant, Ritschl or Harnack?

That the search for the essence of Christianity comes down to the question of what constitutes genuine, original Christianity is confirmed by the method that is followed in this search. When mention is made of the essence of Christianity, one might think that Christianity is here understood in the widest sense as that special religion that is confessed by Christian people in faith and morals, in worship and governance. In that case, the search for the essence of Christianity should consist of meticulous study of all Christian churches, confessions, liturgies, and so forth, in order to penetrate, by the inductive method, to the original essence common to all and foundational to all. However, this inductive method is not followed in the search for the essence of Christianity. It is true that Harnack discusses Catholicism and Protestantism, but he comes to this discussion only after he has, long before, found the essence of Christianity in a different manner, and then he evaluates the various views about the gospel in the churches against his view.

Actually, the inductive method proposed above would probably lead to poor results. The search for the essence of religion in comparative religious history provides vague generalities, with which one can do little. In the same way, the attempt to capture the essence of Christianity from comparative research in various Christian churches and confessions leads only to an abstract formula, a formula that would completely lack any understanding of the fullness and richness of life. And when afterward one would test, as one should, the concrete confessions of the church against this abstract formula, hardly anything would remain, and all this research would lead only to the effacing of historic Christianity.

That danger is not imaginary. Hegel's system was stranded on this rock. [25] Out of historic Christianity he lifted the idea of the oneness of the divine and human, and with this idea he dissolved all of the Christian religion into symbolic images. Scholten in Leiden applied that same method to the confession of the Reformed churches and found that God's complete sovereignty was the chief principle of the confessions; using this principle he argued the Reformed confession into nothing. Both of them forgot that Christianity is not a philosophy, but a religion. Christianity is not an abstract, formal principle that can be derived from or constructed by logical deduction; it is a historical given, a positive religion. God's grace and mercy, the incarnation of Christ, reconciliation, faith, justification, and whatever other doctrines there may be—these are not derived by our logical thinking from an abstract principle about the unity of the divine and human, from God's complete sovereignty, or something like that. Rather, they were given to us in history, or according to our confession, from God's revelation. That and not a philosophic principle is the fundamental principle of knowing [*principium cognoscendi*] of religion and theology. And whoever does not accept these teachings from revelation in faith will never find them, even if he possesses the intellectual strength of a Kant or a Hegel.

Actually, after Strauss nearly everyone took the route of historical criticism to arrive at knowledge about the essence of Christianity. And thus everyone acknowledged that the question about the essence of Christianity comes down to another question: What is original, genuine Christianity as it was proclaimed in the New Testament by Jesus and the apostles? Without doubt the historical method has its place in this search. After all, Christianity is a historical religion; it was prepared, originated, and developed in history and as such constitutes a subject for historical research. In itself there is thus no difference of opinion about the right of the historical method in this research. Moreover, the dogma of the church is not an ingeniously invented philosophical construction but an interpretation of original Christianity that arose in history and rests on a historical knowledge of the gospel. One can contend that the churches in earlier times had a very imperfect knowledge of original Christianity and that their view was often wrong and inexact. However, the churches wished to put into their dogma only what, according to their conviction, were the facts about original Christianity. When they confessed that Christ was the God-man, they only did so because they, along with the apostles, heartily believed [26] that in Christ the Word was made flesh.

Therefore, here also there is no ground to posit with Harnack the historical-critical interpretation of Christianity over against the doctrinal one. Both interpretations want to provide "the historic, authentic, and original understanding of the gospel." But the difference concerns the facts: for Harnack, Jesus was an ordinary even though highly exalted human being; for the Christian churches, he is God revealed in the flesh. And throughout the ages the churches have maintained that their confession of the Christ corresponds to the facts much more than Harnack's so-called historical views.

But why, then, the truly sad phenomenon that there are so many different views about original Christianity? This finds its explanation (in addition to other reasons that need not be discussed here) in the extremely divergent ideas about the nature and import of the historical method itself. Under the influence of the modern outlook, the historical method is understood by many to require in the subject a complete so-called setting aside of presuppositions [*Voraussetzunglosigkeit*] and require in the object a complete subjection to natural law. If this view of the historical method is correct, then Christianity is judged a priori because it does not just appear in history as one great miracle of God's grace and mercy; it also requires, in those who want to know and accept this miracle, a childlike spirit and a receptive heart. If you do not become like little children, you shall in no wise enter the kingdom of heaven.

However, one can prove that, in the whole area of historical research, the historical method (understood and applied in the positivistic sense described above) does violence to phenomena and is nowhere capable of consistent application. After all, in history there are altogether different factors at work than in nature. In history, we do not come into contact with mechanical and chemical powers but rather with the spiritual energy of personality, and we are forced to choose—either to reduce such energy to a blindly operating force of nature or to accept it and to honor it in its wonderful character. Moreover, in history we meet all kinds of religious, ethical, and aesthetic phenomena that do not let themselves be perceived and observed by us without a spiritual relationship on our side. Actually, these phenomena are not satisfied with only observation; they insist on appreciation and assume in our soul a certain criterion for such appreciation. For Christianity one must add that it must go against man with his sinful [27] thoughts and desires because it is a religion of deliverance that wants to free man from sin and also from error and the lie. If the gospel is indeed *for* man, for his needs, and for the total man, then it cannot be *according to* man, and it may not be in accord with the depravity of his heart.

The proof for this is provided by Harnack himself. He begins by saying that for him the question of what constitutes Christianity is a historical question and will be answered by historical research. But with the historical method he wants to apply, Harnack unavoidably brings along a certain view. Thus, on the one hand, Harnack understands the method in the sense that it excludes all miracles, because miracles would be a violation of natural laws. On the other hand, he does acknowledge that even though history itself cannot supply absolute judgments, the question about the essence of Christianity must be answered from the "life experience that is derived from experiential history." When Harnack appreciates and defends Christianity as the absolute religion, then he owes this judgment to his own moral experience that accompanies his historical research and not to his positivistic historical research. His historical method is also applied in his own way; it is in the service of his personality. This is unavoidable and always happens to everyone. There is therefore no ground for the opposition between church-dogmatic and historical-scientific views of Christianity. Both contend to be the "historical, authentic understanding" of the gospel. And principally there is no objection to the demand of the gospel that whoever wants to acknowledge Jesus as divine must be minded to do the will of the Father. "The pure of heart shall see God": this is not only a glorious, religious statement but also a rigorously scientific statement.

The diversity of views about Christianity is unusually great, but still not so great that it would stop further discussion or make discussion useless. There are indeed countless views about the essence of Christianity, such as the Greek, Roman Catholic, Lutheran, Reformed, Anabaptist, Sicilian, rationalist, Pietist, and so forth, and to those one can add the views that Kant, Schleiermacher, [28] Hegel, Schelling, Harnack, and many others have proposed. One can reduce these latter ones to one of the historical views from the first list. What appears to be new is often very old. But let us acknowledge the originality and independence of each view; one view more or less does not matter. Still, in all this diversity one can find important agreement on some points; such agreement makes further discussion about the essence of Christianity possible.

First, there is no church or community or party or opinion that identifies its view of Christianity completely with original Christianity. It is true that each considers its view as the true one and defends it as such against anyone who differs from it. Nevertheless, each one, also every church, makes a distinction between the truth revealed in Christ and the understanding that we have received from this truth. Here Rome is an exception, because it assigns infallibility to the church and presents its teaching as the only true and absolutely correct interpretation of the gospel. However, even Rome makes a distinction between Christ and the pope as his vicar, between the inspiration of the apostles and prophets and the assistance of the Holy Spirit enjoyed by the supreme head of the church. One cannot predict how long Rome will insist on maintaining this distinction. Even those who do not overestimate the significance and influence of the Reform Movement in Catholicism cannot suppress a certain fear. This fear concerns the concessions in that movement to modern science in the areas of historical criticism, teaching about evolution (even by someone like Loisy), and the presentation of the historical Jesus. The word of God in Scripture is more and more subjected to and sacrificed to the word of the church. But for the rest there is no one who principally opposes the distinction between the truth of Scripture and the dogma of the church.

Second, there also is agreement that the question about the essence of Christianity coincides with the question about the original, genuine, and true Christianity and [agreement] that we must return to Scripture, specifically the New Testament, to discern this. Again, there is much difference of opinion here. Some consider only the New Testament, others also the Old; some acknowledge as sources for the knowledge of original Christianity only the Synoptic Gospels, others all the books of the New Testament; some assign to these sources only historical authority, others also moral authority. Still, all this does not take away that there is agreement about the point that there is a [29] source and a norm for knowing original Christianity. Thus no one may determine on his own what constitutes original Christianity, but this issue is decided for all by the history of that original Christianity. What Christianity is (to put it briefly) is not determined by Christians but by the Christ.

Third, there is also agreement that not only historical but also a certain doctrinal authority is ascribed to Christ. There are those who have broken completely with Christianity, who see absolutely no honor in the name of Christ, and who do not care about the word of Christ. But apart from these radicals, various theological directions and parties generally value the name of Christ, and the authority of Christ still carries weight. The attempt to fashion the historical Jesus as much as possible according to their own imagination proves that in the search for the essence of Christianity they are personally involved. Everyone believes that he has captured original Christianity and understands it better than anyone else. As long as others who differ from us attach worth to the name of Christ, there is no reason to contest this and to drive them to denial with our whip of consistency and consequence. Rather, it becomes us to encourage them to hold fast to the name of Christ and to lead them back to the fullness of truth and life that this name implies.

The quest for the essence of Christianity thus leads naturally and with the consent of all back to the other question: Who was Christ and what did he teach and do? "What do you think about the Christ?" is and remains the principal question in religion and theology. Certainly the church of all ages confesses this Christ as the incarnate Word, as the mediator between God and men. However, throughout the ages people have tried to show in many ways that this confession was not the confession of the first congregation but arose only in the second century under the influence of philosophical ideas. In this connection, most New Testament writings had to be moved from the first to the second century. However, some writings, such as the four main letters of Paul, continued stubbornly to resist this displacement. Consequently, scholars began to realize that the church's Christology had its origin primarily in the first century. Thus, the reason to move various New Testament writings to a much later time disappeared. Nearly all successively moved back to the first century. In 1897 Harnack said there was a time when people saw in the oldest [30] Christian literature a web of deceit and falsification, but that time is past. The chronological listing in which the tradition arranged the documents is in all main points correct, from Paul's letters to Irenaeus. If Christianity is to be explained from foreign sources, then such sources must have been operating in the congregation much earlier than scholars were at one time inclined to accept.

Thus the idea arose that Paul was the real founder of ecclesiastical Christianity. The most ancient churches in Palestine did not yet have the confession of Christ as the incarnate Word. With Jesus, religion was still pure inwardness, but Paul made Christ the content and object of religion. His falsification of Jesus's religion consisted specifically in the following:

First, Paul introduced the deification of the man Jesus and turned the historical Jesus into a heavenly creature, who was preexistent and who rose from the dead and ascended into heaven after his earthly appearance. Second, Paul added a supernatural salvation, which takes place objectively and is brought about apart from men. Third, he imported into original Christianity the concept of the atoning, sacrificial Christ and thus prepared the way for the Roman Catholic sacrifice of the mass. Fourth, to all of this Paul added the doctrine of the sacraments as objectively operating mysteries. Several years ago Lagarde already spoke in this manner.

Harnack does not go this far and still tries to appreciate Paul as someone who understood Jesus well. However, at a crucial point Harnack sees himself forced to admit that Paul shifted the original gospel of Jesus. With Jesus, the gospel was a matter between God and the soul, and salvation was a subjective experience; but with Paul, Christ comes to stand between God and man, and Christ brings about our salvation apart from ourselves. Others express their views much more crassly and call Paul the great corruptor of the gospel; they (loudly or silently) join in the slogan, "Away with Paul; back to Jesus!"

However, to elevate the Apostle to the Pagan in this way to be the real founder of Christianity does not simplify the problem. In that case one has to face a question about Paul, the student of Gamaliel, the proud Pharisee, the passionate zealot for the law of the ancestors. How could Paul incorporate these ideas about the preexistence of the Messiah, his satisfaction for sin, his resurrection, his ascension, and so forth into his framework? And how could he apply these ideas to the crucified Nazarene whose congregation he subjected to bloody persecution? [31] But even if this could be explained (which is not at all true), there is always another mystery. How could Paul present his "falsification" of original Christianity and experience with virtually no opposition from the existing congregations or from the apostles in Jerusalem?

There was some difference between Paul and some of the brothers among the Jews, but this difference was limited to the consequences that flowed from the gospel in relation to Old Testament law. There was no difference about the person of Christ, about his death and resurrection. All the apostles were in complete agreement here; there is not a hint of a struggle about Christology in the oldest congregations. And thus there is no other conclusion than that the first churches already had a Christology that did not originate with Paul.

However, if the oldest church, from the first moment of its existence, already confessed that Christ was the promised Messiah, the Son of God, Lord of the congregation, judge of the living and the dead, then only two explanations are possible: Christ is the product of the church, or the congregation is the product of Christ. If the first explanation is true, then one must imagine the following: because of some situation or because of social circumstances, a social group formed that took all kinds of features of the Christ figure from Jewish, Indian, Babylonian, Egyptian, and other sources and applied them to a real (or not real) Jesus. However, this attempted solution is so artificial that one would not dare to predict that the "solution" would stand up. There are unanswered questions about this group of people: What brought them together, and what united them? From where could these simple people derive the characteristics of the Christ figure? How could they combine these characteristics into a harmonious whole and actualize the characteristics in a certain person, Jesus? What were the reasons that they believed in the existence of this Jesus? There are so many riddles and mysteries here that the theological escape that seemed to open itself for a moment soon turned out to be an impasse. Thus there seems to be no other answer than that one cannot explain Christianity without Christ.

Most theologians therefore accept that Jesus really existed and lived. But then something strange happens. The many attributes that were once ascribed to Christ by the church but are denied to Jesus—these must be, [31] in ever greater number, explained from the fantasy of the church, a fantasy derived from all kinds of influences. And when this seems impossible, one must again assign these attributes to the historical Jesus. This development is the reason for the great variety in the portrayal of the Christ image. According to Kalthoff, this image is indeed different in every university. According to one scholar, Jesus did exist, but another says that he did not. The one believes that Jesus considered and revealed himself as the Messiah while another denies this strongly. The one asserts his sinlessness, another denies it. And so it goes with all the words spoken by Jesus, all the works done by him, all the events that took place in his life. Historical criticism always tries to make one or another view plausible. It goes up and down with the waves of shifting opinions. There is absolutely no indication of quiet progress. Every moment it turns back on the road it entered, because it was soon obvious that the road was a dead end.

Historical criticism, which does not want to explain Christianity from the person of Christ, always founders on the rock of Christ's self-witness. Historical criticism allows very little of the historical Jesus to remain certain. But even this little is always too much for a view that believes in the indissoluble dominion of the laws of nature and allows no exceptions to that law. Jesus appears before us as the completely other among men, not only in the Gospel of John and the apostolic Letters, but also in the Synoptic Gospels. He is clearly conscious that he is the Son of God and the Son of Man. He knows that he knows the Father in a completely unique sense and that he was sent by the Father as the Messiah of Israel, as the one promised to the fathers. He always lives in uninterrupted communion with the Father and fulfills his will. Jesus connects forgiveness of sins and eternal salvation to his death, he predicts his own resurrection and ascension, and he announces his return as judge of the living and the dead.

Harnack definitely denies all real miracles, but he accepts this ethical miracle that Jesus knew the Father in a completely unique sense, lived in uninterrupted communion with the Father, and saw himself as the Messiah. Harnack does not attempt to explain this ethical miracle; he appeals only to the mystery of personality. This, however, is playing with words; in this way Harnack could just as well justify all miracles. Paul also spoke of a mystery, and he called it a mystery of godliness. [33] Even though he could not understand it, he knew the content of the mystery. The content was that Jesus, who was God, was revealed in the flesh, was justified in the Spirit, appeared to angels, was preached to the heathen, was believed in the world, and was taken up into glory.

Open-minded historical research thus leads to the conviction that Jesus, according to his own words and the faith of the church from the beginning, was the Christ. But here the ways part, not between Roman Catholics and Protestants, between orthodox and liberals, or between whatever churches and parties, but between those who accept this witness of Jesus in a child-like manner and those who reject him, if not by mouth, certainly with their hearts. Today there are many who seek a middle road, who are willing to know about Jesus but only a Jesus who was the first and the clearest in explaining the gospel of the fatherhood of God. They talk about the Christianity of Jesus [*Christentum Jesu*] as true Christianity. They consider Jesus not as the Christ but as the first, outstanding Christian. They are willing to be part of a faith like that *of* Jesus, or a faith *through* Jesus, meaning a faith that was first made possible through Jesus and that is created and strengthened by being impressed with his person. But they have no need for a faith *in* Jesus, a faith that is directed to Christ himself, and in him directed to the Father. Such people are in an equivocal position: they appeal to Jesus but actually deny him. If Jesus is not the Christ, the anointed of the Father, the mediator of God and men, then he is nothing special to us. He is on a par with all other founders of a religion and with all preachers of morality, and our Christian religion is no more than a *sublimer Nomismus* [loftier legalism], as Lepsius called it, and does not rise above the Jewish view of the gospel.

Jewish scholars who praised Harnack's book understood this clearly. Jews and Christians are one if the doctrines of the Logos, the Trinity, original sin, predestination, and so forth are all foreign imports and if original Christianity contains no more than the ideas of the fatherhood of God and the value of the human soul. At the September international congress of liberals in Geneva, no one was applauded more than Doctor Rabbi Levy. If Judaism lets go of Talmudism, and if Christianity gives up Christology and everything connected with it, then all difference between the two religions is wiped out. Christianity rises and falls with Christ. Whenever the Christian church has realized and acknowledged this, [34] it always has had the witness of Jesus himself and the witness of all his prophets and apostles on its side. As the practitioners of historical criticism became less interested in the results of their research, the more readily they agreed with this position.

The church's view of Christianity is always attacked anew, but it is also constantly justified anew through the searching of Holy Scripture. In the end, the church always proved to be historically more untainted than the historically authentic understanding [*geschichtlich authentische Verständnis*] that offered the shifting opinions of the day about the gospel.

But if Christ is truly whom the church confesses him to be, if he is not just the preacher but also the subject and the object of the gospel—yes, in his person and work he is the gospel itself—then the search for the essence of Christianity has not yet been brought to a conclusion. It is true that we then have the starting point and the center of Christianity, but we have not yet unfolded its full content. We cannot stop with Christ. Just because he is the subject and the object, the core and the center of the gospel, he is not its origin nor its final destination. He is the mediator of God and men and therefore points from himself back to the Father, just as he points forward to the future, wherein God will be all in all.

There is no opportunity in this essay to broaden these thoughts. However, let us in conclusion be permitted to make this one remark: Dogmatics that takes its point of departure in Christology cannot, as we explained, stop there but must stride from here to the unfolding of the rich content that God has granted to the congregation in his Word.

What is the point of a complete dogmatics and the whole history of Christianity, of which dogma is, after all, but a part? In its essence it is no more than determining and maintaining the place that, according to his own witness, belongs to Christ. It is Christ's place in his relation to the Divine Being, to creation, to the world, to humanity, to the church, to culture, and to all things. But in the determining and maintaining of this place, the church is only an instrument; actually it is Christ himself who has attained this place and maintains it in spite of all opposition. If we consider this and work it out, then Christianity finally appears to the eyes of our souls in all its beauty and glory. Christianity is no less than the real, supreme work of the Triune God, in which the Father reconciles his created but fallen world through the death of his Son and re-creates it through his Spirit into the kingdom of God.

# 3

## THEOLOGY AND
## RELIGIOUS STUDIES

[35] One can speak about theology[1] in its true sense only from the position of faith in a special revelation. Certainly, words and names have their history; language changes and varies, just as everything that is living. The etymological meaning of words is often completely lost through everyday use. However, among all other changes the word *theology* has maintained its original meaning. We thus have a moral obligation to use this word with the meaning that it has always had, and with no other meaning. Words are not arbitrary signs that anyone may change at will; all words represent a certain thought. To force another meaning on a word than what is commonly used is a misuse of language and introduces endless confusion. Locke already noted that most disagreements in philosophy arise from a false use of words.

The Greeks, from whom the word *theology* is derived, understood the word to mean the teaching about the gods, as written by Homer and Hesiod, and believed by the people. The Christian church could adopt this word, because it believed in the God who had spoken through the prophets and, in the last

Ed. note: Originally published as "Godgeleerdheid en godsdienstwetenschap," in the journal *De vrije kerk* 18 (1892): 197–225. The Dutch term *godsdienstwetenschap* has been translated in this essay as "Religious Studies," though a more precise and technical translation would be "scientific study of religion(s)" (cf. the source note to chap. 1). Bavinck also treated this topic on the occasion of his inauguration as the professor of theology at the Free University of Amsterdam, December 17, 1902: *Godsdienst en godgeleerdheid* (Wageningen: Vada, 1902).

1. Ed. note: Bavinck uses the words *theologie* and *godgeleerdheid* interchangeably.

days, through his Son and had revealed himself in his Word to the church
of all ages. Thus we have theology in the true sense of the word; the Christian church had knowledge of God himself on the basis of his self-revelation
in his Word and through his Spirit. Theology was the knowledge of God.
The object of theology was God himself, as he had made himself known to
people in nature and grace. The whole discipline of theology was unfolded
and ordered from this principle.

Everything that was discussed in theology came to the fore only because
(and insofar as) it had a certain relationship to God, and in this way our
knowledge of God was increased. [36] The world, humanity, angels, Scripture,
Christ, the church, and so forth all found their place in theology because they
were, directly or indirectly, subsumed under God. The knowledge of God was
the life principle, the organizing principle, of all of theology. This view of the
essence of theology was, with few exceptions, common to the church fathers
and Scholastics, Roman Catholic and Protestant theologians; this view was
generally dominant until the end of the eighteenth century.[2]

Still, we must remember that at one time the word *theology* suggested
only dogmatics or systematic theology. Even when exegesis of Scripture
or church history was mentioned, these were often placed separately, next
to the theological disciplines, and were sometimes designated as auxiliary
disciplines. There was no attempt to develop an organic arrangement of
all the theological disciplines. There was virtually no comprehension of an
encyclopedic system of theology. One can detect only beginnings and feeble
attempts at such an arrangement.

It is even surprising how little the principle of faith that people confessed
was developed in different directions or applied to various areas of life in the
centuries of orthodoxy. After a time of struggle, when a firm doctrine was
established, there soon appeared a traditional dogmatics. Later theologians
simply agreed with the earlier pronouncements and naively copied them.
Hardly anyone felt a need for development. They rested on the laurels that
the fathers had achieved, keeping what they had, but they did not sufficiently
consider continuing reformation. That is why in our century there is so much
for Reformed people to do, not only academically but also practically.

Since the conclusion of the previous [eighteenth] century, however, a
great change has come about in the concept of theology. The word *theology*
is still generally used, but just as the slogan "Christian virtues" serves as a
false label for the neutral education in the elementary state schools, so the
word *theology* is used as the ancient banner under which a completely new
cargo is imported. [The discipline of] religious studies has gradually replaced
theology in our country, and theology is no longer taught in the [Dutch] state
universities. [37] This significant change took place under the influence of

2. Cf. H. Bavinck, *De wetenschap der heilige godgeleerdheid* (Kampen: Zalsman, 1883).

philosophy. The rationalism that gained importance in Descartes's philosophy made natural theology more and more independent of a theology of revelation. Reason, which had been placed under the discipline of faith by the Reformers, gradually ignored this restriction. At first this took on a friendly tone. Reason certainly did not want to destroy faith but only wanted its independence and claimed only to have its own domain next to faith where it could be master. Reason wanted to see with its own eyes and even thought it could obtain rational knowledge from God himself.

However, once reason had gained this place *alongside of* faith, it soon began to take a stand *against* faith, to extend its territory at the cost of faith, and it concluded with the assertion that faith in supernatural revelation was completely unnecessary. True religion was a religion of reason, which was more or less the basis of all religions. Thus the distinction between true and false religion disappeared. The essence of religion was present in all religions, but it was also seen as buried under a number of useless ceremonies and arbitrary commandments, in Christianity as well as in heathen religions.

With his *Critique of [Practical] Reason*, Kant destroyed the foundations of this proud building of the reasonable knowledge of God and caused the rationalistic science of the supernatural to collapse into a heap of rubble. Kant declared that we are in touch with a real world only as long as our senses guide us; a generally valid science is possible only via sense perception. But as soon as we reach something beyond our senses, we wander in the dark; then it is no longer possible to speak of a science that all must recognize. All that is left is subjective conviction and moral certainty, with one person thinking differently from the next. Nonetheless, however much Kant destroyed rational theology with his critique, he himself continued to be caught in the rationalism of his time. In its main features, his view of religion agreed completely with that of his contemporaries.

First, Kant saw morality as the basis of religion. Religion is thus grounded in human nature only insofar as it is a necessary result of the postulates of *practical* reason. It is not provided directly and immediately with human nature, but it arises only by means of a sense of duty and conscience. The psychological explanation of religion, however, cannot come into its own from this position.

[38] Second, with Kant the content and object of religion are no different from that of all other rationalists. True religion was natural and reasonable and had only belief in God, virtue, and immortality as its content. However, such a purely natural religion is not found anywhere in reality. All religions consist of completely different elements that are generally and necessarily unique to that religion. Kant, however, abstracted what he wanted from reality; he determined religion according to a rationalistic framework and had neither eye nor heart for the real essence of religion.

This approach is, third, related to Kant's lack of historical sensibility. Kant cannot close his eyes to the fact that all religions, except his religion of reason, also consist of doctrinal, historical, and ecclesiastical faith. But Kant does not know what to do with that kind of faith. He explains that people are not easily convinced that a virtuous walk of life is all that God demands of us. People think that God also desires special services from them, and thus "religious practices" arise next to and in place of purely moral religion. All religions therefore consist of two elements and flow from two sources—from moral consciousness and from the weakness and ignorance of man.

Rationalism thus furnished this contribution to the rise of current religious studies, claiming that true religion is not present in only one certain religion but in all religions and that the differentiation between true and false religions must be abandoned. However, rationalism almost completely ignored the psychological, historical, and metaphysical side of the question of religion. This would become clear only in the philosophy that arose after Kant and Fichte. The transition, or rather the reversal, occurred when Kant and Fichte were followed by Schelling and Hegel. The main idea in the philosophy of Kant and Fichte is that man is intellectually and morally autonomous; he is not a product but the creator and shaper of the world. Man lays down the law, and the world must be explained from the human point of view.

However, history and experience soon taught that much can be said against this independence and freedom. Rather, man himself is part of a whole, taken up in a connection with things that all together have their source in an absolute force. Thus a completely different philosophy came about. Not the subjective "I" but the absolute force above everything became the principle of philosophy. That absolute, self-existing force objectifies itself in nature and then turns from there in spirit back to itself. [39] All things are taken up in one mighty process. Development becomes the basic idea of the whole system. Everything unfolds itself in due time, according to a logical law. Religion also forms a moment in that process. It is not an accidental phenomenon, not an invention of priests; it is based on human nature. It is not a motley collection of arbitrary ceremonies and laws; instead, it contains deep thoughts in all the forms of its appearance. It gradually rises through various historical religions to its highest and purest form in Christianity. Such was the view of religion in Hegel's philosophy. He was the first to highlight the psychological, historical, and metaphysical side of religion. A number of minor points in his philosophy of religion have been abandoned and put aside. But the spirit that gave birth to his views still reigns to the present. Hegel can justifiably be called the father of modern religious studies.

This scientific study of religion is exactly what its name indicates. It strives for a complete knowledge of that important phenomenon in our life called "religion." Usually this study is divided into a historical and a philosophical branch. The first not only describes the history of various religions separately but also tries to know these in their mutual relationships. All religions are seen as links in one chain, as different evolutions of the same process. The history of religions must lead into one history of religion that through all these stages reaches its highest form and purest shape. The task of the philosophical branch is to describe the origin, essence, right, and value of religion. This philosophy asks, for example: How is religion rooted in human nature? How does it interact with human capacities and powers? In which dispositions, emotions, and acts does it reveal itself? What is the basis of its right of existence? What value does it have for humanity? How is it related to culture, especially morality, art, science, and so forth? There is enough material here to split this branch into psychological, phenomenological, and metaphysical studies.

For the purposes of this essay, it is important to trace how and to what degree this religious studies approach has thrust aside theology in the state universities of our country.[3] Already in 1848 (when the Netherlands' parliament passed a new liberal constitution) the Dutch government came under pressure to remove the faculties of theology from the Dutch state universities and replace them with departments of religious studies.[4] After numerous fits and starts, proposals and counterproposals, and much parliamentary maneuvering, the 1876 Law on Higher Education created a curious anomaly: The *name* of the faculties of *theology* was retained, but the *content* of what was to be taught effectively made them departments of religious studies. *In this way theology was maimed and robbed of its heart and life.*

The reason for this odd development was that the state did not wish to relinquish its influence in the training of ministers for the Dutch Reformed Church (*Nederlands Hervormde Kerk*) while at the same time *the synod* [of the NHK] *was unable or unwilling to create its own institution for the training of its ministers.* The result was a strange mixture of incompatibles lacking all integration and unity of conception. Some of the subjects taught remind one of the old theology programs; others clearly belong to the field of religious studies. This unfortunate development also places the professors who must lecture in these departments in a difficult situation. Professor J. H. Gunning of the University of Leiden, for example, came to the conclusion that he, as a believing professor of theology, could not teach philosophy of religion in

3. Ed. note: What follows in the next few pages is the editor's significant abridgment and rewriting of pp. 39–48 in the Dutch text, which contain an extended discussion of the 1876 Law on Higher Education in the Netherlands that effectively changed the faculties of theology at the state universities into departments of religious studies. We have included enough detail in this abridgment to establish Bavinck's main point of critique against the new law without unnecessarily bogging down the reader. Since the detailed history is of interest to specialized scholars in the history of religious studies, the entire detailed narrative has been placed in appendix B. The sentences and clauses that are italicized in the paragraphs that follow are taken directly from Bavinck's text.

4. Ed. note: We shall be translating Bavinck's word *faculteit* both as "faculty" and, in keeping with English usage, as "department."

the new arrangement. A general religious studies program requires that one be neutral about the Christian faith, treating it simply as one religion among many, and that was something Gunning could not do. With this approach forced on one, *the Christian who practices religious studies* [in this manner] *forsakes his confession and crosses over into the territory of his opponents.*

It has become clear that *theology and religious studies are incompatible and cannot be contained in one department.* Because theology is always tied to a specific religion, it naturally excludes other religions. It is important for Christian theologians to have some knowledge of the history of religions and philosophy of religion, but they are sizeable disciplines on their own and do not fit neatly in the encyclopedia of theology.

It is equally impossible to absorb theology into religious studies. This would treat Christian theology on a par with other theologies and reduce it to historical value only. Both dogmatic theology and practical [church] theology then would have no place. In the departmental conflict between theology and religious studies, it should be noted that while a department of religious studies does not tolerate a place for theology anywhere in the university, a department of theology can fully recognize and honor religious studies.

In addition, an increasing number of people feel *the indispensability of good theology.* While a desire to have more-certain, normative, positive answers to life's big questions before God's face grows, so do concerns about and objections to the latent agnosticism of religious studies. Kant's claim that God is unknowable and the subsequent reduction of religion to morality—*"No doctrine but life; religion is not a matter of the mind, but of feeling, of the emotions"*—is too one-sided to satisfy. *Everywhere one sees the awakening of the need for explicit doctrine, for a certain content of faith. Religion is also serving God with the mind, and it therefore must be the truth and must provide knowledge (John 17:3). Religion cannot be found in unconscious, dark, emotional sensations.*

On the other hand, the objections against a department of religious studies are certainly not to be considered minor. If religious studies are to have a real object for examination, then the existence and knowability of God must be assumed. Whoever completely denies God's existence and revelation can discern in religion only a pathological phenomenon of the human spirit.

Other objections against the study of religions as it exists in Dutch universities today include its problematic character as a genuine science. One person cannot deal with the data for all the religions of the world. It thus is a fair question *whether a truly scientific study of the material is possible in this case and whether a study of the sources (a first requirement of science) is not virtually impossible.*

Finally, a department of religious studies is hampered by yet another objection. If it were established true to its ideal, and not because of practical obligations, it would not prepare for any profession and thus would not appeal to any student. Students in the university seek not only knowledge; most of them also want, in the first place, a preparation and training for a profession in church or society. A department of religious studies, however, is completely outside everyday life and does not prepare [a student] for anything. And even in our country, where theology has in various ways compromised with the "real world," one often hears complaints that theological study does not sufficiently take into account the office and ministry for which students are to be trained. "For all these reasons one must disapprove of the law that in our country in 1876 changed the [university] departments of theology into departments of religious studies."[5]

However, the question that we have studied so far has not been answered. Let us assume that theology and religious studies cannot be brought together into one department and that theology deserves its own department. Nevertheless, religions also have the right to be studied and to become known, because religions are the subject of scholarship. No one will be able to or want to deny this. The material that is presented from all sides about the various religions has increased and broadened so incredibly that there is urgent need for scholarly work. We can no longer be satisfied with the old formulas and ideas. It is no longer possible to declare that Buddha, Zoroaster, and Muhammad are simply deceivers and instruments of Satan. Psychology and the philosophy of history have brought significant changes in our ideas. Christians especially, who stand on the foundation of faith, have a difficult and serious task in this study of different religions. They must penetrate more deeply than they have thus far into the importance of all peoples for the history of God's kingdom. They must search for the relationship and the difference that exists between pagan religions and the Christian religion, and they must discover God's plan, insofar as Scripture and history reveal it.

[49] But this study of religions, an obligation one cannot deny, according to its nature belongs not in the theological but in the literary department.[6] The latter researches a special and distinct subject: human beings as spiritual, rational beings. All its disciplines concentrate on our spiritual nature and focus on its disclosure and phenomena. The complete, rich psychic life of humanity—intellectual, ethical, aesthetic—is researched and studied. And therefore the literary department is the most natural place for the study of human religious life. Just as moral life is not and cannot be the object of a separate academic department, the same is true for religion. Religious life, just like ethical and aesthetic life, is a phenomenon of the psychic nature of

5. Ed. note: This concludes the abridged, rewritten material. The remainder of the essay is a translation of Bavinck's full text.

6. Ed. note: The European university traditionally had four major faculties: law, medicine, theology, literary (arts and humanities). With this emphasis on placing religious studies in the literary faculty, Bavinck is clearly distinguishing it as a *descriptive* science from theology as a *prescriptive* and *normative* science.

human beings, and thus its study belongs in the department of literature and philosophy.

However, one can do justice to the study of religions in this department only if it deserves its importance. As we saw above, from a scholarly point of view there is strong objection to the current classification of religious studies. It is not in agreement with the scholarly requirement that the study of all religions, except Judaism and Christianity, is to be assigned to one person. This task is much too demanding for one person, no matter how excellent a scholar. In the literary department, however, this serious objection can be completely overcome. The disciplines in the literary department consist of three groups: philological, historical, and philosophical. The history of religions belongs to the middle group.

The more recent view of history leads to this conclusion. History is no longer a recitation of facts and dates, a chronicle of monarchs and wars, but a description of the development of a people. General history has not been absorbed by cultural history, but general history now includes cultural history. History is no longer the description of just the political significance of a people; [it is] also [a description] of its social development, its morals and customs, its thoughts and labors—in other words, its whole culture. And the history of its religion belongs to this culture. Religion is one of the most potent factors in the life and aspiration of a people. The scholar of the history of a certain people cannot ignore its religion but is driven to this study by research and by the place of religion in the life of the people. For this reason many of the standard works in the field of the history of religions are produced not by theologians but by those whose studies are in the areas of the literary department. [50] Experts in Indology, Sinology, Persology, Egyptology, Assyriology have generally provided the finest knowledge of the various religions.

Nevertheless, just because the field of history has expanded so significantly at present and the material has increased so amazingly, it is no longer satisfactory to have only one professor in general history in the literary department. Here one needs a division of labor. Good scholarship demands that separate professors be appointed for the language and history of the most prominent peoples and that the history of various religions be related to that study. Only when this is done can one practice sound scholarship, and this study will find the proper place it deserves in the university because of its weight and significance. However, because our small country has four state universities and the funds distributed over the four institutions are already scarce, no one university in our country is equipped as it should be, and we still lack several chairs for important disciplines. And even if the funds were sufficient, there would not be enough scholars to fill the chairs at the four universities. For that reason, a reduction in the number of universities would be desirable.

If the history of religions could be incorporated in this way into the department of literature and philosophy, then the objection of Prime Minister

Heemskerk to the law for higher education would disappear. The prime minister had first proposed placing religious studies in the literary department
but later changed his mind. As reason for this change, he said the following:
The professors of religious studies would really be theologians, but in the
literary department they would have to vote about doctoral degrees, and
vice versa; the professors in literature would have to decide about degrees
in religious studies.[7] However, this objection rests on the idea that religious
studies is, at bottom, theology, and is part and parcel of the same discipline.
We have proved both assumptions to be wrong. The study of religions is
not a theological but a literary discipline, just like the study of languages,
moral phenomena, and the customs of a people. That a certain religious and
theological knowledge is desirable and necessary for this study does not
change the basic principle. [51] And a separate doctorate in religions is just
as impossible as a separate doctorate in languages. If doctoral degrees were
desirable, these could be achieved only in the religions of certain peoples or
people groups in connection with their language and history, as is now done,
for example, in classical, Semitic, and other literatures.

The philosophy of religion also belongs in the literary department. Professor Gunning and Doctor [H. H.] Meulenbelt appear to be of the opinion
that not only should this discipline not be a part of theology but also that it
is a modernistic discipline and cannot be practiced and taught by a confess-
ing Christian without betraying his principles. Their first opinion is true,
but not the second. After all, religion is a general human phenomenon that
fully deserves our interest and research. Why should this phenomenon not
be studied? Why should or could one not ponder how religion is rooted in
human nature or how it is related to other human abilities? In what emotions
and actions does it reveal itself? On what basis is religion justified? Or what
significance does it have for human life?

And on the other hand, philosophy is a universal discipline that considers everything in its purview. It contemplates the idea of the true, the good,
and the beautiful. It tries to discover the deepest reflections about history,
nature, justice, morality, art. Since philosophy considers all these areas, why
could and should it not also consider religion and contemplate this crucial
phenomenon in the life of the human soul and what significance it has for
all of human life?

Professor Gunning is certainly correct when he judges that in theology
there is no place for philosophy of religion. Even though religion is discussed
in theology, for example, in dogmatics and ethics, nevertheless philosophy of
religion is philosophy and not theology, and thus it naturally belongs in the department of literature and philosophy. It differs from theology in principle, in

---

7. Cf. B. J. L. de Geer van Jutphaas, *De wet op het hooger onderwijs* (Utrecht: Bijleveld, 1877),
159.

method, and in purpose. It belongs with anthropology, with knowledge about humanity—not knowledge about God, which is the object of theology.

Currently our educational law lists only the following disciplines under philosophy: history of philosophy, logic, metaphysics, and psychology. However, everyone realizes that philosophy includes other and more subjects. [52] Philosophy has always strived for a unified worldview [*einheitliche Weltanschauung*], a systematic world-and-life view. In its own way, every philosophic system has been an attempt to understand the universe. Every philosopher has tried to reduce countless phenomena of nature and history, of the material and spiritual world, to a single cause, to discern their essence, to expose their relationships, to discover their significance and purpose.

However, if this is the essential task of philosophy, then it is virtually impossible for anyone to occupy a chair in philosophy. Where could someone be found who is a philosopher in the true sense, who comes with a personal full-blown philosophic system? Kappeyne van de Coppello said correctly in the Upper Chamber: "In the narrow sense of the word, a 'philosopher,' the founder of his own system, is not available for the asking. I don't even know if in our country we ever had such a founder of a system, except Spinoza, and it is still debated whether he was Dutch." But van de Coppello solved this dilemma partly by adding, "In the meantime it is sufficient if we have a scholar in philosophy, someone who knows how to penetrate into the various philosophic systems, who can choose one of the systems as his own, and who with the methodology of philosophy can communicate the various systems and disclose the reasons for his preference of one of the systems."[8]

If we take into account this undeniable fact, then the practical objection disappears that could be aimed at the philosophy of religion in the literary and philosophic department. It is no different for the philosophy of religion than for the philosophy of law. Our [Dutch] education law places this discipline under jurisprudence [*Rechtsgeleerdheid*]; this placement was against the advice of the University of Utrecht's senate and in spite of Mister Kappeyne's opposition. He noted correctly that the philosophy of law was a facet of general philosophy, just like philosophical ethics.[9] After all, philosophy of law is no more than a specific application of a general philosophical system to a specific case. And the philosophers of law were not jurists but philosophers, such as Plato, Aristotle, Kant, Fichte, Hegel, and so forth. The same applies to the philosophy of religion. The scholar is a philosopher, not a theologian, even if he were incidentally a professor of theology or a minister in a congregation. [53] In this respect, the philosophy of religion, morals, art, law, and history are all on the same level. They all are just special applications of a general philosophical system that one agrees with. Each application is

8. Ibid., 193.
9. Ibid., 181.

decided by the philosophical principle that one accepts. Then the only question is whether one can consistently and logically apply the relationships to the various areas of life.

Naturally, the obligation rests on the Christian to practice and teach the history of religions and the philosophy of religion (and all scholarship) from a Christian point of view. The fact that these disciplines actually belong in the literary department makes no difference. After all, the gospel of Christ is a joyous message not just for some people in certain circumstances, but for *every* person and for the *whole* person, for the learned as well as the simple, and no more for the theologian than for the literary scholar, the historian, the philosopher. I therefore fail to see why a Christian treatment of these disciplines is not permitted or not possible.

The objections of Professor Gunning against these disciplines on the basis of faith do not touch these fields as such but [two other matters]: (a) merging them into one department that takes the place of theology; (b) the principle of religious neutrality that gives rise to this arrangement. It is understandable that someone might object to teaching in a department that was organized in this way. But if there is no principle that forbids this, there can hardly be an objection against the study and teaching of these disciplines as classified by law. Certainly these disciplines are not evil. The various religions have a right to be researched and known. Neither Scripture nor church forbids this research. Philosophy may be condemned by Scripture because of its meaningless misuse, but philosophy itself is, according to Calvin, a *donum Dei* [gift of God].

The law also allows a Christian approach to these disciplines. The law does not require it, but neither does the law forbid it. The law for elementary education requires that a Christian teacher conceal his convictions when teaching in the public school. But it is very different for a professor at a university. As a scholar and professor he may also profess his faith. It is even a right of scholarship for a professor in the department of religious studies to have the freedom to attack vigorously, verbally or in writing, the principles and organization of the department. [54] Actually, there is not a single professor at our universities who would defend the arrangement of disciplines in the religious studies department that is established in our law. The state is not a schoolteacher, not even in the area of higher education. And thus the law must fully honor someone in our state universities who teaches the history of religions and the philosophy of religion in a positively Christian spirit.

Protests against this view will come only from those who still view neutrality as a guarantee for virtue and scholarship and who maintain (not from a neutral point of view, but a priori) that scholarship and positive faith cannot exist together. It is, of course, certainly true that Christian scholarship in the disciplines mentioned above is not unbiased. But the demand for unbiased scholarship is theoretically false and practically impossible. The modernists have already softened the severity of this demand considerably. They not only permit but also desire that the scholar of the history of religions and of the philosophy of religion be a religious person and have religious sensitivity. If the modernists have the right to demand this over against the positivists (that is, to demand that the scholar in these disciplines be a liberal Christian), why then would Reformed, orthodox, or ethical Christians be denied the right to use their positive convictions in scholarly research? One "bias" is just as good as another.

Whether or not one theoretically accepts the demand for such neutrality, practically it is impossible for any person to comply with that demand. Every scholar takes his heart, his inclinations, his passions to his research. The individual does not cease to exist when carrying out research. There is only the question who one is and what one takes to the research. And then the profession of the believer is that the Christian is again the true person who in principle has died to sin and error, is re-created to be a person of God, and thus is equipped for every good work—also the work of scholarship.

# 4

# Psychology of Religion

[55] The psychological study of religious phenomena (origins, nature, and value of which I will attempt to summarize briefly) is a fairly recent discipline but has been in the making for quite a long time already. Because of the extensive religious changes that occurred in the latter part of the seventeenth and at the beginning of the eighteenth century—such as Pietism in Germany, Methodism in England, and "the Great Awakening" of 1740 in America—the center of gravity shifted away from the objective in religion to the subjective. Before that time religion was considered to be an objective reality whose truth and legitimacy were beyond all doubt, or in any case could readily be proved, which a person had to experience, and to which he had to conform himself. But now the more subjective state rather than the objective truth of religion began to assert itself, and the significance of doctrine became secondary to the significance of life.

This new trend in religious life found its philosophic interpretation in Kant and its theological interpretation in Schleiermacher. These two men differ rather substantially. With Kant, religion is built on morality and hence is a complement, an ornament (albeit an indispensable one), of man's moral nature. With Schleiermacher, religion is rooted in a feeling of dependence that precedes all thinking and willing, and it forms the mystical foundation of man's entire life and development. Yet with both it is not considered, at least not in the first place, as a commandment or a gift from God but as a

Ed. note: Originally published as "Psychologie der religie," in *Verslagen en mededeelingen der Koninklijke Academie der wetenschappen, afdeeling letterkunde*, series 4, vol. IX (Amsterdam: Joh. Muller, 1909), 147–78.

human quality. Both men have greatly affected religion and theology with this new concept of religion. The change became most obvious in dogmatics. Whereas dogmatics used to be an exposition of the doctrine of Scripture or of the church, it now became a description of conscious religious ideas or pious emotions. And even though as a rule an attempt [56] was made to break through to the religious reality behind those ideas or emotions, dogmatic theology nevertheless found its foundation and basis in subjective experience.

The study of religions, which became prominent in the nineteenth century as a result of the expansion of our ethnological knowledge, benefited from this new concept of religion. Not only did this study make it necessary to classify the many and various religions and to determine their mutual relationship; it also appeared more and more that religion was characterized always and everywhere by one and the same human quality or tendency. Very much like, for example, the ability to speak, religion was able to express itself in the most diverse forms of ideas, emotions, and actions. The various religions and creeds presented themselves as "varieties" of the one "religious experience." This change received its official endorsement in this country [Netherlands] when the university faculties of theology were converted to departments of religious studies.

In this study of religions, attention naturally was focused, at first exclusively or for the greater part, on objective elements, the components of dogma and cultus, which appear in all religions, and therefore the historical method was preferred. First, the material that was brought in from everywhere had to be gathered and organized; but from the start the hope was cherished that in this way scholars might also solve the issues of origin and essence, the truth and legitimacy of religion. Although there are still a few who cling to this hope, nevertheless the number of those who believe that the historical method is insufficient and unsuitable for achieving *this* goal is steadily increasing.

After all, the *origin* of religion cannot be discovered historically, because whenever history allows us to view the past, we find that everywhere religion had already existed for a long time. About the *essence* of religion, history provides little or no light, because the many and various religions are so far apart that, once the particular has been extracted, nothing remains of the general and communal essence except a vague definition, which everyone interprets differently. The *truth* and the *legitimacy* of religion in general, or of a specific religion in particular, is not susceptible to proof historically, while the categories of truth and error, of legitimacy and illegitimacy, belong to another order of things than the mere facts offer us.

This result of the study of religions explains why, on the one hand, some insist on the return of philosophy, metaphysics, [57] and dogmatics to religious studies, and on the other hand, why many practitioners of this discipline proceed from the historical to the *psychological* method, expecting it to provide the solution of religious issues. The metaphysical approach is after all, so they reason, blocked for good after Kant's criticism of human cognitive powers. Speculation about God and the world—about the origin, being, and end of the world—do not move us forward one step. The truth and legitimacy of religion cannot be determined dogmatically. The only thing that remains is to study religion from a psychological and social point of view and in that way to show the significance and value it has for the life of the individual and for society at large.

Such a study of religion will also have its benefits. Of late, many have become estranged from all religion and can no longer be reached or rescued by means of evangelistic efforts or missions. However, when religion is studied, not metaphysically or historically but psychologically and socially, in its relation to the whole person and all of society, then its importance, its indispensability, and its usefulness will be acknowledged once again. Acknowledging its value could then lead to showing the truth and legitimacy of religion. Pedagogy and pastoral work, religious and ecclesiastical life, evangelism and missionary work—all will benefit from the fruit yielded by the psychological study of religion.

With these expectations and promises, the psychological study of religion was first undertaken in America, where the soil was ready for it. The so-called religious revivals among Americans have been prominent in that country since 1740. It was to be expected that these frequently recurring revivals would attract attention also in scientific circles. The great American theologian, Jonathan Edwards, under whose leadership these revivals first occurred on a broad scale in America, himself wrote an important treatise titled *The Religious Affections*.[1]

Later the revivalists adopted the habit of providing reports of their gatherings and drawing up a list of the number of converts, including sex and age. These reports attracted the attention of G. Stanley Hall, now president of Clark University.[2] He began a serious study of the data that came to his attention through these reports, and he soon came to the conclusion [58]

1. Ed. note: This treatise is available in several editions. The definitive critical edition is volume 2 of *The Works of Jonathan Edwards*, ed. John E. Smith (New Haven: Yale University Press, 1959); the full text of the treatise is also available from The Banner of Truth Trust, Carlisle, PA; a useful edited, abridged edition is available as *Faith beyond Feelings: Discerning the Heart of True Spirituality*, ed. James M. Houston (1984; repr., Colorado Springs: Cook Communications, 2005).

2. Ed. note: Granville Stanley Hall (1844–1924) was a pioneer in American psychology, the first president of the American Psychological Association, founder of the *American Journal of Psychology*, and the first president of Clark University. He studied under William James at Harvard University and was instrumental in the development of educational psychology, particularly concentrating on the effect adolescence has on education as well as religious experience. Bavinck rather thoroughly discusses the importance of psychology of religion for theologically understanding conversion in the order of salvation, in *Reformed Dogmatics*, 4 vols. (Grand Rapids: Baker Academic, 2006), III:556–64 (#427). This entire section is new material in the revised and expanded second Dutch edition (1910)

expressed in the second of his twelve Harvard Lectures in Boston on February 5, 1881, that "adolescence was the age of religious impressionability in
general and of conversion in particular." In other words, there is a close connection between the physiological and psychological changes that take place
during puberty and the religious experiences that occur in those years. Later,
Stanley Hall not only continued this study for himself, but he also gathered
a number of talented students, such as Burnham, Daniels, Lancaster, Leuba,
and Starbuck, who joined him in researching the same area of study and who,
since 1906, have their own publication, the *American Journal of Religious
Psychology and Education.*

In Europe the importance of these studies was recognized especially after
William James, professor at Harvard University, delivered his Gifford Lectures
on *The Varieties of Religious Experience* in Edinburgh during the 1901–2
school year [published in 1902]. In France, for that matter, the empirical,
experimental, and comparative psychology of Théodule Ribot and his school
had cleared the way for it long before. In Geneva, Professor Théodore Flournoy
began a series of twelve lectures in 1901–2 about religious psychology. The first
one, *Les principes de la psychologie religieuse,* was published already in 1902
in the *Archives de psychologie,* [and the remainder] were printed separately
the following year. In the countries mentioned, many are engaged these days
in psychological studies of religious phenomena; many special studies have
been published already, not only about the psychology of religion in general
but also [about a host of topics]: the psychology of faith, prayer, conversion,
revivals, sin, forgiveness, sanctification, immortality, inspiration, prophecy,
mysticism, asceticism, ecstasy, the ills of religious life, sects, religious ideas,
and feelings in children, farmers, laboring circles, and so forth. We may
expect that these studies will be expanded considerably and will increase in
the coming years.

To date, the attitude in Germany toward these studies has been somewhat
reserved. In spite of the popularity that the study of psychology enjoys in
that country, and contrary to the religious-historical method whose strict
application in theology was demanded the last few years, interest in a proper
psychology of religion has been minimal until now. But a change is on its
way; the first issue of a *Zeitschrift für Religionspsychologie,* with Pastor Doctor Vorbrodt and medical officer Doctor Bressler as editors, saw the light
of day in April of this year [1909]. [59] The religious phenomena that this
psychology prefers to study constitute a specific group. It does not study *all*
religious phenomena without distinction but leaves the study of the objective elements in religion, such as dogma and worship, up to the historical
and philosophical disciplines. The psychology of religion limits itself to the

---

of the *Reformed Dogmatics* and indicates the high value Bavinck placed on interdisciplinary reflection
for Christian dogmatic theology. See "Editor's Introduction," *Reformed Dogmatics,* III:19.

study of subjective religion [*religio subjectiva*] and to the religious experience of the [individual] subject, which is, as Flournoy puts it, "religious life considered from within, even as it develops in the personal consciousness of the subject." And it draws attention, furthermore, not so much to religious ideas as to religious feelings, affections, and passions, "the feelings, acts, and experiences of individuals in their solitude."

This is why the psychology of religion instinctively or intentionally prefers to study such religious phenomena or persons that represent departures from what is ordinary and what belongs to the more interesting cases. Included here are mystics, ecstatics, fanatics, enthusiasts of all sorts and degrees, because, as James comments, they express personal religion the clearest, and their religious life is the most original; they are the geniuses, the "classics" in religion. Sometimes it even looks as if psychology of religion considers the pathological phenomena in religion as being more remarkable and instructive than the healthy ones. Here it applies the rule of [Philippe] Pinel: "One has to first hear how fools spout nonsense in order to know how wise men think."

Religious psychology tries to get acquainted with and study these phenomena quite impartially and objectively. It proceeds from only two presuppositions: The first one is that religion is a phenomenon in human life that not only exists but is also worth investigating. Even the person who considers it to be a delusion must, so it maintains, consider religion worthy of study because of its importance and influence. It may not correspond to any reality, yet as a phenomenon of central significance in human life religion deserves serious investigation. And second, psychology of religion proceeds from the supposition that—just as in nature and in natural life, so also in the life of the soul and even more precisely in man's religious life—law, order, and rules govern. Every discipline proceeds from this supposition either silently or explicitly. For if any area were governed by complete arbitrariness, blind fate, or chaotic confusion, it would, from the nature of things, not be amenable to scientific research and knowledge. The laws may be different in the psychical, the ethical, and the religious realms [60] from those in nature, but if the psychology of religion is going to be a discipline, then it assumes and demands that religious life in its origin and progress is also bound by laws.

For the rest, it claims to proceed completely impartially and unbiased and is unconcerned with objective truth that undergirds religious phenomena. Naturally, this study does take into account the psychological fact that the believer is deeply convinced of it. But since it desires to be and remain a pure discipline, it only investigates empirically and objectively. It makes absolutely no pronouncements about the truth or falsehood of the religious phenomenon but takes the phenomena as they present themselves. It makes a sharp distinction between two questions: What are the religious propensities? What is their philosophical significance? It is careful not to mix and confuse judgments of fact [*Seinsurteile*] with judgments of value [*Werturteile*], and it considers the latter to be independent of the former. In the abstract, it is quite well possible that supernatural forces are at work in religious life. However, even if this might be true, the psychology of religion sees as its task only the investigation of the conditions under which the religious phenomena appear and run their course and the laws to which they conform. All this, when based on different factors and viewed from a different perspective, may then be designated as products of a supernatural activity. It is assumed that no one can object to this, for an issue does not lose its value by being known and understood. And there is less reason for fear, because psychology of religion does not pretend to solve the mystery of religion once and for all; instead, it only hopes to discover the order and connection in truly present religious phenomena and the knowledge of these phenomena that helps us to better understand and appreciate them.

The application of this empirical, inductive method occurs already immediately in the manner in which the religion-psychologist obtains the material for his research. He does not derive it from some theological or philosophical system, nor does he produce it through introspective consideration of the life of his own soul; rather, he studies religious persons. He tries to get acquainted with them and to learn about their religious experiences by visiting their religious gatherings, by attending their revival meetings, or also by living in their circles for a while and by sharing their lives. Second, as a source of knowledge about religious phenomena, he also takes into consideration the writings in which people of every persuasion, age, gender, time, and place have deposited their religious experiences, intentionally or not. He also considers writings in which these are described by other people.

[61] Third, it deserves special attention that some in this field—such as Stanley Hall, Edwin Diller Starbuck, [George Albert] Coe, and others— have used the so-called questionnaire or inquiry method just as this has been practiced elsewhere for a long time already. Professor Starbuck of the Leland Stanford Junior University, for instance, did a special study of the development of religious life, [focusing] specifically on the time in which sudden conversions, such as often happen in America, ordinarily take place.[3] To that end he asked eleven questions of a number of reliable persons who were conscious of such a turning point in their lives and who for the greater part were Americans and Protestants but belonged to different churches. These questions all related to the circumstances and experiences that preceded, accompanied, and followed this decisive moment in their lives. The "cases" that he gathered this way and processed numbered 192, of which

---

3. Ed. note: Bavinck is likely referring to Edwin Diller Starbuck, *The Psychology of Religion: An Empirical Study of the Growth of Religious Consciousness* (London: W. Scott; New York: Scribner, 1901).

120 were women and 72 men. For the study of the *time* of the conversion, he used a much larger number of responses, 1,265 in total, of which 254 came from women and 1,011 from men. Further, he also investigated the religious development of those who were *not* conscious of a decisive turning point in their lives; for this he consulted not only the biographies of Harriet Martineau, Mary Livermore, Frances Power Cobbe, George Eliot, Tolstoy, Carlyle, Ruskin, Frederick Robertson, Charles Kingsley, and Goethe but also the answers that he had received to eight questions from 237 persons, of whom 142 were women and 95 men.

Processing this material was even more difficult than gathering it. First, each of the replies received had to be analyzed and its proper significance understood and explained so that the scientific researcher would be able to obtain a pure and accurate image of the religious development that had taken place in this [particular] instance. This required hours, sometimes days, and often more information as well. Once this analysis was finished, comparison and classification came next; differences and similarities had to be considered carefully. Quite often there was uncertainty about which group a certain case should be placed in. Analysis and classification were followed by the difficult task of "generalizing," which was the effort to deduce from the factual data the laws that govern religious development.

But however difficult all of this may be, the psychology of religion must follow its conviction in this matter if it wants to be a discipline, [62] because every discipline tries to understand the laws that direct the development of the phenomena. To understand religious life in a scientific, psychological way, research must be related to the entire person, exploring one's physical and psychical life, origins, sex, age, temperament, health, and so forth. Furthermore, it is necessary to learn all the causes, circumstances, and conditions that bring religious life into being, develop, alter, revive, or decline. According to Flournoy, the psychology of religion must be physiological, genetic (or evolutionary), comparative, and dynamic. For that reason others have called it a religious biology or psychobiology.

On the basis of such research, some psychologists have already given us the following outline of the development of religious life in the individual: There is as yet no private religious life in children. Just as the human embryo moves through the various stages of development that organic beings preceding humankind did, so childhood represents the original, the oldest, condition of the human race. Ontogeny is repetition and recapitulation of phylogeny. Just as the first humans in their evolution from lower beings remained partial animals for a long time, so animal life is also natural in a child. The baby enters life with virtually the same instincts that exist in animals. The truth of the ecclesiastical doctrine of original sin is that man still lives up to and shows the aftereffects of his animal origin. The child, therefore, is by nature selfish, stubborn, and belligerent. He carries with him the human race's instinct for self-preservation that reveals itself in anger, sensitivity, jealousy, and the like.

Related to this, the child demonstrates the same selfishness when it comes to religion and morality. For the child, the worth of religion consists only in what it can bring or give him. And though the child does not have independent insight, he is gullible and accepts as truth whatever he is told. For the greater part, religion for the child consists in instructions, in dogmas imposed by the authority of the parents or the church; he believes and lives by authority; religion for the child is something entirely external and objective; "Religion is all external to him. God is a being above and beyond him." When puberty arrives, ordinarily in the fourteenth year for girls and in the sixteenth year for boys, a great change takes place. The nature, extent, and significance of this change, which happens in early adulthood, have been the object of [63] serious and extensive scholarly research in the last few years.

Stanley Hall recently published a book of more than 1,300 pages in which he traced, meticulously and exhaustively, all the changes in human development that take place during the years of puberty.[4] They affect all of life and at the same time are of a physiological, psychological, biological, and social nature. Just as the child is a reminder of the oldest condition of the human race, so also the time of youth is neoatavistic. In it the conquests of the race in an earlier period are relived and repeated. The development that takes place at this time is in general characterized by it happening more by leaps than gradually. It repeats that earlier period of storm and stress, when humanity broke the old restrictions and raised itself to a higher level of civilization. Height, weight, and body strength increase much more than in the earlier years. And important functions that did not exist before arise and gain significance. The voice changes, hair growth increases, the size and proportions of limbs change, and the cerebral nerve system required for a richer psychic life reaches its full scope. It is as if nature, with all the powers at its disposal, equips man for the struggle that awaits him; it makes the man aggressive and prepares the woman for motherhood.

Psychologically the change during this stage of life is no less great. While boys and girls enter into a different relationship with the world and acquire different interests, their sense organs also change in structure and function. The senses of touch, smell, taste, and hearing as well as the face undergo important changes. In general, sensory perception diminishes and remarkable progress takes place in the development of deliberation and reflection. The mind, reason, and the self-conscious personality awaken and appropriate

4. Ed. note: The volume Bavinck refers to is G. Stanley Hall, *Adolescence: Its Psychology and Its Relations to Physiology, Anthropology, Sociology, Sex, Crime, Religion, and Education*, 2 vols. (New York: D. Appleton, 1904).

entirely new, more-general, abstract spiritual truths. While a child is governed by heredity and imitation, now its own individuality is formed. What is commonly human differentiates itself and presents itself in special, divergent traits of character and face. And with all these new ideas, another world of emotions also enters the person; new feelings of lust and unease, sympathy and aversion, inclinations and desires, wants and ideals—often unconscious and not understood—intrude on a person's mind. This human being, the individual with his or her own personality, own insight, own "I," emerges in a young man and a young woman. They now want to be themselves and live their own lives.

[64] Puberty also causes great biological and sociological changes. Puberty is the awakening of the sex life, the awakening to the reproductive life. The boy becomes a man, the girl becomes marriageable. This sexual development does not run parallel with the physiological and psychological, but actually constitutes its center. Though sexual development may not cause or explain every other development, it nevertheless adds color and tone to the whole and is its powerful impulse and stimulus. And with this awakening to the reproductive life, the person also increases in stature in the society that surrounds him. He becomes conscious of the fact that he is not here to live only for himself but that he is also destined to live with and for others. The new personality—with its much richer world of ideas and emotions, of wants and desires—transitions from the small, confined circle of childish, selfish living to that large society with many, complex relationships. The center of activity is shifted from interest in self to interest in the totality of life—the whole. In a word, puberty is a second birth, a regeneration, the birth of a new private and at the same time social personality.

But just as with the first, this second birth also is accompanied by grief and labor pains. Puberty brings with it its own ills and dangers, its own digressions and sins. It is, just like the corresponding period in the history of the human race, a storm-and-stress period. The quick, asymmetrical growth of the body and its members causes a feeling of incompleteness. The great potential energy that accumulates in the nerves and has not yet found an outlet causes restlessness and tension by being hindered in its activities. The appearance of all kinds of new sensations and ideas in the consciousness causes constant commotion and turmoil in the life of the soul. It resembles a sea that is tossed to and fro and up and down by the wind. The new personality that awakens to independence and wants to uphold itself feels itself enclosed, thwarted, hindered by society, which wants to lead it into the altruistic life. The subject and its environment clash, and it often appears as if the two egos in a person are on opposite sides and battle each other for victory.

This is the reason why this age is characterized, on the one hand, by a sense of incompleteness and dissatisfaction, which comes to expression in all kinds of doubt, restlessness, grief, depression, melancholy, daydreaming, introspection, and brooding. [65] On the other hand, there is a craving for freedom and independence, a desire to examine things, an idolizing of great ideas and great men, a proud generosity, faith in the future, high idealism, and a desire to reform everything. Just as with any period, so also and especially, this one has its own peculiar virtues and vices. In this period, life swings back and forth between wisdom and folly, admiration and contempt, interest and indifference, overexertion and relapse of strength, self-sacrifice and selfishness, credulity and skepticism, honorable inclinations and sinful passions. The young man stands at a fork in the road. His future depends on which road he takes. The boy is father of the man.

All these situations and experiences are the birth pangs of the new personality. Having been driven out of the paradise of childhood, the young man enters the world in order to assure himself a place of his own. Growing up to freedom and independence, he adapts to his environment and accommodates himself to the social milieu. The storm and stress he must undergo are beneficial and good. They strengthen his personality, enrich his insight, and deepen his life. From childhood the person transitions through the critical period of puberty to the age of male and female maturity. In this physical and psychical process of the years of puberty, the religious development assumes a special place. The discovery of the connection between these two processes has been such a surprise to some that they thought they could explain all of religion from the sex urge, and they saw in religion nothing but "perverted sexuality."[5]

But most of the psychologists of religion oppose this medical materialism. There may be a connection between sexual and religious development that coincides in part, for a while. But whoever wants to explain religion completely [by reference to] to sexuality may, according to them, just as well derive it from breathing and digestion because they also are connected to religion and sexuality. And they may as well regard science and art, for which interest also awakens in the years of puberty, as perverse sexuality. According to Starbuck, it is quite possible that sexual development is the cause and condition of religious awakening. But in that case one has to keep in mind the great difference between condition and cause. In religious development, not only the physical but also the psychical exerts an influence. All kinds of suggestions and ideas, especially of a moral nature, have a bearing on it. The religious process is much too complex [66] for it to be simply explained from a single cause and one single formula. Add to this that the content of religious consciousness often differs entirely from sexual consciousness, and it therefore also later maintains a place and worth of its own. The soul is dependent on the body, and vice versa, but the life of the soul and its religious content

---

5. Ed. note: Bavinck provides no reference for this (English) quotation or for those that follow. It is most likely that the phrases and clauses Bavinck cites are from Starbuck (see n. 3 above).

nevertheless are entitled to an independent worth; in the end, not its origin but its reasonable content and its moral fruit determine its worth. "By their fruit you shall know them (the mental states), not by their roots."

The rejection of this materialistic theory, however, does not alter the fact that all psychologists of religion acknowledge a close, although often not further defined, connection between religion and love, and they see religious development in the years of puberty to be a natural and necessary developmental process in a young person's life. Of course, this religious development does not happen with all people in the same way and the same form. There is a difference depending on nurture and environment, character and temperament, sex and age. Specifically there is a difference in religious development between healthy and sick souls, the "healthy-minded" and the "sick soul." There are people who do not need a conversion, and there are others who do need it. There are "once-born" and "twice-born" people. Some people enjoyed a religious upbringing in their youth and continue to feel at home in the religion of their childhood all of their lives. They do not need to experience a crisis; they do not know what a broken heart or what struggle with sin is. They do not know the fear of punishment or the anguish of judgment. They go through life as free, happy children, rejoicing in the good that surrounds them, believing in the progress of the human race, and they are possessed by good hope for the future. They are the fortunate people who because of their good humor and their positive frame of mind conquer the sorrow of this world; they are held up as examples by the "mind cure movement" when it wants to banish fear from the human heart through suggestion and destroy all sin and sickness through thought.

Nonetheless, in the years of puberty even these privileged people often experience perhaps not a definite conversion but still a more or less powerful religious revival. With the child, religion is still external and objective; if this is not to remain a memorized lesson but a matter of private, free, personal conviction, a matter of the heart, then [67] an awakening, a revival, a deepening and internalizing of religious life must take place. And such a development of religious life usually occurs at the same time that the independent personality is born in the person. There are, however, many types of religious experiences. One standard does not apply to all. The universe is much broader than we suspect and does not fit one system. There are sick souls, people who have a totally different outlook on life, who understand the misery of the world and the vanity of all things, and who in their own soul struggle with sin, with its guilt and power. These are the deeper natures who are in need of a religion of redemption, people with a low pain, fear, and misery threshold who only achieve rest and peace through a crisis.

Such a crisis usually is called conversion, and Christianity views it as the fruit of a supernatural action. But according to the psychology of religion, there is no scientific necessity to resort to a supernatural factor as an explanation of this religious crisis. Conversion, however strange and abnormal it may seem, is a completely natural process that has a satisfactory psychological explanation.

First, the psychological study of religious experiences has shown that there is a close connection between the physical-psychical development of the years of puberty and religious awakening and deepening that takes place during this same time period. The inquiry into this, and the statistical processing of the obtained data, have shown that religious awakening ordinarily falls between the tenth and the twenty-fifth years of life. Leaving out the details, it may be said that it occurs sometimes already in the seventh or eighth year, then rises sharply into the sixteenth, and then quickly decreases until the twentieth, after which it diminishes until the thirtieth year, while after that time it hardly ever occurs anymore. Attention should also be called to the fact that even though puberty and conversion may not exactly coincide in time, the religious crisis in girls usually occurs somewhat earlier than in boys. In girls it occurs especially in the thirteenth and sixteenth years, and also, but much less, in the eighteenth year. In boys, by contrast, it occurs very little before the twelfth year but happens most often in the sixteenth and also very often in the eighteenth and nineteenth years of life.

This coincidence is already remarkable and makes one surmise that there is a close connection between puberty and conversion, love and religion, sexual emotion [68] and religious awakening. This surmise is reinforced, in the second place, by a profound connection and a striking resemblance that may be observed between the above-mentioned private experiences of young people at that age and the religious findings that are made in the same years. During the years of puberty, the life of the soul is subject to a continual restlessness, turmoil, doubt, vacillation, and so forth. Well then, religious experiences display the same character. A consciousness of sin, a feeling of guilt, fear of punishment, depression, dejection, repentance, fear, and the like are all part of it. At the moment of conversion, which may last for a shorter or longer period, it is as if two forces, which then are represented differently, struggle with each other—such as the old man and the new man, darkness and light, sin and virtue, Satan and Christ—so that the persons themselves are not so much one of the competing parties but appear to themselves much more as the spoils for which both forces contend. In that struggle, experiences of sin, misery, wretchedness make room gradually, but sometimes also suddenly, for feelings of peace and joy, forgiveness and reconciliation, of God's grace and fellowship with him. The religious experiences are thus qualitatively identical to those of puberty; such events differ from pubertal ones only in that, when transported to the religious arena, they are naturally also colored religiously and are interpreted accordingly.

In the third place, according to the psychology of religion, we must keep in mind that the religious experiences that we call conversion, awakening, revival, and so forth definitely do not happen in only one religion but in all peoples and religions. Not only did Paul, Augustine, and Luther, but also Buddha, Muhammad, and others experience a religious crisis. It is not only Christianity that can tell stories of both individual and mass revivals, but so can every religion. All religious phenomena, both objective ones (dogma, worship, congregation, and so on) as well as subjective ones (mysticism, asceticism, ecstasy, revelation, inspiration, and so forth) are part of all religions. And not only that, but all religions agree in assuming, consciously or unconsciously, that there is a connection between religious development and puberty. For this age period, all religions practice certain ceremonies of separation, testing, circumcision, tattooing, and so forth, all of which are intended to initiate the young man or woman into full religious fellowship. Among us, the Roman Catholic person has first communion, the Lutheran has confirmation, and the Reformed [69] has public profession of faith. Puberty is the age of the second birth, of the birth of an independent religious and religiosocial personality.

Finally, in the fourth place, the new psychology considers itself able to provide a very acceptable explanation of the change that occurs in a person's conversion or awakening. In the last few years many psychologists have understood the great significance that must be attributed to the unconscious in human life, or better, to the subconscious or subliminal cerebration. Thus ideas that reside at a specific moment in human consciousness are only a very small and minute part of those that are actually found there. Sensations, impressions, lusts, desires, and so forth, brought about or awakened earlier, do not disappear altogether, but sink below the threshold of consciousness into the unconscious, leaving behind traces in the paths of the nervous system of the brain, where they continue as though it were their own life and activity. Through continual changes in our unconscious as a result of the garnering of new sensations, the unconscious material of ideas is constantly kept in motion. And on some occasion or other a certain category of ideas can easily rise to the surface from that unconscious and may correct ideas present in the consciousness, or totally expel and replace them.

Such transformations of consciousness, such alterations of the personality, constantly take place in human life. Today we are very much interested in a certain cause, and tomorrow we have lost interest in it. "Hosannas" are replaced every moment in the individual and the masses with the cry "Crucify him." A number, a name, an incident will not come to mind at a certain moment in spite of all our efforts, but it occurs to us a little later without any effort. An arithmetic or other problem or an argumentation looks insoluble in the evening, and the next morning a ready-made solution comes to mind. President [Theodore] Roosevelt finds himself in a totally different environment of ideas when he enjoys a hunting trip than when he devotes himself to matters of state in the White House. At that moment he is externally and internally a different person, a different personality.

So then, a conversion, a revival, an awakening is nothing more than such a transformation of consciousness. It means that "religious ideas, previously peripheral in his consciousness, now take a central [70] place, and that religious aims form the habitual center of his energy." Conversion *appears* to be sudden, immediate, unprepared, just as a thought that occurs or the inspiration of a genius. But this actually is not the case. All converts speak afterward of earlier received religious impressions. Such impressions, sensations, ideas sometimes received in early youth long ago are not destroyed, but only submerged in the unconscious. When there is an occasion from the outside that corresponds to a disposition of the soul—for instance, a word in a sermon that strikes home, a remembered or an opened text in Scripture, a moving revival meeting, and so forth—then whatever lived, stirred, and worked in the unconscious until now suddenly leaps into the conscious, expels the presently reigning ideas, and there assumes the central place itself. One's consciousness changes radically and receives an entirely new content; and with that transformation of consciousness the second birth, the birth of a new religious personality, takes place. "Spontaneous awakenings are the fructification of that which has been ripening within the subliminal consciousness."

The sudden nature that sometimes characterizes religious awakening is therefore not only no proof of its miraculous, supernatural origin, but it also does not distinguish itself in essence from that slow, steady growth to which other religious development testifies. Neither does the value of religious awakening depend on its origin; rather, it depends on its essence and fruit. The question is not "How does it happen?" but "What is attained?" Whether or not religious development experiences a crisis depends on the particularity of a person's being and is determined by earlier and present circumstances. Conversion is therefore not an event in a class of its own and experienced only by some. Rather, it is a communal experience of all; it is an expression of the awakening of the religious personality during the years of puberty, a natural, necessary, normal, psychological process during the period of youth.

This psychological explanation of conversion is supported by the religious development that becomes evident at a later age and that is generally called sanctification. Then it appears to be impossible to distinguish people who have experienced a religious conversion from those who are not aware of such an experience. "Converted men are indistinguishable from natural men." Quite often the latter are even on a higher moral plane. A situation of peace and quiet, of harmony with and adaptation to the environment, does not exclusively characterize those who are converted, [71] or only Christians, but other people as well. A feeling of certainty and joy is found in Tolstoy as well as in Bunyan. On the other hand, "twice-born men" are no more set free later from all doubt and struggle than "once-born" or "healthy-minded men." Total apostasies may be rare, but it is quite common that a period of enthusiasm and activity is followed by a time of depression and fatigue. It also holds true here that the bow cannot always be drawn. High tide is followed by low tide.

Furthermore, it is a remarkable phenomenon that when human beings reach the age of maturity, they usually conquer their doubt and begin to reconstruct their faith and life. The number of those who continue to adopt a purely negative attitude toward religion once they are adults is relatively small. With nearly all of them, their religious development results eventually, in spite of all kinds of wanderings, in a positive and active religious attitude. Reconstruction appears to be a law of religious life in later years. Once a person becomes an established citizen, becomes a man or a woman and a father or mother, and begins to assume his or her own place in society while becoming attached to it through all kinds of relationships; when they listen more quietly and seriously, with a sense of duty and a feeling of responsibility, to the voices that come to them from science and philosophy, religion and art, after the storm-and-stress period; and when they become acquainted with the disappointments and calamities of life—then their judgment often changes and becomes more tempered, and they reconstruct their religious faith. Some will return to the religion of their youth; others through change and connections create for themselves a new religion. Religiously, there remains a great diversity among people. As life develops, it differentiates and grows more complex. At times religious life may, for some people, take on a variety of pathological forms.

But nevertheless, says Starbuck,[6] the differentiation leads to unity, specifically in three respects. First, with all [Christians] there is an increasing agreement of faith in a personal God, in the existence of an immortal soul, and in an appreciation of the person of Christ, be it as Redeemer or example. Second, although many religious ideas are restored, in the thinking of all, dogmas continue to diminish in importance, more and more worth is attached to religious feelings instead of to religious belief, and more emphasis is placed on the inward aspect of religious life [72] than on its external forms. And third, according to prevailing opinion, motives and good intentions exceed faith and feelings in religion because the aspirations in all are directed more and more toward altruism. Egocentric leanings yield to others, of which society, the world, and Godhead are central.

Thus there is—to summarize Hall—thought and law, movement and plan in religious development, both in humanity at large and in the individual. There is no recapitulation. We may discern three moments here. First, the

6. Ed. note: Here is the clearest evidence that the material (phrases, clauses, and sentences) that were placed in quotation marks in the preceding paragraphs are indeed from Starbuck's work (see n. 5 above).

evolution of man into a private, independent personality, responding to the ages-long birth of humanity from animal; then the development of individual persons into social beings responding to the slow birth of society, with its endless forms and complicated relationships; and, finally, the evolution of social persons to be part of humanity, of the world at large, of the Godhead, of "The Power that makes for righteousness." According to Stanley Hall, we are now in the midst of this period. The evolution of humanity looks back on endless centuries and also faces endless centuries. We do not live in an ancient and hoary world, as Christians often think, but we live in its time of youth. The twilight we perceive is not of the evening, but of the dawn. The soul *is* not but is in the process of *becoming*—the soul is still in the making: it contains forces that now still slumber like the sleeping beauties in the woods but that will awaken and will promote, more powerfully than we can manage, the coming and the reign of the human kingdom, "the kingdom of man."

When assessing the value of the psychology of religion, for which I now ask your attention for a while, I will abstain in this context from all theological objections that could be raised against it, limiting myself to a few comments of a generally scholarly nature.

First of all, it is a reason for joy and thanksgiving that not only objective but also subjective phenomena in religion have in the last few years caught the attention of science and have been turned into objects of careful and systematic research. Even if people would want to deny all objective truth with respect to these phenomena and consider them to be nothing more than a delusion and figment of the imagination, they still deserve to be studied because of their importance and significance in the life of humanity [73] and, if possible, to be explained in their origin and essence.

There can be no doubt about the possibility and the legitimacy of this research. For even though, in my opinion, essence and perception definitely do not coincide, the world exists for a person only in and through consciousness. The content of this consciousness can therefore be seen and studied objectively, in and for itself, but also subjectively from a psychological perspective. This psychological consideration supplements the former [i.e., objective] in a remarkable way and often spreads a surprising light on religious phenomena, which it seems to view from below. This is the case in art, science, philosophy, the study of society, and so forth, and now it has been already shown in the study of religion. The difference in the religious life of the child, the youth, the man, and the old man; the connection between the religious revival and puberty; the explanation of conversion through repeated transformations of consciousness; the working of subliminal forces in the religious process; all of this, and more, expands the horizon, deepens the insight into religious life, and yields benefits that are not to be despised by the theologian, the pastor, the homiletician, the missionary, the teacher, or the educator.

But psychology of religion is still a recent discipline and therefore sometimes eager to pick fruits before they are ripe. Even though an inquiry is extended quite far, it nevertheless always remains limited to between ten and a few hundred people. And what are their claims over against the millions who have not been questioned and whose answers might completely upset the conclusion that conversion or awakening is a natural, necessary process of the years of puberty? Furthermore, though the persons to be studied may have been selected with great care and the questions put to them may have been composed with much tact, yet the responses—just as all autobiographies, diaries, confessions, conversion histories, and descriptions of personal experiences of the soul—cannot be used and assimilated for the intended purpose except with the greatest of care. Intentional dishonesty is out of the question. But there is such a lack of self-knowledge here, such danger of deception, such a great distance between being and consciousness, that it is hard to construct anything on the basis of such descriptions. And when these religious experiences, which often attach such different meanings to the same word, are processed, categorized under the same formula, arranged in [74] categories, and finally generalized into laws—then difficulties mount up so that people shrink back from drawing a general conclusion. In the history of religions, just as also in sociology and history in general, searching for fixed laws has thus far not been crowned with success. For that reason there is a legitimate fear that the psychology of religion will not see its efforts rewarded as soon as some think.

Thus, for instance, there is most likely a connection between religion and love, between religious awakening and the development of puberty. But the nature of that connection is still a mystery, just as is the connection between body and soul. Moreover, many religious awakenings have undoubtedly taken place during the years of puberty, yet the number of those that happen before and after that time is not small. There is an exception to every rule. Furthermore, sudden conversions do occur fairly often, although by no means generally, in Methodist circles; but the large Christian churches have never encouraged them and have a different idea of the manner in which this usually takes place. And finally, it is difficult to refute the fact that many, when questioned about the religion of their youth, would sooner speak of loss than of gain. Apart from this, Starbuck and Hall also acknowledge that in the years of youth not only religious-ethical personalities but also criminals, lechers, and drunkards are being formed. If over against all these facts people maintain that conversion is a necessary moment in the development of the pubertal years, then this can only happen by detaching conversion from its entire content and putting it on a par with every transformation of the consciousness. In that way there would be a conversion, as James once said, that would be without any idea of God, which could equally well be from virtue to sin as from sin to virtue. Detached from all content, thus purely psychological, and seen as a transformation of the consciousness, both puberty and religious awakening are indeed completely equal. But in that case the preconceived principle actually serves not only to correct history but, worse, to destroy the object of research rather than to explain it.

These comments lead us, furthermore, to seriously doubt the possibility of demonstrating the legitimacy, truth, and value of religion by means of the psychology of religion, as proposed by [William] James. For as long as we do not hold everything to be true and good and beautiful in religion—just as in jurisprudence, morality, aesthetics, and so forth—[75] but also acknowledge abnormal and pathological phenomena, as James and others indeed do, in order to judge we must either bring in a norm from another field, or we must try to borrow a norm from the religious phenomena themselves. The latter is the aim of so-called pragmatism, a philosophical trend that also counts James among its followers. Not the "roots" but the "fruits" are to constitute the standard for the truth and rightness of religious phenomena. Religion belongs to the "sthenic [strong] affections"; it is a life force, one of the most important biological functions of mankind. Its emphasis is not so much what God is, but how we use God. "Not God, but life—more life—is the end of religion. God is not known, He is used." By being such a life force and by applying it, religion proves its truth and legitimacy.

This is a striking viewpoint insofar that James here takes up a position diametrically opposed to Kant, with whom he otherwise agrees quite strongly. Kant tried to divest virtue completely of all *eudaemon*, that which produces happiness and well-being. With James, religion and virtue are recommended precisely because they promote general well-being and thus are socially useful. Still, even with this utilitarian norm James does not overcome the difficulty. When only the life force decides what is true and right in religion, the serious question remains whether Islam and Buddhism might not have a firmer basis than Christianity and whether superstition, which carries through to the present among a large part of the population, might not prevail over a purified religion. But aside from that, even when determining what is meant by life force and the promotion of general well-being, one cannot do without a firm standard. With the life force, we surely do not think only of strength, power, and brute force but of its content as well. If "value" or "worth" is to be the proof of "truth," then there has to be, first of all, concurrence about value and worth.[7] To be consistent, pragmatism would have to say that this value/worth can only be proved from its value or worth, and thus ad infinitum. Since this is impossible, pragmatism comes to a dead end unless it reverses itself and demonstrates the truth and rightness of religion from a different perspective than that of value or worth.

7. Ed. note: Bavinck here plays on two Dutch words, *waarde* (value, worth) and *waarheid* (truth).

James must have felt this himself when at the end of his work he asks whether, and how far, the psychology of religion proves the existence of an objective reality that it corresponds to and that proves the truth and legitimacy of religion. He answers his own question by saying that mysticism with its appeal to [76] immediate revelation, and theology and metaphysics with its speculation, are both incapable of doing this. Yet a person has not only a mind but also a heart, emotions, and a will. With the mind we only reach phenomena, "the symbols of reality." But with the heart we come into contact with real, objective reality, with the *noumenal* world, "with realities in the most complete sense of the term." For that reason the heart must be honored again. Stronger yet than the mind in scholarship, this emotional and motivational aspect of the person asserts itself in the practice of life. It leads us to a world and life view other than what scholarship alone gives us. All appreciation, particularly of things religious and ethical, depends on our personal will and is rooted in our emotions. "Le coeur a ses raisons que la raison ne connaît pas [the heart has its reasons that reason does not know]."[8]

Actually, with this conclusion James returns to the mysticism he once rejected. On the basis of a positivistic science, he tries to construct a building of an idealistic worldview. For this he divides humans into beings of mind and will, and he divides the world into a phenomenal and *noumenal* one. He now claims that these two are related to each other as symbol and reality, as menu and dinner. With respect to the unconscious, therefore, James—just as do Myers in his *Human Personality* and many members of the Society for Psychical Research—holds to the mystical theory in spite of the fact that it is opposed, on very strong grounds, by Peirce, Jastrow, Hall, and others. Granted that James does not go so far that he sees in the unconscious—in the heart, in the emotions of human beings—the lodging and working of all sorts of supernatural or *jenseitige* [otherworldly] beings. Nevertheless, he does say that reality reveals itself and is experienced there, that hidden ideas and forces work there, that God's grace comes and works through "the subliminal door." Not without reason, therefore, he calls himself a supernaturalist, albeit in a very modified sense.

Nonetheless, the knowledge that James acquires in this way, the way of Schleiermacher and Schopenhauer, is minimal. It comes down to this: the truth of religion can only be proved through psychological studies when there appears to exist a "More"—a "More" than scholarship—that researches the phenomena and lets us know. Such a "More" is objectively the essential in all religions, just as the corresponding emotions in man constitute the kernel of subjective religion. Of course, no one is satisfied with such a "More" in religion; everybody dresses it up differently and interprets it in his own way. [77] These dressings and explanations form the contents of the "overbeliefs,"

---

8. Ed. note: This saying is from Blaise Pascal (1623–62).

which are "absolutely indispensable" but which, at the same time, cannot lay claim to objective legitimacy. Thus everybody has and must have his own religion and his own God. "All ideals are a matter of relations." It may even be asked whether religious experience proves or demands the oneness of God. Religious experience does not need an absolute power or a being with absolute, metaphysical properties—such as independence, simplicity, personality, and so forth—for all such properties are empty titles, stones rather than bread: they offer "a metaphysical monster to our worship." Religion only needs a higher power. That may be the reason why polytheism contains an important truth. It shows the endless variety of the world better.

With this result for his research, James himself proves that the psychology of religion, although it can provide important contributions to a better understanding of religious life, can never replace or make up for dogmatics, philosophy, or metaphysics any more than can the history of religions. It does teach us, at least to a certain degree, what religion is, how it is rooted in and is connected to human nature; but it does not tell us anything about its content, its truth, its legitimacy. Therefore, Troeltsch comments correctly in his lecture [at the World Fair] in Saint Louis [in 1904] on *Psychologie und Erkenntnistheorie in der Religionswissenschaft* [published 1905] that psychology of religion as practiced in America, England, and France certainly offers much that is important, but because of its lack of a good theory of *Erkenntnis* [knowledge], it does not ask the question about truth. And in the final analysis in the discipline of religion as well, knowledge is all about truth.

# 5

# CHRISTIANITY AND NATURAL SCIENCE

[78] When the budget of the Dutch East Indies was discussed in the Upper Chamber [of the Dutch Parliament] in December 1911, Mister C. Th. van Deventer delivered an important speech in which he mentioned various matters, but especially the educational policy of the government in our colonies. In that connection he asked the basic question: "What is to be the foundation of the education of the natives? Is it to be based on religion or on general humanism? Is it to be confessional or neutral?"

Mister Deventer's choice was decidedly in favor of a neutral, generally humanistic education, and he adduced various considerations as the reason for his choice. Circumstances in Indonesia are quite different from ours. [The substance of his remarks follows:][1]

In our country there definitely are parents who desire an education for their children that is based on Christian principles, but in Indonesia this is, of course, out of the question. It is hard to assume that parents in Muslim areas will prefer a Christian education. When there is an expressed desire to establish such schools, this desire does not originate with the *parents* but

Ed. note: This is a rewritten version of remarks Bavinck delivered in the First Chamber of the Dutch Parliament on December 29, 1911, on the matter of the budget for the Dutch East Indies for the fiscal year 1912.

1. Ed. note: This editorial insertion was added to make it clear that in what follows Bavinck is not stating his own views but summarizing those of parliamentarian Mr. van Deventer. Bavinck was himself a member of the Upper Chamber for the Anti-Revolutionary Party (see n. 2), and this essay represents his own response to the Deventer speech.

with *others*. It has been shown, however, and there is continued evidence thereof, that parents do greatly desire a *Western* education that leaves religion untouched. This explains the undisputed popularity of the public, native school. Even the fanatic people of Aceh send their children gladly and without objection to government schools. But they certainly would not do so if the schools were used to serve the spread of teachings that were contrary to Islam. In our country many may be convinced that education requires a religious foundation, but with the great majority of natives, this is not the case. The neutral school, which for so many here [79] is a source of offense, is a much desired good for the great majority of natives.

Add to this, as Professor Snouck Hurgronje says, that orthodox Muslims today trust our public education because they know that in those schools religion is left alone. But if a strong missionary action should be conducted and supported by the government, this would certainly generate a reaction sooner or later, causing a most serious conflict in our relationship and creating difficult opposition. At the most, it would mitigate the urge for intellectual development greatly, since the native culture as yet does not have the means to establish schools on a grand-enough scale to apply for subsidies.

To misuse these circumstances, however, and to force institutions on native Muslims that to a large extent would be paid for from the taxes they paid and would also serve directly to propagandize Christianity—[that strategy] would be incompatible with prudent politics and also with the principle of the free education that the Anti-Revolutionaries so strongly advocate.[2] If native culture has shown a strong inclination during the last quarter century to be incorporated into our culture—an inclination, however, that has nothing to do with and operates outside the area of religion—then it would be totally compatible with the principles of the Anti-Revolutionary Party regarding free education to grant the natives not a positively Christian but a neutral and humanistic education, just as has been provided for years already in our public schools to the growing satisfaction of parents.

At the conclusion of his remarks, Mister van Deventer did add that he liked the idea of the Christianization of Java's Muslims very much, but we ought not to close our eyes to reality. Muslims on Java and everywhere else are rarely inclined to renounce the faith of their fathers and to accept the teachings of Christianity, which the majority of them regard as inferior. Indeed, history shows that where Islam with its consequent monotheism has established itself, chances for Christianity are as good as nil.

For that reason, in the opinion of Mister van Deventer, the mission would be much wiser to concentrate its efforts on the regions of the [Indonesian]

2. Ed. note: The Anti-Revolutionary Party (ARP), founded in 1879 by Abraham Kuyper, was the political party of the Dutch neo-Calvinists. Here it is clear that Mr. Deventer's policy remarks are directed especially at the Calvinists in the Dutch parliament. Bavinck is responding on behalf of the Anti-Revolutionary Party's point of view as well as for himself.

Archipelago that have not yet been taken over by Islam, where it could be active with a much better chance of success, [80] than to conduct a campaign among Muslims, [a campaign] that is usually hopeless and leads to Islamic opposition. In the meantime let Western humanism—which need not be irreligious, as witnessed by the positive book by Raden Adjeng Kartini[3]— continue to awaken the spirits, placate the emotions, and ennoble morals. Perhaps by following this pathway an attitude will be created among Muslims that will make them more receptive to the teachings of Christ.[4]

After Misters Hovy and Woltjer [from the ARP] had made known their objections to statements in this speech, I took the liberty of advancing objections against it as well. The first objection was that our modern culture, which in general and in our colonies in particular has been appreciated in the East during the last few years, cannot be divorced from Christianity and from religion in general. According to the report, this was stated as follows: The culture craved more and more in the East is a craving that will increase in our primary school education but even more so in our secondary and increasingly also in our higher education. In the broader sense of the word, this culture, in my opinion, is intimately connected to religion and Christianity. We could discuss this at length, but for brevity's sake I will limit myself to the following comments:

It is undeniable that our modern culture indirectly owes its existence mainly to the extraordinary progress of natural science and the application of its technical inventions, and in the second place to historical scholarship. And no one less than the renowned professor [Paul David Gustav] Du

3. Ed. note: Raden Adjeng (Ajoe) Kartini (1879–1904) was a Javanese noblewoman who became a national heroine for her pioneering work in the education and emancipation of women in Indonesia. Her collected letters were posthumously published in 1911 (The Hague) under the Dutch title *Door duisternis tot licht* (Out of Darkness Comes Light); it was translated into English and published under the title *Letters of a Javanese Princess* (New York: Alfred A. Knopf, 1920). This is undoubtedly the volume referred to here.

4. *Report of the Acts of the Upper Chamber of the States-General, 1911–1912*, 10th meeting, December 29, 1911, 113–14. After Mr. van Deventer made the long journey to the Dutch East Indies, returning in the beginning of December, he delivered a speech in the Upper Chamber on December 30, [1912,] that attracted major attention. Of course, the "Christian educational policies" of the government were also mentioned again. As I see it, this second speech in 1912 distinguished itself from the first one in 1911 in that Mr. van Deventer (1) made a much stronger plea for neutral government schools, also in Minahassa and among the Moluccans; (2) however, this time, in agreement with the Minister of the Colonies, he made a sharper distinction between the educational provisions of Muslim regions, on the one hand, and pagan regions in the outlying areas, on the other; (3) on his part he did not object that part of the educational task would be provided by Christian missions in pagan areas; on the contrary, he appreciated the work done in those areas; at the same time, he considered all missionary education and, in general, Christian education in Muslim regions definitely undesirable. His reason now was that we must accept Islam as a world religion to be respected since it is quite compatible with a higher culture. *Report of the Acts*, 12th meeting, December 30, 1912, 177.

Bois-Reymond, formerly professor in Berlin,[5] has stated that the [81] natural sciences, however paradoxical it may sound, owe their origin to Christianity. In fact, they cannot be divorced from it because Christianity is the religion that asks us to consider nature as something that is an independent entity, a position not possible in polytheism or polydaemonism. As far as the discipline of history is concerned, Professor Rudolf Eucken[6] of Jena has not just once but repeatedly acknowledged and stated that the discipline of history, as we know it today, is intimately connected with Christianity in both its essence and its value. Once again, it is Christianity that has made possible a uniform history and made it known to us as one mighty, gigantic drama that includes all peoples, the entire world, and all of humanity. On that basis I believe that we have to dispute the claim that culture without religion and without Christianity would definitely be adequate for the population in our colonies in order to give that population what it needs.[7]

A year after these words were spoken, an article appeared in [the journal] *De Gids* by Doctor Ch. M. van Deventer (not to be confused with the member of Parliament, Mister C. Th. van Deventer) that disputed this way of reasoning.[8] Or rather, he leaves the argument alone but lifts one single sentence from it, divorces it from its context, and aims the weapon of his sharp criticism against it. The sentence that is attacked, as it is cited by Doctor van Deventer in quotation marks, reads thus: "Natural science, however paradoxical it may sound, owes its origin to Christianity, from which it really cannot be divorced, because Christianity is the religion that makes us look at nature as something that is an independent entity, a position not possible with polytheism or pandaemonism."

This quotation is not literally correct, especially not when one considers the context. My reasoning was clear, I believe. It concerned the Christian politics of the government, and I tried to show briefly—in opposition to those who disapprove of this and who advocate neutral schools in the Dutch East Indies, for both higher and secondary education as well as the lower grades—that Christianity and culture cannot be separated and that any dualism supporting

---

5. Ed. note: Paul David Gustav Du Bois-Reymond (1831–89) was trained in physiology but turned to mathematics and contributed significantly to modern calculus in the area of differential equations.

6. Ed. note: Rudolf Christoph Eucken (1846–1926) was a German idealist philosopher who was awarded the Nobel Prize in Literature in 1908. The flavor of his idealist (antinaturalist) thought is clearly expressed in the following passage from his Nobel Lecture (1909): "Naturalism cannot give to literature an inner independence or allow it an initiative of its own; for if literature is only a hand of life on the dial of time, it can only imitate and register events as they happen. By means of impressive descriptions, it may help the time to understand its own desires better; but since creative power is denied to it, it cannot contribute to the inner liberation and elevation of man."

7. *Report of the Acts of the Upper Chamber*, 1911–1912, 17.

8. Under the title "Het breede betoog: Onuitgesproken rede," *De gids* (December 1912): 481–96.

such a view is untenable in theory and practice. In [82] order to have a strong argument against those who are proponents of neutral education, I appealed to an authority who is also recognized in their circles and cannot be suspected of a bias toward orthodoxy, Professor Du Bois-Reymond of Berlin. I said, verbatim: "Now no one less than the famous professor Du Bois-Reymond, formerly professor in Berlin, has stated that natural science, however paradoxical it may sound, nevertheless owes its origin to Christianity," and so forth.

However, Doctor van Deventer changes the beginning of the quotation; he omits Du Bois-Reymond and justifies it with these words: "Such was the main thesis, and that it comes from the great Du Bois-Reymond is of less importance right now: Professor Bavinck adopts it as 'a thesis in its own right.'"[9] It seems that Doctor van Deventer wants to reject what he does not consider to be an apparent but truly paradoxical statement—that the natural sciences owe their origin to Christianity—detach it from Du Bois-Reymond and his authority, and charge it to my account. Nevertheless, he is somewhat perplexed over what to do with the statement of "the great Du Bois-Reymond," next to whom all of us do not hesitate to "call ourselves but children." On page 493[10] he says that the aforementioned scholar, though renowned in physiology, was never an expert on antiquity. And in a postscript to his article, he feels compelled, for honesty's sake, to acknowledge that Du Bois-Reymond did indeed make the comment about the origin of natural science, but his reasoning in that respect, says Doctor van Deventer, is very weak, and besides, "The opposition was not against him, but against Professor Bavinck, who contended a certain thesis to be correct" (496).

With this, Doctor van Deventer totally ignores the intent for quoting this comment of the Berlin professor. If I myself had simply made such a statement about the origin of natural science, such a statement, especially without further explanation, would have been of little worth. But when a man like Du Bois-Reymond makes such a statement, all of us do well to reflect on it and decide whether his words are correct or not. For that reason it is mostly immaterial whether the person who made it part of his speech agreed with it or not. The thesis of the Berlin professor nevertheless remains valid. And for that reason the argument of Doctor van Deventer, even though he wants to avoid it, is not [83] directed in the first place against me—I merely quoted it—but against the author of the quotation.

In this I can even meet Doctor van Deventer quite a way. If I had wanted to speak about the relationship between Christianity and the natural sciences in my own words, I certainly would have expressed myself less dogmatically and less forcefully than Du Bois-Reymond. I do not say this now because

9. Ibid., 481–82.
10. Ed. note: This and following page numbers in the text are to the speech/essay "Het breede betoog."

of the criticism of Doctor van Deventer, for I have always thought this way. Years ago I put it as follows:

> Christian theology did not deny these things. On the contrary, following the example of Scripture, it has always emphatically upheld the natural order and the causal nexus of the phenomena. It is not true that Christianity with its supernaturalism was hostile to the natural order and made science impossible, as Draper, for example, and others have sought to demonstrate with such relish. Much more in line with the facts is the judgment of Du Bois-Reymond when he wrote: "Modern natural science, however paradoxical this may sound, owes its origin to Christianity." In any case, Christianity made science—specifically natural science—possible and prepared the ground for it. For the more the natural phenomena are deified—as in polytheism—and viewed as the visible images and bearers of deity, the more scientific inquiry is made impossible since it becomes automatically a form of desecration that disturbs the mystery of deity. But Christianity distinguished God and the world, and by its confession of God as the Creator of all things, separated God from the nexus of nature and lifted him far above it. The study of nature, therefore, is no longer a violation of deity.[11]

These words clearly interpret the intent of the brief remark I made during the debate in the Upper Chamber. But Doctor van Deventer may possibly counter that on that occasion I expressed myself not weaker but much more forcefully than Du Bois-Reymond, who only said that the *newer* natural science owes its origin to Christianity. But I omitted the adjective and claimed the same for the natural sciences in general. This omission in the ad-libbing was, however, wholly unintentional and happened involuntarily. I only intended to quote Du Bois-Reymond without any further [84] meaning than he himself attached to it, as I did in my *Reformed Dogmatics*. For that matter and in that connection, it would have been difficult to refer to anything else *but* the newer natural science, for the discussion was about the connection of Christianity and culture, which, I believe, should go together in the education of the people of the Dutch East Indies. Mention was made specifically there of "our modern culture," in which people in the East have expressed an interest in the last few years. It was said of this modern culture that it was derived mainly from the extraordinary progress of the natural and historical disciplines, of course in the last century or centuries, for that is the only meaning that could be given to it.

And speaking of the discipline of history, I added immediately and deliberately, "as we know it today." Finally, in the rest of my speech I intentionally made a distinction between animism and Islam as practiced by the people of the Dutch East Indies, leaving it an open question whether and how far our

11. Herman Bavinck, *Reformed Dogmatics* (Grand Rapids: Baker Academic, 2004), II:611.

culture could be adopted by Islam and grafted on their own worldview; but I definitely mentioned my belief that such was not possible with animism. No one in the place where the speech was held could think of any other culture than our present-day culture, including the natural and historical disciplines. With a little bit of goodwill, my opponent could have surmised that by referring to natural science, I specifically meant what emerged toward the end of the Middle Ages and now has reached such an admirable height, or that, at any rate, my thesis was not to be taken in the absolute sense in which he understood it. However, if natural science in general had been meant, a reasonable interpretation would have inferred from it only that natural science, although also often practiced elsewhere quite productively, nevertheless first came to its full development under the influence of Christianity. [Furthermore], the natural sciences that owe their existence to a theistic worldview achieved unprecedented unity, expansion, and significance among the Christian nations. The same can also be said of the discipline of history.

But Doctor van Deventer did not do this. With a certain amount of pleasure he pulls the aforementioned sentence from its context, divorces it from the authority of Du Bois-Reymond, [85] gives it independent status, takes it in the most absolute sense of the word, and now attributes to me the strange claim that Christianity is the only source of natural science and that there has never been anywhere else, neither in Greece nor in Arabia, anything that resembled investigation of natural phenomena.

In so doing, of course, he won the argument already before it began. If one takes on oneself the liberty to determine the position of the enemy and indicate where and how he has to stand, the victory is easy. The entire argument of Doctor van Deventer about the existence and the flourishing of the natural and historical disciplines in antiquity could therefore have been omitted completely. It is directed against a straw opponent. He must know that Christians at all times, since the beginning, thankfully acknowledged—albeit with the benefit of past records—and adopted whatever had been achieved by antiquity in the area of science and art and culture in general. On page 490 he then reminds us that the Christian world in the Middle Ages had to relearn astronomy from the Arabs and natural sciences from Aristotle, and he concludes these reminders by asking, "Isn't it foolish that we have to rattle off such facts?" I am much inclined to respond to that question in the affirmative. We don't battle facts that are irrefutable. We tend to acknowledge and respect them, as God in his providence presents them to us.

We do, however, often have objections against the explanations given of these facts and against opinions that are tied to them. The article of Doctor van Deventer also forces us to point out this necessary distinction once again. It was his right, when he thought that I stood where I certainly do not stand, to gather all kinds of facts from the history of antiquity as witnesses against me. But he did *not* have the right to attach such personal attacks and general observations as he permitted himself in his criticism, which betrays more fierce passion than wise thoughtfulness. Thus he portrays his opponent as a person of gigantic boldness, who dares to turn facts into fables (488), who reminds him of men such as Cortez, Pizarro, and the conquistadores, who wanted to conquer a kingdom with only a handful of soldiers, and where they won the battle, first destroyed temples and idols to the greater glory of Europe and Christianity (488–89). He also portrays me as a hot-tempered person not receptive to reason, [claiming that] it is folly to try to offer [86] him gentle counsel, whose rapacity blinds him to facts as large as the sun and who can only be rescued from his intoxication by fierce resistance.

These outbursts do not contribute to a high regard for Mister van Deventer's tolerance. One detects very little of what the member of Parliament [also named] van Deventer considers necessary, as he stated at the conclusion of his last speech, for the Dutch to fulfill their great task in the Archipelago: to bring knowledge and wisdom, justice and strength, self-denial, tolerance, and above all, love.[12] But, so much for the personal. Much more serious are the conclusions Doctor van Deventer draws in his article about Christianity, not only about Christians or the Christian churches, but also about Christianity itself. He does assure us that he does not want to malign Christianity, but everyone can see from the following quotations how much stock to put in this assurance. That he would mention Galileo, who was tormented; Bruno, who was burned; Bekker, who was dismissed (490)—this was to be expected, although it is surprising that Servetus is not mentioned here.[13]

But, furthermore, we learn from Doctor van Deventer that Christianity does *not* necessarily drive away polydaemonism (489), for in many countries belief in evil spirits, devils, fairies, elves, goblins, and so forth continued to reign centuries after Christianity was introduced. Back in 1600 or there-abouts, Father Delrio stated that there are evil spirits and that it is heresy not to believe this. Thus, according to Doctor van Deventer, we may well be afraid "that the natives will find support in Christianity for their national belief or superstition for a long time to come" (490). "For a Christianity that believes in saints, angels, devils, or whatever transcendental spiritual beings; and acknowledges miracles, just as popular Greek polytheism does; the possibility exists that nature can be disturbed by a force from outside itself, provided that it attaches such power of intervention to saints, angels,

---

12. *Report of the Acts of the First Chamber*, December 30, 1912, 181.

13. I certainly do not condone these and similar actions by Christians and Christian churches, nor the Bulgarian atrocities, which, as is claimed, are no match for those of the Turks. Nevertheless, a fair verdict demands that one should take into account all the circumstances, as, e.g., Professor [B. H. C. K.] van der Wijck does in his well-done, impartial study about Giordano Bruno and his statue, in *Gestalten en gedachten: Verspreide opstellen* (Haarlem: De Erven F. Bohn, 1911), 159–203. Furthermore, it makes a great deal of difference whether one grieves about these matters or takes offense at them.

and devils" (491). "Any religion that acknowledges such beings stands in this respect on a par with ancient polytheism (490), so that actually the question of mono- or polytheism is of minor importance." "The issue therefore is not whether this [87] intervening force is one or more but whether there is such a force and whether it and faith in it and strict natural science can coexist" (491). "If any form of whatever religion considers that the natural order can be disturbed by many gods, angels, devils, or saints, or by the one God himself, then this form is just as damaging to a strict training in natural science as ancient polytheism in general is more damaging than the various purified forms of it, and certainly much more damaging than the polytheism of Epicurus" (491).

All these statements have the advantage of telling us plainly where we stand, and they give us a clear indication what the judgment will be about Christian politics and Christian missionary work in the Dutch East Indies. "Gentlemen," Doctor van Deventer said in his undelivered speech, "we want to move faster in the Dutch East Indies rather than wait for centuries (during such centuries Christianity was prevalent in many countries and yet permitted all kinds of superstition to exist), and thus we prefer to put education in the natural sciences under the protection of the Enlightenment and proceed from the thesis that phenomena can be explained from natural causes. Similarly, in Greece the Enlightenment opened the way during the Middle Ages against all resistance and fought daemonism. Therefore, the Enlightenment must be brought to the Dutch East Indies lest a knowledge of natural science enter it too slowly; we must be very careful that the natives do not receive a poor understanding of Christianity, turn it into a weapon for animism, and in that way thwart the Enlightenment" (489–90).

No wonder that Doctor van Deventer, who posits with so much fervor and passion the antithesis between the Enlightenment and Christianity, even begins to speak of a religious war toward the end of his presentation. "The term *religious war*," he says on page 492, "sounds very painful, and yet we will wind up with such a war if you agree with [Bavinck's] presentation and act accordingly."

Doctor van Deventer says all of this and more in reaction to the fairly innocent and insignificant fact that I expressed an opinion in the Upper Chamber about the relationship of Christianity and natural and historical science, which I made with an appeal to the authority of Du Bois-Reymond and Eucken. And even if I considered that relationship as stringently as Doctor van Deventer unjustly attributes to me, what justification did he have [88] to lash out the way he did and to get so excited as to conclude by speaking of a religious war? Is it no longer even possible these days to discuss such an important matter as the connection of Christianity and culture without immediately arousing passions? I do not wish to follow Doctor van Deventer any further in this matter. But I gladly take the opportunity to set forth my opinion in somewhat greater detail on what the relationship of the newer natural sciences to Christianity is and what it ought to be.

To prevent misunderstanding, it is well to state in a few words, in this connection, what is meant by Christianity and [what is meant] by natural science. Regarding Christianity, we may assume that it is an established fact that it is not an art, a science, a philosophy, and so forth. It is a religion, and furthermore a religion of redemption that has the person of Christ at its center and that aims at the redemption of man from the guilt and power of sin in and through Christ and the restoration of man's fellowship with God. As such it involves a certain view of God, and therefore it can engage with natural science and possibly even clash with it. If the Christian religion consisted only of a mood, a feeling, or emotion, this would be impossible. But, however Christianity may be reduced, it always implies some religious *ideas*[14] that touch upon the realm of natural science. Nevertheless, not everything in these ideas, however important in other respects, is of importance to natural science. Many ideas, such as those concerning the church, the sacraments, and so forth, are never touched by the natural sciences, or are touched on only occasionally. But Christianity and natural science do engage each other, particularly in the area of the religious-ethical, the teleological, or in other words, in the theistic worldview as it comes to expression in the doctrine of creation—its sustenance and government—which is confessed by the entire Christian church in the first article of the Apostles' Creed.

The idea of a natural science can be considered in a broader or narrower sense depending on whether the concept of nature is taken in a broader or narrower sense. Formerly all of creation, the spiritual as well as the material, was often subsumed under nature, and the concept was expanded to include God when speaking of him as *natura naturans* [nature naturing/creating]. But even when the latter was avoided, "nature" often was considered to involve much more than in our day, including the doctrine of souls and spirits (or angels). When thinking of nature today, however, we only think of the visible, physical world, "das sinnlich Äusserliche und dem Geist Entgegengesetzte [which is the sensorially external and is set over against the spirit]."[15] But even in this limited sense, it is the object of various disciplines. In the first place, when speaking of natural science, one thinks of physics, chemistry, and engineering, but however important, they are not the only disciplines that investigate nature. Many others can be mentioned as well, such as astronomy, geology, mineralogy, paleontology, [89] geography, biology, botany, anthropology (somatology), and so forth.

These natural sciences often go by the name of exact sciences, because in many instances and on a rather broad scale, they use experiments. However,

---

14. Rudolf Otto, *Naturalistische und religiöse Weltansicht* (Tübingen: Mohr, 1904), 2ff.
15. [Rudolf] Eisler, *Wörterbuch der philosophische Begriffe* (Berlin: Mittler, 1899–), s.v. "Natur."

one should remember that this has its limits and that natural science also cannot confine itself to observation and experiment. In both instances it cannot avoid thought, speculation, precisely because as a discipline it looks for the universal, the systematic, the logic in the phenomena; *scientia non est singularum* [knowledge/science is not singular]. For that reason Wigand stated quite correctly: "Without speculation there is no hypothesis; without hypothesis no science is possible."[16] Similarly Louis Pasteur: "The illusions of an experimenter constitute a large part of his strength. Preconceived ideas serve as his guide."[17] Such speculation is necessary today in every natural science because of the grouping of the phenomena under one general heading but comes to expression especially in the discipline that had been neglected for a long time, but which has been restored to its proper place of late and is called "philosophy of nature." It is here that natural science reaches its conclusion. For the final, or if you will, the first questions are the most important ones in every discipline.

Physics and chemistry are praised greatly, and the results with which they have enriched the practical life of people in so many ways are greatly admired. After all, we like to know everything: what constitutes nature, what are its origin, its essence, and its end. It is important and useful to know the quantitative relationships that exist between things. But for us it is of much more value to know what the things are in themselves since the essence has to do with their quality, material and force, space and time, cause and movement, effect and purpose. Everyone, therefore, harbors such a philosophy of nature, consciously or unconsciously, whether they want to or not, and it impacts all scientific research. But although formerly there was great unanimity in this respect, today opinions differ greatly. Materialistic and psychical, mechanical and dynamic, monistic and pluralistic views of nature (and worldviews) challenge each other and compete for priority.

When we consider Christianity and natural science with these issues in mind, the question of the relationship between the two is hardly absurd. [90] Some rather easily dismiss this matter with a few words. They know only one thing, that religion, and particularly the Christian religion, has meant only trouble for culture in general and for natural science in particular. It would be quite easy to mention a great number of witnesses who represent this mindset. For the sake of brevity, I refer the interested reader to some works where one can find them in abundance.[18] On reading them one will soon recognize

16. Albert Wigand, *Der Darwinismus und die Naturforschung Newtons und Cuviers: Beiträge zur Naturforschung und zur Speciesfrage*, 3 vols. (Braunschweig: F. Vieweg & Sohn, 1874–77), II:68.
17. "Louis Pasteur," in Doctor J. V. de Groot, *Denkers van onzen tijd* (Amsterdam: Veen & van Langenhuysen, 1910), 156.
18. John William Draper, *History of the Conflict between Religion and Science* (New York: D. Appleton, 1897); L. Büchner, *Force and Matter, or Principles of the Natural Order of the Universe*, 4th ed., trans. from 15th German ed. (New York: P. Eckler, 1891); [Karl August] Specht, *Theologie*

that for many the struggle is not only against some ecclesiastical creed but also against Christianity itself and even against all religion. Still, this consideration is very superficial. It is refuted immediately by the meaningful and ever more acknowledged fact that for all people, culture since antiquity has been very closely connected to religion, in part originated from it and in part promoted by it. This holds for the Babylonians and the Assyrians, the Phoenicians and the Egyptians, the Chinese and the East Indians, the Greeks and the Romans, and in even greater measure for all so-called primitive people who are never devoid of culture. And it is also applicable for the knowledge of nature and research into nature to the extent that one can speak of this with these various peoples.[19] The origins of the various branches of knowledge and of all of culture go back to hoary antiquity, even to the first inhabitants of the land of Sumer and Akkad. Specifically, astronomy and arithmetic had their beginnings there under the influence of and in connection with the religious-astrological worldview.[20] When the Babylonians adopted this culture from the original inhabitants, they expanded it increasingly around them, and with their calendar they became, for instance, the teachers of all of humanity.[21] From Babylon this ancient civilization traveled to the East, to India and China, and to the West, to all of Asia Minor, Northern Africa, and—as the most recent discoveries increasingly demonstrate[22]—also to [91] Greece.

But in Greece, scholarship chose its own direction for the first time. Because it was able to free itself from popular religion and attain a purer concept of the Godhead and the world, it conquered for itself an independent sphere that assured its progress and success. An absolute separation of religion and civilization (scholarship) was unknown to them, except in a few instances. Anaxagoras and Socrates might be called atheists by the standard of folk religion, but in fact they were not. The most important practitioners of scholarship in Greece saw in nature the work of an ordering spirit, even though they did not yet know him as a holy and gracious God.

---

*und Wissenschaft*, 3rd ed. (Gotha: Stollberg, 1878); Ernst Haeckel, *The Riddle of the Universe at the Close of the Nineteenth Century*, trans. Joseph McCabe (New York: Harper & Brothers, 1900); Andrew Dickson White, *A History of the Warfare of Science with Theology in Christendom* (1896; repr., New York: Free Press, 1965).

19. For that reason it is true not only of our culture that it is connected to religion (the Christian in this case) but also of all cultures always and everywhere. One never encounters a religiously neutral culture.

20. Cf., e.g., H[ugo] Winckler, *Die babylonische Geisteskultur in ihren Beziehungen zur Kulturentwicklung der Menschen* (Leipzig: Quelle & Meyer, 1907). One ought to keep in mind that the Panbabylonists are often guilty of exaggeration, also with respect to the astronomical knowledge of the ancient Babylonians; cf. Friedrich Küchler, "Die altorientalische Weltauffassung und ihr Ende," *Theologische Rundschau* 14 (1911): 237ff.

21. R[udolf] Eisler, *Geschichte der Wissenschaften* (Leipzig: Weber, 1906), 8.

22. R. H. Woltjer, *De beteekenis van het Oosten voor de klassieke oudheid* (Utrecht, 1912), 18ff.

When in the second century Christianity became better acquainted with this classical culture, the question naturally arose how to relate to it. There were extremes on the right and on the left; some wanted to reject it totally, while others wanted to adopt it uncritically. But the Christian church and theology were, generally speaking, more sensible; adopted a critical, eclectic point of view; and tried, while investigating everything, to retain the good.[23] That it did not always succeed in this and often made too many concessions to pagan civilization and the superstitions of the people is readily granted by all who acknowledge the right and duty of the Reformation in the sixteenth century. Even though it is not correct to assert with [Arnold] Dodel that the system of Ptolemy was an accommodation to the biblical tradition,[24] it remains difficult to refute [Wilhelm] Dilthey when he says that theology was intertwined with components of ancient scholarship about the cosmos.[25]

This intimate connection with antiquity and its tradition even held up and impeded the rise and success of independent scholarship. In addition, the Christian church, after the fall of the Roman Empire in the West in 476, when its dogma had been formed and its organization completed, was faced with the gigantic task of educating the people who, with the migration of the nations, had invaded Europe. In spite of all its shortcomings, it acquitted itself of that task most admirably. This great achievement on the part of the Christian church cannot be rated high enough and ought not to be forgotten, for the church thereby safeguarded the cultural treasure of antiquity in monasteries and afterward delivered it to the new [92] nations that gradually gained their independence. Already under the influence of Charlemagne, monastery, cathedral, and canon chapter schools were established all over the realm. And when Christendom had sufficiently entered and formed the German national spirit, a thirst for knowledge and learning arose that since the twelfth century has sought fulfillment in the universities.

However, a forceful, external impetus was added here. The Germanic peoples at first had only an imperfect knowledge of classical antiquity. A great change occurred, however, when after the beginning of the twelfth century, through the medium of the Arabs, the Jews, and especially after the fall of Constantinople, the learned works of the Greeks—of Aristotle and others—about metaphysics, physics, psychology, and ethics were conveyed to Western Europe. After the decline of philosophy among the ancient Greeks, the schools of the Syrian Christians in Edessa, Nisibis, Damascus, and other places became the seats of learning. There the Arabs became acquainted

---

23. [Joseph] Mausbach, *Christentum und Weltmoral*, 2nd ed. (Münster: Aschendorff, 1905).

24. Cf. Eberhard Dennert, *Die Religion der Naturforscher*, 4th ed. (Berlin: Berliner Stadtmission, 1901), 8.

25. W[ilhelm] Dilthey, *Einleitung in die Geisteswissenschaften* (Leipzig: Duncker & Humbolt, 1883), I:369, 377. [ET: *Introduction to the Human Sciences*, edited with an introduction by Rudolf A. Makkreel and Frithjof Rodi (Princeton, NJ: Princeton University Press, 1989).]

with philosophy and in an unbelievably short time succeeded in appropri-
ating it and bringing it to the pinnacle of success. Their acquaintance with
Christian theology, such as that of John of Damascus, and the necessity of
controversy promoted the rise of Islamic theology and the development of
dialectics. The study of the Qur'an and the study of language were the result
of this, but that was not all. Soon all kinds of disciplines of nature and history
came to new life, especially after 750 AD among the Abbasides, who made
Baghdad a center of culture. Following the example of the academy in the
capital, schools and libraries, sometimes also observatories and hospitals,
were established in many other places. The scholarship of classical antiquity
was not only preserved in those schools; it was also augmented and expanded
in many respects.[26]

Opinions are divided about the value of this Islamic culture. Whatever
one may think of it, it perished in the Islamic world for all kinds of external
and internal reasons, and until today it has not been revived there, although
it has been transferred to Christian Europe. Here it found a receptive environment; the seed fell into fertile soil. To be sure, at first there was some
opposition to the introduction of Aristotle into the schools, but this resistance was of a relatively short duration. Once he became better known [93]
and was understood to be free from Platonic and Neoplatonic speculation;
and once his idea about God, the creation of the world, and the immortality of the soul had been more or less brought in line with the Christian
creed; then he gained great authority and became the precursor of Christ
in natural matters [*praecursor Christi in naturalibus*], as John the Baptist
had been in matters of grace [*praecursor Christi in gratuitis*]. Aristotle was
actually thought to be a monotheist, and his theistic worldview was one of
the reasons why Arabic and Jewish philosophy were so readily received in
Christian Europe.[27]

All these factors worked together to form the medieval scholarship that is
known as Scholasticism; although it is often greatly scorned, it is usually little
studied or understood. The Middle Ages continue to remain known in some
circles as the Dark Ages, but this judgment rests on ignorance and is very one
sided. One loses the desire and the courage to look down contemptuously on
this important period in the history of Christian culture (not to speak of other
elements of culture such as, for instance, the arts) when only the following
three factors are kept in mind: (1) medieval Christianity brought about the
Christianization and civilization of the new peoples; (2) it gave life to the
oldest and most famous universities; (3) it tackled the most basic issues with
tremendous intellectual power and raised the humanities to an exceptional

26. Alfred von Kremer, *Culturgeschichte des Orients under den Chalifen*, 2 vols. (Wien: Braumüller,
1875–77), II:396ff.; Joseph Hell, *Die Kultur der Araber* (Leipzig: Quelle & Meyer, 1909).

27. Friedrich Ueberweg, *Geschichte der Philosophie*, ed. Max Heinze, 4 vols. (Berlin: E. S. Mittler
& Sohn, 1901–5), II:271, 276–77; Dilthey, *Einleitung*, I:385, 393.

height never achieved before. Of course, with respect to this, the question is not whether we can adopt this medieval scholarship as our own and whether it suffered from many deficiencies. Even Roman Catholicism acknowledges that it awarded too much authority to antiquity, neglected observation, and believed that it could find all wisdom in books.[28] How much more should Protestants acknowledge this! However, this medieval deficiency could be explained historically, and it was not a mistake of principle, for Scholasticism taught unanimously, while rejecting the doctrine of innate ideas, that observation was the path to knowledge.[29]

The idea of evolution, which is still more of a frame of mind than a system that governs all of us, often plays tricks on us and makes us unreasonable with regard to the past. It involuntarily leads us to believe that former things are of themselves inferior, transitory, and have had their day; that they only served as a preparation for what was to come; and that they lacked any independent worth. [94] But this is highly biased. Besides leading toward what is to come, every period in history also has its own lasting significance. "We are not all capable of everything [*non omnia possumes omnes*]."[30] Therefore, quite correctly Paulsen says, referring especially to medieval scholarship: "It is a foolish idea that asks that every human being should live for the sake of his fellow man and every historical period for the sake of the future."[31] He considered it to be a judgment that was just as unwarranted as that of Romanticism concerning the Enlightenment and that of social-democracy concerning today's society.

Besides this, however, the Middle Ages were also a positive factor in preparing people for a new day. Many factors contributed to this: the Germanic spirit, the Crusades, the rise of the cities and a free citizenry, social and political conditions, the invention of gunpowder, the printing press, Arabic and Jewish philosophy, the discovery of America, and so forth. The new day is to be explained not only as a result of the Reformation, nor exclusively of the Renaissance, nor can the scholarly spirit that arose toward the end of the Middle Ages be reduced exclusively to humanism. "It is a foreign idea," says Dilthey, "to reduce the change of the scholarly spirit since the fourteenth century to humanism. The increase in knowledge through books and with the help of antiquity took place during the entire Middle Ages."[32] And it is true that this increase of knowledge benefited the humanities first of all. Nevertheless, theological metaphysics ceased to be the center of European thought when the

28. Cf., e.g., T[ilmann] Pesch, *Die grossen Welträthsel*, 2nd ed., 2 vols. (Freiburg: Herder, 1892), I:118, 138, etc.
29. Ibid., I:250, 106, 134. For that matter, men such as Albert the Great, Roger Bacon, Nicholas of Cusa, and Leonardo da Vinci taught the contrary by their example.
30. Ed. note: Virgil, *Eclogue* 8, line 63.
31. F[riedrich] Paulsen, *Geschichte des gelehrten Unterrichts* (Leipzig: Veit, 1885), 21.
32. Dilthey, *Einleitung*, I:452.

knowledge of nature and the philosophy of nature of the Greeks and Arabs invaded Western Europe, bringing about, according to Dilthey, the greatest intellectual change that took place there during all of the Middle Ages.[33]

But Christianity also exercised its unmistakable influence in this process. In the first place, the Holy Scriptures—through psalmists and prophets, Jesus and the apostles—presented a view of nature so rich and beautiful that it not only produced an unsurpassed poetry of nature in Israel but also brought into being in the Christian church a lofty, and yet basically very sound, philosophy of nature as is found nowhere else,[34] through men such as Gregory of Nyssa, Athanasius, Saint Augustine, and Thomas Aquinas.

[95] While paganism always hovers between reckless abuse of the world and a childish fear of its mysterious forces, the Hebrew with sovereign self-assurance encounters nature without being afraid of it and yet with an awareness of being highly responsible, because as a man of God he has the calling to subdue and manage it.[35] At various times in antiquity, natural philosophy, especially with Aristotle, rises high above the theogonic and mythological ideas of popular belief; but even where the ideas come close to monotheism, the Godhead remains as a cosmic power, without holiness and without love, which arranges everything toward its reasonable end. To understand the rich significance of this, it is well to point to the Christian view of history. No one disputes that Herodotus may be called the father of history. But there remains, nevertheless, a significant difference between the Greek view of history and that of Christianity, which is rooted in Holy Scripture, understood best by Saint Augustine, and described by [Rudolf] Eucken as follows:

> Although in its ecclesiastical form Christianity clung firmly to the doctrine of unchangeability, its thought world was not lacking in fruitful impulses of an opposite character. History meant far more to Christianity than it did to the ancient world. It was the Christian conviction that the divine had appeared in the domain of time, not as a pale reflection but in the fullness of its glory; hence as the dominating central force of the whole, it must relate the whole past to itself and unfold the whole future out of itself. The unique character of this central occurrence was beyond all doubt. Christ could not come again and yet again to let himself be crucified; hence as the countless historical cycles of the ancient world disappeared, there was no longer the old eternal recurrence of things. History ceased to be a uniform rhythmic repetition and became a comprehensive whole, a single drama. Man was now called on to accomplish a complete transformation, and this made his life incomparably more tense than it had been in the days when man had merely to unfold an

33. Ibid., I:379.
34. Cf. Bavinck, *Reformed Dogmatics*, II:408ff., 416ff.
35. According to Rudolf Smend, *Lehrbuch der alttestamentlichen Religionsgeschichte* (Freiburg im Breisgau: Mohr, 1893), 458.

already-existing nature. Hence in Christianity, and nowhere else, lie the roots of a higher valuation of history and of temporal life in general.[36]

In this view of history the new element that Christianity introduced is shown even more clearly than in [the view] of nature. [96] However much medieval thought depended on that of the ancient peoples, here in the philosophy of history and society it was "schöpferisch [creative]," as Dilthey calls it. Christianity was conceived of as a cooperation of the will of reasonable creatures with divine providence, which wants to lead people to an established goal: the kingdom of God. This view is totally different from that of antiquity, for the classics continued to derive their view of the Godhead from the cosmos, and where they constructed teleological systems, they never got any farther than a "Gedankenmässigkeit des Weltzusammenhangs [feeble understanding of the world order]." But with Christianity, God himself enters history and leads people to the realization of his goal. In Christianity, God becomes the God of history. For the ancient peoples, God always remained a force of nature to which also society, meaning humanity, was in the end subjected; but in Christianity, God is the God of history, who fulfills his counsel in the world. There [with the ancients] God is supreme reason; here [in Christianity] he is the almighty, holy, gracious Will. There he is substance; here he is a person. There the world is a development of nature; here it is a wonderful drama.[37]

And this again has a bearing on one's view of nature, for the first and the second article of the Apostles' Creed are mutually related. Nature is a mechanism in which everything moves according to a fixed order, measure, and number. We see this more clearly today than in former days, but the biblical authors and Christian theologians and philosophers such as Saint Augustine also essentially knew this. We should not presume, therefore, that we understand the essence of causality or, for instance, the law of gravity better than in earlier times because we have learned to use this term "gravity," for it remains true, before and after [modern science], that no created spirit penetrates the essence of nature. But Christianity gave to the newer natural science the realization that nature, however mechanically it may operate, is subject to the spirit and that the whole world is an instrument, an apparatus, for the realization of an eternal divine plan.

Something was added to this. People in the Middle Ages displayed a strong desire for world domination along with a deep hunger for world flight. Both

36. Rudolf Eucken, *Main Currents of Modern Thought: A Study of the Spiritual and Intellectual Movements of the Present Day*, trans. Meyrick Booth (London: T. F. Unwin; New York: Charles Scribner's Sons, 1912), 246; cf. idem, *The Problem of Human Life as Viewed by the Great Thinkers from Plato to the Present Time*, trans. Williston S. Hough and William Ralph Boyce Gibson (New York: Charles Scribner's Sons, 1910), 143–44, 147–50.

37. The reading of the entire, thoughtful chapter in Dilthey's *Einleitung*, I:418–46, "Die mittelalterliche Metaphysik der Geschichte und Gesellschaft," is recommended.

were born from a dualism between matter and spirit that was derived not from Scripture but from Plato's philosophy, [97] a dualism that in Christianity, the more it became Roman Catholic, was transferred to the distinction between the natural and the supernatural. We do not do justice to Rome when we assume that Rome identifies the natural and the material with what is sinful, or deems it to be the principle of what is evil. But Rome does consider the natural to be somewhat inferior, something of a lower order, which must be curbed by supernatural grace. In the same measure, as medieval Christianity brought this distinction into opposition and tension, it prepared a strong reaction and greatly promoted this distinction through its educational system. Toward the end of the Middle Ages, a desire awakens everywhere and in every sphere of life for liberation: liberation from the pope, from the emperor, from the church, from the hierarchy, from the priest, from the tradition, from Scholasticism, from barbarous Latin, from the philosophy of Aristotle, from "gothic" art, from the unnatural. It is as if humanity has come of age and refuses to be led by the church. The spirit of Protestantism is born. And in this emancipation movement the Reformation assumes a central place, for it grants the individual—who had lost the support of the infallible church—a religious certainty through preaching justification of the sinner by faith alone. Every person needs this certainty in order to work energetically, to understand his earthly task to be a divine calling, and to devote all of natural life to the service of God.

Natural science was undertaken in this way and in this spirit. From the beginning it was marked by [Francis] Bacon's word: "Superficial science leads away from God; thorough, sound science leads toward God." For it should not be forgotten that the awakening of the newer natural science coincides with the Reformation and contemporary developments and that all these different movements, however distinct, are nevertheless disclosures of the new spirit and mutually demonstrate a great degree of kinship. We see this not only negatively in their opposition to medieval Scholasticism but also positively in retrieving the natural everywhere and restoring it to its rightful place as a result of a specific, new religious point of view. The Reformers are known for this. They replaced the Roman Catholic quantitative antithesis of inferior nature and supernatural grace with the ethical or qualitative one of sin and grace.

We find a similar reformation in those days with the founders of natural science. Influenced by mysticism, just as Luther, they found God again [98] in their own lives and hearts, and they also again discovered him all around in nature. This nature remained the same, but the human person had changed. They viewed nature differently, looking at it in a new light, in the light that had arisen in their own soul through God's revelation. And when such people looked at nature from that perspective, they stood amazed at its beauty and glory. Admiration again became the beginning of science. Nature, seen in

God's light, was not a seducing, satanic power but a revelation of God's glory and a marvelous creation of unity and harmony. God's unity brought about the unity of the world. And subject and object, microcosmos and macrocosmos, all felt a kinship in God, who created both [elements as paired]. In his *Table Talk*, Luther said that by God's grace we begin once again to acknowledge his glorious works and wonders in the formation of the fruit in the womb and the flowers of the field. Calvin testified that there is no minute part or piece of the world that does not reveal God's glory. And in the Belgic Confession we read that nature is like a beautiful book in which all creatures, great and small, are as so many letters, an image that already appears with Raymond of Sabunde.

Thus spoke all those men who introduced the newer natural science. Faith and science are not antithetical with them and not even independent from each other. But faith stimulates them to investigate nature scientifically. Columbus was a hero of faith who derived strength and courage from his faith to make his way westward in spite of all opposition. He even considered himself called by God to discover the lost paradise in the Far East, so that when he discovered the Orinoco River, he thought that he faced one of the streams of paradise (Eden). Copernicus, "the Luther of astronomy," also felt attracted to the heliocentric system because it was simpler and more in accord with the wisdom of the Creator. Paracelsus, "the Luther of medical science," recommended the study of nature because alongside Scripture it is God's book, with each country as a page. These people strongly encouraged observation and sometimes even experiments, because they wanted to know God from his works, a desire expressed by Huygens, Newton, Boyle, Harvey, Swammerdam, and by far the majority of astronomers and naturalists in their scientific work and also in their explicit testimonies.

To be sure, all of this is being suppressed and ignored in certain quarters. Under the influence of a false view of the world, many have begun to believe that natural science has [justifiably] robbed us of the Bible, Christianity, religion, morality, justice, and yes, even God himself. [99] Hence they take pleasure in portraying almost all men of renown as materialists and atheists and incorporate them into their own ranks. Specht, for instance, says that the materialist understands that a spirit cannot have generated matter and that therefore only the knowledge of matter can lead to an understanding of its potency and laws: this explains the fact that most and the greatest naturalists choose materialism.[38] But history shows us something different. It would speak even more forcefully if we knew what was in a man. But in the books that treat the history of the sciences, the religious convictions of its practitioners are rarely, if ever, mentioned. Even books about the history of philosophy usually fail to take note of them, as if they did not have the

38. Specht, *Theologie und Wissenschaft*, 355.

slightest bearing on the thinking of the philosophers and as if all these men were only thinkers and not people of flesh and blood. It is also often difficult to find out what their innermost thoughts were about God and religion, because they never spoke about it, or perhaps only among friends, and thus nothing of their thoughts on this subject is preserved for posterity. But we may be sure that, as [Louis] Pasteur once said in the Academy of Medicine, there are two people in each of us:

> Each one of us is made up of two persons: the intellectual person with a mind that is without presuppositions, who through observation, experimentation, and reasoning wants to bring himself to a knowledge of nature; and also the sensitive person, the man of tradition, of faith or doubt, the man who has feelings, the man who weeps because his children are no more and who cannot prove—sad to say—that he will see them again, but who believes and hopes that he will, who does not want to die like a microbe, and who tells himself that the force that is in him will bring about a transformation.[39]

But even if we consult only what is known for certain about the faith of the greatest men of our race in all centuries and among all peoples, including what they believed about natural science since its revival from the beginning of the new history, the proponents of a theistic natural science may confidently say: Those who are with us are greater than those who are against us. Groen van Prinsterer was fully justified when, as a man of his own age, he called on all the preceding centuries to be witnesses as he disputed the constitutionality of the French Revolution. And in like fashion the great majority of those who practiced natural science from the end of the Middle Ages until approximately the middle of the eighteenth century were adherents of the magnificent Christian confession: [100] "I believe in God, the Father Almighty, Creator of heaven and earth."[40]

But in the eighteenth century a gradual change took place. Its way was prepared by Deism, and it emerged for the first time clearly and plainly in Baron [Paul-Henri Thiry] d'Holbach's *Système de la nature*, published in 1770, which has rightly been called the bible of materialism. The naturalism it promulgated—which, judging by the time in which the work appeared—was

---

39. In J. V. de Groot, *Denkers van onzen tijd*, 171.

40. For the sake of brevity I refer to a few books that show the truth of this contention: Rudolf Eucken, *Beiträge zur Einführung in die Geschichte der Philosophie*, 2nd ed. (Leipzig: Dürr, 1906), 1–54 (about Cusanus, Paracelsus, and Kepler); Otto Zöckler, *Gottes Zeugen im Reich der Natur*, part 2 (Gütersloh: Bertelsmann, 1881); Karl Alois Kneller, *Das Christentum und die Vertreter der neueren Naturwissenschaft* (Freiburg: Herder, 1903); E[berhard] Dennert, *Die Religion der Naturforscher*, 6th ed. (Berlin: Berliner Stadtmission, 1901); idem, German 7th ed., trans. G. Steenkamer, titled *Zijn de natuuronderzoekers ongeloovigen?* (Baarn: Hollandia, 1910). See also Karl Joël, *Der Ursprung der Naturphilosophie aus dem Geiste der Mystik* (Basel: Reinhardt Univ.-Dr., 1903); and Élie de Cyon, *Gott und Wissenschaft*, vol. I, *Psychologie der Naturforscher* (Leipzig: Veit, 1912).

not the fruit of an exact science but the product of a philosophic worldview that dated back already to some Greek philosophers of antiquity. Nevertheless it was accepted more and more in the nineteenth century following the collapse of speculative philosophy. Further, it was supported by, or at least sought the support of, the teaching of the variability of the species first advocated by de Lamarck and Geoffrey Saint Hilaire, Darwin's theory of descent, and the mechanical explanation applied with such extraordinary success in physics and chemistry in the nineteenth century. Among scholars there is virtually no objection to the mechanical explanation. No protest was ever raised against it based on any article of the Christian confession. There is no talk of a battle against physics and chemistry, just as there is none with mechanics (engineering), astronomy, mineralogy, and so forth. Nor does it concern even geology and paleontology, as long as a distinction is made between the facts and the theories built on them. But this changes as soon as we come to the doctrine of life, the origin of organisms and specifically of humanity. We do not have to look far for the reason for this. The mechanical explanation of nature is not science but a specific viewpoint among the practitioners of science who are intent on drawing all these phenomena of organic life within the circle of physics, chemistry, and engineering (mechanics) in order to explain them in a purely mechanical and merely quantitative fashion.

[Ernst] Haeckel teaches this most clearly. His idea of the monism he preaches is that there is only one "Weltgesetzlichkeit [world order]," [101] causal mechanism, and he calls every other theory simply dualistic, transcendent, supranaturalistic. When Du Bois-Reymond deems that life and consciousness cannot be explained from metabolism, he offers, according to Haeckel, a program of metaphysical dualism.[41] If [Wilhelm] Wundt still maintains that psychology is a special discipline, then he has exchanged his monistic, materialistic point of view for dualism and spiritualism.[42] When Karl Ernst von Baer speaks of a "Zielstrebigkeit [purposefulness]" in connection with organic bodies, then [Haeckel claims that] because of increasing age and the influence of mysticism, von Baer modified his original monistic views and made them dualistic.[43] But in this respect, Haeckel is definitely not the only one [so speaking], even though he perhaps goes farther than others.

Many agree with Haeckel in principle, even though when they come to a certain point in the road they suddenly stop and refuse to proceed. So, for instance, Du Bois-Reymond hides behind his seven mysteries of the world and considers these beyond explanation by science, but actually he reasons this way because he thinks about science the same way as Haeckel does. The purpose of all study of nature, the ideal of theoretical natural science, is

41. Haeckel, *Riddle of the Universe*, 180–82.
42. Ibid., 100–101.
43. Ibid., 266–70.

for him "the dissolution of all natural phenomena in the mechanism of the atom," so that someone equipped with sufficient understanding to survey the entire world at a particular moment would be able to read from it infallibly its entire past and future.[44] Even here it is a matter of indifference whether the original elements of the world are called atoms, molecules, dynamids, monads, energies, or whatever else. What matters above all and what is the deciding factor is the question of whether the scientific explanation coincides with the reduction of all natural phenomena—even of life, consciousness, the will, and so forth—to a mechanism of atoms.[45]

Such a mechanical explanation of the world, I am convinced, constitutes a danger not only for Christianity and religion in general, but also for our entire culture and for all our ideals. We ought to be grateful, therefore, that in recent years a few reactions have arisen in scientific circles in opposition to it; that psychology and history have tried to regain their independence; and that in opposition to or next to materialism, idealism once again asserts itself. But this reaction often [102] displays a more conservative character rather than a character based on principle, and it therefore is not capable of stemming the tide. It pins its faith on dualism, which makes a distinction and separation between the known and the unknown, between the area of scholarship and fantasy, between man's head and heart, between his intellect and instinct (intuition), and so forth, and thus in principle between two supreme powers in the world. And in the meantime, materialism and the mechanical worldview gradually invade all segments of the population, and there they undermine all notions of religion, morality, and justice. In a certain sense it is therefore possible to separate Christianity and culture. But to the degree by which it detaches and withdraws itself as a culture from Christianity, and natural science withdraws from the theistic confession, it ceases to be culture in the real sense of the word or true scholarship and thus it loses its beneficial influence. What [Uriel] da Costa said about the printing press—that it was a giant step toward heaven and hell—holds true for all culture. Dynamite is a marvelous invention and greatly useful. But in the hands of the anarchist, it becomes a means for arson, destruction, and murder.

This view of the relationship between Christianity and culture is especially important for the Dutch East Indies. Here in Europe we live in a society that to a large degree is still permeated by the Christian spirit and has its religion, morality, justice, and so forth resting on Christian principles. However, suppose that Christianity with its religion, church, institutions of mercy, Sundays and feast days, marriage, the oath, moral and judicial principles, art and culture, and so forth were suddenly removed from our

44. [Emil Heinrich] Du Bois-Reymond, *Über die Grenzen des Naturerkennens: Die Sieben Welträthsel; Zwei Vorträge*, 5th ed. (Leipzig: Veit, 1882), 10ff. Cf. the criticism of Wigand, *Darwinismus*, II:433ff.

45. Cf. also Otto, *Naturalistische und religiöse Weltansicht*, 17–18.

midst: our poverty would be incalculable and our loss unequalled! And then imagine that one of the newer worldviews and personal outlooks such as the materialistic monism of Haeckel became the faith of the masses. Would it be possible to build a church, a worship, a religion, morality, a judicial system, a society, a civil state on it? There certainly are a few reasons that make it doubtful. Fortunately today there are no longer any official restrictions to free speech. But this does mean that with this freedom of speech the moral responsibility of all practitioners of scholarship and of all bearers of culture becomes even weightier and that all of them have to conduct themselves the more according to Kant's principle: Conduct yourself in such a way that the basic tenet of your will could apply at the same time as a general law.

As stated, this is doubly important for our colonies. For there is no [103] Christian society that can offer a counterbalance and resistance to worldviews that undermine all religion and morality. There is no doubt that many have honest intentions with regard to the neutral culture that they want to pass on to the Dutch East Indies. But it is equally certain that this culture, by itself and involuntarily, affects the religious and moral convictions of the native population in many respects, in addition to its civil and social life. This is admitted quite generally today with regard to the animistic peoples, and many acknowledge the right and the benefit of Christian missions. But this mission is considered unnecessary and dangerous in regions and countries with a Muslim population. In fact, a distinction should be made between these two aims of missionary work; missions experienced this and complained about the powerlessness and lack of results that characterized the efforts to Christianize Islam; [missionaries] will be the last to say that they have already found the proper method and the right path. But this does not mean that mission work should cease and that neutrality is the correct attitude that Christianity is to assume toward Islam.

The proponents of neutrality do not remain true to this point of view even when it comes to the schools. As soon as they demanded neutrality in education, they immediately described it with the term "humanistic education," which does not even need to be irreligious, as the book by Kartini proves. This humanism, however, undoubtedly includes a particular worldview, or at least a philosophy of life that is different from the Christian one and that is diametrically opposed to the Muslim faith. To be sure, humanism, at least as it emerged from the Renaissance toward the end of the Middle Ages, contains different elements that are also appreciated by Christianity, for Christianity wants to form people of God who are perfectly equipped for all good work. However, if people use neutrality in order to make propaganda for humanism, what are we to say to those who use the same neutrality to achieve acceptance of agnosticism, skepticism, atheism, materialism, and socialism, or to generally recommend a mechanical worldview that mocks God and religion, in the name of unbiased scholarship and modern enlightenment? This danger is no longer imaginary.

Finally, in the Christian world, culture has achieved an extraordinary height, but when we consider the mass of humanity, [we know that] relatively few enjoy it. Whoever does not [104] know it from personal observation finds it hard to imagine how simple and sober most peoples' lives are, not to mention those who suffer from poverty and want. And that will never change, of course, in spite of all efforts to spread knowledge, culture, and prosperity to an ever larger circle. It is clear that the earth is not rich enough to let all its millions of inhabitants live in luxury. In the sweat of his brow a man is to earn the bread that he is modestly apportioned, to sustain himself and his family. That by itself is not an unfortunate circumstance, for peace of mind is not found in riches and luxury, but godliness with contentment is great gain. But if European culture makes its way into the Dutch East Indies, it will take with it not only its advantages but also its disadvantages, such as capitalism, the proletariat, class distinction, the big cities, luxury, and also poverty, grim labor in mines and factories, not to speak of the importation of alcohol and opium.

Without idealizing the circumstances of uncivilized people as Rousseau does, the question is nevertheless pertinent whether they would grow happier and more content simply because of our culture. Nonetheless, the cultural process proceeds under God's providence and cannot be reversed. But in that case is it not our calling and duty to offer—if at all possible, to all those peoples whom we want to raise to our level of civilization—the comfort of faith in their dire struggle of life? And tell them about God, the Father of our Lord Jesus Christ, who by his almighty and ever-present power upholds, as with his hand, heaven and earth and all creatures; who so rules them that leaf and blade, rain and drought, fruitful and lean years, food and drink, health and sickness, prosperity and poverty—all things, in fact, come to us not by chance but from his fatherly hand? Essentially, the church's mission has no other aim than this. And thus it does not stand in opposition to culture but connects with every culture that merits the name. The same is true with natural science, according to the words of Friedrich Rückert:[46]

> Nature is God's book,
> but man will experience
> that without divine revelation
> his attempt to read it will fail.

---

46. Ed. note: Friedrich Rückert (1788–1866) was a German poet and professor of Oriental languages who translated poetic works from Chinese, Persian, and other Oriental languages.

# 6

# EVOLUTION

[105] The idea associated with the word "evolution" is so unstable and changeable that we should first give a clear definition of what is meant by it.

The word appears already in classical Latin, but at the time it had a different connotation from what it has today. In the first place, the verb *evolvere*, from which it is derived, means to roll into the open something that is within and hidden and is therefore used, for example, of intestines that fall to earth. It also acquires the meaning of unfolding, dispersing, opening, and is used of a garment that is unfolded, of a scroll that is opened. Furthermore, it acquires the meaning of treating a subject that has to be unfolded orderly and gradually in a speech or essay. That is why *evolutio* appears in Cicero in the sense of consulting and reading a book, and it also referred to the regular treatment of a subject. The words *evolvere* and *evolutio* were therefore used originally in a methodological sense, and they retained this meaning for a long time. It is not until the eighteenth century, especially with Leibniz, that the Latin *evolutio*, the French *développement*, and the German and Dutch word *ontwikkeling* were applied to the real becoming, the becoming of things in nature.

Much older than the word is the thought expressed by these designations today. In antiquity, according to [Rudolf] Eucken,[1] the idea of *being* was

Ed. note: Originally published in *Evolutie*, in the series Pro en contra betreffende vraagstukken van algemeen belang [Concerning Questions of General Concern], series 3, vol. 3 (Baarn: Hollandia, 1907); the companion piece was written by P. G. Buekers.

1. Ed. note: The reference, not provided by Bavinck, is probably to Rudolf Eucken, *The Problem of Human Life as Viewed by the Great Thinkers from Plato to the Present Time*, trans. Williston S. Hough and William Ralph Boyce Gibson (New York: Charles Scribner's Sons, 1910), esp. 18ff.

prominent, and the Eleatic school pushed this concept to the limit to such a degree that multiplicity and movement were dissolved in appearance. But over against this, Heraclitus made himself guilty of a similar exaggeration when he rejected all *being* and subjected [106] not only particular things but also the entire world to eternal change. This philosopher claimed there is no *being*, only *becoming*. Only *becoming*—what happens, movement—is God. The philosophy that succeeded these trends was marked constantly by its attempt to avoid both extremes, and by trying as much as was possible to combine being and becoming, unity and multiplicity, rest and movement, the absolute and the relative. This not only occupied Empedocles, Anaxagoras, the Atomists, but also Plato and Aristotle. And one can rightly say that the last named philosopher was the first to devise a "system of development."

Aristotle conceived of *that which is* as the being that is developing in the phenomena. True being does not consist in isolation above and beyond, but it is *within* things. However, it does not immediately and initially fully exist there, but it gradually comes into being by way of a process. All becoming (happening, moving) consists in the transition from potential to actuality. Aristotle, therefore, does not explain what comes to pass—as the Atomists do—from mechanical pressure or impact, but he borrows his idea of development from organic life. For him becoming is an actualizing, a realization of what is potentially and germinally present in the phenomena; he explains the *becoming* from the *being*; for him the *genesis* exists for the sake of the *ousia*. With this thinking, Aristotle is far ahead of the Atomists because he considers becoming not as determined entirely from the outside through accidental circumstances but as guided from the beginning in a certain direction. The nature, the character, the being, the idea of something indicates the direction in which the development will take place. Since evolution is thought to be organic, it is also thoroughly teleological. And since Aristotle applies this idea of development not only to particular things but also to the world in its entirety, he discovers order and planning, movement and upward mobility in the world of creatures. The higher always presupposes the lower and is built on it, but the higher is never the mere product of the lower; it in turn is something independent that rises above the lower. Evolution is organic and teleological, and for that reason it has a progressive character.

Christianity did not replace or dispute this idea of development but took it over and enriched it. The idea of development has profited from the Christian worldview especially in two respects. First of all, by the doctrine of creation. Aristotle, in his system, did not know what to do with matter. Just like Plato and most of [107] the Greek philosophers, he remained a dualist: spirit and matter, the divine and the physical stood next to each other from eternity. Matter was originally and remained to the end an unruly mass, an irrational remainder, from which one could not determine how it could become part of the idea. But Christianity taught that matter also originated from and through the word and therefore was a part of divine thought. This then clarified how the world could share in the idea: the world did not merely have fellowship with the idea, but it proceeded from the idea. The world was the incarnation of thought. *Vernunft* [reason] was the foundation of all things. Nature is not a dark, demonic mass but incarnate word, infinitely deep qua content and yet clear to the very bottom. Still, with this view Christianity did not fall into the error of Hegel, the mistake of calling all of reality reasonable. It did allow for all the discord that is present in this world, but it conceived of it as a temporary, occasional deformity; Christians explained discord not from the essence of things, from matter, but from the anomaly, from the *anomia* of things—not physically, therefore, but ethically. Christianity did not bring a dualistic division, but it did make an indelible distinction between the physical and the ethical process. By doing so, it has immeasurably enriched the theory of development.

This becomes even more apparent when we consider, in the second place, what new, important idea Christianity has given to history. Only recently [Ulrich] von Wilamowitz-Moellendorff expressed it as follows: "The Greeks have never developed a real theory of history." Their horizon was too limited. They knew people, but not humanity, and for that reason they could not arrive at a uniform history. History was caught up in the rising and falling of nations, in a monotonous repetition of the past. What happens today has already happened many times before and will happen again. There is a restless coming and going of worlds, but in that endless process there is no progress, no hope of an eternal rest. By contrast, Christianity presents a history of humanity, a development that proceeds from a certain point and moves toward a specific goal, progressing toward the absolute ideal, toward true being, toward eternal life. History becomes an immense drama that leads through suffering to glory, a divine comedy that shows the gradual but certain realization of the kingdom of God and that casts glimpses of divine glory over this sad world.

This Christian idea of development also made its way into the newer philosophy. [108] We find it in its purest form in Leibniz, but we also encounter it essentially in Herder and Goethe, Hegel and Schelling, and actually in all well-known historians. Indeed, with many the idea of development is detached from the theistic foundation on which it rests in Christianity, and thus it is seriously flawed. These historians often exchange theism for naturalism, but in that case their naturalism is of a special kind. For Goethe, to whom [Ernst] Haeckel likes to refer, and for all his sympathizers, nature was not an inanimate machine but was bursting with divine life, an eternally generating force, a never-exhausted, creative artist. The change that one observes constantly in this world is seen therefore as a development from within; the whole is at work in its parts. The development is thus conceived organically and for that reason retains its teleological character; it is the work of an absolute "Reason" [*Vernunft*]. Goethe's well-known lines,

What would he be, a God from outside prodding,
Who spun the spheres around a finger, nodding?
The world to move from inside suits his pleasure,
Himself in nature, nature in self to treasure,
So that the life in him that weaves and is
May never lack his Mind, his energies.[2]

are the poetic interpretation of this philosophical idea of development. When these men therefore speak of unity in the development, not wanting to acknowledge any *saltus* [a leaping], or leaps in nature, while searching everywhere for gradual transitions, they do not mean a physical descent, but a logical, ideal order in the progression of creatures. The abundance of forms is their proof of the eternal, ever-rising, creative force of Nature, which they have deified.

In the nineteenth century this concept of development was replaced for many with a totally different idea. This modern idea was not completely new, for it had been proposed already in antiquity by Leucippus, Democritus, and Epicurus; it reemerged in the newer philosophy with [Pierre] Gassendi and with [René] Descartes in his teaching about the animal body, and it found acceptance with some French Encyclopedists. But for various reasons it gained a new and vibrant life in the nineteenth century. First of all, it was prepared for by the idealistic philosophy insofar as it had detached the idea of development from its theistic root. Second, it was advanced by the enormous flourishing of material culture and the extraordinary flight of natural science, which the nineteenth century witnessed since its second quarter. And third, it was seized and defended with youthful enthusiasm by a host of men such as Vogt, Büchner, Moleschott, Czolbe, who viewed it as the solution to all the mysteries of being. [109] Nevertheless, with all these proponents the idea of development displayed a character that was much too philosophic for it to capture and dominate the minds for long.

But then it was privileged to receive a scientific foundation through the serious, accurate, and shrewd research of Charles Darwin. The modern idea of evolution existed already before Darwin, just as socialist expectations had prophets already before Marx. But Darwin endeavored to give this idea of

---

2. Ed. note: These lines are from Goethe's "Prooemium," in Johann Wolfgang von Goethe, *Selected Poems*, ed. Christopher Middleton, *Goethe Edition*, vol. I (Boston: Suhrkamp/Insel, 1983), 227. Bavinck only cites one line from this poem: "Was wär ein Gott, der nur von aussen stiesse . . . ?" To understand the line better in its context, the five lines that follow are also cited. The point Bavinck is making is even more clear when we consider the opening two lines of the poem:

Now in his name who made himself creation! [better: "in the name of Him who created
   Himself (*sich Selbst erschuf*!)"]
Eternal act his single occupation [*Von Ewigkeit in schaffendem Beruf*].

The editor is grateful to Professor Barbara Carville of Calvin College for assistance in tracing this quotation.

evolution a solid foundation in the facts, in the same way in which Marx, according to the opinion of his followers, changed utopian socialism into a scientific socialism. And Darwin did not leave it at that. Not only did he show us, in an amazing mass of facts, striking analogies that exist between organic creatures, which had been categorized in species by [Carolus] Linnaeus and on which he constructed his theory of descent; he also tried to explain this descent by his hypothesis of "natural selection," which in the "struggle for life" assures the "survival of the fittest," and thus assures the development also as progress.

As a result, evolution received a completely different meaning in the newer science than it had before. Formerly, development was understood generally as an organic, progressive, teleological process, and it was used to posit a logical, idealistic order between creatures. Today the idea and system of development carries the following characteristics:

1. Evolution is to be understood especially in the sense of descent. Humans originated from animals, animals from plants, plants from cells, cells from inorganic matter. All that is higher derives from what is lower: spirit from matter, soul from body, thought from brains, life from death; there is no new beginning anywhere, no new force ever appears in the endless series of creatures.
2. The forces that cause this evolution are all of a mechanical and chemical nature, and thus work according to fixed, unchangeable laws of nature.
3. There is no room for an essence and nature of things, nor is there a plan and a goal in the process of development; whatever is necessary from the standpoint of causes is, from the point of view of teleology, accidental.

There is no dissent about these three characteristics of the modern theory of evolution. However, there are a number of opinions about the question of whether this development is to be identified with progress or decline. Development by itself is a neutral word [110] and may connote either progress or decline. Besides, these terms imply a judgment call and therefore assume a standard for judging. Since the modern theory of evolution denies any guiding thought and aim, it also is not able to provide norms by which to measure progress or decline. Nevertheless, development is understood almost always and involuntarily in the sense of progress. Based on the theory of descent, evolutionists prophesy a continuing improvement of the human race, and spiritist schools expand these expectations to the other side of the grave. If a wild horde can develop into a well-ordered society, there is good hope that this well-ordered and yet very flawed society may evolve into a socialistic Utopia. And if a monkey can evolve gradually into a human being, there is a good possibility that in the next life humans will gradually change into angels. But here we do not have to discuss the question of whether the modern theory of evolution offers sufficient grounds for faith in such a this-worldly or otherworldly progression. For our purpose, suffice it to know that the newer theory of development presents itself to us in the form of a mechanical, nonteleological theory of descent.

So many and such weighty objections exist against this theory that it is impossible to consider it seriously as a solution to the problems of this world. The short space available for this controversy permits only a few comments, but these may already be sufficient to justify any counterargument that mechanical monism experiences in many circles, both within and outside the realm of scholarship.

In general, the mechanical worldview suffers immediately from a much too naive and superficial idea of the mystery of being. [The claim] "The world is a machine" sounds simple, but it demands too much of our faith that this brief formula should contain the answer to all that moves and lives, and that all thinking and striving, struggling and suffering on the part of man and humanity could be reduced, in the end, to a mechanical movement and would be the result of the pressure and thrust of soulless atoms. The world is never something that is self-evident. The more scientific research reaches deeper into the phenomena, the more complex they become and the mysteries increase.

This becomes clear as soon as the question about the origin of things is raised. It is true that when natural science limits itself to its own realm, [111] it does not have to concern itself with this question. Standing on the foundation of what is, it cannot make a judgment about the genesis and the origin of things. But because its practitioners are also people with human hearts who are not above metaphysical need, natural science often, imperceptibly, transitions into natural philosophy: observations of facts transition into theoretical considerations. The mechanical idea, which is fully justified in some areas of nature, is then expanded into a mechanical worldview and proclaims the dogma of the eternity of matter. The person who acts that way speaks no longer as a naturalist but as a philosopher, as a believer, just as much as the person who explains the origin of things from creation. And in distinction from the latter, he involves himself in an insoluble contradiction.

After all, the world that physics reveals to us consists of categories of space and time. These categories make it impossible to think of the world in absolute, eternal, and endless terms. In his antinomies of reason, the philosopher Kant has irrefutably shown that when we consider this world to be the only true reality, we come to a dead end. Neither time nor space categories allow themselves, from the nature of things, to be transferred into the absolute. The thought that the world did not have a beginning and knows no boundaries takes us to the antinomy of infinite time and infinite space. The sum of finite parts, no matter how large, never leads to infinity. Thus time and space are existential categories of the world and thought forms of our observation, but they cannot be part of what is the absolute ground of all being. Infinite time and infinite space include an inner contradiction.

The same holds true for the movement of the world. Now that science understands, much more than before, the use of energy and the mechanical theory of heat, it cannot put the world on a par with a machine. For if the world were indeed a machine, it must have begun its movement at some point. A perpetual motion machine is a self-contradiction. If the world, thought of as a machine, were eternal, it would have used its power eternally and would already have stood still eternally. Today it is, therefore, generally accepted that *this* world had a beginning and will have an end. If this is true, one is faced with the question of how and through what this world-machine was put into motion. If this motion is due to a prior motion, one has to assume a *regressus in infinitum* [regression into the infinite], [112] which actually means that one abandons the mechanical worldview. If, however, motion first began at that time, there is no explanation for it from a mechanical standpoint, for how rest changed into motion, and even much less why the movement of matter assumed such a direction that it created the present world. In a word, it is impossible to identify the absolute and the relative, the necessary and the accidental, God and the world. Whoever tries it uses words, not concepts. The world is not necessary: it can, without contradiction, be thought of as not existing; it carries a contingent character. Therefore, the question always reimposes itself: Where does it come from, and why does it exist? That is the mystery we face. Being itself is a mystery. And the mechanical worldview must acknowledge and respect this just as any theology or philosophy does.

Against this one can say that the origin of things is indeed a mystery, but that it is the only mystery in the mechanical worldview. However, immediately a second mystery joins the first when one considers the essence of things. We often talk about matter and forces and natural law as if they were the most common things in the world. But the reality implied in these words too is full of mystery. For a long time the theory of atoms was valued; extremely small particles of matter were considered to be the basic elements of the world, and these particles were thought to be the carriers of power. This became an accepted theory even though neither the essence of matter nor the essence of power nor their mutual connection had been clarified in the least. Upon further research, however, newer physics and chemistry discovered that atoms are not the basic elements of the world. This has caused the entire theory of atoms to waver. At the meeting of naturalists in Kassel in September 1903, the renowned English chemist [Sir William] Ramsay stated: Today nobody believes anymore that the world can be understood by reducing all phenomena to atoms, which supplied with power move like suns and planets. We have begun to see that, in spite of the fact that we partially know the laws that cause the phenomena, they themselves in their very nature remain a mystery to us. "What happens at the very core that causes a hidden event to transition from one state to another remains forever a mystery to us" ([via Alexander] Classen).

[113] This is why more recently atomism is being replaced more and more by dynamism. Here material atoms are seen not as the basic elements of all that is but as energies or centers of power, which then either are powers without carriers or must exist independently, just as is attributed to souls or spirits. This energetic worldview seeks support from the positivistic *Erkenntnistheorie* [theory of cognition]. If science may proceed only from what is given in the strict sense of the word, then no atoms outside of us may be considered for this, but only inner sensations. Only ideas in our consciousness are positive in the real sense of the word. Even though this idealistic standpoint does not allow us to speak of powers as atoms outside of us, and even though it consequently leads to solipsism and skepticism, it nevertheless has rendered this service over against mechanism: it reveals the superficiality of the theory of atoms. Matter and power and their mutual connection are certainly not as simple as materialism may want us to believe. It uses an important word [atoms] very quietly.

Even less understood, if that is possible, is the phenomenon called *life* that we encounter in this world. The development of biology has been extraordinarily successful in the nineteenth century. A striking similarity has been discovered between products and phenomena in nature at large and in living organisms. Inorganic chemistry and organic chemistry seem to be closely related. Plants and animals display a fundamental similarity in elementary structure, in the phenomena of life, and in the way they function. The living organism includes organs and functions, such as metabolism, blood circulation, and the feeding process, that are subject to mechanical and chemical laws. Organic substances, which in natural circumstances only occur in a living body, have also been produced artificially in the laboratory. The irritability and spontaneity of living organisms find remarkable analogies in the phenomena of inorganic nature, as in the formation of crystals.

It therefore is even more remarkable that the mystery of life remains unsolved to this day. Continued microscopic research has led not to simple atoms but to the minutest units of life. Following preparatory work on the part of biology in the nineteenth century, the most remarkable discovery is that of the cell. And with cells, the last elementary components of an organism, we encounter the same problem that we face with every living being. The question about the origin and the essence of life is reduced to that of the origin and being of a cell. [114] We will leave to later research whether these cells, of course not chemically and physically, have even more components biologically. Today we only note that with cells we are dealing with the final biological units of an organism. Likewise, there is no difference of opinion that these cells do not originate of themselves through mere mechanical powers from inorganic matter. Whether it will be possible later to produce life from what is lifeless is a question about which people may differ. But today *omnis cellula e cellula* [each cell stems from another cell] is the end of biological wisdom. The people also who consider the *generatio aequivoca* [spontaneous generation] as the final answer of their system will have to acknowledge that as yet the origin and the essence of life are unknown to us. We should not be surprised, therefore, that many naturalists have lately replaced mechanism with vitalism.

Proponents of the mechanical evolution theory may say that spontaneous generation, though not yet proved, should nevertheless be adopted as a postulate of science. The only thing correct about this assertion is that spontaneous generation is a postulate of their own premise in the mechanical worldview. However, this does not yet coincide with *science*. On the basis of revealed facts, one may reject the mechanical explanation of life and become convinced that in life a power is at work other than [what is active] in inanimate nature; such a person is scientifically just as much entitled to his opinion as the proponent of the mechanical worldview. This has nothing to do with a dualistic supranaturalism. What nature is, nature is in its totality, thus also including plants, animals, and human beings; and in the name of our understanding of science, we may not prescribe which powers are at work in nature, but we must learn from nature itself, humbly and childlike: *Naturae parere, libertas* [the freedom of nature to bring forth].

This rule demands an even-stronger application when we get to the problem of the origin of humanity. The danger is not imaginary that the hypothesis of humanity's animal descent is identified with the facts on which it is built. The facts are no other than the many points of similarity that have been identified in anatomy, physiology, and psychology between man and animal. Of course, this great similarity was also well known formerly, for it is evident and obvious to all. The definition of man as a rational animal clearly and succinctly expresses the agreement and the difference between man and animal. Nevertheless, through and since Darwin, the data that demonstrate the similarity [115] have increased considerably, and the particulars have been pointed out. The similarity does not manifest itself only in the skeleton, bone structure, spine, skull, brains, lungs, genital organs, placenta, and so forth but is also apparent in the rudimentary organs, in the development of the embryo, and, as Doctor [Hans] Friedenthal of Berlin determined through his experiments, in the blood relationship between man and the so-called anthropoid apes.

The conformity between these and similar phenomena is so strong and surprising that, with the abandonment of faith in creation and the neglect of other data, the thought could easily arise that man gradually evolved from an animal. Nevertheless, this hypothesis must be strictly distinguished from the facts on which it rests. In the theory of man's animal descent, we are not dealing with an observable and well-established fact but with an argument built on the facts mentioned above; in other words, a hypothesis—which is not to say that for this reason, and as such, it should already be rejected. Hypotheses in science have an undoubted right to exist and are indispensable for the progress of science. Provisionally posited as an explanation of various phenomena that were observed, a hypothesis may be confirmed through further research and gradually assume the character of a theory. But of course, it is also possible that later and better observations may weaken it and cause it to be discarded.

The theory of animal descent now appears to be an idea that, with continued research, is losing probability instead of gaining it, although initially it was acclaimed as the only true solution. Consider that the theory of descent implies, according to its proponents, that man evolved gradually from an animal merely through the working of mechanical and chemical powers, just as the organic came into being from the inorganic. According to Haeckel, whoever espouses another power, a life force, for instance, or an independent life of the soul, fractures the system, brings in dualism and supranaturalism, and suffers—as do such as Kant, Du Bois-Reymond, Virchow, Wundt, Pasteur—from mental deterioration. The mechanical system demands that all of life, and thus also human life, is a form of motion, a complex machine. Without grounds, we cannot say whether continued research will confirm or weaken this hypothesis of human descent.

The comment should be made beforehand that one can hardly be careful enough with the construction of a genealogical kinship on the basis of a series of analogies in science. [116] The comparison method undoubtedly has a right to exist and possesses great value, but it very easily entices one to make hasty conclusions. The religious-historical method so widely applied today supplies many remarkable examples. People detect slight corresponding traits between two stories, sagas, myths, and immediately they are ready to claim that both are in fact identical, that the differences merely concern the form, and that they are related to each other historically. Various sides have protested these premature conclusions. But even in natural science such a warning is not superfluous. The theory of descent leans primarily on comparative anatomy, physiology, and psychology. But these are driven involuntarily by the desire for analogies, to give them full exposure, and to push differences and peculiarities into the background and to denigrate them.

And yet there are such differences between man and animal in spite of all similarities. As a group of living beings, humankind is separated from all other kinds of beings by various marks. Physiologically there are especially the upright gait, the shape of the hand, the skull, and the brain. And these, although small in number, are nevertheless of such great significance that no one errs in making the distinction between man and animal, and the system analyst does not have the least trouble with organizing them in different cat-egories. This classification itself proves that there is a considerable difference between human and animal, because if they were related genealogically, there would have to be many forms that could not, or only with great difficulty, be classified under the main headings.

However, of greater significance are the peculiarities that come to expres-sion in the higher life of the soul of man, in his mind and reason, heart and conscience, will and freedom, and also in all those spiritual matters of language and religion, morality and justice, science and the arts, which have been ac-quired and depend on man's rational nature. For that reason the descent of man is not decided by natural science alone. Psychology, religion, and ethics also have a right to speak on this issue. And they are even more entitled to it when these human peculiarities in anatomy and physiology do not naturally receive their due or are even denied their due. This is the case when the theory of descent also tries to explain the origin of language, religion, morality, and so forth. However many attempts [117] have been made to that end, until now none of them has succeeded; they always result in misunderstanding the phenomenon that they want to explain. For the sake of brevity, we will mention only the explanation of human consciousness.

If the materialistic theory of descent is right and thought is related to the brain as gall to the liver, then consciousness is nothing other than an accompanying reflection of some material processes in the brain, having no bearing at all on the course of events and being totally disassociated from them. World history would then have run the same course, even if man would have been devoid of consciousness and thought. However, this conclusion, which follows logically from the principle, is being rejected by all who have not been blinded by materialism. For the weakest sensation is in nature and essence so different from the material processes that it is impossible to de-rive an explanation of the first from the latter. [Theodor] Ziehen therefore correctly states that materialism has not only failed to solve the problem, but it also did not even understand it and put it correctly. In psychology, materialism has been replaced by many with psychophysical parallelism or with psychic monism.

If man's animal descent were a *fact*, it would have to be accepted in spite of all this. But such is definitely not the case. There are no direct proofs. No one has ever observed them. Today we live in a time in which species are constant. Even the strong, though often much exaggerated, similarity between the em-bryonic development of man and animal does not obviate the fact that both of them from the beginning develop in a different direction. And inasmuch as scientific research enables us to judge matters, this also seems to have been the case in the past. As far as we can determine, human beings have always been human and animals always animals. One cannot speak of a slow, gradual transition. Thus far the "missing link" has not been found. According to the judgment of many experts, fossils, such as the Neanderthal man's skull and the *Pithecanthropus erectus*, deserve no consideration. Besides, these cases are much too isolated to justify such a far-reaching conclusion as the theory of descent. If the descent had taken place through an enormous number of small changes, divided over a countless number of years, there should be a great number of transitional forms. But paleontology teaches that, although there has been a succession in the origin of organisms, various species have always lived side by side, and no proof exists of [118] their genealogical kinship through transitional forms.

Besides, the selection theory that tried to explain the manner in which higher organisms could originate from lower ones, and with it Darwinism in a narrower sense, has been all but abandoned and replaced by a more acceptable explanation. The thesis of [Rudolph] Virchow that was insisted on for years, that the theory of descent has not been proved, is acknowledged by many today as correct. At the zoological congress in Berlin in 1901, Professor [Wilhelm] Branco said that in the diluvial period, man suddenly appeared, without ancestors. And a year earlier Reinke testified in his speech about the development of the natural sciences in the nineteenth century: "Without reservation we must acknowledge that we do not have a single totally unobjectionable proof of its correctness."

Since this is the situation with the theory of descent, it shows clearly that it is more a matter of wishing and believing than of knowing. It is not proved by the facts, but demanded by the system. If creation is rejected a priori and the existence of a power higher than mechanical and chemical power is placed outside any scholarly discussion beforehand as dualistic and supranatural, then it is obvious that man must descend from animals. Human beings have to come from somewhere. And in referring to Virchow's position, Haeckel is right when he asks, "Then where does he [man] come from?" But the entire view of scholarship that underlies this argument proceeds from a wrong supposition. It is thought that we can speak of knowing in the true sense only when things can be dissected chemically and all their workings reduced to mechanical motion. This, however, is overrating the "chemical-physical knowing," against which [Karl Wilhelm von] Nägeli and Oskar Hertwig justifiably warned: "One overlooks here that also this knowledge, like all human knowledge, is only piecework, and it pushes against every junction of natural science, which at the moment appears to us to be invincible, and that chemistry and physics in principle have no advantage in this connection over biology."

Not only in biology and anthropology but also in inorganic nature we will not find our way without an almighty and omnipresent power by which God sustains and governs all things. As Professor [Johannes Diderik] van der Waals said in his well-known article in *De gids* of March 1903, everything in nature is the realization of an all-encompassing and yet indivisible thought of God. Behind everything stands a great, superior mind, for laws and rules are everywhere. And in 1904 Professor [Hendrik Willem] Bakhuis Roozeboom concluded [119] his speech "The Present State of the Problem of Chemistry" with these words: "The farther our knowledge reaches into as yet virgin territory, the more reasons there will be for admiration of God's world order, which also manifests itself in this area of nature and which reduces that manifold diversity to a few basic thoughts."

The relationship between faith and science will certainly improve when the latter surrenders the mechanical worldview; when the hostility toward religion, specifically the Christian religion, is laid aside; and when the other side acknowledges, more so than heretofore, the important element of truth that undoubtedly is implied in the theory of evolution and descent. That evolution exists, provided it is not limited to mechanical motion and chemical connection and division, is after all proved throughout the history of peoples and humanity by every organism that comes into being and perishes. There is heredity but also variation, as appears from the difference in children born to the same parents, the races among humans, plant culture, and animal husbandry. The extent of this variation is unknown at this point. But it certainly is not limited to the boundaries of the species, which Linnaeus indicates in his *Systema naturae*. Our understanding of species is unsure and is far from being fixed. It may be changed, reduced, or expanded at any moment by scientific research. The species that we accept today in the plant and animal world do not coincide therefore with those that God by his creative power called into being at the beginning. Most likely the latter [at the beginning] were much fewer in number than Linnaeus could surmise in his day. In that case descent takes place in a wide circle of organic beings not only through evolution, but also either through gradual change or sudden mutation.

Provided that evolution is not understood in a mechanical sense, there is, therefore, no antithesis between creation and development. But it should not be understood that way either. In his writings Professor Eucken repeatedly emphasizes that today's advanced culture, which after all is the product of the labor of the human spirit, proves the superiority of that spirit. In the life of the spirit of humankind with its imperishable norms, its searching for and partial possession of the truth, its vast inner life, its desire and striving for independence and personality, liberty and infinity—in this life of the spirit a different, higher reality manifests itself than the one that meets us in nature.

[120] All of this sounds true and beautiful; the life of the spirit is more than nature and cannot be understood as the product of mechanical motion. But this does not say enough, for it did not bring us any farther than to the ancient dualism of spirit and matter. Still, natural mechanism cannot be explained without an intelligent cause. Already, insofar as it is a machine, it points back to an intelligent cause just as each implement made by human ingenuity and energy bears the stamp of its maker. Natural mechanism cannot be the final

cause and explanation of everything, since it asks for an explanation itself: natural mechanism is not lord of the world, but servant of the spirit. The forms in which it operates—time and space, measure and numeral, order and law—are basic categories of the spirit [*Urverhältnisse des Geistes*]. Just as a machine serves man, natural mechanism must be subservient to the governing and leading of a divine mind that rules over all.

This does provide room for development in the true sense of the word. If the whole world is nothing but one big machine, then development is excluded. Whoever says development says plan and law, direction and goal. Development stands between beginning and end; it leads from beginning to end. Development is not a mechanical concept, but an organic, teleological concept. For that reason it can only receive its full due on the basis of creation, which grants the world its being and which at bottom and in principle is what it has to become. Aristotle already understood that becoming exists for the sake of being, not the reverse. There is *becoming* only if and because there is *being*.

# 7

# CHRISTIAN PRINCIPLES AND SOCIAL RELATIONSHIPS

[121] There is a wide divergence of opinions regarding the attitude of our Lord Jesus Christ toward society and its problems. Many claim to belong to the Social-Democratic Party [in the Netherlands] or are sympathetic toward its principles; in Jesus they see first of all a social reformer. Christianity, they say, is born from the social needs of that time, just as later Calvinism's doctrine of predestination issued from uncertainty about economic conditions at the beginning of the sixteenth century. After all, [they say,] all spiritual ideas and powers in state and church, religion and society, science and art are caused ultimately and fundamentally by social conditions in the manner in which material goods are produced and distributed. Social conditions in the days in which Jesus was born were very distressing. They aroused in his soul a deep concern and a great measure of compassion. The gospel that he came to bring was therefore a gospel for the poor. In those days, sins and misery, just like today, were the result of the way in which society was organized. It is the law that makes sinners. Mammon creates thieves. Marriage causes adultery. Persuaded of this, Jesus wanted to return to nature, away from artificial society. Instead of justice and law, government and force, humans needed love and liberty. Jesus was the first socialist and anarchist.

Or, if this proposition seems to be somewhat exaggerated, Jesus was nevertheless a man of the people and for the people. He always spoke in defense of the poor and against the wealthy. He always derided the rich and mighty

Ed. note: Originally published as *Christelijke beginselen en maatschappelijke verhoudingen* in the series Christendom en Maatschappij, series 1, vol. 1 (Utrecht: Ruys, 1908).

yet looked with compassion on all who were wretched. The battle of his life was against the patricians, the profiteers, the priests; and in that battle he perished. Today's Christianity is [122] narrow-minded and selfish. One evil day it enlisted in the service of wealth and power, thus positioning itself over against the sick and the weak. The altar today serves only to protect the throne. The priest has lowered himself to be an accomplice of the monarch, and the church has become a mainstay of capitalism. But original Christianity had an entirely different purpose. It opposed all competition between social classes. It wanted community and cooperation of its members. It recommended harmony and love such as exist between members of the same body. If the Christian religion of today wants to regain its lost influence and become a blessing to society, its attitude will have to change radically. It should not lock itself up in large cathedrals, where only the prominent and well-to-do appear; it has to come down to people from all walks of life; it has to go out into the highways and byways of life and seek those who are lost. Christianity must become socially minded or else it will disappear.

Over against these proponents of a social and socialistic Christianity are others who believe the very opposite: that the Christian religion has nothing to do with society and the state and that it has no message for either. Jesus was a religious genius, to be sure, and answered to a high moral ideal, but the interests of society did not concern him in the least, nor did he have anything to do with the affairs of the state, just as he was totally indifferent to all of culture. Religion and morality are on the one side, and society, state, and culture are on the other; each live their own lives and follow their own course. Religion's place is in the heart, the inner chamber, the church; but politics and the economy go their own way and, as such, have nothing to do with religion.

In Germany this viewpoint is advocated especially by the well-known Fr[iedrich] Naumann, a present member of Parliament. At the beginning of his career, he intended to reconcile religion and politics. He considered Jesus to be a social reformer and wanted to restore and expand Jesus's rule over the German people through social politics. Naumann therefore believed that Christianity and social democracy were compatible, just as [Fritz] Küster, [Hans] Stoelke, [August Hermann] Francke, and others still believe today. But Naumann's trip to the East in the year 1898 and his experiences there changed his perspective. The more he became acquainted with economic and political life, the more he became convinced that it has a life of its own in today's world and that Jesus knew nothing of this and had not been concerned about it.

[123] Upon his return to his own country, Naumann became a proponent of a radical separation of religion and politics. Jesus was no longer the ideal for his activities, although he does retain some importance for morality, just as there remains a certain value in Christianity for the inner life. But for the

rest, Christ and Christianity have nothing to say to our present-day culture. State and society, industry and commerce, science and art have assumed a totally different character in our day, and there is nothing they can learn from Scripture anymore. Politics, for instance, has nothing to do with moral principles; it is only concerned with the interests of the state and the people. As such in our day it ought to be pure *"Realpolitik* [politics based on practical and material factors]." Others go still further. Because Christianity, in their opinion, is completely indifferent toward culture and is even hostile to it, it is no longer suitable for our day. It denigrates human beings. Today we need a different religion and another morality; all the values we have known thus far must be exchanged and traded in for those given to us by the doctrine of evolution and cultural development.

Over against these diverse opinions, the best we can do is to let Scripture itself speak and say what it thinks and has in mind. Naturally it is not possible to briefly explain everything Scripture says about society and its relationships, but the main issues can be spelled out clearly enough so as to give us a solid and practical result.

It is at once quite remarkable that until today science, in spite of all its research, knows nothing for certain about the origin of things. Because it always takes a position on the basis of what exists, it cannot penetrate to the origin of things. As soon as it wants to go to the origin behind history, it enters the area of speculation and has to be satisfied with assumptions. From a scientific point of view, we know nothing with certainty about the origin of heaven and earth, of plant and animal and human, of husband and wife, of marriage and family, of society and the state, of religion and morality and justice, of language, art, and science. All these institutions and phenomena exist everywhere already, and we examine them in the light of scientific research, even though that research is still in a primitive stage; but never and nowhere are we witnesses of the origin of these phenomena.

[124] What science withholds from us, however, is given to us by special revelation that comes to us from Scripture. It gives us a story of the origin of creatures; this story has foundational significance for their existence and destination. Since we think differently about their origin, our knowledge of them and their development—their nature and goal—assumes a different perspective for us. If human beings, comprised of soul and body, come from animals through slow evolution, then they essentially remain animals. And if originally society was nothing more than a horde, then it will retain this character also in its further development.

But Scripture teaches us something totally different. And what it teaches about the origin of creatures determines our entire worldview. Without further elaboration one only has to think of the following: (1) Heaven and earth, invisible and visible things, are created by God. Moreover, matter, no less than spirit, is of divine origin. (2) Humanity, according to body and soul, is created by a special act of God's power; we are distinguished from all creatures by being image bearers of God. (3) We humans are created immediately as male and female; God willed the gender difference, and marriage was instituted by him at once. (4) This marriage receives God's special blessing; it is for the multiplication of the human race. Implied in marriage is the family; in the family [is implied] society; in society [is implied] unity, community, and cooperation of the human race. (5) Though sharing the same image of God, male and female are given their own organization and entrusted with their own tasks. The difference and inequality is not even caused by sin but is willed by God from the beginning and is soon confirmed and expanded by children who are born of the first marriage. Marriage and family contain the point of departure and principles of all kinds of relationships that will later develop in society. (6) Husband and wife receive the assignment to help each other in the calling entrusted to the human race: to multiply and thus to subdue the earth. Human beings are not called to idleness but to work; cultural work has a divine origin. (7) But just as God created heaven and earth in six days and rested on the seventh day, so also in human life do labor and leisure alternate. Labor is a means, not a goal. The ultimate goal is that man with his labor may enter into rest and serve God on the seventh day in God's temple. The origin of man determines his destination: [being] from God, he has to return to God; God is the highest good for man and humanity.

[125] All of this prepared the way for a healthy, normal development. But, as everyone knows, this development became abnormal. Even the person who denies the fall into sin cannot contradict this. Those who deny the fall must explain sin from the original nature of humanity, allowing it to coincide with being, as Buddhism teaches, and thus declaring it to be invincible except by annihilation. Nevertheless, Scripture maintains that sin is not part of creation, that it came into the world by human will, and that it therefore is moral in nature and for that reason also ineradicable. The history of the human race is therefore one mighty struggle between God's grace and our guilt. Immediately after the fall, God's grace begins to work already. God places his covenant with humanity over against our covenant with Satan. And the more guilt increases, the more grace abounds. Even the punishment pronounced on the woman changes the curse into a blessing. The woman will give birth with pain, but she will be saved by her childbearing. And man's toil by the sweat of his brow will serve to subdue the earth. In spite of sin, God maintains his original intent for the human race.

This even shows up in paganism. For although God let pagans follow their own way, he did not leave himself without witness. He made himself known to them in the works of his hands, assigned them a place to live, gave them rain and fruitful seasons, filled their hearts with food and laughter. He also made it possible for them to live their lives, through the testimony of their conscience, by maintaining marriage and family, by the institution of society and the state, by maintaining religious and moral beliefs, by the labor of culture, by all sorts of blessings and benefactions. But in the centuries that preceded the coming of Christ, nowhere did God's grace and power oppose sin more forcefully than in the holy line of Seth and Shem and thereafter in the people of Israel, which he freely chose for special honor. He made known his words to Jacob and his ordinances and his precepts to Israel. Thus he treated no other nation, and they did not know his precepts.

Among these demands we must consider, first of all, that with no nation did the significance of the family, as foundation of all of society, feature so prominently as with Israel. The nation was divided patriarchally and genealogically into twelve [126] or thirteen tribes, depending on whether one considers the two sons of Joseph, Ephraim and Manasseh, as taking his place and whether or not Levi is counted. Among these tribes Judah received the place of honor (Gen. 49:8–11). Every tribe was subdivided into generations [clans] (Num. 26:50; 1 Sam. 10:19–21), who were the descendants of a grandson, great-grandson, or another descendant of Jacob (Num. 26:21, 29–38, 40). A generation in turn was divided into a number of families or groups of families [ancestral houses] (Num. 1:2, 18; 1 Chron. 7:7). Each family was eventually composed again of a number of households (Josh. 7:14–18). Each tribe, generation, family, and household had its own head, and all of these elders together constituted the "elders," the rulers (Exod. 5:6; 16:17, 22; 19:7; 1 Chron. 29:6), the called of the assembly (Num. 1:26; 26:9). These were the representatives of the people, who already in Egypt (Exod. 3:16; 4:29) and later repeatedly (Exod. 19:3–8; etc.) gathered in a council meeting to decide about proposals that Moses submitted (Deut. 1:9–14) or who themselves came with proposals and made decisions (Deut. 1:22, 23).

Of course, all these elders did not always gather (as in Num. 11:16; 16:2; 27:21; Deut. 31:28); sometimes the meeting was limited to the heads of tribes, who also were called the heads of the thousands, and thus they formed, in a sense, a limited council in distinction from the large council (Num. 1:16; 10:4). But both of these councils could not take care of everything; permanent officials were needed to take care of current affairs. These were divided into two kinds. First there were the so-called *šōṭĕrîm*, or writers, officials who in Egypt were charged with supervising the work of making bricks (Exod. 5:6, 10, 14) and whose task it was, in general, to keep the genealogical records of Israel up to date and to indicate who had to go to war (Deut. 20:5; Josh. 1:10–11; 3:2–4). In addition, there was another group of officials, the *šōpĕṭîm*, or judges, who were chosen by Moses from the elders of the people to assist him, and who were placed over smaller or larger groups of people to settle differences, as in Exodus 18:13–23. Later such officials, *šōṭĕrîm* and *šōpĕṭîm*, were appointed in all cities (Deut. 16:18; 25:1); at the head stood a supreme court, which was established in Jerusalem (Deut. 17:8–13; 19:17–18). It is remarkable that no priests or Levites are mentioned in connection with these councils and officials. It is possible that sometimes priests were members of local courts (Deut. 21:5; cf. 1 Chron. 23:4; 26:29–32), but this was not prescribed. Only in the supreme court did priests [127] also have a seat; this was because difficult cases often required a good explanation of the law, and the priests were obviously the right persons for this.

For the rest, Israel was the opposite of a hierarchy precisely because it was a theocracy. God was Israel's lawgiver, judge, and king; and Israel was God's people, his inheritance, his kingdom (Exod. 15:18; Num. 23:21; Deut. 33:5; Judg. 8:22; 1 Sam. 8:7; Isa. 33:22; etc.). The only thing required of Israel was to live according to the law that God had given, not only religiously but also morally, as well as civilly and as a society. Thus all power in Israel had a servant character; it was tied to God's law in every respect. Israel did not become a "religious community" only after the exile; it had already been one for a long period before the kingship of Saul; Israel was united through religion, through the legislation of Moses.

Except being instructed by ordinary officials, Israel was taught on behalf of God and in accordance with his law by the priests and the prophets, and it was rescued in times of distress by the judges. There was therefore no room for a king as other nations had. An autocratic and despotic kingship was actually a rejection of God's kingship (1 Sam. 8:5, 20). The first king of Israel could only be a foreshadowing, a type of the Messiah (2 Sam. 7:12–16; 1 Chron. 17:14), constitutionally bound in all things to God's law (Deut. 17:14–20; 1 Sam. 10:25). Of course, this kingship in Israel was therefore also called on to maintain the service of the one, true God in public life; kings were to honor and maintain not only civil law but also the religious and moral laws, and not only the laws of the second table but also those of the first table. Idolatry, soothsaying, sorcery, image worship, blasphemy, Sabbath desecration—these were forbidden in the law and punishable with exile or the death penalty (Exod. 18:20; 20:23; Lev. 20:6, 27; 24:11–16; Deut. 13:1–5; 17:2–7); [violators of the law] had to be banned and eradicated by the governing authorities, and godly judges and kings acted accordingly (Num. 25:5, 7; 1 Sam. 15:33; 1 Kings 15:12; 18:40; 2 Kings 9–10; 12:2–3; 18:4; 23:20).

However, to prevent any misunderstanding, we should add here that church and state, however closely allied, were nevertheless also different, not only so far as members were concerned, but also in offices and administrations, in institutions and laws. Foreigners could participate in the spiritual privileges of Israel, and thus, so to speak, be members of the church without being citizens; and lepers, unclean persons, and people banished did remain citizens, but they were nevertheless isolated and taken outside the community.

[128] Priests and civil authorities were invested with distinct offices that were hardly ever combined, and the one law contained special civil and religious laws. Consequently priests and Levites, even though they served in the temple, had to explain the law and instruct the people. They did not have

an inheritance in Israel but lived in separate cities on the donations of the people. Thus they were very dependent. They possessed no secret creed or art and certainly had no hierarchical, conscience-binding power. When we take into account here that killing the Canaanites, Agag, the priests of Baal at Mount Carmel, and the house of Ahab were isolated incidents, prescribed in most cases by special divine command, and that the work of the godly king was usually confined to removing idols and the restoration of public worship, we see that Israel, also religiously, enjoyed a great measure of freedom. Unbelief and heresy were not punished; there was no inquisition; restraint of conscience was totally unknown. And when the prophets testify against a turning away from God and resist kings and priests, they avail themselves of the word, call for a return to the law, but never insist on using force.

Another peculiarity of Israel's legislation was that not only the people but also the land was seen as the Lord's property. According to God's sovereign will, he gave Canaan to Abraham and his seed for an inheritance and later divided it among the tribes, generations, families, and households (Josh. 13ff.). Thus the Israelites lived with God actually as strangers and aliens and received the land from him on loan (Lev. 25:23). The law was intended to perpetuate this state of affairs by safeguarding the families for the property, on the one hand, through the promise of children (Deut. 28:4) and the institution of the levirate [marriage] (Deut. 25:5–10), and on the other hand, by safeguarding the property for the families through the institution of the Year of Jubilee (Lev. 25:23). These and similar provisions counteracted poverty and begging, and an accumulation of capital and landownership, but did not erase all social differences. Differences remained not only between husbands and wives and between parents and children, but also between rich and poor and between freed and slaves. Prosperity and riches were seen as a blessing (Gen. 13:2; 14:23; Deut. 28:1–4; 1 Kings 3:13; Job 1:1–3; 42:10–17).

In addition, slavery, which was a phenomenon in nearly all nations, was permitted also in Israel. Abraham already had a great number of slaves, some born in his house [129] (Gen. 14:14) and others purchased with money (17:23). When leaving Egypt, Israel took along many aliens (Exod. 12:38; Num. 11:4), who were used for menial work (Deut. 29:11). The original inhabitants of Canaan had made themselves deserving to be eradicated because of their wickedness (Deut. 20:16–18), but were often spared and then made slaves, if possible, or forced laborers and conscripts (Deut. 20:10–11; Josh. 9:21; 16:10; 17:13; Judg. 9:28, 38; 1 Kings 9:20–21). Nonetheless, a real slave trade did not exist in Israel; at least we do not read about it anywhere in the Old Testament, although in the surrounding countries this trade was practiced on a large scale (Gen. 37:28). The number of slaves was therefore relatively small. In 2 Chronicles 2:17 we find 153,600 "aliens" listed; and according to Ezra 2:65 and Nehemiah 7:67, there were 7,337 slaves among the 42,360 Jews who returned from Babylon—in other words, about one sixth [of the total]. The proportion in other countries was much less favorable. This also explains why slaves never played a role in Israelite history; a slave rebellion is never mentioned.

The requirement of mercy that had to be practiced according to the law, also toward slaves and all lowly and wretched, certainly had a bearing on this. And here we have a third peculiarity that should be noted. [Franz Clemens] Brentano [1838–1917] was quite correct when he observed that Old Testament morality is written from the point of view of the oppressed. In addition to justice, mercy was widely practiced. People had to freely lend to the poor (Deut. 15:7); taking interest from a brother [an Israelite] was not allowed (Lev. 25:36; Deut. 23:19); pledges were not to be taken forcefully from the poor and had to be returned by sunset (Exod. 22:26; Lev. 25:35–37; Deut. 23:19; 24:6, 10); debts had to be canceled in the seventh year (Deut. 15:1). [Furthermore], a hired man and an alien were not to be oppressed (Deut. 24:14); wages had to be paid on time (Deut. 24:15); the stranger, orphan, and widower had to be treated justly (Exod. 22:21–22; Deut. 10:18; 24:17; Isa. 1:17, 23; 10:2; Jer. 7:6; 22:3; Mic. 2:9; Zech. 7:10). [For this reason] the poor, strangers, widows, and orphans were entitled to the gleanings of the harvest (Lev. 19:9; Deut. 24:19); in the year of the Sabbath they were entitled to the entire harvest (Exod. 23:10–11; Lev. 25:5). They [the needy] were also to take part in the meals of the sacrifice and of the tithes (Deut. 14:28–29; 16:10; 26:12). [In addition,] people with physical handicaps were not to be mocked or cursed (Lev. 19:14; Deut. 27:18), and the elderly had to be shown respect (Lev. 19:32). Animals also had to be treated well (Exod. 22:10; Lev. 22:18–28; Deut. 22:6–7; 25:4); [130] a righteous man cares for the needs of his animals (Prov. 12:10).

This entire ethic of mercy was urged on Israel by the consideration that the God of Israel was merciful and that in his mercy he set his people free from the bondage of Egypt (Exod. 22:21; 23:9; Lev. 19:33–34; 25:38, 42; Deut. 5:14; Ps. 94:6; 146:9). Slaves in particular benefited from this. First, Israelites were not allowed to be enslaved to each other since they after all were servants of the Lord, set free by him (Exod. 13:3; 19:4–6; 20:2; Lev. 23:43; 26:13). For that reason they were not allowed to be sold as slaves. The service of one and the same God therefore meant, in principle, the abolition of slavery. The Israelites were, however, allowed to work for wages (Deut. 24:14–15), and in special circumstances they could also become serfs. An Israelite who had become poor could sell himself to someone else (Lev. 25:39–47). If someone had stolen something and was not able to make restitution, the court could assign him to the aggrieved party as a servant (Exod. 22:1–4). In certain instances a father could sell his daughter to someone else, but [he could] not [sell] his son (Exod. 21:7–11), and perhaps a creditor was also entitled to sell an insolvent debtor or his children (Lev. 25:39, 47). But even in such cases serfs were not to be used for demeaning work (Lev. 25:39–40, 42; 1 Kings 9:22); they were not to be treated ruthlessly or abused but rather used as day laborers (Lev. 25:43; Deut. 24:14–15); and they could be redeemed at any time (Exod. 21:2; Lev. 25:25, 47; Deut. 15:12–15). If such a servant wished to remain with his master, the latter had to take him to the doorpost and pierce his ear with an awl, and he would be his servant for life [Exod. 21:6; Deut. 15:17].

Actual male and female slaves, however, had to be treated mercifully. The Israelites were to remember that they themselves had been slaves in Egypt (Deut. 5:14–15; 15:15; 16:11–12; 24:18; etc.). Slaves were to be considered members of the household: they were to be circumcised and incorporated into Israel (Gen. 17:12; Deut. 5:14–15); they too were to rest on the Sabbath (Exod. 20:10; 22:21; Deut. 5:14–15); they were allowed to eat of the Passover (Exod. 12:44) and partake of the sacrificial meals (Deut. 12:12, 18; 16:11, 14); and they were often treated well. A slave could even own property (Lev. 25:49); if Abraham had remained childless, Eliezer would have been his heir (Gen. 15:3); and sometimes a slave, in the absence of a male heir, was adopted as a son-in-law (1 Chron. 2:34–35). Quite often a master would take a female slave as concubine for himself or his son (Gen. 30:3; Exod. 21:9). While corporal punishment of slaves was permitted (Prov. 29:19, 21; [131] Job 7:2; Ps. 123:2), such chastisement was considered necessary also for children; furthermore, [it was] also limited by law. Whoever killed a slave while beating him had to be punished himself (Exod. 21:20); if he knocked out the tooth of a servant or hit him in the eye and destroyed it, he had to let him go free (Exod. 21:26–27). He who brings trouble on his family will inherit a storm (Prov. 11:29); the slave also is a human being, created by God (Job 31:13–15).

Of course, theory and practice are often far apart, and this held true for Israel as well. When Israel entered Canaan, it underwent a great change. It slowly transitioned from a nomadic life to being a settled agricultural nation. However, it is incorrect to say, as claimed these days, that the service of the Lord was inextricably linked to nomadic life and was hostile to all culture. For although Jeremiah praised the Rechabites because of their obedience to the command of their forefathers not to build houses, nor to sow seed, nor to plant vineyards (Jer. 35), he nevertheless does not recommend such a life of abstinence to any of the prophets. On the contrary, just as he bought a field at Anathoth (32:8–9), so an ideal for all the prophets was to sit under their own vine and fig tree (Deut. 8:7–9). Idleness was looked down on (Prov. 19:24; 22:13; 26:15); diligence was praised (10:4; 12:24); money was seen as a shelter (Eccles. 7:12); and wisdom, art, wealth, song, music, and dance were also considered legitimate (Exod. 15:1; 25:17–40; 31:2; 1 Kings 4:29–34). But as an agricultural people, Israel came in contact with the Canaanites who were left and ran the danger of adopting their idolatry, image worship, sorcery, and immorality. When as a result of unfaithfulness they began to experience oppression by the other nations, Israel was rescued time and again and its independence restored, but the many smaller and larger wars broke the unity of the tribes and occasioned lawless circumstances, when everybody did what seemed right in his own eyes. The monarchy brought about a favorable turn in this situation, but when, during and after Solomon, gold flooded the country and wealth made its entrance, idolatry and iniquity increased markedly. The division of the kingdom, which for political reasons also broke up the unity of worship and instituted an independent temple, priesthood, and worship, paved the way for the apostasy of the people. Under Ahab this image worship actually took the form of idolatry, and Baal worship replaced the service of the Lord. Even more pernicious was the Babylonian-Assyrian influence, which since the days of Hezekiah had asserted itself more and more forcefully. Idolatry and superstition, lust and cruelty, [132] temple virgins and child sacrifices, despotism and bribery, injustice and oppression—all made their entry into the kingdom of Judah and became more and more dominant. A situation arose religiously and morally—affecting civil and social life—that was diametrically opposed to God's law and that made exile as punishment necessary for both Israel and Judah.

But, ever since Joshua's time, there remained a remnant that stayed true to the word of God and seven thousand who did not bow the knee before Baal and the queen of heaven. This godly circle brought forth the prophets, the psalmists, and the authors of the proverbs. In one long, unbroken line they raise their voice against the religious and moral apostasy of the people. They do not act as political agents or social reformers, as party leaders, as preachers of a new religion and morality; and yet they take note of all the social abuses, and they measure these by the law of God, which the people know and which is a blessing for all of their lives. Then they fulminate and weep in turn about the sin to which the people have surrendered. They complain about robbery and intemperance, bribery and miserliness, hunger for money and pleasure, injustice and deceit in goods and measure and weight, holding back wages, selling the righteous, oppressing the orphan and the widow, hatred against the godly, and so forth.

The books of all the prophets, the songs of all the psalmists, the proverbs of all the wise—these works are so filled with such critiques that there would be no end to quoting them. They did not excuse or ignore a single sin against the first or second table of God's law. They disclose Israel's transgressions and Jerusalem's gruesome deeds. And in the process they do not spare anyone; they accuse the entire nation, not only the lowly, but also and especially the wealthy and the powerful, the kings and the judges, the priests and the false prophets. They never look for the reasons of the misery in the ordinances and laws, in the institutions and regulations, in the poor organization of state and society, in the inequality between rich and poor, for God made them both; but they always look into the hearts of the people, at their apostasy and their breaking of the covenant, at their idolatry and world conformity, at their abandoning God and his word. Therefore they do not expect restoration from a political revolution or social legislation, but only from a true return to God and his service. They called the entire nation back to the law and the testimony, to justice and righteousness, and urged people to humility and repentance. And if the present offers little or no hope for this, [133] they look forward eagerly and with great longing to the future, when God will write his law on the hearts of all people. Then the kingdom of the Anointed of David's house will flourish in righteousness and peace, and everyone in the Holy Land will receive an inalienable inheritance (Ezek. 46:18; 47:14) and sit down under his own vine and fig tree in safety. There will be no more slaves, for men-servants and maid-servants will also receive the Spirit of the Lord, and even aliens will share in Israel's privileges.

These prophetic expectations were not fulfilled immediately and fully but initially and in principle in the person and work of Christ, and they will continue to be fulfilled in the entire New Testament dispensation until the end of time. This Christ is what the church confesses concerning him, for otherwise his significance would be far inferior to philosophers and artists, statesmen and social reformers. The novel, the unique thing, about Christ is that he is more than Solomon and Jonah and any other prophet (Matt. 12:41–42), that he is the Messiah (Mark 8:29), the Son of God (Matt. 11:27), sent by God (Matt. 10:40) to seek and to save the lost (Matt. 18:11; Luke 4:18; 19:10) and to acknowledge them as his own before the face of his Father (Matt. 10:32; Mark 8:38; 12:10). He is the mediator between God and humanity; the [one who as God] gives us the knowledge of God, a knowledge that can only be given by God himself (Matt. 16:17). He alone reveals the Father to us (Matt. 11:27). What he came to bring to earth is therefore something of inexpressible worth—the kingdom of God, not as a moral community that men would create, but as a heavenly, imperishable treasure (Matt. 6:20; Luke 12:33). The content of this kingdom is righteousness (Matt. 6:33), salvation from destruction (Matt. 7:13; Mark 8:35; 9:48), and eternal life (Matt. 5:3–9; 7:14; 13:43). The kingdom is thus of absolute, world-transcending worth (Matt. 6:33; 13:44; Mark 8:36; Luke 10:42), and citizenship in it is only possible by way of regeneration (John 3:3), faith, and conversion (Mark 1:15).

From this standpoint Jesus evaluates all natural things. He does not despise them, he is not an ascetic, he does not impose fasting (Matt. 9:14); he is hated as a glutton and a drunkard (Matt. 11:18); he celebrates a wedding (John 2), participates as a guest at many a meal (Luke 7:36), and considers food and drink, garment and clothing as good gifts of the heavenly Father (Matt. 6:25–33; Luke 11:3). He also honors marriage (Matt. 5:28; Mark 10:2–12), loves children (Matt. 18:2; 19:14), prizes a person's own home (Luke 9:58), and especially in [134] his parables speaks openly about all of nature and the natural life, about all circumstances and relationships. The ascetic outlook on life is, in principle, foreign to Jesus. On the other hand, he is even much

farther removed from Epicureanism, which cares only about self, conde-
scendingly looks down on the common people, and is not concerned at all
about the fate of the poor and the sick (Matt. 15:14; 3:4, 15; John 7:49). On
the contrary, Jesus is constantly moved with compassion for the multitudes
that surround him.

This compassion not only encompasses spiritual ills and distress but also
is prompted as much by physical misery and material want. Jesus heals the
sick, cleanses the lepers, delivers the possessed, gives sight to the blind, makes
the lame to walk, raises the dead, and proclaims the gospel to the poor (Matt.
11:5). He is drawn to the poor and needy, calls the weary and the heavy-laden
to himself (Matt. 11:28), and is known as a friend of publicans and sinners
(Matt. 9:10; 11:19). People who depict Jesus as a true humanist are just as far
removed from the truth as those who see in him an ascetic who bears ill will
toward all culture. Neither superficial optimism nor gloomy pessimism finds
an ally in him. He stands outside and above both parties, always assumes a
place of his own in his own sovereign sphere, and maintains himself against
our efforts to turn him into a party member.

On the one hand, therefore, Jesus certainly does not deny or despise
natural goods, yet he is far from valuing them in themselves or determining
their worth. He did not come to earth for that reason; it was not the task,
the calling, or the work that God had given him to do. This is why he never
stood up directly for the poor and oppressed, the widows and orphans, the
slaves and the day laborers *as such*. He never urges improvement of their
lot or pay increases, life insurance or pension plans. Jesus is not a man of
science or art, nor is he a politician or an economist; he is no social reformer
or demagogue, nor a party man or a class struggler. He accepts social conditions as he finds them and never tries to bring about a change or improvement in them. He acknowledges the right of the emperor and orders paying
him tribute (Matt. 22:17–22). He pays the two-drachma [temple] tax (Matt.
17:24–27); he honors those who occupy Moses's seat (Matt. 23:2–3), refuses
to act as arbiter in a dispute between brothers about an inheritance (Luke
12:14), and [135] fulfills the righteousness of the law in this respect (Matt.
3:15). He assumes the difference in possessions between the poor and the
rich; speaks of owners who possess a house or a vineyard, lands or goods
(Matt. 21:40; 22:2; 24:43; Mark 12:1; Luke 12:16; 13:25; 16:1; etc.); and says
that there will always be poor people (Mark 14:7). He accepts existing differences in property without criticism. Similarly he also presupposes without
comment the existing regulations governing buying and selling, leasing and
letting, earnings and wages (Matt. 13:44; 19:21; 20:11; 21:33); and he starts
from the idea that servants are obliged to submit to their masters and obey
them (Matt. 10:24; Luke 17:7–10). He leaves all political and social circumstances and relationships for what they are; he never intervenes in any of
this, either by word or action.

But while Jesus leaves all of this untouched, he nevertheless comes into the world with the newness of his person and work. To all ranks and classes he preaches the same gospel of the kingdom of God. This is the treasure, the imperishable good, that he comes to bring to earth. And now he reveals that everything—whatever it may be, food and drink, dress and clothing, marriage and family, vocation and social standing, riches and honor, and so forth—qualifies as nothing in comparison to the treasure of the kingdom of heaven and ought to be surrendered willingly and without hesitation. Jesus judged earthly circumstances and relationships from the perspective of the kingdom of heaven; it was the standard according to which he judged. It was the way he looked at things. As far as food and drink, dress and clothing are concerned, these things will take care of themselves for all who seek the kingdom of God and his righteousness (Matt. 6:15–34). Husband and wife, parents and children, brothers and sisters, houses and acres must be abandoned as soon as they are at variance with the demands of the gospel (Matt. 10:37; Luke 9:59–62; 14:26); soul and life must be denied for the sake of Christ and for the sake of the gospel (Matt. 10:39; 16:25).

Above all, *riches* constitute an impediment to entering the kingdom of heaven. Jesus does not oppose the wealthy as such; he does not challenge capitalists merely because they possess large capital; after all, he also associates with wealthy people, partakes of their meals, does not always depict them as evil, but even occasionally portrays them as good, generous people (Matt. 20:1–15; 22:2; Luke 15:11–12; 19:12–13). He never considers the contrast between rich and poor from an economic point of view. He does not want to help the poor as such to a better position, higher wages, or more possessions; [136] and he does not want to move the wealthy as such to abandon their possessions and to distribute them among the poor. Instead, he views riches from a moral standpoint: he compares them with the goods of the heavenly kingdom and then says that, when compared with these, all earthly treasures are worthless because of their transitoriness (Matt. 6:19–20). In fact, they are often even a great *hindrance* for entering into the kingdom of heaven (Matt. 19:21, 23–24) because they cause so much anxiety (Luke 14:18–20); they produce a false sense of ease (Luke 12:16–20) and seduce us toward a life of luxury (Luke 16:19). Neither conservatism nor mammonism, neither socialism nor communism, appeals to Jesus, for he did not come to earth to provide a decent [material] existence for the poor and the proletariat. Rather, he came into the world to save his people from their sins, to serve and to give his soul as a ransom for many.

In teaching his disciples, Jesus wants to raise their standard of judgment to this level. To understand his teaching, we must note before all else that Jesus never developed a political or social agenda. It is a different question, of course, whether one can learn something from his teaching for the organization of state and society. But, as such, it is not a lesson in politics or economy, no agenda of principles or of action. Christ's teaching is totally of a religious-moral nature; it is not intended for the state, for society, but is directed to his disciples and indicates how they are to conduct themselves in their private lives. That this view of Jesus's teaching is correct is already made plausible beforehand by the sad conditions that prevailed in state and society when Jesus began his ministry. The people wandered like sheep without a shepherd (Matt. 9:36; 10:6); the leaders seduced the people and led them from bad to worse (Matt. 15:14; 23:15); the Sadducees did not bother with the people, and the Pharisees imposed burdens that they themselves did not touch (Matt. 23:4). Such was the situation religiously and morally; the political and social situation was even worse. There was no justice and no legal certainty; prevailing justice equaled violence; the rulers did not dispense justice; the people were handed over without pity to the capriciousness of the rulers and the exploitation of lower officials, the publicans and soldiers (Matt. 20:25; Luke 3:12–14; 19:8).

In such circumstances, the disciples were left to their own devices; [137] they could expect nothing from the world, the authorities, or from the judiciary. And Jesus does not conjure up visions of a great future for them; instead, he promises them nothing but the cross and oppression and persecution (Matt. 10:16–42). This explains why in the teaching of Jesus and of his apostles there is no direct command to become involved socially or politically while the so-called passive virtues of self-denial and long-suffering, of humility and love are so prominent.

The Sermon on the Mount makes this quite clear. It is dominated completely by the contrast between the righteousness that God requires and that which the Pharisees in Jesus's day demanded. By drawing attention to this contrast, Jesus in the first place tells us who, in his judgment and in the judgment of the Father, are blessed. Not the people who by external observation of the commandments seek to establish their own righteousness, but those who are mentioned in the Psalms and the Prophets as the wretched, the needy, the poor, and so forth. These Jesus now calls the poor in spirit, the people hungering and thirsting for righteousness, the pure in heart, and so forth. When Jesus therefore pronounces these people blessed, he does not violate but endorses the Old Testament completely. He is not a new lawgiver who supplements or improves the Law and the Prophets, and thus actually dissolves them, but he fulfills them totally and therefore demands another and better righteousness than that of the Pharisees and scribes (Matt. 5:17–20).

This sharp contrast between Jesus and the Pharisees, and this total agreement of Jesus's teaching and the Old Testament—all come to expression not only in the general Beatitudes but also in the explanation of each commandment: in the commandment concerning murder, which forbids also anger and even the least unkindness toward the neighbor (Matt. 5:21–26); in the commandment regarding divorce, which condemns adultery of the heart

(Matt. 5:27–32); in the commandment concerning the oath, which considers perjury at all kinds of occasions [as coming] from the evil one (Matt. 5:33–37); in the command concerning repayment of debts, which remains valid for civil life but according to the Old Testament (Lev. 19:18; Prov. 24:29; 3:27–30) is superseded by the disposition of love and forgiveness. This new disposition reaches so far that the person who treats us unjustly must be met more than halfway, with the result that coals of fire are heaped on his head (Matt. 5:38–42 [cf. Rom. 12:17–21]). [The contrast also comes to expression] in the command to love the neighbor, which applies not only to friends and benefactors but also to enemies and those who hate us (Matt. 5:43–48).

Jesus [138] emphasizes the disposition of the heart, inner conformity with the law, and internal *spiritual* righteousness when he explains each commandment over against the Pharisees. This is the reason he opposes the hypocrisy that was demonstrated in his day, especially when giving alms (Matt. 6:1–4), when praying (6:5–15), and when fasting (6:16–18). Therefore he admonishes his disciples not to love the external, the treasures of this earth (6:25–34). In other words, while the disposition of the heart is the main thing, be careful when judging a brother (7:1–6) and entrust everything to God in prayer (7:7–12). The person who chooses this road walks a narrow, difficult road, to be sure, with temptation and deception threatening from all sides (7:13–23); but he is sure of the future, for he has built his house on a rock (7:24–29).

Whoever understands the Sermon on the Mount this way and enters into its spirit discovers that no explanation violates it more than the one that presents itself as the literal one. Some people—such as the ascetics of all times, the monks, the Anabaptists, the Quakers, and more recently the authors Jozua Davids, Tolstoy, [Charles M.] Sheldon, Marie Corelli, and others—support this exegesis sincerely and with great hopes, but they only succeed in presenting a copy of the life and teaching of Jesus that then quite easily degenerates into a caricature. Others—such as [Heinrich] Grätz, Renan, Schopenhauer, [D. F.] Strauss, [Friedrich] Paulsen, Theobald Ziegler, Nietzsche, and others—favor this explanation to show the impossibility of following Jesus's teaching or to point out to Christians their pitiful inconsistency. But this explanation is diametrically opposed to the one Jesus himself gives of the Law and the Prophets in the Sermon on the Mount. Unlike the Pharisees, Jesus does not view the Old Testament literally. He enters into its spirit and wants his disciples to agree with him at the core of their being, spiritually, internally.

The true following of Christ therefore does not consist in copying him, in replicating him, in imitating his life and teaching but is found in the inner conversion of the heart, which gives us a true desire and choice to walk according to all, not just some, of God's commandments in spirit and truth. Therefore the words of Christ do not contain a political or social agenda;

they cannot be imposed by means of the authority or force of a government and cannot be exacted with violence or under threat of punishment. At the moment someone does this, the words of Jesus are robbed of their spiritual essence and their core. They are religious-moral [139] commandments that can be honored only in the way of liberty, spontaneously, from an inner compulsion of the regenerated heart. Only a good tree can produce good fruit.

This was the content of the gospel of Christ, and it was proclaimed as such by the apostles and confessed by the church. But it is not surprising that the spiritual liberty that the gospel grants was soon abused by many and became an occasion for the flesh. Some, thinking that being a Christian prohibited associating with fornicators, idol worshipers, and so forth, wanted to break off all fellowship with pagans. Women who had been converted sometimes believed that they were not allowed to live together with their husbands. Jews who learned that circumcision was of no value wanted to become uncircumcised. Subjects who had heard the word that believers have no other master than Christ considered subjection to the government to be in violation of that. Male servants and female servants, knowing that in Christ there is neither slave nor free, refused to obey their lawful masters. The moral order that prevailed in the kingdom of heaven soon clashed with the rule of law in state and society.

In reaction, all the apostles at that time began unanimously to oppose this abuse of Christian liberty by supporting the natural order, institutions, and relationships. Like Christ, they admonish fellow Christians to be long-suffering and patient, to be gentle and forbearing, to be humble and loving, to endure persecution and abuse quietly and obediently, so that evil may be conquered by the good. This becomes evident already in the first church in Jerusalem. On the basis of Acts 2:44–45 and 4:32, 34, many have assumed that in this congregation people had all things in common. But a careful reading shows that this assumption is untenable. After all, the context in which these words appear clearly indicates that they intend to depict the harmony, the mutual love, and the willingness to sacrifice for one another in this first church.

This mutual love is shown quite unambiguously in Acts 4:32: No one claimed any possessions as his own. He owned and possessed things that belonged to him, but he did not look at them as such; he was willing, if need be, to help other members in their need. In Acts 2:44 and 4:32, the words "They had all things in common" therefore do not imply that private ownership had been abolished and all possessions given to the church; they only intend to say that all members of the congregation considered [140] their own property to belong to all; this is how ready they were to share and thus to help others. This is proved rather powerfully by the fact that some went further: they sold their property and gave the money to the apostles. First of all, this was a completely free, voluntary act (Acts 5:4); second, it was an exception through which Ananias and Sapphira sought to distinguish themselves; and third, such an act is mentioned later as something unusual (Acts 4:36–37), which definitely was not imitated by [many] others: according to Acts 12:12, Mary had a house of her own. The purpose of the generous sharing practiced in the first church was therefore by no means intended to establish a community of goods, but only to take care of the poor. The money gathered by the sale of goods was not divided evenly among the members of the congregation, but it was used exclusively for the support of the needy (Acts 2:45; 4:35; 6:1–6).

Just as with private property, so all natural ordinances and institutions are maintained by the church. The wealthy are nowhere called to divest themselves of their property, although they are urgently and often admonished not to put their trust in worldly goods, to guard themselves against miserliness, and to be compassionate and share (Rom. 15:26; Gal. 2:10; 1 Tim. 6:9, 17–19; James 1:10–11; 5:1–6). The poor are never encouraged to demand their share of earthly goods but rather to be satisfied and to work faithfully in their occupation (Eph. 4:28; 1 Thess. 4:11; 2 Thess. 3:7–12; 1 Tim. 6:6, 8; Heb. 13:5). To associate with others in the community who are not members of the congregation is permitted, for otherwise one would have to leave the world (1 Cor. 5:10). A believing spouse may not leave his or her unbelieving spouse (1 Cor. 7:12–13); a circumcised man should not become uncircumcised, and whoever has not been circumcised should not be circumcised (1 Cor. 7:18). Nothing is impure of itself (Rom. 14:14); all that God created is good, and nothing is to be rejected if it is received with thanksgiving (1 Tim. 4:4); every good and perfect gift comes down from the Father of the heavenly lights (James 1:17). Marriage is honorable and the bed undefiled (Heb. 13:4). Men are to love their wives, and wives are to obey their husbands (Eph. 5:22, 25); children are to obey their parents, and parents may not exasperate their children (Eph. 6:1–4). Governing authorities are to be obeyed and feared for the Lord's sake, for there is no authority except that which God has established (Rom. 13:1; Titus 3:1; 1 Pet. 2:13).

Similarly, each person should remain in the situation to which God has called him or her (1 Cor. 7:24). [141] This also holds specifically for the relationship between masters and servants, between freed persons and slaves. According to Leviticus 19:13; 22:10; 25:50; Deuteronomy 15:18; 24:14–15; and Isaiah 16:14, in earlier times in Israel, as well as in the days of Jesus and the apostles, there were slaves but also hirelings and day laborers, who were hired for a shorter or longer time and paid wages (Matt. 20:1; 21:28; Mark 1:20; Luke 15:17, 19; John 10:12; etc.). This was also the case outside of Israel. The ancient world, in Greece and Rome, and earlier also in Egypt and Babylonia, employed a considerable number of free laborers. Incidentally, polygamy and slavery are from the nature of things confined to the higher classes. Indigent people could not support more than one wife and a single slave. As soon as industry develops, there are therefore not enough slaves, and one has to resort to free laborers.

But when the apostles in their Epistles speak of *douloi*, they are undoubt-edly speaking of slaves. After all, during the early days of the apostles, the gospel was preached especially in the big cities, in the centers of civilization, in Antioch, Ephesus, Thessalonica, Corinth, Athens, Rome, and from there it spread ever farther into the countryside. In those big cities it was accepted—for the greater part, although not exclusively—by the lowly people of the world, and then especially by slaves (1 Cor. 1:26–28). Slaves addressed by the apostles in their epistles were ordinarily domestic slaves whose living condi-tions, generally speaking, were much better than land [agricultural] slaves, who worked outdoors on rural estates and who frequently were delivered up to the capriciousness of cruel supervisors and suffered a great deal. But the lot of slaves who served in the house of their masters in the cities was not only bearable but sometimes they also received excellent care. Just as today, in those days there were hard and stern masters, but also gentle and kind ones. There were slaves who were on very friendly terms with their masters, who were highly educated, who were allowed to devote themselves to art and science, and who occupied important positions. But, of course, however comfortable their circumstances, legally they were not free; they were a thing, a piece of property that belonged to the master.

This legal status is fully acknowledged by the apostles. Nowhere do they assert, either directly or indirectly, that slavery is wrong, that it did not exist in the beginning, and that it has no right to exist today; they do not distinguish between the relationship between the government and subjects, between husband and wife, [between] parents and children, and [between] masters and servants. [142] Of course, such a distinction does exist, for marriage, the family, and the state are instituted directly by God, while God never commands or establishes slavery anywhere. But the apostles do not pay at-tention to this distinction and treat all of these as if they were of the same sort. In Ephesians 5:22–6:9 (cf. Col. 3:18–4:1), Paul deals in turn with the duties of wives, husbands, children, fathers, servants [slaves], and masters. In the case of Peter, the admonition to servants to be subservient to their masters follows immediately upon the admonition of subjects to obey and honor the authorities (1 Pet. 2:13–18). However, the admonitions to servants to be subservient to their masters are much more numerous than those to masters to be just and compassionate to their servants.

This does not mean that the duties of masters toward their servants were of less importance. But at first it did not happen very often that slave owners would join the congregation. In a few instances when this was the case, there certainly was little danger that they would misuse Christian teaching to treat their slaves harsher than before. On the other hand, a large number of slaves were members of the congregation, and they certainly were in danger of dis-obeying their master in the name of Christian liberty, of putting themselves on a footing of equality if their masters also were Christians and of scorning them if they remained pagans. Therefore the apostles admonish slaves repeatedly and emphatically, first of all, to be subservient to their masters and to obey them as unto Christ, acknowledging the will of God, who meets them in this authority of their master, and in that way to serve not men, but God (Eph. 6:5–7; Col. 3:22–23; 1 Tim. 6:1; Titus 2:9; 1 Pet. 2:18).

Second, to render this obedience, [slaves are to serve] not merely to win favor when the master's eye is on them, as pleasers of men, and not with reluctance and resistance but as servants of Christ; wholeheartedly, in simplicity of heart, with dedication, with fear and trembling; to avoid not only punishment but also [the act of] disobedience itself (Eph. 6:5–6; Col. 3:22; Titus 2:9; 1 Pet. 2:18). And third, [slaves are] to let this obedience encompass everything that is commanded, which has to be consistent, of course, with their service "in the Lord" and which therefore, because of this addition, is limited in character and degree; to render it not only to good masters but also to the harsh ones, not only to believing ones but also to unbelieving ones; not to scorn the former and not to serve the latter with less [zeal] but with even more faithfulness than usual (Col. 3:22; 1 Tim. 6:2; Titus 2:9–10; 1 Pet. 2:18). [143] All of this is seriously pointed out to servants so that they, as serving the Lord Jesus Christ, may receive the reward of their inheritance and especially so that the name of God and the Christian religion may not be slandered but may be praised because of their godly walk (Eph. 6:8; Col. 3:24; 1 Tim. 6:1; Titus 2:10).

All these admonitions, therefore, serve obviously not to turn slaves into nonslaves but to make them humbly accept their situation as God's will and in that way to be good slaves. Nowhere are they advised directly or indirectly to try to gain freedom, and nowhere do masters receive instructions to set their slaves free. In fact, in 1 Corinthians 7 Paul urges everyone to remain in the situation they were in when God called them. Today many even doubt that the translation and understanding of 1 Corinthians 7:21b, "But if you can gain your freedom, do so," is correct. It seems that the apostle wants to show here that external circumstances do not contribute anything to or take away anything from being a Christian. Circumcision is nothing, and the foreskin is nothing; the important thing is to keep God's commandments. Thus everybody is to remain, is to continue in, is to consider only the situation in which he found himself when he was called to the kingdom of God. If therefore someone was called and converted when he was a slave, he ought not to be troubled by that; yet Paul goes on to say, "If you can gain your freedom, do so." This can hardly mean, "If you can gain your freedom, see to it that you become free; seize the opportunity."

First, Paul wants to show that external circumstances are not important to being a Christian; the important thing is to keep God's commandments, and that can be done in any situation. Second, if he had meant this [to seize the opportunity to become free], it would have been strange to read in verse

22, "For he who was a slave when he was called by the Lord is the Lord's freedman," since this explanatory sentence indicates that also the slave who became a Christian, in his situation as a slave, is inwardly and spiritually a free person in Christ. The other exegesis, favored by many today—that Paul intends to say here, "Even if you could obtain your freedom, it might be better for you to remain a slave, so you can show your Christian calling in it"—is not plausible. For the sentence "but even if you could obtain your freedom" begins with the word "but," and thus it contradicts the preceding. The conjunction "but" would be completely superfluous and would obscure the sentence if Paul had only wanted to say, "Even if you can gain your freedom, you should prefer to remain a slave."

The thought of the apostle seems to be a different one and comes down to this: [144] external circumstances do not diminish being a Christian; one can be a Christian in any social position. Therefore everyone is not to look at his position in life, whether slave or free, but at his calling, what he is in Christ. Thus, if someone is a slave, this ought not to trouble him; in a sense it is regrettable and not a desirable state (as is expressed in the words "ought not to trouble him"), but it detracts nothing from his being a Christian. "But even if," Paul continues, "you can gain your freedom, use it not just for the sake of being free but so that in this newfound freedom your being a Christian can be better displayed as you live out your Christian calling. For the slave called by the Lord is the Lord's freedman, is inwardly free. But similarly the free man, called by the Lord, is and remains in his freedom a servant of Christ." Paul, therefore, does not say that the slave who has the opportunity to be free should be preoccupied with that freedom as such. Instead, he says that a Christian slave who has the opportunity to be free certainly may take it, not merely for its own sake, not for the sake of calling attention to his freedom once he is free, but so that through that freedom he may show his servitude to Christ. Therefore, use this freedom, which is given you, the more to show that you are a servant of Christ!

Thus Paul maintains also in this letter to the church of Corinth the high, ideal standpoint that Christ himself adopted in judging earthly things. As a result, compared with the great good given us through faith, all earthly distinctions and relationships do not disappear, but nevertheless they diminish in significance. According to the apostles the relationship of master and slave is parallel to that of husband and wife, parents and children, government and subjects. Nevertheless, they do not seem to ignore the distinction. Marriage, family, and the state are divine institutions, but slavery is a social arrangement, and a widespread and significant institution in those days. Christianity had to deal with that arrangement and show its strength. Slavery can, just like wealth and poverty, be tolerated and used in a Christian way. Christianity does not say that slavery is the only mode of existence in society, that it is necessary or lasting or a Christian institution. It does not abolish slavery either, not out of respect for a direct divine command but to honor historically grown ordinances in state and society. Paul calls it a yoke (1 Tim. 6:1), just as is marriage with an unbeliever. But a Christian is not allowed to reject it on his own.

[145] A Christian slave may not think that in order to be a Christian, he cannot be a slave. If he is able to gain his freedom, there is no obligation whatsoever for him to remain a slave. Freedom is to be preferred over slavery, and striving to improve your lot is permitted. But if he is a slave and has to remain one, then he is indeed called to apply his being a Christian to this situation—to be obedient, faithful, diligent in his work—and thus to be a *better* slave than other, unbelieving pagan slaves.

That this was Paul's thinking is confirmed by his cordial letter to Philemon. Philemon and his wife, Apphia, most likely lived in Colossae and belonged to the local Christian congregation that met at his home (v. 2). He was a zealous colaborer in the gospel of Christ (v. 1) and showed the believers great love (vv. 5–7). Paul hoped to be able to take up residence at his house when he would go to Colossae later (v. 22). A certain slave named Onesimus, who belonged to Philemon, had run away. We do not know the reasons for this, but most likely they were not the result of bad treatment received from his master, for then Paul would have mentioned something about it, or at any rate he would not have praised Philemon the way he apparently does in his epistle. But Onesimus was disappointed in freedom; a runaway slave was nowhere welcome, could not get help anywhere, and was constantly in danger of being arrested and severely punished. Maybe that was why he fled to the big city of Rome. Here, more than anywhere else, he had the opportunity to hide and find a place to stay. But even this did not work out for him, and thus he turns for protection to Paul, whom he probably had come to know, at least by name, in the house of his master.

At any rate, Onesimus came to Paul, through whose witness, as blessed by God, he was brought to faith in Christ. Then Paul urged him to return to his master and gave him a letter of recommendation, intended not only for Philemon and his family but also for the entire congregation that gathered in his home. Paul can recommend Onesimus with full candor; he had come to know him and can personally vouch for his reliability. Onesimus has become a dear son to him, whom he has raised in his captivity. The apostle would have liked to keep him to use him for his work of the gospel. But Paul did not want to do this, so as not to force Philemon involuntarily to show Paul the kindness of giving Onesimus to him. For that reason he sent him back.

[146] But what a difference between the Onesimus who ran away from his master and the one who returned. Philemon had to do without his slave for a short time, but now he received him back for eternity. He received him back not as a slave but as more than a slave, as a dear brother, who could be of service to him "in the flesh" as well as "in the Lord," as a slave and as

a brother. Paul therefore does not comment about the servant relationship between Onesimus and Philemon. He does not say that Onesimus is now no longer a slave, but he sheds light on the fact that Onesimus's conversion has caused his relationship to Philemon to be totally different and much more intimate. The latter receives him back not as a slave but as more than a slave, as a dear brother in Christ, who now can be of service to Philemon in this double relationship of slave and brother. Neither does Paul ask Philemon to grant his slave freedom since his words "I know that you will also do beyond what I tell you" (v. 21) are much too general to allow for such a special interpretation. If Paul would have wanted it [said], he certainly would have said so clearly and forthrightly. But even if these words should be interpreted that way, one could conclude from them at the most that Paul asked for this release as a favor, but certainly not as a right. Even in this case he does not touch the institution of slavery with a single word. He accepts it for what it is and acquiesces to its existence.

Although the gospel left everything unchanged in the natural relationships, it nevertheless preached a principle so deep and rich and extraordinarily powerful that it was bound to exert a reforming influence on all earthly circumstances. The gospel has to be understood clearly. It must be accepted the way it presents itself without turning it into a political or social system, and then it will reveal its permeating power. For what does this gospel proclaim? What was this new element that was unknown to all of antiquity and that made the ancient world shake to its foundations? It was this, that heavenly, spiritual matters, that the kingdom of God and his righteousness in Christ, are a tangible, completely trustworthy reality and that their value infinitely exceeds all visible and temporal things. There is absolutely nothing that is considered great and glorious among men that can be compared with it. In order to be a Christian, a citizen of the kingdom of God and heir of eternal life, it matters not at all whether one is a Jew or Greek, barbarian or Scythian, male or female, free or slave, rich or poor, socially important or unimportant.

[147] The only way to enter the kingdom of heaven, which is available to all, is by way of regeneration, an inner change, faith, conversion. No nationality, no gender, no social standing, no class, no wealth or poverty, no freedom or slavery has any preference here. The old has passed; behold, all has been made new. The walls of division have fallen away, the palisades taken down; the gospel is intended for all and must be proclaimed to all. The despised and those without rights in antiquity—the barbarians, the uncivilized, the ignoble, women, slaves, publicans, sinners, whoremongers, idol worshipers—are all people of God's family, destined for his kingdom. Yes, if there is any preference, then the poor, the ignoble, the unlearned, the oppressed are the ones who are considered first for the gospel. God chooses the poor, the despised, and the ignoble, so that no one should boast before him.

What a revolution this gospel brought about in the ancient world: it gave a reforming power to humanity! All people are equal before God. He rates no one inferior because of social standing or rank, because of simplicity or unimportance. God loves everyone who fears him from all peoples and generations and social classes. This is a raising in status, this is the birthday of a new humanity, the beginning of a new society. Christians, however different they were among themselves in origin and social status, were an elect family, a holy nation, a people made his own, a holy priesthood, one body with many members. Even if Christianity had resulted in nothing more than this spiritual and holy community, even if it had not brought about any modification in earthly relationships, even if it, for instance, had done nothing for the abolition of slavery, it would still be and remain something of everlasting worth. The significance of the gospel does not depend on its influence on culture, its usefulness for life today; it is a treasure in itself, a pearl of great value, even if it might not be a leaven.

Although the worth of Christianity is certainly not only, not exclusively, and not even in the first place determined by its influence on civilization, it nevertheless is undeniable that Christianity indeed exerts such influence. The kingdom of heaven is not only a pearl; it is a leaven as well. Whoever seeks it is offered all kinds of other things. Godliness has a promise for the future, yet also for life today. In keeping God's commandments, there is great reward. In its long and rich history, Christianity has borne much valuable fruit for all of society in all its relationships, in spite of the unfaithfulness of its confessors.

[148] Space prevents us from pursuing this any further. In conclusion, we will present a brief summary of the teaching of Scripture regarding societal relationships.

Scripture's point of departure is creation, because essentially all relationships are connected with it, and thus can only be known from it. Science offers us only conjectures about the origin of things. Scripture teaches us that God is the almighty Creator of heaven and earth and that man, in distinction from all other creatures, is made in his image. Also [Scripture teaches] that the distinction of soul and body, of man and woman, of parents and children, of authority and obedience, of inequality in gifts and powers, in talents and goods, in calling and task; the duty to work and the privilege of rest, and thus the change of day and night, of work days and the Sabbath; the earthly calling and man's heavenly destination—all these are founded in creation, called into being by God's will. Therefore they have to be acknowledged and honored as unchangeable ordinances.

The intent of grace, which entered immediately after the fall, always and everywhere has been to maintain and restore these original relationships. This characterizes both general and special grace, although general grace works only from the outside to the inside and special grace works from the inside to the outside. Israel's legislation united both operations because it rests in the covenant of grace and yet observes the law. Although it has been fulfilled in Christ, just as prophecy [has been fulfilled], it [Israelite legislation] nevertheless remains valid for us insofar as in its purely moral aspects it carries a responsible character; maintains the divine will as rule for all of life, including the life of the nation; desires to regulate all relationships, including property, according to the principle of righteousness; and gives a great deal of prominence to charitableness in social life.

While the gospel that Christ brings us in his person and work is not the abolition but the fulfillment of the Law and Prophets, it presupposes creation, honors the work of the Father, and concurs with all natural relationships in human life that exist by virtue of God's will. In itself the gospel, the proclamation of the kingdom of heaven and his [God's] righteousness, is the good news of reconciliation and redemption from sin through the blood of the cross. This is the gospel that must remain, first in church and missions, but also beyond it, everywhere. It may not be robbed of its contents or dissolved into a political or social program. Only in this way can the gospel be maintained in its everlasting, all-surpassing value.

[149] The gospel that therefore only battles sin looks at all men from the same perspective. It knows no social positions or classes, no rich or poor; it only knows sinners and offers the same grace to all indiscriminately. Thus it proclaims the eternal worth of every human being. It also maintains the possibility of redemption for those who have fallen the lowest, points all people to the same way of redemption—the way of regeneration, faith, and conversion—and subsequently creates a spiritual community for all believers, which is rooted in Christ and for that reason permanently surpasses all human associations and survives them by far.

Because the gospel is exclusively directed to the redemption from sin, it leaves all natural relationships alone. It is in principle opposed to all socialism, communism, anarchism, which after all never only oppose sin, but by their denial of the fall identify sin with nature, unrighteousness with the very institution of the family and the state, and therefore creation with the fall.

For the same reason the gospel shuns every revolution that arises from the principle of unbelief, since by its overthrow of everything a revolution makes no distinction between nature and sin and eradicates the good with the bad. The gospel, on the other hand, always works reformationally. It creates the greatest reformation by setting people free from guilt, renewing the heart, and thus in principle restoring the right relationship of man to God.

And so from this center it influences all earthly relationships in a reforming and renewing way. The various walks of life—family, society, the state, occupation, business, agriculture, industry, commerce, science, art, and so forth—each have a certain measure of independence, which they owe to the will of God as it manifests itself in their own nature. In time, by God's providence, they develop and are changed in accordance with their nature. The authority of the government over its subjects, of the husband over his wife, of the father over his children, of the master over his servants—this authority is considerably different today from what it was in the days of Paul. The gospel fully honors this development, today as well as in the time of the apostles; it puts no pressure on it and does not impose a single obstacle. The gospel is gospel, good news for all creatures, not a proclamation of destruction and death, but of resurrection and life.

[150] So that everything may revive and become again what it ought to be and can be, the gospel tests all things—all circumstances and relationships—against the will of God, just as in the days of Moses and the prophets, of Christ and the apostles. It considers everything from a moral point of view, from the angle in which all those circumstances and relationships are connected with moral principles that God has instituted for all of life. Precisely because the gospel only opposes sin, it opposes it always and everywhere in the heart and in the head, in the eye and in the hand, in family and society, in science and art, in government and subjects, in rich and poor, for *all* sin is unrighteousness, trespassing of God's law, and corruption of nature. But by liberating all social circumstances and relationships from sin, the gospel tries to restore them all according to the will of God and make them fulfill their own nature.

While conservatism closes its eyes to changes in society, and radicalism fails to have a solid standpoint in the stream of events, a reformation that proceeds from a Christian principle combines both: being and becoming, the absolute and the relative, the unity of the divine will and the wonderful leading of his providence. The name "Christian-Historical" combines both elements, and the term "Anti-Revolutionary" adds to it that historic Christian principles are to be applied in the practice of everyday life, not by way of a radical revolution, but in that of a reformation that retains all that is good.[1]

---

1. Ed. note: The term "Christian-Historical" harks back to the father of distinctly Christian political thought and action in the Netherlands, Guillaume Groen van Prinsterer (1801–76), the primary influence on Abraham Kuyper, founder of the Anti-Revolutionary Party (see chap. 5, nn. 1 and 2).

# 8

# ON INEQUALITY

[151] Thoughtful people have always been troubled by the problem of unity and diversity, oneness and multiplicity. We always perceive within and outside ourselves an ever-changing world of phenomena; nowhere do we find anything that is abiding and lasting; everything is in flux; nothing is stable except instability. If in these busy, stressful times we look beyond ourselves at world events, we are constantly deluged by an overwhelming mass of incidents and events that are impossible to categorize or to understand. And when we look inside ourselves, we see a restless sea of impressions, emotions, and moods, and we feel like a ship that is tossed to and fro. Sometimes in that vast restlessness of existing reality, we see things that weary us because of a certain monotony, but we also encounter things that move us and even bewilder us by their impenetrable mystery. In both instances questions arise: What accounts for such infinite variety and endless diversity in this one, vast universe? Might it be possible that this endless variety can be reduced to, or is derived from, one single source that might quiet our souls?

It is true that we can take some aesthetic delight in the variety and diversity that surrounds us even without understanding it, since there is beauty in diversity. But this variety also hides a great many contradictions, for diversity is often a pseudonym for a mysterious struggle between clashing powers. Just as nature has its days and nights, its summers and winters, so humanity faces good and evil, truth and falsehood, beauty and disgrace. According to the book of Genesis, enmity has been put between the seed of the woman and

Ed. note: Originally published as "Over de ongelijkheid," in *Stemmen des tijds* 2 (1913): 17–43.

[the seed] of the serpent. We recognize this all around. There is no peace or harmony anywhere; instead, [152] dissonance and struggle are everywhere. People, social classes, nations, political parties, principles, and interests have clashed throughout the centuries, while inside each person the head and the heart, flesh and spirit, duty and desire, conscience and lust are constantly at war with each other. Is it perhaps possible that all these harrowing contrasts can be reconciled and brought together in a nobler synthesis that might satisfy us in our day and eventually conquer and destroy them?

It goes without saying that over time many and varied efforts have been put forth in trying to resolve such an enormous, all-encompassing problem. Yet it is possible to categorize these efforts. Two groups especially have become prominent. They are, on the one hand, the pantheistic or monistic systems that have tried to reduce variety to an appearance of reality with the slogan "variety is basically one reality." Thus they treat variety either as modifications of a single reality, or they see it merely as man's imagination, which does not correspond to any objective reality. These are the views of the Greek Eleatic[1] and Stoic schools of thought that, overlooking gnosticism and Neoplatonism, have become part of the more recent philosophy of Spinoza, Hegel, and Spencer. They may even have found a more consistent voice in the philosophy of Buddhism, which views the entire world as *maya*, the representation of the one, unknowable, and unutterable *It*.

On the other hand, there are the pluralistic systems that despair of ever finding one single reality and that do not go beyond accepting an original, eternal multitude of gods or spirits, of powers or matter. These philosophies also date back to antiquity. They were not only embraced by the earlier and later schools of materialism but also formed the basis of polytheistic and polydaemonic paganism; the same holds true for the dualism of the Persians and Manichaeans, for the theosophical distinction of the dark and bright aspects of God. And it is remarkable that they have reappeared more recently in this form as a reaction to monism. Not only is the pluralism of William James proof of this, but also the dualistic representation of a morally good God next to the mysterious power of nature and the even more prominent superstition and magic that increasingly spreads to our centers of culture.

This is how, to date, religious and philosophic systems have approached the gripping problem of unity and multiformity. It is quite remarkable that in our day, more so than ever before, this idea of diversity has become a *practical* problem. The great diversity in our world is seen by many people today, especially in the social realm, as inequality.

1. Ed. note: The Greek pre-Socratic philosophical Eleatic school (at Elea, a Greek colony in Lucania, Italy) began with Parmenides (5th–6th c. BC), the great philosopher of "being" who taught that everything is fundamentally "One."

[153] It is true that this inequality, which is only one instance of a worldwide problem of multiformity, is very important to people. The reason for this is not only that it presents a theoretical problem, but even more so because it calls attention to the many highly deplorable disparities that exist in real life. What is the reason and why is it necessary that a few may live in luxury and that many may live a fairly carefree life but that the mass of humanity has to earn a living through hard labor? Who or what accounts for the difference between those whose homes are furnished lavishly or comfortably and the many who have to endure living in stuffy rooms, narrow alleys, and dreary slums that lack light and fresh air?

In more recent times the first person to seriously ask this question is the man whose two-hundredth birthday was joyfully commemorated this year [1912] on June 28, especially in Geneva and Paris. This celebration once again focused attention on the importance of this man. His name again became a party slogan. His advocates and his opponents squared off stridently. In Paris the celebration took place under strong protest from the adherents of the royal party, while in Geneva nature even seemed to take the protesters' side, for it turned out to be a stormy and rainy day there. Some called the man whose birthday was being celebrated a loathsome creature, someone who poisoned the people, a destroyer of society, a precursor of Kropotkin,[2] and even of outlaws like Garnier and Bonnot.[3] Others, however, deemed him the father of all the great ideas that shaped our lives after the Revolution, calling him the first true Protestant. As in earlier days, his name once again aroused feelings of love and hatred, reverence and contempt, enthusiasm and bitterness. And no wonder, since the name of this man is none other than Jean-Jacques Rousseau.

For this man, who was born in Geneva in 1712, the year 1749 became a turning point in his life when he was thirty-seven years old. Before that time Rousseau was a drifter, spiritually and physically, searching and wandering; he was a man who did not know what he wanted and did not want what he did know. He was like a ship without both rudder and compass. After moving to Paris in 1741, he had made a name for himself, at least to a degree, by his new method of writing music. He also had managed to become accepted in the drawing rooms, where he got acquainted with the critics of the day, such as Diderot and Holbach, Helvétius and Grimm. But at that time Rousseau had not yet found himself, and as he said later, he never felt at home in those circles.

[154] But on an exceptionally hot summer day in the year 1749, Rousseau walked the two leagues [4–5 miles] from Paris to Vincennes to visit his friend

2. Ed. note: Prince Peter (Pyotr) Alexeyevich Kropotkin ("the Anarchist Prince," 1842–1921) was a Russian anarchist and advocate of a communist society free from central government.

3. Ed. note: Octave Garnier (1889–1912) and Jules Bonnot (1876–1912) were the two leaders of the Bonnot Gang (la bande à Bonnot), a French criminal, anarchist gang that operated in France and Belgium from 1911 to 1912.

Diderot. The latter was held prisoner in a castle surrounded by a large park for having committed a literary faux pas (he had used a careless expression in his *Lettres sur les aveugles* about a princess of the royal court, who felt that he had insulted her). It was two o'clock in the afternoon. There was no shade to walk in because the trees had been trimmed short, according to the custom of the day. Rousseau rested on occasion, and upon resuming his walk, he tried to slow down by reading. He had taken along a copy of the *Mercure de France*. Suddenly his eye caught an announcement of an essay contest by the Academy of Dijon on the topic "whether the progress of the sciences and arts has tended to corrupt or purify morals."[4]

At that very moment a tremendous change took place in him. Suddenly a light went on in his mind. Rousseau writes in his *Confessions*: "At the moment of that reading I saw another universe and I became another man."[5] In the second of his four letters to Malesherbes, he elaborates on this. He experienced a moment that had such a unique impact on his life that he would never forget it. If anything ever resembled a flash of inspiration, it was the emotion that overwhelmed him at that moment. "Suddenly I felt my mind dazzled by a thousand lights; crowds of lively ideas presented themselves at the same time with a strength and a confusion that threw me into an inexpressible perturbation; I felt my head seized by a dizziness similar to drunkenness."[6] His heart was beating so fast that he could hardly breathe; he sat down under a tree and spent the next half hour being so moved that when he arose, he noticed that the front of his vest was soaking wet from tears. When Rousseau arrived at Diderot's [confinement], he was still in a state of mind that bordered on delirium. He asked Diderot what he should do, and Diderot told him that he should not only enter the competition but do so in a way like no one else would: "You must approach it altogether different from anyone else." And Rousseau responded, "You are right." Diderot seemed to have known his friend Rousseau very well. He understood that a negative response would be totally in line with Rousseau's way of thinking.

[155] One may differ with Vinet, who calls this change in Rousseau's life a religious conversion.[7] But it certainly was a remarkable and extremely important change. One could almost say that it inaugurated a new era. And it ran

---

4. "Si le progrès des sciences et des artes a contribué à corrompre ou à épurer les moeurs."

5. Jean-Jacques Rousseau, *The Collected Writings of Rousseau*, vol. V, *The Confessions: and, Correspondence, Including the Letters to Malesherbes*, ed. Christopher Kelly, Roger D. Masters, and Peter G. Stillman, trans. Christopher Kelly (Hanover and London: University Press of New England, 1995), book VIII of *Confessions*, 294.

6. Ibid., 575.

7. Cf. *Alexandre Vinet, "Rousseau," *Foi et vie* 1 (1912): 399. But E. Doumergue, who for the rest praises Rousseau's spirituality, observes correctly that the gospel was merely a law for him and that Rousseau, who considered sin only to be a human weakness, did not see the need for Christ as Savior and that therefore Rousseau's Christianity lacked precisely . . . a conversion ("Jean-Jacques Rousseau et la Déclaration des droits de l'homme et du citoyen," *Foi et vie* 1 [1912]: 419).

much deeper and was much more radical than one might have expected of a man like Rousseau. It started in his head, but then penetrated his heart and brought about a transformation of his entire life. From then on he abandoned the world, its praise, its pomp, and its honors and became even more than before a lover of solitude, a loner. He broke with society, with friends, and also with the philosophers of the day, those ardent missionaries of atheism. He cleansed his heart of greed and created for himself a different, moral world. Until then he had been a good person; now he became a virtuous person or at the least intoxicated by virtue. He resigned from a fairly well-paying banking position with [the financier] Francueil and decided to make a living by copying music for so much a page.[8] When he lived in Geneva for a few months in 1754, he rejoined the Reformed Church on April 1; he had left it for the Roman Catholic Church on August 23, 1728, under the influence of Mrs. Warens.[9] In 1756 he left Paris for good to start life as a hermit in l'Hermitage, a residence outside of Paris that Mrs. D'Epinay had kindly offered him, but which he soon exchanged for a small home in the park Montlouis in Montmorency. This had been made available to him by the fiscal plenipotentiary of the prince of Condé.[10] Here he stayed only a few years in order to move restlessly from one place to another, as if being persecuted, until his death in 1778. But Paris never again became his regular home.

The transformation of his life even affected the way he dressed. Until that time he had worn a powdered wig, as was customary, and also knee breeches and white hose, but he gave it all up and started wearing the solid and durable dress of a simple citizen. He sold his watch and with a great deal of satisfaction told himself that from now on he did not need to know [156] what time it was.[11] Even his linen became part of this transformation. When earlier he had been secretary of the French ambassador in Venice for eighteen months, he had acquired a considerable quantity of linen of exquisite quality. But unfortunately he lost it on Christmas night of the year 1751 when all his linen, including forty-two shirts of the finest texture, was stolen, most likely by the brother of his landlady Thérèse Le Vasseur. And thus he was delivered also of this passion for fine linen.[12]

The great change that Rousseau experienced at that time, though in a way somewhat related to his former way of life, consisted in his sudden renunciation of the corrupt culture of his day and his return to the simplicity and truth of nature. Both of these were total opposites in the eighteenth century. No one was aware of or cared about nature. Country residences were characterized

8. Rousseau, *Confessions*, book VIII, in *Writings*, V:303–5; cf. idem, *The Reveries of the Solitary Walker*, trans. Charles Butterworth (New York: New York University Press, 1979), 31.
9. Rousseau, *Confessions*, book VIII, in *Writings*, V:327ff.
10. Ibid., 331ff., 408.
11. Ibid., 305; cf. *Reveries*, 31.
12. Rousseau, *Confessions*, book VIII, in *Writings*, V:305–6.

by square buildings, straight avenues, geometrically planted bushes, and trees
that were pruned like pyramids or globes. Medieval art was despised as being
"Gothic." Voltaire considered the Notre Dame in Paris an architectural mon-
strosity.[13] By the beginning of that century, the Renaissance had degenerated
into an arbitrary, oftentimes unnatural baroque style, which soon was joined
by a stiff, pedantic pigtail period. Science consisted of abstractions that were
the fruit of human reasoning but that had no connection with reality. Society
was divided between the court, nobility, and clergy, who enjoyed all kinds
of privileges, and a population steeped in poverty, whose tax burdens grew
increasingly heavier. The contrast of all this pierced Rousseau's soul. He did
not merely notice it or make it the object of ridicule, as Montesquieu did, for
instance, in his *Lettres persanes* of 1721, in which he made the France of his
day the object of satire. Instead, Rousseau felt it with all the warmth of his
heart and seemed to experience it in his very own soul.

His birth and youth in Geneva on the banks of Lake Léman and at the
foot of the Alps undoubtedly prepared him for this. And so did his sensitive
nature, which he had received from his parents and which was shaped by
growing up in the great outdoors. Add to this not only his rich imagination,
which, as he indicated, blossomed in the country and in the forests but pined
away when inside house or city,[14] [157] but also his strong, almost passionate penchant for turning himself into an object of meditation. But it was the
Dijon contest that first made him unmistakably aware of the sharp contrast
between nature and culture. It led to a crisis that determined the course of
the rest of his life. For the first time he clearly saw that the teachings of our
wise men were faulty and foolish and caused only oppression and misery in
our social order.[15] The emotion he experienced at that moment was so deep
that he, though not a man of willpower and action, broke with his past and
entered upon a new life that was inspired and governed completely by one
thought: We must return to nature!

Until then he had lived at odds with himself and his surroundings. But
now he rediscovered himself and nature at the same time, and he found the
two to be in deep harmony. The language of his soul and of nature were one.
Until that moment both had been buried in his thinking under the results of a
rationalized reason and a corrupt culture. But now Rousseau had discovered
both in their originality and truth and in their simplicity and beauty. And
thus they became for him something different and much more meaningful:
nature without and his soul within now set free from the unnatural trappings
imposed on them by reason and culture, suddenly turned into revelations of
one and the same God: a God who is pure goodness and from whose hands

13. Felix Bungener, *Voltaire et son temps: Études sur le dix-huitième siècle*, 2 vols. (Paris: J. Cher-
buliez, 1851), II:93.
14. Rousseau, *Confessions*, book VIII, in *Writings*, V:360.
15. Ibid., 349.

nothing evil can come. The multitude of wrongs and all the misery in our world can only find their origin in society and the culture it has created. And having understood the original relationship of soul and nature, of man and the world, of subject and object, of myself and not-myself, he became the powerful, influential fighter for the rights of naturalness.

In his 1750 *Discourse (First Discourse)*,[16] he tried to show that the arts and sciences resulted from human vices and would without fail lead to religious and moral degradation. In this treatise and in its defense before the king of Poland, he had already intimated that the prime reason for evil is inequality and that it gradually produced wealth, luxury, idleness, and also the arts and sciences. He developed this thought further in his second *Discourse on the Origins of Inequality*,[17] where he posits over against the real, miserable conditions of the society of his day the fiction of the "nature state." In it, people did not confront each other in warlike and combative ways, as with Hobbes, but rather as those who lived together as free, sane, good, [158] and happy people. In his *Social Contract*,[18] he has the state emerge from a hypothetical contract in which each citizen does not relinquish his liberty and rights but in which these coalesce into one voluntary sovereign entity that does not put limitations on peoples' freedoms and in which no person is able to commit crimes but in which all strive for the well-being of all citizens equally.

In his *Émile*,[19] he proceeds from the thought that everything that comes from the hand of the Creator is good but that it degenerates when man takes over; thus the matter of educating people consists of seeing to it that natural man remains good by improving society. And in the *Profession of Faith of a Savoyard Vicar*,[20] he admits to a natural feeling of religiosity, which he identifies with the original gospel of Christ. In one word, Rousseau tries constantly to reduce human work to what existed originally, and then he identifies the latter suddenly with freedom and rights, with religion and virtue. So redemption consists of turning from culture to nature, from a society that is complex

16. Ed. note: Jean-Jacques Rousseau, *Discourse on the Sciences and Arts (First Discourse); and, Polemics*, vol. II of *The Collected Writings of Rousseau*, ed. Roger D. Masters and Christopher Kelly, trans. Judith R. Bush, Roger D. Masters, and Christopher Kelly (Hanover and London: University Press of New England, 1992).

17. Ed. note: Jean-Jacques Rousseau, *Discourse on the Origins of Inequality (Second Discourse); Polemics; and, Political Economy*, vol. III of *The Collected Writings of Rousseau*, ed. Roger D. Masters and Christopher Kelly, trans. Judith R. Bush, Roger D. Masters, Christopher Kelly, and Terence Marshal (Hanover and London: University Press of New England, 1992).

18. Ed. note: Jean-Jacques Rousseau, *The Social Contract; and, Discourses*, trans. G. D. H. Cole, rev. and augmented by J. H. Brumfitt and John C. Hall, Everyman's Library 162 (New York and Toronto: Alfred A. Knopf, 1973).

19. Ed. note: Jean-Jacques Rousseau, *Émile: or, On Education*, trans., introduction, and notes by Allan Bloom (New York: Basic Books, 1978).

20. Ed. note: The *Profession of Faith of a Savoyard Vicar* is part of *Émile* and also separately published (New York: P. Eckler, 1889).

and corrupt to the original natural state of innocence, from the deceptiveness of the mind to the pure dictates of feeling.

The ideas that Rousseau promulgated in his writings are by no means new or original, because most of them are found in his predecessors, especially the English Deists, and were already more or less consciously part of the thinking of his contemporaries. Madam de Staël put it well when she said, "He has invented nothing new, yet he has set the whole world on fire."[21] The latter part of the statement is even truer than the first. No one's influence in the eighteenth century could be compared to Rousseau's. He might say the same thing others had said, yet he said it in his own way, and in a way no one had said it before or could say it. He had the ability to express his thoughts in such a simple and clear manner, with such deep feeling and conviction, that everyone was charmed by them. He captivated his readers by the brief, forceful, and beautiful sentences with which he began his books and chapters. And when he later developed his initial thesis, it was done in such eloquent language and with such passion that readers were entranced even before they had time to think it through.

Actually, Rousseau represented the thinking of the day. He spoke the language of his day. He gave voice to what people thought subconsciously, and he could do so because he was a man with a heart. That distinguished him from the men of the Enlightenment. [159] He shared their loathing of tradition, of what had developed historically, and particularly of Christian dogma. But while the Encyclopedists idolized reason and science, using it to mock God and religion, Rousseau's heart was homesick for a return to the innocence of nature. Behind the arts and sciences, the riches and opulence that were the pride of the Enlightenment, Rousseau saw the misery of the masses, their spiritual poverty, and their empty hearts. Its [the Enlightenment's] atheism and materialism did not satisfy him, and although he was a son of the Enlightenment, he became its most powerful opponent. Although he was mocked because of [the Enlightenment], not to mention persecuted, even if this was more imagined than real, he left the movement. He dared to be his own person, to stand on his own two feet, to say "no" when the whole world said "yes." This is the reason why the lonely walker became the leader of many and the person in charge.

Rousseau's influence on his contemporaries and those who followed him was powerful. When he appeared on the scene, Voltaire's glory was past, and Rousseau became the man of the hour for the common people as well as for the better situated. Although he wanted to withdraw from the world and be by himself, people did not leave him alone. He was feted and celebrated.

21. Ed. note: Anne Louise Germaine de Staël (1766–1817) was a French-speaking Swiss littéra-teure, an enthusiast of Rousseau, and an influence on nineteenth-century Romanticism. Her most famous written work is *De l'Allemagne*.

People learned from him to idolize the outdoors, as well as humanity in its natural state, the Bushmen and Hottentots. In the name of nature, people began to despise not only industry but also agriculture, for it was seen as the root cause of property and inequality. The corn that now provided food had also been, on further reflection, the cause of human ruin and therefore of much less value than carrots and cabbage.[22] Just as gentlemen began to dress in coarse clothes, put on thick-soled shoes, and sport gnarled walking sticks, so the ladies decked themselves à la Jean-Jacques Rousseau with sentimental bonnets, practiced bloodletting, and drank buttermilk in order to create a wan look.[23]

Even though Rousseau had not been born to be a revolutionary, nevertheless his teachings were thoroughly revolutionary. Without Rousseau, as Napoleon said, France would not have had a revolution. According to Taine,[24] 1789 is the commentary on the text of the *Social Contract*, and [Maximilian] Robespierre is its incarnation. Granted that there are many differences between Rousseau's *Social Contract* and the 1789 [160] [French] *Declaration of the Rights of Man and the Citizen* [drafted by Robespierre].[25] Nevertheless, the basic thought in both is that man should abandon society as it has developed historically, with its differences and inequalities, and return to nature and its original rights. One must also remember that Rousseau never intended to introduce the natural state in its absolute sense; he understood quite well that this would be impossible. Nor did he portray the natural state as a situation that had really existed once upon a time. He only used this idea as a means to portray what he thought a desirable arrangement of society and the state should look like, with common interests for all, and in which everything was to be done for the people and by the people.

Contrary to the existing state of affairs of his day, he wanted a state that was based on freedom for all, in which no class or persons would enjoy privileges that had been obtained illegally or by force. And with the creation of such a state, he was not concerned about historically developed circumstances, or privileges that have been obtained historically, or parties, or factions. Instead, relying on his feelings, he used his unrestrained imagination, and as a result he constantly contradicted himself. At the same time Rousseau was never a socialist or communist. But the thoughts he expressed about

22. Bungener, *Voltaire*, II:136–38.

23. D. P. D. Fabius, *De Fransche revolutie* (Amsterdam: J. H. Kruyt, 1881), 63.

24. Ed. note: Hippolyte Taine (1828–93) was a French historian, a literary critic of a positivist bent who sought to apply the scientific method to literature and the humanities.

25. É[mile] Doumergue points out the differences in his article, "Jean-Jacques Rousseau et la Déclaration des droits de l'homme et du citoyen," *Foi et vie* 1 (1912): 424–30, 447–51, and concludes that the *Declaration of the Rights of Man* was taken not from the *Social Contract* but from the American Bill of Rights and therefore is not derived from the philosophy of the eighteenth century but from Protestantism and the gospel. Who has the time and inclination historically to test this rather interesting opinion?

inequality and its source, about rich and poor, about masters and servants, and especially about the ways in which the rich and powerful used social and political institutions to serve their own interests—these thoughts became the material on which socialist and communist systems after him were built. And Rousseau's influence went far beyond this: the philosophical systems of Kant, Fichte, and Jacobi; the literature of Herder, Schiller, and Goethe; the Romanticism of Schlegel and Tieck; Schleiermacher's theology of feeling; and in general the newer lyrics, nature and civic poetry, modern religion, ethics, and pedagogy—they were all baptized more or less by Rousseau's spirit.[26]

Finally, although the criticism of his social and philosophical theories had been merciless, [161] his sermons castigating the misery of society, and his forceful fight against the political and social inequality among people caused a tremor to go through the world and brought about a reversal in the way many people think. The powerful words with which he concluded his *Discourse on Inequality* still resonate in many places:

> It is manifestly against the Law of Nature, in whatever manner it is, that a child command an old man, an imbecile lead a wise man, and a handful of men be glutted with superfluities while the starving multitude lacks necessities.[27]

Especially this idea of the injustice of social inequality has become deeply rooted in the hearts of men and has found wide acceptance. It may be said that the basic thought patterns of our century oppose such inequality and want to get rid of it completely. Rousseau made another distinction between natural or physical inequality as it comes to expression in sex and age, in gifts and abilities, and in moral or political inequality that consists of wealth and power, honor and social status, and that rests totally on convention. But he deemphasized and limited natural inequality considerably, recognizing that first of all the natural differences in physical or mental strength often were the result of lifestyle and nurture. Furthermore, such differences were of much less significance in the state of innocence, because there was no art or science as yet and no property and servitude; everybody was able to look after his own needs; if there was inequality, it was hardly noticeable, and its importance was almost negligible.[28] No wonder that others went even further and called all differences in human mental abilities acquired differences[29] and that in the nineteenth and twentieth centuries, insofar as they remained true to the principles of the Revolution, they began to oppose the inequality even

26. Cf. P. J. Molenaar, "De Invloed van Jean-Jacques Rousseau," *Stemmen des tijds* 1 (July/August, 1912): 17–43.
27. Rousseau, *Discourse on Inequality*, in *Writings*, III:67.
28. Ibid., 41–42.
29. As, e.g., Claude Adrien Helvétius in *De l'esprit; or, Essays on the Mind and Its Several Faculties* (Paris, 1759; New York: B. Franklin, 1970).

more forcefully and on a much broader scale than initially had been done in .
the eighteenth century.

This inequality is hard pressed in our day by opposition from two sides. On
the one hand, it is attacked as though from above by the evolutionist mind-set,
which may be either pantheistically or materialistically colored. This mind-set
governs scientific thinking, either consciously or unconsciously, and tries hard
to destroy all basic differences. The destruction concerns, first, the difference
between God and the world but also the difference between man and animal,
soul and body, truth and lie, good and evil, Christianity and paganism, and
so forth. [162] On the other hand, differences are attacked as though from
below, by all those modern movements that seek to obliterate the differences
between husband and wife, parents and children, the government and the
governed, employers and employees, rich and poor, and so forth. Both movements are undoubtedly related, and it would not make much sense to fight
against pantheism and materialism in the realm of thought while supporting
socialistic or communistic emancipation in the realm of trade.

The name "citizen of Geneva," as Rousseau liked to call himself after his
second discourse,[30] makes us think of another man who lived and worked in
Geneva two centuries earlier: the powerful Reformer John Calvin. But what
a tremendous contrast arises the moment these two names are mentioned
together. Calvin, the classically formed humanist, a man distinguished in
manners and appearance, with a sharp mind and an iron will; over against
Rousseau, the restless wanderer, who was often moody, whose thinking lacked
logic, whose life was rudderless, who was a dreamer and a fanatic, and the
first great romanticist of the eighteenth century! Both experienced a transformation in their lives, but with Calvin it consisted of a turning away from
the errors of the Roman Catholic Church and an embracing of the truth and
the freedom of the gospel, while with Rousseau it was no more than a breaking with all culture and a return to the instinctiveness of nature. Calvin had
learned to see human nature as culpable and polluted in the light of Scripture,
while Rousseau taught that nature, before it was contaminated by culture, was
good and beautiful and without any corruption. Calvin sought the cause of all
misery in sin, which was a personal act consisting of disobedience of God's
law. Rousseau blamed society and civilization, and he was moved to tears
when he thought of his own goodness; no one had ever existed who was as
good and compassionate as he! Calvin did not expect anything from nature
but expected everything from God's grace in Christ. In one word, Calvin cast
man and all creatures in the dust before the overwhelming majesty of God.

---

30. When his *Émile* was condemned in 1762 by the magistrate, he was exiled from Geneva and
lost the title of "citizen of Geneva," and the relationship cooled considerably. Ed. note: Bavinck supplies
here the reference in the *Collection complète des oeuvres J.-J. Rousseau*, 24 vols. (Geneva, 1782–89),
I:206, which places it at the beginning of book IX of Rousseau's *Confessions*. However, the discussion
of Rousseau's banishment from Geneva takes place in book XII (*Writings*, III:493ff.).

Rousseau, on the other hand, put man on the throne, himself first of all, at the expense of God's justice and holiness.

[163] But the demolisher of the eighteenth century was not the only one to contemplate the immense problem of inequality: the Reformer of the sixteenth century did the same. However, he [Calvin] approached it from a different angle: it was not political and social inequality that struck him first of all, but religious inequality. When human nature in all men is equally polluted, how does one explain the profound and ever-continuing difference between those who accept the gospel and those who reject it, between those who are saved and those who are lost? For Calvin and all the Reformers, this was the central, all-important difference that superseded all other differences because it was everlasting. And in answering this serious and deeply moving question, Calvin saw behind all culture and nature the good pleasure of God, his sovereign and omnipotent free will as the ultimate and deepest cause. He did this in the company of Luther and Zwingli, while following in the footsteps of Augustine and guided by Paul, disregarding culture and nature.

This confession of God's good pleasure was taken from Scripture by the *religious* consciousness and used in the first place to establish the certainty of faith; yet from the outset this confession had and continued to have a much deeper meaning especially for Calvin. God's preordaining was the final, most profound cause of all differences among creatures, such as kind, gender, gifts, and in all that is (*zijn*) and is just so (*zóó-zijn*). It is neither the free will of man, nor merit and worth, nor culture, nor even nature that is the source of all multiplicity in creation, but God's almighty and all-powerful will, which at the same time is wise and holy, though inscrutable and inexplicable. Culture, nurture, or free will is not the cause, for the fundamental differences precede these and are already present in nature. Nature is not the cause either, for it did not come into being and does not exist on its own but is carried by the word of God's power from its beginning and always. By his will all things are and have been created.

Through this confession, which only a strong generation can accept, Calvin taught his followers first of all acceptance, submission, and contentment in times of struggle and oppression. However, few people today will thank him for this. Sowing discontent and systematically goading people to be hostile toward all prevailing conditions and arrangements are held in much higher esteem by many. Rousseau is their great example, for he is the one who, blaming everything on society and culture, made people proud and rebellious, but he also caused them an endless series of disappointments, for revolution that runs counter to nature [164] is a sword that always turns against the one brandishing it. "You can drive nature out with a pitchfork, but it always comes back."[31]

31. "Naturam expellas furca, tamen usque recurret." Ed. note: Bavinck refers to an event at the time he was writing this essay involving the French antimilitarist anarchist Gustave Hervé (1871–1944): "It

Still, acquiescence is not nearly the only and most important thing that Calvin impressed on his faithful followers. The will of God, according to Calvin's confession, may be absolutely sovereign, totally all-powerful, and inscrutable and therefore to be acknowledged with holy awe and deep reverence; yet it is for everyone who believes the will of a merciful and gracious Father, who loves all his children with an eternal love; his will may be hidden, but he always has wise and holy reasons for all the dark ways in which he often leads them. Such a will is not fate, in which a person acquiesces willy-nilly, but an object of childlike trust, an inexhaustible fountain of comfort, and the strong anchor of a firm and solid hope. Remember that in spite of—no, in keeping with—the teaching of predestination, the abundant grace of God in Christ constitutes the heart and soul of Calvin's *Institutes*. For him this was the essence of Christianity, through which God tells us how much he loves us. He saw the will of God revealed in all things, even in the iniquities of mankind. But basically and in essence this will is the saving grace that leads the world and mankind through the darkness to the light and through death to eternal life.

This comfort was unknown to Rousseau, but Calvin made it known to the Christians of his day for their comfort and assurance. Through the preaching about God's holy and gracious will, Calvin furnished faith, heroism, and inspiration to the least and simplest, to those persecuted for the sake of the gospel, to prisoners in their jails, to martyrs on scaffold and pyre, making them scorn all suffering and glory in oppression. And this kind of comfort we need just as much in our day. For nothing is easier than to join Rousseau in sowing discontent in the hearts of men and to make them rebel against their own fate and society at large. The danger is even great for each of us, as Busken Huet said, that out of fear for the little man, we become flatterers of the people and courtiers of that which is common.[32] But fundamentally such flattery is cruel, like offering a stone and a serpent [165] to someone who prays for a loaf of bread or a fish. For when a person loses his faith in a higher, better world, life here on earth begins to look more and more like a jail against whose walls he butts his head senselessly.[33] Even Nietzsche said, "Maybe nothing is more commendable in Christianity than the art of teaching even the least to transport themselves through piety to a higher order of things and thus

---

was instructive a few weeks ago to see the reversal of Gustave Hervé, whose revolutionary-anarchistic preaching had reduced many who practiced it in life to poverty and misery." The larger context of Hervé's revolutionary thought is covered by Paul B. Miller, *From Revolutionaries to Citizens: Antimilitarism in France, 1870–1914* (Durham, NC: Duke University Press, 2002).

    32. Conrad Busken Huet, *Het land van Rembrandt: Studien over de Noordnederlandsche beschaving in de zeventiende eeuw*, 2 vols. (Haarlem: H. D. Tjeenk Willink, 1886), II:2, 139.

    33. Benjamin Constant, in B. H. C. K. van der Wijck, *Gestalten en gedachten: Verspreide opstellen* (Haarlem: De Erven F. Bohn, 1911), 274.

to be at peace with life, which is difficult enough as it is and which can only be difficult."[34]

But this comparison would be incomplete if it did not point to a third area in which Calvin differs from Rousseau. The latter did indeed rail at society and taught people to do the same, and in keeping with the custom of the day, he turned the monarch into a scapegoat and made him responsible for their miserable condition. Yet in the end he quietly withdrew into seclusion without moving a finger to reform society. Calvin, on the other hand, derived from the same will of God, which he had come to know in Christ as a will of grace, the motive for strong, energetic, and far-reaching actions. I know that when the flourishing period of the Reformation was past, the faith that at one time had brought comfort to people had changed for many into a doctrine that frightened them and that the doctrine of predestination often was abused as an excuse for the flesh, an abuse that still lives on in certain spiritual fringes like the ones in Rotterdam that made the headlines recently. That, however, is a caricature of the Reformed confession. If we steadfastly believe that the *will* of God is the cause of all things, then our reverence for that same will, which has been revealed in Scripture as the rule for our lives, must compel us to promote its dominion everywhere and as far as our influence reaches. If you believe, with Rousseau, that society is the cause of all evil, then you have pronounced its death sentence: you have given man the right to execute people, and you have legitimized the Revolution. But if you believe with Calvin that the will of God, his will of good pleasure, is the cause of all things, then that same will becomes his revealed will and the moving force and rule for our living. The words "Your will be done" encompass and provide not only strength to acquiesce but also strength to act.

Furthermore, without mentioning Calvin by name, Rousseau nevertheless expressed admiration for him and for the results of his work. There is a great difference between Calvin and Rousseau, [166] but the difference does not totally erase their affinity. The "citizen of Geneva" in his wanderings did not lose all the traits of his origins. Voltaire was and remained a Roman Catholic, even in his unbelief. Rousseau was and remained a Protestant, even when he joined the Roman Catholic Church and embraced Deism. Rousseau said that Voltaire actually only believed in the devil, even though he gave the appearance of believing in God.[35] Indeed, Voltaire was a vain scoffer, and his laughter was a sneer. Rousseau never scoffed; in his own way he was a serious seeker. After being struck by the infinite goodness of nature, he even discovered "the gift of tears" and delighted in it with weak

---

34. Nietzsche, in B. H. C. K. van der Wijck, *Gestalten en gedachten: Verspreide opstellen* (Haarlem: De Erven F. Bohn, 1911), 218.

35. *Confessions*, book IX, in *Writings*, V:360.

sentimentality.[36] Sometimes he would speak in enchanting language about God and his providence, about the soul and immortality, about virtue and conscience, about Scripture and the gospel. Still more, both Calvin and Rousseau proceeded from their most intimate self-consciousness—the first one from the self-consciousness of faith confirmed by the testimony of the Holy Spirit; the latter from the self-consciousness of his feelings, as derived from nature, which he, sadly enough, considered to be unpolluted. Both proceeded directly from their inner life to what was original in God's world. For Calvin this was the original gospel of Christ, and for Rousseau it was the original speech of nature, which he experienced aesthetically. Both were men with a heart, and both were masters of French prose.

Nevertheless, Rousseau, in spite of himself, acknowledged the greatness and superiority of Calvin.[37] In the dedication of his *Discourse on Inequality*, which he offered to the "magnificent, much-honored, rulers of Geneva," he states that he is happy that he was born in Geneva, where equality and inequality are so well aligned. If he would have had a say in where he would have been born, he would have chosen a city that was not too big, where the citizens knew each other, where people and government all worked for the same goal, and did so together; in other words, where there was a democratic government characterized by tempered wisdom. He would have chosen a happy and quiet republic that had already existed for centuries and had shown durability, where the citizens were free and independent, as they deserved to be, a republic that was not bent on [167] expansion and that was safe from being conquered by surrounding nations, where the government was chosen by the people and legislation took place with its approval. And if Providence would have added a proper location, a temperate climate, fertile soil, and a beautiful vista, he would have no other desire than to be allowed to spend all the days of his life peacefully and quietly in such a republic. Well then, all such privileges are part of the city of his birth. One cannot imagine a better

36. D'Alembert stated correctly, "The excitement of Rousseau appears to come more from his mind than his feelings," in Bungener, *Voltaire*, II:168; in the same spirit Bungener himself said, "He did have a feeling for virtue; but, he did not know where it came from" (ibid., 164), and "It is quite clear that he mistook the feeling for virtue for virtue itself" (ibid., 165).

37. In his *Lettres écrites de la montagne*, Rousseau makes the following comment about Calvin: "Calvin, no doubt, was a great man, but ultimately he was a man, and what is worse, a theologian. For the rest, he had the pride of a genius who knew that he was superior and who became indignant if you disagreed with that." Ed. note: French text is available in *Rousseau: Religious Writings*, ed. Ronald Grimsley (Oxford: Clarendon, 1970), chap. 17; the specific quote regarding Calvin is found on p. 335. Rousseau's comment on Calvin is more muted here than his earlier rave in *The Social Contract*:

Those who know Calvin only as a theologian much underestimate the extent of his genius. The codification of our wise edicts, in which he played a large part, does him no less honour than his *Institutes*. Whatever revolution time may bring in our religion, so long as the spirit of patriotism and liberty still lives among us, the memory of this great man will be forever blessed. (Rousseau, *Social Contract*, book II, chap. 7, note)

political and civil situation than there. Happiness is complete; all that is left is to enjoy it. Its independence, obtained by the sword and guarded for two centuries, is generally well known.

The makeup of the government there is exceptional and is the product of excellent reason. The only masters the citizens have are wise laws that they themselves have made and that are maintained by government officials whom they themselves have elected, officials neither rich enough to allow themselves to be demoralized by wealth and its pleasures nor poor enough to require the help of others. Only one desire remains: that such a wise and happy republic may continue to thrive, and there is only one concern: that all citizens will work toward this goal through mutual unity, obedience to the laws, and respect for the government. And it deserves such respect. Nowhere in the world will one find a body that is as honest, as enlightened, as respectable as Geneva's magistrates. They are all examples of moderation, plain morals, respect for the law, and a sincere conciliatory spirit. And the citizens add more and new luster to this government by their own virtues.

Just as Rousseau's own father made a living from the labor of his hands, but also read Tacitus, Plutarch, and Grotius, so all the citizens of Geneva, and even the most common among them, work diligently, and at the same time they are well educated. Among the best citizens are, to name some, the ministers whose eloquent words are well received, the more so because they apply the principles of the gospel to their own lives. In their midst the spirit of Christianity truly reigns, as well as moral holiness, self-restraint, strictness, and gentleness toward others. The hope for the future well-being of the state depends to a large degree on their acknowledged wisdom, temperance, and diligence on its behalf. And finally, one certainly ought not to forget the other half of the republic, which looks after the well-being of the other person and which by its meekness and wisdom maintains the peace and good manners: those lovely and virtuous female citizens, whose destiny it will always be to care for what is ours.

[168] They [female citizens of Geneva] maintain love for the law in the state, and concord among the citizens. They are chaste guardians of morality and the gentle restraints of peace. At every opportunity they affirm the rights of the heart and of nature in the interest of duty and virtue. In other cities so-called sophisticated men admire the size of palaces, the magnificence of carriages, the splendor of theaters,[38] and all the dainties of weakness and wealth. In Geneva, however, only human beings can be found; but this spectacle is

---

38. In the seventh volume of the *Encyclopédie* [ed. Denis Diderot and Jean d'Alembert], d'Alembert had written an article about Geneva in which he expresses the wish that before long a theater might be built, would operate under stringent laws, bar all licentiousness, and attract actors of impeccable conduct. But Rousseau protested this in his *Lettre à M. d'Alembert*, dated March 20, 1757, and still worth reading. Ed. note: French text is included in Grimsley, *Rousseau: Religious Writings*, chap. 9, pp. 72–78. Though d'Alembert's article appeared in 1757, Grimsley dates Rousseau's letter in 1758.

well worth it, and those who seek it are worth as much as the admirers of the rest.[39] Rousseau's words are certainly full of praise for the Geneva reformer. It would even be worthwhile for someone to make an intentional study of how much the republican government of the city of his birth influenced his political and social ideals.[40]

Yet further, the example of Geneva proves that Calvin's religious philosophy of life, when applied, also contains a promise for today's society. Has it not often been shown that to a large degree Protestantism has benefited civilization and the prosperity of nations? Has it not been claimed in the last few years by influential people, though with a great deal of bias, that the capitalism of our [169] day is linked to Calvinism? As Christians, as Protestants, as Reformed Christians, there is therefore no need at all to confront the modern age antithetically, for it is governed by the same will of the heavenly Father who has assigned us a place to live and work. If we were Rousseau-like naturalists, we might easily revert to stark conservatism if we did not have a standard from above and beyond reality, or if we would borrow such a standard from the realm of imagination, we might easily seek our well-being in an unhistorical radicalism. However, when we believe in a higher order of things, the holy and gracious will of God, which comes to us not only through the facts of history, but also through the testimony of his Word, then we have found a norm with which to measure the present and change

---

39. Rousseau, *Oeuvres*, I:526–31. Later he had a less-favorable opinion about the form of government in Geneva. His two books *Émile* and *Social Contract* were condemned by the Geneva City Council, without the council hearing the author, and were burned in public, and his citizenship was revoked. Then Rousseau mounted a defense in his *Lettres écrites de la montagne*. [Ed. note: see n. 37 above; a good discussion of Rousseau's letters appears in *The Political Writings of Jean-Jacques Rousseau*, introduction and notes by C. E. Vaughan, 2 vols. (Oxford: Blackwell, 1962), II:173–96. This volume, however, only contains letters vi–ix.] In it he did not recant his earlier favorable opinion, but he did make a distinction between the legitimate state and the actual state: "Nothing is more free than your legitimate State, nothing is more slavish than your actual State" (*Lettres écrites de la montagne*, in *Oeuvres*, III:67). In Rousseau's day Geneva did number among its 24,000 inhabitants five distinct social classes that were sharply delineated: citizens (born in Geneva of citizens), bourgeois (who had been granted citizenship), inhabitants (who had bought the privilege of living in the city), natives (children of these inhabitants born in the city), and subjects (living in the surrounding area of the city). The citizens and the bourgeois numbered at the most 1,600 souls. They alone were members of the general council, which had the right to accept or reject proposals of the executive council (of 25 members). From their number all the members of the executive council, of the council of 60, and of the council of 200 were chosen. They held the important positions and offices. In actuality, a hereditary aristocracy ruled with more-or-less democratic forms. Note a picture of the constitution of Geneva dating from the time when Rousseau published his *Lettres écrites de la montagne*, located before these *Lettres* in the *Oeuvres*, III:1–4.

40. In his *Lettres écrites de la montagne* (Grimsley, *Rousseau: Religious Writings*, 325ff.), Rousseau summarizes the main thoughts of his *Social Contract*; he himself says that this brief and accurate analysis of his work is nothing other than the history of the government of Geneva, that all the main thoughts of his book reflect trait for trait a representation of "your republic," and that he took the government of Geneva as a model for political institutions.

it. And then we overcome the danger to condemn reality unconditionally or to justify it, at least in principle.

On the one hand, we will then refrain from condemning society in the way Rousseau and his superficial followers have made themselves guilty, and we will sooner learn to respect it as a wonderful artificial organism that developed under God's guidance and that has been a blessing for millions of people for centuries. As van Houten has said, even though we deplore the want and misery that people endure, when we consider the struggle of mankind against nature, and besides that the helplessness, weakness, and depravity of so many individuals, we are amazed that there is not more suffering and that there are even countries with tens of millions of people where it is so rare that someone starves from lack of food that if it should happen all the newspapers in the world would trumpet it. It is a greater miracle indeed that the great majority of those huge masses of people receive their daily bread, rather than that many are not provided for regularly and suffer want.[41]

However, at the same time we certainly ought to appreciate all that happens, simply because it happens, and we should try to understand the signs of the times, which show us how new circumstances and new relationships are constantly gaining ground in every area. The so-called social question has undoubtedly a spiritual background; it is rooted in Rousseau's false theory of equality and for that reason [170] is not susceptible to be solved by social legislation. Whatever was done by the state and society and individuals to bring about improvement of conditions—efforts that were necessary and deserve praise—has not contributed in the least to create contentment or gratitude or to curtail the demands. Nevertheless, who among us would wish for a return of the time in which the social classes were separated from each other almost like castes, and people were expected to praise whatever their masters decided, and the practitioners of the sciences looked down on everyone who had to earn his keep by manual labor? The more we approach the middle of the seventeenth century, the more we notice how professors tended to avoid their fellow citizens and began to constitute a separate caste. They did not participate, or very little, in social life, were very seldom seen in the circles of the unlearned, and demonstrated a formality and decorum that dismayed everyone but that was quite in keeping with their dress, especially with their awful wigs that fell down from the head to their waist. Many wanted to be honored as deities. Their pride and conceit were often boundless, so that even learned people who associated with them complained about their conceit.[42]

---

41. Samuel van Houten, "Paus Leo XIII over het arbeidersvraagstuk [ed. note: question about labor, in *Rerum novarum*]," taken from the *Vragen des tijds*, p. 2.

42. [Gilles D. J.] Schotel, *De Academie te Leiden* (Haarlem: Kruseman & Tjeenk Willink, 1875), 232.

In contrast with this—and we are seeing that this is becoming more and more a reality—it appears that the center of gravity in society is shifting, that the value of manual labor and technical skills are appreciated much more, and that another state of affairs is in the making, [one] in which the tremendous wealth of material and spiritual goods of this age is divided more equally among all social classes. At any rate, we face a future in which the wealthy, in fact all the wealthy and all who are endowed with many worldly goods and much property, will be asked to demonstrate a much greater measure of self-denial and devotion than in previous centuries. Riches, both spiritual and material, will become much less a privilege to be enjoyed entirely for our own pleasure and only for self. It will assume more and more the character of a duty, according to Paul's word, for all the members of the body to care for each other with equal concern, or to quote the Heidelberg Catechism, each member should consider it his duty to use his gifts readily and cheerfully for the service and enrichment of the other members.

When considering the inequality in society, we therefore face the same problem we touched on at the beginning of this chapter: what is the relationship of the one [171] to the many, the absolute to the relative, the eternal to what constantly changes, between the timeless principles and their application in changing circumstances? No one has a ready answer for that question, least of all those who rely on big words and resounding slogans. In order to find the answer, serious study is required both of the principles that are to serve us as a guide and of the extremely complicated circumstances in which we live. But perhaps we will find the answer gradually, over time, in the same way in which the kingdom of God came about in the parable: "This is what the kingdom of God is like. A man scatters seed on the ground. Night and day, whether he sleeps or gets up, the seed sprouts and grows, though he does not know how."

# 9
## TRENDS IN PSYCHOLOGY

[172] Just as other sciences, so also psychology has experienced great changes in the previous century for all sorts of reasons. These changes involved methods, the nature of psychology, and its intent. The distinction between the old and the new psychology is not stated quite accurately, and even less adequately, when it is said that the one was based on speculation and the other on pure observation. For it definitely is no invention of recent times that observation and experience are the sources of all knowledge. This was known already for centuries. The old psychology was also built on empiricism, even though it was not nearly as accurate and extensive as today. Conversely, the new psychology is certainly not built on observation alone, for true observation presupposes thought and is impossible without it. Thought is the indispensable means to abstract phenomena that are to be observed and are observed from their actual environment, and thought is, furthermore, even more indispensable for categorizing and describing those phenomena in order to discern and explain a common norm.

Nevertheless, there is a grain of truth in the distinction indicated above: Thus in previous centuries a rather commonly accepted theory about the

Ed. note: Originally published as "Richtingen in de psychologie," in the journal *Paedagogisch tijdschrift* 1 (1909): 4–15. The first page of this essay in *Verzamelde opstellen* (see n. 2 of Editor's Preface) contains footnote 1 without a corresponding superscript in the text, and presumably (from the content) it was intended as a footnote to the title itself: "Cf. Professor C[arl] Stumpf of Berlin, 'Richtungen und Gegensätze in der heutigen Psychologie,' *Internationale Wochenschrift für Wissenschaft, Kunst und Technik* 1, no. 29 [(October 19, 1907): 904–13]; and Doctor C[onstantin] Gutberlet, 'Der gegenwärtige Stand der psychologischen Forschung,' *Philosophische Jahrbuch* 21 (1908): 1–32."

essence of the soul already existed. It was considered to be a spiritual entity that was united with the body in an intimate way. At the same time, the soul was thought to possess such a measure of independence from the body and its metabolism that when separated from the body by death, it was able to continue an independent existence. Before Christianity was known, this idea [173] of the spiritual and immortal nature of the soul was already more or less known in all nations and in all religions, but it was strengthened considerably through the preaching of the gospel and seemed to be elevated above all doubt. The result of this conviction was that when people observed and studied the phenomena of the soul, they did not proceed purely empirically, but also already made use of the light that the knowledge of the soul's nature as related to those phenomena had provided, just as conversely the knowledge of the soul's nature was supplemented and enriched by what had been obtained from observing the phenomena. The method used in psychology was therefore neither one-sidedly speculative nor one-sidedly empirical; rather, it was both: it was deductive and inductive at the same time. The nature of the soul clarified the phenomena of the life of the soul, and these phenomena spread light on its nature.

But gradually a big change took place here. After the sixteenth century all sciences, one after the other, began to disassociate themselves from theology and also from revelation and the Christian faith: they tried to become totally independent. As far as psychology was concerned, at first it was thought that one could deduce the knowledge of the nature of the soul sufficiently from natural revelation and thus retain it in an unadulterated and unimpaired form. But this proved to be difficult in the long run. Descartes already had assumed a separation between the rational soul, which consisted purely of thought, and the vegetative-animal life that arose from the body and was purely mechanical in nature. Later the distinction between rational and empirical psychology was added to this, a distinction already predisposed to give the empirical predominance. And when empirical psychology—made ready by all kinds of research done in England, France, and Germany—was reinforced considerably by the support of the natural sciences in the nineteenth century, it felt strong enough to become independent and to remove metaphysical and rational psychology from the area of science.

This *empirical* psychology that gradually gained supremacy in this way, is, of course, not wrong by itself. The more accurately the phenomena of the soul are studied, the better. However, it [empirical psychology] often assumes a somewhat hostile attitude toward *metaphysical* psychology. In this case it objects to the fact that research of the phenomena of the soul already assumes the idea of the soul's existence. And on behalf of an impartial, unbiased science, empirical psychology demands that all such [174] presuppositions be discarded and that one start the research as a blank sheet of paper and then wait quietly and without a personal interest for the outcome. When this demonstrates that the soul is merely the result of metabolism, people will have to accept this truth, however painful it may be, for truth is more valuable than false comfort.

This empirical psychology did not stop with observation only, but following the example of the natural sciences, it gradually started making use of experimentation, and in that way it developed into *experimental* psychology, at least in a number of areas and insofar as this was possible. The naturalist, for instance, does not limit himself to observing the phenomena that occur in nature independently from himself; he also intervenes in the development of these phenomena; he makes the powers of nature run in a specific direction, and thus he seems to force nature to reveal its secrets to him. In the experiment, he presents nature with a certain question and then waits for the answer. In the same way, an experiment in psychology provides [the researcher with] the opportunity to create a certain state of consciousness and thus to be able to observe it more accurately, for a better understanding of its relationship and temperament.

This empirical experimental research can also try to approach psychic phenomena in two ways. It can draw attention directly to those phenomena, but it can also try to come close to them via a detour. After all, soul and body are closely related; psychic phenomena are often accompanied by larger or smaller changes in the organism. So for instance, psychic sensation depends on the strength of sensory stimulation. Though the latter can be changed at will and calculated quantitatively, the degree and extent of the sensation can be determined accordingly. The science occupied with this and generally tracing the relationships and interactions between psychic and physical phenomena is called *physiological psychology.*

In this experimental and physiological research, the direction empirical psychology is taking seems to be governed by the desire to divest psychology, as much as possible, of its subjective character and to turn it into an exact science. While in former days people studied psychic phenomena mainly through introspection, today the emphasis is on studying the life of the soul as much as possible in others. Subjective psychology [175] then becomes *objective* psychology, and this in turn leads of itself to *comparative* and *genetic* psychology. The area of research expands endlessly when one wants to study the life of the soul in others. Thus one can make a study of the life of the soul of children and infants, boys and girls, men and women, social classes, societies and nations, civilized and uncivilized people, lunatics and geniuses, the sick and healthy, criminals and upstanding citizens, godless and pious people, yes, even animals and plants.

The results of this extensive and multifaceted research demand comparison. Multiple facts require unity and order. Questions arise as a matter of course: What is the difference and what is the similarity between all those disclosures of the soul's life? Is there a discernible plan and direction? Are there laws possibly or is there perhaps one law ultimately that governs all of life in all its manifestations? Is the teaching of evolution also applicable here? And thus the horizon expands and even looks backward to the past, in search of sources from which the soul's life may have originated and to discover its paths of development. Objective psychology becomes comparative psychology, and this in turn becomes genetic psychology. For example, [Ernst] Haeckel in his *Welträthsel* does not think much of mathematical and physiological psychology and recognizes its limitations; instead, he values comparative and genetic psychology much more. These, he believes, show us the steady progress the lowest one-cell organisms have followed in the course of many centuries on their way to becoming mammals. And then he points out how gradually man has evolved from these mammals and how he has lifted himself up through the centuries to become the present-day civilized person. This slow process of becoming human in the past still finds its corresponding development in every individual experience as he goes from embryo to infant and from a boy to a young man. The history of every single individual is a brief repetition of the history of humanity; the one serves as a commentary and confirmation of the other. Genetic psychology is true psychology because it shows us laws that govern both the history of the soul's life in humanity as well as of the inner life of every nation and every human being.

However, this development of psychology did not please everyone. Just as in the latter part of the previous [nineteenth] century, a general reaction [176] arose on the part of those who favored feeling and will over the supremacy of the intellect, philosophy over science, idealism over materialism, liberty over coercion, the individual over the community—so also many psychologists, seeing the outcome of their actions, are coming back.

Upon some reflection it became clear as day that materialism cannot be the explanation of the world and humanity, of life and consciousness. Haeckel may have thought that he had solved every riddle in the world, or at least had reduced the world to one single substance, but others began to realize more and more that matter cannot be the origin of the spirit and what is lifeless cannot be the source of life, nor can the unconscious be the root of the conscious. They spoke of seven and many more mysteries that were not explained by the natural sciences and especially not by materialism.

This one fact by itself—that knowledge of nature, matter, the atoms, or whatever the names of the elements that make up the sensory world may be, comes by way of the spirit and in the form of mental pictures—already squarely opposes materialism. We know nothing of the entire external world, including our body, except through our consciousness. Before we can know what matter and forces in nature are all about, we have to investigate what consciousness and spirit are and what perceptions and ideas are. The soul comes before nature, and psychology before physics.

The soul cannot be reduced to nature because it is always accompanied and presupposed, even by the simplest perception of the external world. The same thing also holds for research into psychic phenomena. These also, in self and in others, are only observed by means of one's own consciousness. If psychology, therefore, tried to become purely *objective* psychology, it was on the wrong track and set before itself a totally unreachable ideal. It is no more possible to ban the subjective element when observing the phenomena of the soul than when observing natural phenomena. If someone wants to remove it, all science becomes impossible. But with this recognition the validity and value of introspection as the source of knowledge of the soul was restored. The French philosopher A[uguste] Comte had tried to demonstrate that introspection was unreliable and could not be classified among the sources of psychology. But today it is fairly well acknowledged generally that it is indispensable, not only in subjective, but also in objective psychology. All of us are conscious of our inner condition: we are aware of our perceptions and ideas, our [177] feelings and passions, our thoughts and intentions. And precisely because we are conscious of ourselves and have some knowledge of our own spiritual life, we are able to observe and study the spiritual life in others. Even *experimental* psychology is built on this self-knowledge and becomes impossible without it. We can comprehend others only because and insofar as they are related to us. Generally speaking, it is therefore not true that the soul of man can be explained from the soul of a child and the soul of man from the soul of animals, but, as [Wilhelm] Wundt says correctly, the only possible road of comparative psychology leads from the human to the soul of the animal and not vice versa.

The reaction that arose in psychology against materialism can be put this way: of late the soul has returned to psychology. For a long time the idea prevailed that the soul was not important at all, that its relationship to the brain was like gall to the liver, and like urine to the kidneys; psychology became part of natural science. But it seemed that this did not work, and thus the life of the soul returned as a peculiar phenomenon and psychology as an independent science.

But there is no further agreement. It is true that people speak more openly about the soul and the life of the soul than in former days, but psychologists immediately go their separate ways and are quite different from each other when it comes to the question of what the soul might be after all, and how the life of the soul functions.

When observing and describing psychic phenomena, a big difference of opinions presents itself at once. The life of the soul displays many phenomena, such as sensations, ideas, concepts, judgments, feelings, temper, inclinations, passions, desires, and so forth. But what are all these phenomena? Naturally and seemingly, there is a mutual and multifaceted relationship. But taken together, do they exist independently as, for example, clouds that float in the sky? Or do they point back to something that appears in it? Do they come from forces, organs, abilities (or whatever they may be called) that somehow precede or are basic to it? In a word, are they pure phenomena, or are they the outcome of some force? Proponents of *phenomenal* psychology assert the first; those of *functional* psychology maintain the latter.

Suppose, however, that the phenomena of the soul's life do not float in the sky, but are functions of organs (powers, energies); where do these organs come from? Are they part of human nature as such, and were they or are they part of all human beings always and everywhere? Or [178] has every human being in particular or at any rate humanity as a whole acquired them and acquired them gradually in the struggle of life? The question, put in these general terms, is open to all kinds of special applications. Take, for example, the phenomenon that every human being perceives in the forms of space and time; or notice that every human being always asks for a reason or a goal; or call to mind that not a single human being can think and judge and act in any way he pleases, but feels a commitment to the laws of thought, morality, and beauty. From where do all these phenomena come, all these ineradicable habits, that entire intellectual, moral, religious, and aesthetic bent of mind that every human being—although in different measure and form—seems to be born with? Pure *empirical* or, in this connection, *evolutionistic* psychology claims that all those habits or abilities were acquired gradually in the struggle for life through natural selection. *Nativistic psychology*, on the other hand, maintains the existence of a human nature common to all people and holds that all those abilities and powers belong to human nature from the very beginning.

If the latter is true, another problem immediately presents itself. Assuming that such innate abilities or powers exist, what are they and how many are there? Since [Johann Friedrich] Herbart, the theory of the soul's abilities has lost its credibility, and everybody parrots him, often thoughtlessly. However, people will then have to make a choice: either the phenomena of the soul's life are nothing more than phenomena (in that case the name also is wrong, for phenomena point back to something that exists and becomes visible; if in the soul's phenomena nothing becomes visible, then they are mere appearances) or they are manifestations and expressions of one or more powers, and in that case the old abilities have been reintroduced by this or another name. Every psychology that does not dissolve the phenomena of the soul's life into appearances, but considers them to be functions, turns around and will have to return in one way or another to the theory of abilities. Nearly all psychologists and also all psychopathologists continue to speak of intellect, feelings, and will as special powers of the soul, even though they reject the name of abilities.

Besides, Herbart himself, who strongly opposed the concept of powers, nevertheless acknowledged one power: the power of the soul to form ideas.

Moreover, he believed that he had explained the entire life of the soul with this one concept. As long as there were ideas, they would get in touch with each other according to set laws—just like material atoms in nature—and thus produce all those phenomena [179] that he then wanted to summarize under feelings, temper, desires, passions, and emotions. But other proponents of functional psychology turned their backs on Herbart's intellectualism and assigned the first place of the soul's life to feelings or the will.

This is why there are differences not only about the number of powers that must be assumed to be part of the soul but also about the place each one deserves. *Intellectual* psychology assigns precedence to the intellectual or more generally to the conscious. *Emotional* psychology is of the opinion that feelings precede all other phenomena of the soul, intellect, or will. And *voluntaristic* psychology maintains the will as the basic force of the human soul, and often also [the will] as the principle and the root of all life and being. Each of these orientations also differs in its understanding of intellect, feelings, or will. With *consciousness*, the question is whether the life of the soul coincides with the phenomena of consciousness, or whether behind it or under it there is another hidden, dark life from which consciousness sprouts, just as the light of a flame evolves from a dark core. Quite a few seek the essence of man in that unconscious life of the soul. They believe that all psychological processes take place there. Whatever emerges into the consciousness is only the result of what is created under the threshold of the conscious. In this unconscious life, man is even connected in a mysterious way to other people far away, to souls and spirits, to the All. And *occultism* tries hard to penetrate into this dark region in order to obtain a certain measure of definite and reliable knowledge.

No less is the confusion about the place, the content, and the significance of *feelings*. The boundary between sensation and feelings, and between feelings and lust (desire, inclination, and so forth), is drawn here today and somewhere else tomorrow. It is, in turn, highly exalted or utterly despised. Concerning the *will*, the big difference is first of all whether it is to be considered an independent force, or whether it is composed of elements of consciousness and feelings. The other question linked to it is then whether the will is capable of intervening in the process of ideas and to guide the process into another direction, or whether it is part of the process itself and is wholly governed by the process. *Associational* psychology says the latter, but *apperceptional* psychology maintains that in the apperception an independent force of the soul appears, which emerges from the will and asserts its influence in consciousness. [180] And finally, when speaking about the will, another serious problem presents itself: whether the will is free or not, first psychologically but then also ethically and religiously. *Deterministic* psychology preaches the total lack of freedom of the will. *Indeterministic* psychology pleads for a larger or smaller measure of freedom. Both trends sharply oppose each other today, not only in psychology, but also in ethics and jurisprudence.

After struggling through all these issues, we still have not reached the finish line. For, whether people favor phenomenal or functional psychology, the question always presents itself concerning what the origin is of the phenomena or functions (organs) of the soul's life. The thought that these are ethereal is unsatisfactory because it is easy to say this, but there is no clear idea to connect it to. Opinions about this issue vary widely again. *Materialistic* psychology, which has been contested and weakened but is far from becoming extinct, still maintains that in the real sense of the word, the soul does not exist: instead, it is matter that under certain circumstances and through a very complex and very refined union produces thought. *Spiritualistic* psychology is diametrically opposed to this; it completely denies the reality of matter and believes only in the reality of ideas. *Pantheistic-monistic* psychology places itself between these two schools and considers both matter and power, body and soul, to be manifestations of one and the same substance underlying everything that exists. Ordinarily this monistic school favors the so-called *psychophysic parallelism,* which is the idea that soul and body do not affect each other but that psychic and physical phenomena each for themselves create an unbroken causal series of forms that proceed parallel to each other.

When this spiritualistic psychology—which denies the reality of matter but affirms the existence of souls or spirits—is excluded, it may be said that all the earlier named orientations have this in common concerning the existence of the soul: they deny its independent existence. For them, the soul is that complex of spiritual phenomena, whether thought of as conscious or unconscious phenomena, and is absorbed by the spiritual phenomena. It does not possess an independent existence that might differ essentially from the Divine Being or from matter. The soul has no *being*; it is *only* process, action, phenomenon. This idea [181] may be called *actuality* psychology and is diametrically opposed to the so-called *substantiality* psychology, which sees in the human soul a spiritual substance distinct from the Being of God as well as from the being of matter. The name "substance" is flawed because it reminds one so easily of something material and expansive, yet the intent is clear: the soul is a spiritual entity created by God and is essentially different from the material world.

Finally, it should be added that there are quite a few differences in attitude toward the relationship of psychology to the other sciences and about the significance that the former has to the latter. In general, today one can observe a strong attempt to establish a close connection between psychology and all sciences and to consider all objects of the various sciences from a psychological point of view. This is possible, of course, because all objects of our knowledge are conveyed to us only through our consciousness; consciousness seems to be the lens through which they cast their image on our souls, and it has a fairly strong influence on the formation of that image. Thus psychology is also associated today with pedagogy, psychiatry, jurisprudence, ethics, the study of art and language, history, religion, and so forth, and everywhere people are rushing to start conducting experiments. Children, men, women, criminals, lunatics, pious people, and the godless—all of them are subjected to experiments by experts and dabblers. The craving to experiment has reached such a dangerous level here and there that a serious warning, such as Wundt and others have voiced, is quite in order.

But with the application of psychology to the other sciences, a distinction ought to be made between a moderate and a radical orientation. The former acknowledges that the psychological consideration of the objects of the various sciences—such as nurture, education, overloading, fatigue, flaws, crimes, and so forth—is a useful means that is able to shed an interesting light on these things. But others go much further and think that psychology is the basis of all spiritual sciences and that all of these can be reduced to psychology and are part of psychology. They are proponents of extreme *psychologism*, which believes that it has dealt sufficiently with religion, ethics, logic and aesthetics, metaphysics and philosophy when it describes how the ideas and norms, the notions and concepts that appear in them have arisen from psychology. The supposition and result of this orientation is that all ideas coming up for discussion in the spiritual sciences lose their objective [182] validity and simply become changeable and variable products of the human spirit. It revives the ancient teaching of Pythagoras that the human being is the standard of all things.

Contrary to this skeptical psychologism, others rightly defend *apriorism* and maintain the objectivity of norms. At the most, *psychologism* can describe, although always very incompletely and inadequately, how all those norms and ideas were formed by humans, but it never gets around to the question of what their inner, independent, objective value is. From a purely psychological perspective, it is just as important to trace how a mistake, a lie, a criminal plan, a horrible intention was formed in the human soul as it is to investigate how a change of mind, a conversion, or a sacrificial act came about in a human being. But this does not mean that the inner distinction between both of these series of circumstances has been wiped out, much less explained. However important psychology may be, and whatever useful contribution it makes, it has its limitations and will never replace logic and ethics, religion and aesthetics; pedagogy also, although thankful for psychology's guidance, maintains its independence, which belongs to it according to its own nature.

# 10

# THE UNCONSCIOUS

## DEFINITION

[183] Consciousness is such a wondrous phenomenon that Du Bois-Reymond rightly called it one of the seven mysteries of the world.[1] And Ernst Haeckel, who thought he had a solution for all the mysteries except one, understood so little of consciousness that the only explanation he had was to push it back endlessly and attribute it, in its simplest form, from eternity to atoms.[2] Consciousness involves an immediate awareness of a state of things, with a direct psychic experience, which we have to create ourselves if we want to understand it at all. Consciousness is an original phenomenon that cannot be reduced any further or dissolved into parts, and therefore it can no more be explained by means of a definition than color or light can be explained to a blind person. Only by being conscious can we understand something of consciousness; it makes itself known by itself; it shines by its own light; it is a law known through itself [*principium per se notum*].

But considered thus in its own light, consciousness clearly includes two elements. First, it is an awareness on the part of the subject regarding phenomena that occur within by which we come to know all sorts of things that

Ed. note: This essay was delivered as a lecture to a scholarly conference at the Free University of Amsterdam on July 7, 1915, and then published as a monograph in Amsterdam by W. Kirchener.

1. Emil [Heinrich] Du Bois-Reymond, *Über die Grenzen des Naturerkennens: Die Sieben Welträthsel; Zwei Vorträge*, 5th ed. (Leipzig: Veit, 1882), 78.

2. Ernst Haeckel, *The Riddle of the Universe at the Close of the Nineteenth Century*, trans. Joseph McCabe (New York: Harper & Brothers, 1900), 225; cf. Du Bois-Reymond, *Über die Grenzen*, 71.

are part of our consciousness. These include observing, remembering, judging, knowing; but also feelings, both sensory and spiritual; wishing, desiring, striving, wanting, and acting experiences such as the following: I am conscious that I know this or that person, that I experience pain or am sad, that I plan and decide to travel, and so forth. Consciousness is knowledge, awareness, "knowing" what goes on inside of me. And second, it is an immediate awareness. It is a knowledge obtained not through external [184] sense organs or through deliberate research and serious study but directly through immediate experience, through "an inner sense" [inneren Sinn], as Kant called it, in imitation of the *sensus interior* of Augustine and the Scholastics. This "inner sense" is nothing but consciousness itself. Some phenomena in the life of our soul (some inner phenomena) have the peculiarity that they are conscious and that they exist in no other way; if I know something, I also know that I know it; without the latter, the former could not happen.

This immediate awareness, which is part of and is produced by certain psychic phenomena, has an attendant character: it is a direct and concomitant consciousness [conscientia directa et concomitans]. And many psychologists today believe that consciousness is absorbed in it and that nothing else can be said of it. In that case consciousness is not independent, is not a force or an activity, and does not exist except for its content. It is only a mirror that reflects some phenomena of human life. But for brevity's sake, leaving behind the objections that could be raised against this, we want to call attention to the fact that common parlance thinks differently. For we use the word "consciousness" also in a different sense from the one just mentioned. Not only do we say, "I am aware of this matter [active]," or "His matter has made me aware [passive]." We also speak more generally and say that this or that is the content of my consciousness, that we are conscious beings, that consciousness resides in our head, and so forth. And thus by "consciousness" we do not mean a consciousness that attends some phenomenon of the soul but the quality or ability on our part to take in [in zich opnemen] something spiritual and to appropriate it as a psychic possession.

The correctness of this common parlance is demonstrated by the fact that the phenomena of consciousness or the contents of consciousness are not only mutually connected into one single unit as association psychologists teach, but they are also related to a definite subject and they are and only can be psychic phenomena because of that relationship. Sensations, observations, memories, thoughts, judgments, and so forth do not exist by themselves or float in the air. They are what they are first because they are my or your or his or her sensations, and so on. The relationship to a subject, to a "self," is always implied in consciousness.

The nature of that "self" is distinct. Insofar as we are somewhat able to make a judgment by way of analogy, with an animal it is the animal essence that is the bearer of sensitive life. Since an animal cannot say "I" and thus lacks self-consciousness [185], some therefore have also denied that it possesses consciousness. But this goes too far and is refuted by the facts.[3] Not only does an animal have immediate sensations, but it also forms impressions, saves them, and recalls them. And thus it relates them to its own self. For that matter, a child also has a consciousness long before it becomes self-conscious. Preyer[4] and Stern[5] correctly observe that self-consciousness does not awaken in a child until it begins to say "I," because for a long time after it has become conscious of itself, it continues to speak of itself in the third person, having learned to refer to itself that way by following the example of the parents. But that does not alter the fact that the child leads a sensory life at first and then gradually begins to make a distinction between the world, its own body, and the contents of its consciousness as object and itself as subject.

Through this self-consciousness, which underlies all our activities as rational-moral beings and comes to expression in our entire *Geistesleben* [spiritual life], we rise far above the animals. And although it often consists only of a so-called *conscientia concomitans* [associated conscience], just as does consciousness in general, nevertheless it implies the principle that the human "self" is more or less conscious of itself, considers soul and body to be its own, and in the midst of all of life's changes is able to be and remain itself. For even though many recent psychologists say that the notion that we continue to remain the same person is nothing but delusion and self-deception, as was understood already by Indian philosophers,[6] this does not contradict the fact that the continuity of the self-consciousness presents us with a mystery that science has not been able to explain up to now.

Nevertheless, in a limited sense it is completely correct to say that people change daily and from moment to moment. W[illiam] James has rightly portrayed consciousness as a stream in which sensations push each other onward without stopping and without resting. Just as life itself, so also consciousness is subject to growth and development, to being born and dying. And it remains mysterious from beginning to end. We do not know where it begins. Some people even assume that plants have a weak consciousness, and they attribute to all creatures, even to atoms and monads, a dark notion of consciousness. [186] But even when we leave these metaphysical matters for what they are, it remains a mystery when consciousness awakens in a child, at or after or even before birth. The fact that later we do not remember anything of those first

3. Doctor Kohlhofer, "Was ist Bewusstheit? Gibt es unbewusste psychische Akte?" *Philosophische Jahrbuch* 24 (1911): 382–92.

4. William Preyer, *The Mind of the Child*, 2 vols., trans. H. W. Brown (New York: D. Appleton, 1905), II:189ff.

5. William Stern, *Psychologie des frühen Kindheit, bis zum sechsten Lebensjahre* (Leipzig: Quelle & Meyer, 1914), 321 [ET: *Psychology of Early Childhood up to the Sixth Year of Age* (New York: H. Holt, 1924), 471].

6. Cf. C. J. Wijnaendts Francken, *Over het bewustzijn* (Baarn: Hollandia, 1911), 29–31.

days does not seem to be conclusive proof, for consider how much of what happens later in life vanishes totally from memory. There may be consciousness, and it undoubtedly exists apart from self-consciousness.[7]

Furthermore, once consciousness awakens, it moves through the most varied situations. It disappears during sleep, it looms up on the horizon in a haze in dreams, and it radiates brightly during real thinking. Impressions, thoughts, and so forth sometimes assume a central place in our consciousness, and then again roam on the periphery, or they are driven away completely and abandoned to forgetfulness. And it even seems that after consciousness has arisen gradually and reached its zenith at midday, it diminishes just as gradually in order finally to set for good at the night of death. And yet, in and behind all these changes something enduring hides, a "self" that experiences all of this, a physical-psychical being, which we call human and of which consciousness and also self-consciousness (the "I," the ego) do not seem to be the core but rather a property or determination.[8]

So the question arises, of course, what is the connection between our being and our (self-)consciousness? Is there something inside a person or does something happen inside a person that falls outside or beneath their consciousness? This question cannot be avoided, as many people do, with the comment that when such unconscious phenomena occur in a person, we cannot know or say anything about them simply because they are unconscious. For it concerns the question whether such phenomena, which we find in the human consciousness, are perhaps of such a nature that they compel us to acquiesce in accepting factors in the unconscious, because without them there is no explanation. This is a common scientific practice. No one has ever seen atoms (dynamides, electrons) or ether, and yet present-day natural science is built on the supposition of their existence. Contrary to Haeckel, who proposed that faith in the existence of the soul was reverting to dualistic supernaturalism,[9] Ed[uard] von Hartmann maintained correctly that the philosopher who saw himself obliged, for example, to accept the hypothesis of a life force from the observed phenomena formally [187] carries on just as scientifically as the naturalist who on the basis of empirical data concludes that atoms exist.[10]

Nevertheless, the question that earlier was put rather generally needs to be stated more precisely for clarification. In a certain sense everybody assumes the existence of the unconscious, for everybody acknowledges that all kinds of processes take place in the human body that happen entirely

7. Eduard von Hartmann, *Philosophy of the Unconscious: Speculative Results according to the Inductive Method of Physical Science*, 3 vols. in 1 (London: Routledge & Kegan Paul, 1931), II:109ff.

8. Cf. Johannes Rehmke, *Die Seele des Menschen* (Leipzig: Teubner, 1902), 3ff.

9. Haeckel, *Riddle of the Universe*, 89–90.

10. Cf. Herman Bavinck, *Christelijke wereldbeschouwing*, 2nd ed. (Kampen: Kok, 1913), 50–51.

outside of consciousness, specifically also in the brain. Science may be able to give us some information about those processes, but at the moment they take place, they occur entirely outside our consciousness. The question about the so-called physiological-unconscious presents, therefore, few difficulties as long as it remains a general question. These difficulties first arise when a second question is raised, whether there are (besides those physiological and specifically cerebral processes) other phenomena, occurrences, activities that are unconscious and that are at the same time psychic in nature. Here the immediate objection presents itself that it is very difficult to point out the boundary between human physical and psychic life, because of the close connection between body and soul. But this objection is immediately followed by another one: Of what do these unconscious-psychical phenomena consist? Are they references to the soul itself, with its powers and dispositions, its habits or activities? Or do the facts also allow us to speak of unconscious impressions, feelings, and acts of the will? And even if the last question should be answered in the negative, the entire matter of the unconscious has thereby not yet been settled. For besides the unconscious, many also accept subconscious, concomitant consciousness, or weak consciousness. Of course, this can often be distinguished only with difficulty from the unconscious, but it nevertheless needs to be discussed because of its importance for the entire life of the soul.

## History

A brief summary of the history of these questions must precede our discussion of them.

Even though the term "unconscious" is of more recent origin, the matter itself has been known more or less from of old. Just as humanity has always intuitively understood the difference between what is alive and what is lifeless,[11] so it [188] also has been convinced at all times of the distinction between the soul and consciousness. This is shown by the fact that people everywhere attribute to human beings—in addition to the one or more souls that we have in common with plants and animals—a much higher soul, which sometimes existed already before coming into the body, continues to live on in another form after death, and sometimes even transitions into other bodies. In Wundt's language, the "soul that inhabits the body" is to be distinguished from the "breath" or "shadow-soul."[12] Philosophy borrowed all these thoughts

---

11. The boundary drawn between both, especially by animistic peoples, was quite different and much broader than with us; but it is incorrect to assume that these so-called primitive people did not know that boundary at all, and considered everything without exception as being alive and animated; cf. Jan ten Hove, "Animisme," *Theologisch tijdschrift* 48 (1914): 499–513.

12. Wilhelm Wundt, *Völkerpsychologie*, vol. II, *Mythus und Religion* (Leipzig: Engelmann, 1900–1920), 1ff.

from popular religion, and they are actually found among the Orphists, in Pythagoras, and in Plato. The latter combined it with the theory that all true science at bottom, as knowledge of ideas, is a memory of what the soul once witnessed in its preexistent state.

How else could one understand the possibility of learning and refute the objection of the Sophists that it is not possible to learn the known or seek the unknown? Besides, experience also provides positive proof for this, for mathematics can be produced by thoughts that the mind itself experiences, and general ideas could not be deduced from sensory things if they were not known to the mind beforehand, in one way or another.[13]

Granted that Aristotle rejected the preexistence of the soul together with the preexistence of ideas, but for the rest his agreement with Plato is much greater than is often thought. After all, just like Plato, Aristotle also ascribed more than one soul to human beings, and just like his predecessor, he did not succeed in combining these three souls into one organic unit. Furthermore, he taught just as emphatically as Plato an essential distinction between observation and thought, opinion and science, and considered science to be found in the knowledge of causes, meaning causes of general, necessary truths, which themselves in the final analysis rest on axioms that cannot be proved and are fixed by themselves. And third, he too considered the *nous*, the intellect, to be a faculty that had the ability to immediately understand these basic axioms, and a faculty that knew, in general, how to penetrate to the essence and cause of things through sensory perception.[14] This is why it is not surprising that later philosophers (even though Plato and Aristotle had not taught "innate ideas") nevertheless followed in their footsteps and began to speak of innate presuppositions [ἔμφυτοι προλήψεις], common or natural notions [κοιναί or φυσικαὶ ἔννοια], [189] small ideas of great things [*notitiae parvae rerum maximarum*], seeds of innate virtue [*semina innata virtutum*].

Christianity brought little change to this psychological structure. It elevated the value of personality, put the matter of its immortality beyond doubt, broadened the life of the soul, and enriched the religious-ethical knowledge of the soul. But psychology remained true to the Aristotelian system. Both Protestant and Roman Catholic Scholasticism rejected the theory of innate ideas and taught with Aristotle that the intellect contained nothing that was not first experienced. But this was not at all meant in the sense of later empiricism, because at the same time it maintained that the intellect was a

13. E. Zeller, *Die Philosophie der Griechen in ihrer geschichtlichen Entwicklung*, 4th ed., 3 vols. in 5 (Leipzig: Fues's Verlag, 1875–81), II:823ff. [ET by Sarah Frances Alleyne, *A History of Greek Philosophy from the Earliest Period to the Time of Socrates*, 2 vols. (London: Longmans, Green, 1881)]; C. B. Spruyt, *Proeve van eene geschiedenis van de leer der aangeboren begrippen* (Leiden: Brill, 1879), 6ff.

14. Zeller, *Philosophie der Griechen*, III:189ff.; Spruyt, *Aangeboren begrippen*, 18ff.

faculty that was able to rise from the visible to the invisible and that could know intuitively the truth of general principles and penetrate to the essence of things.

When one also considers that Scholasticism considered the soul to be a God-created, spiritual entity, which brought with it from the beginning all sorts of powers, (innate) habits, and gifts and was able through education and nurture to gain all kinds of acquired habits—then this provides sufficient proof that the old psychology, though it never spoke of the unconscious, understood the matter thoroughly, at least in principle.

However, Descartes brought about a great change in this for he was the first to identify the soul with consciousness. In order to be able to sharply distinguish the natural sciences from the humanities, he put the essence of the body in largeness [*extensio, spatium*] and the essence of the soul in the mind [*mens, cogitatio*]. Consequently, the soul ceased to exist as the life principle; it came to stand dualistically over against the body, and the body became an object of the natural sciences, whose task it was to mechanically explain everything physical. All following philosophers now focused their efforts on reconciling this dualism. Among them, Leibniz believed that he had surmounted the contrast by understanding substance to be not an inactive force but rather an active force [*vis activa*], not as a psychic or mathematical atom, but metaphysically as a soul-like unit; substance is something capable of action [*la substance est un être capable d'action*]. In this way Leibniz came to attribute the property of perception to monads; they were powers of perception.[15]

Of course, one had to assume in these impressions endless differences [190] in degree: such as sleeping, dreaming, and waking monads; perception and apperception, soul and spirit; there were obscure ideas and clear ideas and distinctive ideas. Even as hearing the roaring of the sea supposes that each falling drop of water makes a sound that can be perceived only with a very weak consciousness, so we constantly turn infinitely small, hardly noticeable perceptions into clear apperceptions only through mutual multiplication and augmentation. Strictly speaking, all sensory perceptions, all feelings, also specifically aesthetic affections belong to these lower, hardly noticeable, deteriorating perceptions. It is only through his spirit and reason that man is able to form fully conscious clear ideas.[16] Because Leibniz thus discerned degrees in perceptions, he has been called the father of unconscious ideas. Yet this is not quite right, for Leibniz, in the strictest sense of the word, did not assume unconscious perceptions, but an endless series of weaker and stronger ones.[17] In a certain sense, perceiving belongs to all monads, in fact

---

15. Cf. Kuno Fischer, *Geschichte der neueren Philosophie*, 3rd. ed., vol. 2, *Gottfried Wilhelm Leibniz* (Heidelberg: Winter, 1889), 328ff., 464ff.
16. Ibid., 414–15; Hartmann, *Philosophy of the Unconscious*, I:17ff.
17. Hartmann, *Philosophy of the Unconscious*, I:18–19.

all creatures, and observation is not so much the source of knowledge as the occasion through which the power of impression develops and produces what belongs to it by nature. "There is nothing in the mind [intellect] that was not earlier [experienced] in the senses," [said John Locke; and Leibniz added,] "except the mind itself" [*nihil est in intellectu quod non prius fuerit in sensu, nisi ipse intellectus*].[18]

Through these thoughts Leibniz shaped the transition from Descartes to Kant, from rationalism to idealism, from the theory that a human being is essentially *cogitatio* to the idea that the human being is intellectually and morally autonomous. This idealism carried a predominantly critical, epistemological character with Kant, but as is often said, it was developed by Fichte into an ethical idealism, by Schelling into a physical idealism, and by Hegel into a logical idealism. At the zenith of its development, when idealism tried to derive all existence from thought, it evoked a strong reaction in Schelling, when he was in his second phase. Perhaps thought was still able to explain the essence of things, but it would never be able to understand their existence. There is no transition from thought to being: reality does not allow itself to be deduced from logic. And this is even less so because reality is by no means always reasonable; rather, it always includes an irrational element. Over against Hegel's rational optimism, Schelling therefore posited the irrationalism of the will. Behind reason he returned to the will, [191] the blind, illogical will. In the final analysis there is no other being than to will: *Wollen ist Ursein* [to will is original being].[19]

The new theory of the unconscious finds its origin in this philosophy of the will of Schelling. For if the will of the world, man, and God is detached from the mind and precedes it in order, then the way is cleared for all kinds of hidden, mysterious forces to exert themselves. Schelling himself pointed this out already in his *System of Transcendental Idealism*, explaining history and art from the cooperation of freedom and necessity, of the conscious and the unconscious.[20] This theory received a much broader application in aesthetics by Jean Paul Richter, Th[eodor] Vischer, [Karl Philipp] Moritz, and [Jean] Carriès; and in psychology by [Joseph] Ennemoser, the defender of Mesmerism; Carus, the celebrated physician in Dresden; and von Schubert, who preferred to be engaged in the abnormal and mysterious phenomena of the life of the

18. Richard Falckenberg, *Geschichte der neueren Philosophie* (Leipzig: Veit, 1886), 218 [ET by A. C. Armstrong Jr., *History of Modern Philosophy from Nicolas of Cusa to the Present Time* (New York: H. Holt, 1893)].

19. Cf. Herman Bavinck, *Reformed Dogmatics* (Grand Rapids: Baker Academic, 2003–4), I:167, 259; II:230; Wilhelm Windelband, *A History of Philosophy*, 2 vols., trans. James H. Tufts (New York: Macmillan, 1901; repr., New York: Harper & Row, 1958), II:573ff.

20. F. W. J. Schelling, in *Ausgewählte Werke: Schriften von 1799–1801*, 4 vols. (Darmstadt: Wissenschaftliche Buchgesellschaft, 1968), II:587ff., 162ff. ["System des transcendentalen Idealismus," in *Werke* I/3:587ff.; and "Erster Entwurf eines System der Naturphilosophie," in *Werke* I/3:162ff.]

soul.[21] However, this theory received the highest place in Schopenhauer's philosophy, whose main publication appeared already in 1819,[22] and in that of von Hartmann, who published his *Philosophy of the Unconscious* in 1869. The latter, therefore, is not the discoverer of the unconscious: by his own admission he had many predecessors;[23] and he adds that [Wundt at] Leipzig gave him the idea to study the realm of consciousness more closely, that for factual data he owed much to Carus and [Hans] Reichenbach, and that qua intellectual propensity he felt closest to Schelling's positive philosophy.[24] He considered his own contribution to consist of having collected very carefully everything that could be gathered as proof of the unconscious in nature and history, in humanity, and that he had tried "to understand" the unity he had thus discovered as "a multiunit of the Absolute, and to bring it to the center of a philosophical system [*Vieleinigkeit des Absoluten zu begreifen, und in den Mittelpunkt eines philosophischen Systems zu rucken*]." By associating the physiological and psychological unconscious with the metaphysical unconscious, and making the experience-data subservient to speculation, he developed abstract monism into concrete monism.[25]

[192] Nevertheless the development of the idea of the unconscious in psychology was held back for years, on the one hand, by the intellectualism of [Johann Friedrich] Herbart and his school, and on the other hand, by materialism and positivism (agnosticism, neo-Kantianism) that disputed the existence or the recognizability of the soul and was satisfied with a "soulless psychology."[26] But this changed gradually. Materialism appeared to be powerless to explain psychical phenomena from metabolism. Du Bois-Reymond called consciousness one of the seven mysteries of the world. [Gustav Theodore] Fechner placed over against the gloomy *Nachtansicht* [night view] of modern science the *Tagesansicht* [day view] of his metaphysics, according to which the entire world of matter is animated by and united through the spirit. Wundt moved psychology into a different direction through his voluntarism;

---

21. [Carl Gustav] Carus published (among others) *Vorlesungen über Psychologie* (Leipzig: Fleischer, 1831); *Psyche: Zur Entwicklungsgeschichte der Seele* (Pforzheim: Flammer & Hoffmann, 1846) [ET: *Psyche: On the Development of the Soul* (New York: Spring Publications, 1970)]; and *Physis: Zur Geschichte des leiblichen Lebens* (Stuttgart: Scheitlin, 1851). [Gotthilf Heinrich von] Schubert's *Die Geschichte der Seele*, 3rd ed. (Stuttgart: Cotta, 1839), is especially well known.

22. Ed. note: A. Schopenhauer, *The World as Will and Idea*, trans. R. B. Haldane and J. Kemp, 2nd ed., 3 vols. (London: Kegan Paul, Trench, Trübner, 1891).

23. Hartmann, *Philosophy of the Unconscious*, I:16–42; idem, *Die moderne Psychologie* (Leipzig: Haacke, 1901), 32ff.

24. E[duard] von Hartmann, *Philosophie des Unbewussten* (Berlin: Duncker, 1869–), I:preface; VIIff.; III:494–99. [Ed. note: Bavinck's references here to von Hartmann's *Philosophy of the Unconscious* are not available in the English edition.]

25. Hartmann, *Philosophie des Unbewussten*, I:443–44 [ed. note: English is not available].

26. Frederick A. Lange, *The History of Materialism*, trans. Ernest Chester Thomas, 3 vols. in 1 (New York: Harcourt, Brace & Co., 1925), II.3.3:168.

natural science on its part exchanged atoms for monads, dynamids, and energies. Last but not least, so-called occult phenomena increased so much and attracted so much attention that science could no longer afford to ignore them disdainfully but had to subject them to serious scientific research.

All these factors were the reason why the unconscious in psychology began to enjoy increasingly friendlier attention and broader consideration; there is no conceivable psychology today that does not try to pay some attention to it.

## PHENOMENA

Even though all psychologists today are more or less busy with the unconscious,[27] this does not mean at all that they all think alike. Even the word is used in many different ways; some ascribe no fewer than eight meanings to the word, such as the unremembered, the unintended, the unnoticed, the automated, the reproduced, the productive, physical reality, the absolute.[28] This ought to be kept in mind when discussing the phenomena [193] that are considered with regard to the unconscious.

The physiological unconscious presents itself first of all. For all those psychologists who believe the soul and consciousness to be identical, the psychically unconscious is clearly an impossible contradiction. But though it is impossible for consciousness to just hang in the air, they assume that it rises from, or at least that it rests in, and accompanies and reflects the processes of the brain; and thus they do speak of an "unconscious cerebration." It undoubtedly is a very difficult question where to draw the boundaries between physiology and psychology. Many phenomena that at one time were considered to be psychic were later explained quite easily physiologically. Nor will anyone deny that consciousness is very closely related to the brain. But it should be kept in mind that a physiological explanation is still miles removed from a mechanical explanation. And even though present-day science considers the latter its ideal, it remains a fact that this is attained only within a limited area and that until today, just as with consciousness, it also

27. Of the amazingly rich literature, we will mention here—except for von Hartmann's *Philosophie des Unbewussten* and the psychologists he discusses in his *Die moderne Psychologie*, 32ff.—only [Leopold] Loewenfeld, *Bewusstsein und psychisches Geschehen* (Wiesbaden: Bergmann, 1913); Georg Weingärtner, *Das Unterbewusstsein* (Mainz: Kirchheim, 1911); [Wilhelm] Windelband, *Die Hypothese des Unbewussten* (Heidelberg: Winter, 1914); Frederic W. H. Myers, *Human Personality and Its Survival of Bodily Death*, edited and abridged by his son L. H. Myers (London: Longmans, Green, 1907); Joseph Jastrow, *The Subconscious* (London: A. Constable, 1906); [Gerbrandus] Jelgersma, *Ongeweten geestesleven* (Leiden: van Doesburgh, 1914); Wijnaendts Francken, *Over het bewustzijn* (Baarn: Hollandia); [Israel] Zeehandelaar, *Over de mogelijkheid van telepathie* (Baarn: Hollandia, 1911); [J. P. F. A.] Noorduyn, *Het onder-bewustzijn* (Baarn: Hollandia, 1912); etc.

28. *F[riedrich] A[lbert] Lange, *Geschichte des Materialismus*, 2nd ed. (Iserlohn: Baedeker, 1875), 381.

remains an unsolved riddle for life itself. This is the reason why many today despair at the explanation of both from metabolism and turn in a different direction by following [Eduard] Fechtner: instead of trying to explain life from death, they try to explain death from life and darkness from light.

Physiological unconsciousness is nevertheless to be considered here, if it points to the fact that man in his body received a wonderful organ that, even though there is a close connection between it and the soul as the principle of life, for the greater part leads a life of its own and is dependent on consciousness and will. The so-called physiological automatisms serve as proof of this—the functioning of the heart, lungs, stomach, intestines, and so forth—which continue without us being aware of it and which function the better as long as they do not remind us of their existence through sensitivity or pain. And also our reflexes, the involuntary reactions of our body to external stimuli, like trying to maintain our equilibrium when we lose our footing, or lifting our arm when danger threatens, the pupil contracting at bright light, sneezing when the nose is tickled, coughing when the throat is irritated, and so forth—all indicate that much can happen in our bodies over which our will has no say at all, and of which our consciousness becomes aware only afterward. At any rate, it is a fact that the psychophysical life of man runs much deeper and more extensively than his consciousness.

[194] This thesis is confirmed when, in the second place, we investigate such phenomena that point to a psychic unconscious. Instinct belongs to this from the very start: the ability to perform an appropriate action unconsciously. It only happens in the realm of sensory perceptions and feelings and is thus distinguished on the one hand from rational deliberation and on the other hand from reflex movement. With the latter the instinctive action has in common that it is caused immediately as a result of sensory stimulation, is necessary as a means of sustaining life, is innate and unconscious. But instincts are no longer seen as purely mechanical: they allow variations within certain boundaries, do not rule out all exercise, and are coupled with consciousness insofar that they include awareness of the means but not the end, which is nevertheless reached through these means.[29] Usually it is said that animals possess many more innate instincts than people, but Stern comments that this is true only in a certain sense.[30] At birth animals may immediately have more instinctive abilities than people, but the innate is not nearly always developed and ready in the same way; with people, instincts turn up only later and then most of the time in connection with actions of a higher order. A child brings with it immediately the sucking instinct, and

---

29. Hartmann, *Philosophie des Unbewussten*, I:79ff.
30. Stern, *Psychologie der frühen Kindheit*, 34 (ET: *Psychology of Early Childhood*, 70–71); Hartmann, *Philosophie des Unbewussten*, I:205ff.

soon thereafter defense instincts; instincts of certain movements, of play, fear, shame, affection, aversion, and so forth become apparent.

Of much greater significance is the fact that people are born unequal not only physically, but also psychically. This is a dilemma with which religion and philosophy in the East and in the West have wrestled, including Origen and Augustine, Calvin and Rousseau. Locke believed that the soul of man was a tabula rasa at birth, on which people later could write whatever they wanted. In the same way [Claude Adrien] Helvétius and [Étienne Bonnot de] Condillac deduced [afleiden uit] all mental differences between people from environment and nurture. Socialism tried to find a solution for the problem in the same direction. However, the facts about the inequality that is not the result of acquiring but is innate speak so strongly that they could not be denied for long; and under the influence of the theory of evolution and heredity, they are generally accepted today. In fact, in science, literature, and the arts people have often swung to another extreme, so that a reaction in favor of the independence of the personality became a real necessity. But here we do not have to enter any further into the question of heredity; [195] suffice it to say that heredity and variability are always coupled together, and that in spite of all research devoted to this question, no one until the present time has been able to say where the one ends and the other begins; even with regard to inheriting acquired qualities, opinions differ markedly. One thing is certain: every human being has much in common with his parents, family, nation, humanity, and yet at the same time differs from them in certain respects. Every human being, as Emerson said, is a citation of his ancestors; and yet he is also an independent thought and word.

The difference in human beings shows up in everything: in the physical and no less in the spiritual; in sensation, observation, memory, imagination, feeling, emotion, desire, will, character, temperament, and so forth; and not only in these aptitudes by themselves but equally so in their mutual relationships. We have innate capabilities, qualities, habits, dispositions, inclinations, conditions, actions, and whatever else one wants to call them; prior to our consciousness and our will, they shape us to be what we are and lay the foundation for our own thinking and acting. Without our will or knowledge, all of that unconscious [dimension] affects our conscious life and gives direction and guidance. And this does not happen only now and then, by way of exception, but it is the rule: our conscious life is continuously born by and animated by the unconscious. Our becoming aware and our observations, our feeling and our wanting, our thinking and speaking; all our convictions in religion, morality, science, the arts; our insights and prejudices, our sympathies and aversions—these all are rooted far and deep behind the consciousness in our soul. Often they make us impervious to all reasoning and proof, and often so strongly that we ourselves with all our will-power are nevertheless powerless to resist them. Who is able to sufficiently account for the reason why he fosters sympathies for and sides with one or another of the warring nations these days? Later, after having fostered such sympathies and having taken sides, we try to justify them with reasons, but such proof is usually not the basis but the outcome of our convictions. The root of a human being's personality lies in the subconscious, in the soul itself, with all that is innate to it. Soul and consciousness definitely do not coincide. The self is much richer than the "I."[31]

[196] This may certainly be said now of every human being. The human soul contains many slumbering gifts that never will come to full fruition, at least not in this life. But this applies especially to those privileged people whom we call geniuses and who more than others live by grace. Certainly, being a genius does not exclude study and effort. There is truth in the sayings "Luck is pluck" and "No inspiration without perspiration." But it nevertheless is striking that geniuses themselves are the first to call the best and the most beautiful that they produce "a gift" and ascribe it to inspiration. Thinking and writing verses, poetry, and philosophy are therefore closely related. The conscious and the unconscious cooperate incomprehensibly in every human being, but above all in every artist.[32]

In addition to this, it should be mentioned that when growing up, every human being feels restrained in all sorts of ways,[33] not only externally by his surroundings but also internally by laws that apply to his nature and all its activities. He is unable to observe, feel, think, and will the way he perhaps would like to. There are models of observation and categories, norms, and rules that bind people in all their activities; there are logical, ethical, and aesthetic laws from which they cannot free themselves, that are fixed a priori, and that gradually reveal themselves in life. According to the theory of evolution, these forms and norms have come into being little by little as part of the struggle for life and afterward are inherited and then become second nature; but this explanation is not very satisfying, especially when

---

31. Cf. [Abraham] Kuyper, *Ons instinctieve leven* (Amsterdam: Kirchner, [1910]), articles in *De Standaard* of March 18, 1908, and subsequently also published separately [ET: "Our Instinctive Life," in *Abraham Kuyper: A Centennial Reader*, ed. J. Bratt (Grand Rapids: Eerdmans, 1998), 255–78]; Hartmann, *Philosophie des Unbewussten*, I:220ff.; G. le Bon, *Les opinions et les croyances* (Paris: Flammarion, 1913); Camille Bos, *Psychologie de la croyance* (Paris: Alcan, 1905).

32. About geniuses, see F. W. Myers, *Human Personality*, 55ff.; Hartmann, *Philosophie des Unbewussten*, I:278; J[ürgen] Bona Meyer, *Probleme der Lebensweisheit*, 2nd ed. (Berlin: Allgemeiner Verein für Deutsche Literatur, 1887), 85–121; [Anthony] Brummelkamp Jr., *Het genie eene scheppingsgave* (Leiden, 1901). Geniuses became the object of studies especially since Lombroso connected genius and insanity.

33. [Gustave] le Bon in *Psychologie des foules* (Paris: Alcan, 1895) [ET: *The Crowd: A Study of the Popular Mind* (London: T. Fisher Unwin, 1922)] dealt with the influence that a crowd has on each individual. See also [Scipio] Sighele, [*La foule criminelle: Essai de psychologie collective*, 2nd ed. (Paris: Alcan, 1901); idem,] *De menigte als misdadigster*, trans. Anna Polak (Amsterdam: Maatschappij voor goede en goedkoope lectuur[, 1906]).

thinking of the source of religion, so that many today return to adopting a religious a priori view.[34]

For the present, we leave the question of whether the phenomena and facts [that point to a psychic unconscious] discussed in the second place belong to the category of the unconscious or should be assigned there; they themselves, however, stand firm. For that reason we can now, in the third place, proceed to a discussion of another group of phenomena: those that at first were conscious but later disappeared from consciousness. Usually it is then said that they are kept in the memory and can be produced through recall.

[197] However, it needs to be said that not only impressions but also duties and activities can be made our property. For that reason some scholars in recent years have expanded the concept of memory to such a degree that it would include retention of all changes that have resulted from stimuli and that it could even be exalted to a principle that explains the world.[35] This expansion of a known and fixed idea certainly should not be recommended, but it remains a fact nevertheless that we can appropriate many duties through practice and habit so that they take place as though by themselves, mechanically or automatically. Such is the case with all daily activities like walking, speaking, writing, playing the piano, bicycling, using a foreign language, and so forth; all of these took much effort and exertion at first, but gradually they become so customary that our mind does not even have to pay attention to them anymore; our mind is freed for other and more important work.[36] There are innate habits and also acquired habits, as though a second nature acquired by habit.

Now the question is, however, whether such activities happen completely unconsciously, or whether they happen with a very feeble degree of consciousness. And the same question presents itself when it comes to impressions or thoughts, which are said to be kept in our memory. If such impressions or thoughts have actually vanished totally from memory, the question arises whether they then may justly be called impressions or thoughts. It is difficult to speak of impressions that do not present themselves and thoughts that are not thought. And yet, on the other hand, they cannot have totally vanished, for in our memory we possess the ability to recall them to consciousness with more or less effort, without again first going through the experience to which we owed them in the first place. Sometimes it happens that we exert ourselves in vain trying to remember a name or a date and that afterward, when we have given up looking for it, such a name suddenly occurs to us.

34. Karl Dunkmann, *Das religiöse Apriori und die Geschichte* (Gütersloh: C. Bertelsmann, 1910).

35. So esp. R[ichard] Semon, *Die Mneme als erhaltendes Prinzip im Wechsel des organischen Geschehens*, 3rd ed. (Leipzig: Engelmann, 1911).

36. J. V. de Groot, "Lapsing Intelligence," *Verslagen en mededeelingen der Koninklijke Akademie van Wetenschappen, afdeeling letterkunde*, series 4, vol. XV (Amsterdam: Joh. Muller, 1912), 388–416.

Does that not indicate that our mind has nevertheless remained active, and what we could not obtain by means of effort simply fell into our lap? Many try to solve this difficulty by going back to the physiological unconscious and speak of tracks, traces, engrams, and so forth that are left in the brain by the impressions. In that case, memory would be a function of the nervous system or belong to [198] organic matter. But even though there is no doubt about a very close connection between the brain and memory, it remains an absolute mystery how nerve substance thus retains earlier impressions so that the brain later is able to reproduce these impressions and in addition is able to recognize, judge, and compare them.[37] Others are satisfied with the psychic unconscious and have no objection to speaking of unconscious impressions. Still, this also does not remove the difficulty, for in that case the term "unconscious" serves only to hide the ignorance.[38] As far as memory is concerned, we face an unsolved mystery and do not know how it retains impressions, only potentially or habitually, insofar as our mind has the capacity and the agility to reproduce impressions on its own, or also things somewhat real, as though impressions. At any rate, memory and associations do not give us adequate justification to accept, in a strict sense, unconscious impressions.

Our attention is drawn, in the fourth place, to the phenomena that go by the name of "subconscious" (subliminal consciousness) or "conscious." The first term, "subconscious," however, is understood again either in a broader or narrower sense. In the narrower sense it coincides with the absolute unconscious and would not fit into the phenomena to be discussed now. Others use the image of a threshold that separates the first and second floors of the conscious from one another, but this image is not a happy choice in view of the reality of our impressions. For in the cases that we are looking at now, there is no talk of a sharp delineation or a deep chasm that separates the conscious from the unconscious, but rather of a gentle, gradual transition.

Leibniz's terminology was better, therefore, when he spoke of perception and apperception, Fechner of lower and higher waves of consciousness, Wundt of field of vision and focal point, others again of a rustling sound heard from afar and nearby, or of twilight, dawn, or day.[39] It is true that von Hartmann sharply disputes these degrees of consciousness, but this may be explained from his peculiar opinion that consciousness, as it arises from opposition of the will, carries a purely negative character, and also because of his desire (with self-consciousness) to make the sharpest possible delineation between consciousness and attentiveness.[40]

---

37. G. Lamers, *De psychologie van het geheugen* (Nijmegen: Malmberg, 1914), 90.
38. Wilhelm Windelband, *Einleitung in die Philosophie* (Tübingen: Mohr, 1914), 168.
39. Cf. Weingärtner, *Das Unterbewusstsein*, 30, 34, 36.
40. Hartmann, *Philosophie des Unbewussten*, I:59ff.; idem, *Die moderne Psychologie*, 39, 40.

[199] We all know from experience that there are indeed real degrees of consciousness. When we are strenuously involved in some labor, we nevertheless do remain somewhat aware of things happening around us. At that moment it makes no impression on us at all: it does not strike us, as we say. But if we are questioned about it later, we often remember that we did see or hear something. For example, we walk outside, absorbed in thought, and afterward remember that we met someone whom we thought we had not noticed at all. We were totally preoccupied with thinking about something, and yet we heard the clock strike. In an interesting lecture about the psychology of reading, Professor Straub pointed out recently that our eye not only sees letters that fall within its focal point but that it also distinguishes a number of letters more or less clearly sideways and ahead, which actually makes reading possible.[41] And Freud, in Vienna, called attention to the fact that our slips of the tongue or pen are not accidental but must be explained from the fact that when we wanted to speak a certain word, or write it down, we thought of something else that was more or less related to it.[42] And that in this and in similar cases, we were somewhat conscious of what was outside the center of our thoughts, as can be proved by a factory worker who is so accustomed to the roar of machinery that he does not even notice it anymore and is not immediately conscious of the noise suddenly stopping.

These facts prove that there are simultaneously two groups of impressions present in our consciousness, one at the center and one at the periphery, one in the upper floor and one on the ground floor. There is no talk here of the unconscious or of a subconsciousness in the strict sense or that an impression would have totally vanished from the conscious and have sunk below consciousness. It is also difficult to assume that these two groups of impressions would each be connected to a separate part of the brain, as von Hartmann and others maintain. But the mentioned phenomena certainly do give us the right to speak of a division in the consciousness. There is undoubtedly a distinction between dark and bright consciousness, between consciousness, perception, and attention, or attentiveness.[43]

[200] This fact is not only important by itself, but it is also remarkable since it sheds light on other phenomena of the life of the soul. Take, for example, dreams. When we sleep the "I" loses its supremacy; intellect, reason, self-consciousness, attention, awareness all withdraw into that which is hidden; and we further this ourselves when we, upon retiring for the night, oppose the activities of our senses by barring light and sound from the room as much as possible. But the lower impressional life, upon being freed from the

41. Cf. report in *Algemeen handelsblad* of March 23, 1915, morning edition.
42. [Sigmund] Freud, *Zur Psychopathologie des Alltaglebens: Über Vergessen, Versprechen, Vergreifen, Aberglaube und Irrtum*, 3rd ed. (Berlin: Karger, 1910) [ET: *The Psychopathology of Everyday Life*, ed. James Strachey, trans. Alan Tyson (New York: Norton, 1965)].
43. Cf. [Joseph] Geyser, *Die Seele* (Leipzig: F. Meiner, 1914), 74ff.

control of the "I," gains free play and is stirred by external stimuli (sensory perceptions, the fall of an object, the buzz of an insect, and so forth) and by internal stimuli (organic perceptions, illness or pain of some organ, sexual stimuli, and so forth); even during sleep, when not distracted by anything else, we are more sensitive to those stimuli than at other times. As a result of such stimuli, the impressional life inside of us goes to work; it starts to fantasize. The content of the impressions and imagination is derived from the real world, from what we have experienced that day, or more often even two or three days earlier, and also quite often from something that already happened long ago, from experiences of our earliest youth. And we experience all of this so realistically and intensely in our dream, which passes extremely fast, that at that moment we deem them to be real, and we sometimes find it difficult upon and after awaking to distinguish between reality and the dream. Children and so-called primitive peoples believe both to be real; and the sleepwalker behaves with surprising confidence and safety.[44]

In hypnosis the same phenomenon occurs. Suggestion numbs the higher recognition, and the [hypnotist's] ability to pursue something in the sleepwalker paralyzes his thought and will and turns him into an unresisting instrument of someone else's intentions. His lower impressional life becomes a servant of the hypnotist, not only in and during the session, but also often for quite some time afterward, at a specific day determined by the hypnotist. And the person hypnotized carries out the task he was given by the other person. It is somewhat similar to our organism that obeys unconsciously and without resisting when we, at night, before going to sleep, seriously set our mind to wanting to wake up at a specific time.[45]

Many forms of insanity are also related to these dream and hypnosis phenomena. In mania, melancholy, and paranoia; in hysteria [201] and neurasthenia—the division, the discord, the dissociation of the consciousness usually plays a large role. Already in ordinary life, moods are able to so govern us and anxious cares so depress us and all kinds of impressions and ideas so captivate us that we don't have any interest in anything else. Who does not have his favorite ideas and hobbyhorses? How many sleepless hours are spent sometimes at night because we cannot let go of one particular thought that controls us as an idée fixe? Usually a healthy person regains control again and reclaims mastery over his impressions. But in the case of insanity, a person has lost command of himself; his ability to plan and his will have been weakened and sometimes totally destroyed; his consciousness is governed by another force that he is not able to resist or drive away. Delusions, obsessions, compulsions, anxieties, notions of grandeur,

44. D. Schermers, "Het droomleven van den mensch," in the *Orgaan van de christelijke vereeniging van natuur—en geneeskundigen in Nederland*, 1915.
45. Myers, *Human Personality*, 116ff.

insignificance, persecution, and so forth have conquered his consciousness and refuse to be driven out by reasoning or command. The contents of those impressions have been borrowed from reality, just as with dreams, and are therefore connected to the development, the culture, the religious convictions, and so forth of the patient.[46]

This does not mean that the madman has really lost a piece of his soul or, for instance, abilities such as his intellect or reason or will. But just as the illness is unsubstantial and does not take away any substance from the organism but makes the organism itself or a particular member work differently, so insanity does not destroy an organ or function of the soul but deforms it and makes it work in an abnormal fashion. The psychic patient lives in an imaginary world that is forced on him and that detains his thinking and willing. Healing, therefore, only begins when gradually or suddenly another world of impressions and thoughts gains dominance.[47] Hence come the many efforts more recently to restore the dismayed consciousness through psychic therapy, Christian Science, mind cure, new-thought movement, faith cure, divine healing, mental science, and so forth.[48]

In conclusion, mention should be made briefly of that remarkable phenomenon that is given the name of dual personality, depersonalization, or alteration of one's personality. A few pathological cases are known in which someone, [202] for a shorter or longer time, lost his own personality and experienced a totally different impression of self.[49]

From these pathological phenomena more-recent psychologists have tried to derive proof that personality is a group of variable impressions and not a unity. It was difficult for them to think differently because they had first dissolved the soul, the substantial unity of a person, into a series of conscious contents and self-impressions. For when there is no being behind the conscious (except in the physiologically unconscious, in the brain), nothing else remains in the same person, in the discovery of variable contents of the consciousness and various self-images, than also in the case of the same person (who then, however, does not remain the same) to speak of various "I's" and personalities. But this actually is a confusion of the real and the empirical self, of the self and the impression of self, of the self and the ego. Someone's idea about self is as much subject to error, to amnesia, as his idea of the world; already in everyday life we often pretend to be something entirely different from what we really are. How great is human self-deception, and how little

46. P[ieter] Wieringa, *Godsdienstwaanzin* (Groningen: Jan Haan, 1907).

47. Bernard Hart, *The Psychology of Insanity* (Cambridge: Cambridge University Press, 1912).

48. William James, *The Varieties of Religious Experience* (London: Longmans, Green, 1906), 94ff.

49. The best-known instances of Rev. Bourne, Rev. Hanna, Felida X, Heléne Smith, et al. are shared and discussed, among others, by Jastrow, *The Subconscious*, 323ff. See also Myers, *Human Personality*; and [Alfred] Binet, *Les altérations de la personnalité*, 2nd ed. (Paris: Alcan, 1902).

the true knowledge of self! For that reason it is not strange that in abnormal, pathological cases a person can think of himself and pretend for a shorter or longer period of time to be somebody totally different from who he is. But this delusion certainly does not at all preclude the fact that a person remains substantially the same in all these cases.

In the fifth place, the unconscious serves with many today as a means of explaining so-called occult phenomena. The history of mankind is replete with these; everywhere one encounters superstition, mantic claims, and magic as bastard forms of religion. People believe in having their fortune told from the stars (astrology), from the entrails of animals, from the flight of birds, from signs and cards, from the lines of one's face (physionomy) or hand (chiromancy, palmistry), from handwriting (graphology), and so forth. Oftentimes special gifts or powers are attributed to a person or to some persons to reveal things that are hidden or to do wondrous things, such as clairvoyance, second sight (deuteroscopy), premonition, telepathy, telesthasy, teleplasy, hypermnesy, reading thoughts, divining, pointing out illnesses and their cure while in a somnambular state, and so forth.[50] Also quite popular are faith in revelations or [203] promptings through dreams, appearances and materializations of the dead or of good and evil spirits, ecstasies and visions in which heavenly beings appear and heavenly things are seen. Humans have an inveterate need to know the supernatural and seek to satisfy that need in all kinds of ways.

In the days of the Enlightenment, all these phenomena were considered to be aberrations of the human spirit, and it was thought that they could be adequately explained from self-deception or priestly deception, or from bad perception and hallucination. But this changed toward the end of the eighteenth century, and people resorted to hidden powers of nature as an explanation. [Franz Anton] Mesmer, for instance, believed in animal magnetism and used it to heal the sick; Kieser spoke of tellurism, Reichenbach of *Od*, and so forth. The materialism of the middle of the previous [nineteenth] century pushed the study of occult phenomena to the background for quite a while, only to revive it again with even more force after the appearance of spiritism and theosophy. This began in Germany especially with G[ustav] Th[eodore] Fechner, M. Perty, Carl du Prel, and others; and in England and America with the founding of the Society for Psychical Research in London in February 1882, members of which were and still are Sidgwick, Barrett, Bennett, F. W. H. Myers, W. James, G. J. Romanes, W. Crookes, A. J. Balfour, Ol[iver] Lodge, and others.[51] Although all these scholars differ markedly among

---

50. Professor G. Van Rijnberk, *Hedendaags mirakelgeloof* (Amsterdam: F. van Rossen, 1914).

51. The main points of the Proceedings of this Society are briefly summarized by Sir W. F. Barrett, *Psychical Research*, Home University Library of Modern Knowledge (London: Williams & Norgate, 1911). See also Edward T. Bennett, *La société anglo-américaine pour les recherché psychiques*, trans. and introduced by M. Sage (Paris: Boding, 1904).

themselves, they nevertheless agree with each other in trying to explain all occult phenomena from immanent forces within the person, and specifically from the psychic unconscious.

Now it may appear that this is something new, but in fact it is already quite old. Already before the middle of the previous century, Ennemoser said: "True magic resides in the most secret innermost powers of our soul; the nature of our soul has not yet been revealed; all the wonders of the soul dissolve eventually in the wonders of our own soul."[52] Long before him, Agrippa von Nettesheim had already stated: "The cause of all things miraculous lies within ourselves."[53]

Even more remarkable is that mysticism, a general phenomenon in all religions, is based on the same thought [204] and follows practically the same path. There are always three stages to be distinguished in mystical life: asceticism, meditation, and contemplation. The soul detaches itself from the bonds of matter, from the body and the entire outside world, and turns inward through asceticism, which consists of all kinds of physical and spiritual exercises such as prayer, doing penance, abstinence, self-flagellation, suggestion, hypnosis, and so forth. The soul makes itself passive, imposes silence on reason and the will, and seems to descend into the unconscious. Next it lets itself be completely taken up by impressions and thoughts that arise from the unconscious, which it has suggested to itself or which others have suggested to it (concentration, meditation).

And finally, in this way it reaches a state of rapture or ecstasy (trance); it is elevated above space and time, above pain and suffering, and enters a totally different world. It hears and sees wonderful things (vision, visualization, contemplation, clairvoyance, telepathy, and so on) and reproduces the experience in sounds and images that often are incomprehensible to others (mystical language, automatic writing, speaking in tongues, foreign languages, and so forth).[54]

Thus in many respects the occult is a renewal of the old mysticism and the even older animism (preexistence, reincarnation, and so on), but it connects these old ideas with the modern theory of evolution and extends this into the hereafter. In that way it tries to escape the dualism of faith and knowledge; over against materialism, which denies all faiths the right to exist, it wants to maintain the spiritual world. But over against those who strictly separate the area of faith from that of knowledge, it tries to draw the knowledge of that spiritual world within the boundaries of an exact science that is obtainable through experience and research. That there are occult forces—powers that work according to higher and yet fixed laws—is considered to be proved indirectly

52. Julius Becker, *Aberglaube und Mystik im 19. Jahrhundert* (Berlin: Aufklärung, 1902), 44.
53. Ibid., 23.
54. See Bavinck, *Reformed Dogmatics*, III:528ff.; IV:69–75.

through chemistry, X-rays, wireless telephony, and so forth. If official science, they say, would only abandon its bias and research the psychical phenomena with the same open mind as they do the natural phenomena, it would become convinced of their reality and connect knowledge of natural phenomena with knowledge of psychical phenomena into one big unit. The well-being of humanity is found in a merger of the culture of the West with the wisdom of the East, of the rational mind that is nurtured here and the feeling heart that is fed there. Therefore a stream of "psychism" (the cultivation of secret forces of the soul) floods the entire civilized world; by all kinds of means [205] people want to penetrate the secrets of nature, of the soul, of the present and the future, of the spirit world and the world on the other side of the grave. And so is rumored that people often go to extremes, just as it happened long ago in the mysteries and with [other] sickly and degenerate religions.[55]

Whatever the case, it is certain that occultism presents itself as a new religion[56] and elevates the unconscious to a principle that explains the world. Von Hartmann, in particular, joined all those phenomena that plead for the unconscious in man, nature, and history and from this concluded there to be one Agent, which he called the absolute unconscious and which is the cause of all things, the sole *Individuum* that produces and harbors all individual appearances. This Unconscious, which may be called unconscious by negation or the superconscious via *eminentiae*, has two attributes: the will and impression; and it produces the whole world through these two, through the will as father, the *that* of things; and through impression as mother, the *what* of things. Being, therefore, owes its existence to the blind will and is the cause of all misery, but through the impression that becomes awareness in man, world history serves to emancipate itself from the will and to terminate the misery of existence.[57]

We find the same or related thoughts in many other philosophers, which is not surprising since the presently dominating idealistic philosophy, which dissolves the physical world into appearance (*maya*), can only escape solipsism and nihilism by giving the impressions an objective basis in the so-called Unconscious or in a world soul that contains everything. Others rather express themselves by saying that "separate psychic individuals are not to be seen as independent beings that stand next to each other and are forever cut off from each other, but rather as temporarily separated contents of a higher—in the final analysis of a most high—all-embracing consciousness," of an "endless consciousness that develops according to fixed laws."[58] But essentially it makes

---

55. *Cf. *Het Theosophisch Pad*, April 15.
56. Becker, *Aberglaube und Mystik*, 50.
57. Hartmann, *Philosophie des Unbewussten*, II:222ff. Cf. Bavinck, *Reformed Dogmatics*, II:193ff., 231ff.; III:544ff.
58. Thus Professor [Gerardus] Heymans, *De toekomstige eeuw der psychologie* (Groningen: J. B. Wolters, 1909), 25–26. Cf. also Fr. van Earned in his articles: "In het light der oorlogsvlam," *De*

little difference; in both instances theism is exchanged [206] for pantheism, and von Hartmann especially shows how much this pantheism is related to occultism. Consciousness proceeds from the unconscious and returns again to the unconscious; it is a brief light between two eternities of darkness.

## CONCLUSIONS

The theory of the unconscious that has gained such prominence in psychology of late is proof that the "psychology without a soul" is untenable, and in this respect is a recovery of the old theory of the soul, according to which soul and consciousness are distinct and consciousness is not the essence of the soul but a property. Furthermore, though on the one hand it rejects the tabula rasa theory, on the other hand it is a return to the theory of the powers [potentiae] and habits [habitus] of the soul, which, among other theories, is of great importance for the upbringing of children.

Besides that, it shows that the soul is not purely an ens [being] but that it also has to be understood as an agent, and therefore the categories of actuality as well as of substantiality apply to it.

However, although all kinds of conditions and activities in the life of the soul are unconscious, it is at the same time not desirable to devise a special theory of the unconscious for the soul, because the soul with its powers and habits in effect teaches the same thing more simply, and the term "unconsciousness," without explaining anything, requires explanation itself. Nor does it merit any recommendation to apply the term of the unconscious to the processes of the brain (unconscious cerebration, the physiological unconscious), since these are not part of the realm of psychology but rather of physiology.

For the same reason, we should not approve of any talk of unconscious impressions, feelings, and acts of the will, because these phenomena always imply some consciousness.

The unconscious (half, weak, double consciousness) is the name for that important group of phenomena of the soul that may be lying outside the center of the conscious (outside of perception and attentiveness) but which nevertheless do not fall totally outside of it. Although the boundary between this weak consciousness and the absolute unconscious is often difficult to determine, the group of phenomena just mentioned are not a sufficient basis for building a theory of the unconscious on it.

This subconscious, however, does provide a good service when explaining other phenomena of the soul, such as dreams, hypnosis, the alteration of personality, various forms of lunacy; but it cannot offer a satisfactory

---

Amsterdammer (March 21) and following issues of this year [1915]. It would also be interesting to trace this modern idea of God with Lotze, Fechner, Paulsen, Eucken, Windelband (Einleitung in die Philosophie, 414 ff.), Emerson, James, Myers, Boutroux, Poincaré, Bergson, et al., but this is not the appropriate place.

solution [207] of all these phenomena that may be summarized under the name of the occult.

Nor is the theory of the un- or subconscious any more capable of explaining the ethical conflict in human beings:[59] first, because the proponents of the theory of the un- or subconscious are very much divided among[60] themselves about the intellectual as well as the ethical quality of this un- or subconscious; and second, because the struggle between reason and lust (conscience and passion, duty and inclination), just as the struggle in believers between flesh and spirit (old and new man, Rom. 7:14–25; Gal. 5:17; etc.), is totally different from the one between the unconscious and the subconscious.

The theory of the unconscious finds support in Holy Scripture insofar as it definitely takes the view that the soul is much richer and deeper than the consciousness (Ps. 44:21; Prov. 4:23; Jer. 17:9–10; 1 Cor. 14:25; 1 Pet. 3:4; etc.), and it posits this thought as basic to its doctrine of sin (Gen. 8:21; Pss. 19:12; 51:10; Jer. 17:9; Mark 7:21), of regeneration (Jer. 31:33; John 3:8), of the mystical union (Rom. 8:16; Gal. 2:20), of inspiration (2 Pet. 1:21), and of obsession (John 13:2; Acts 5:3).

On the other hand, Holy Scripture distinguishes between the secret things, which belong to the Lord, and the revealed things, which are for us and our children (Deut. 29:29); it teaches that all our knowledge can be obtained only via the normal way, from general and special revelation (nature, history, Scripture: Isa. 8:19–20; 40:21–26; Rom. 1:20; 10:6–8; 1 Cor. 2:9), and therefore forbids all manticism and magic (Lev. 20:6; Deut. 18:10–12; 1 Sam. 28:7; Isa. 8:19–20; Mic. 3:7; Rev. 21:8; 22:15).

All these pronouncements of Holy Scripture are intimately connected with theism, which diametrically opposes pantheism and occultism as well as agnosticism and gnosticism.

59. Cf., e.g., Noorduyn, *Het onder-bewustzijn*, 37.

60. According to Sidis (see Loewenfeld, *Bewusstsein und psychisches Geschehen*, 47), the unconscious is dull, has no critical capacity, is easily persuaded, servantile, cowardly, without morality; and according to Freud, the content of the unconscious is in the final analysis always sexual lust. On the contrary, Maudsley, Carlyle, James, Myers, et al. claim that all that is good and noble arises from the unconscious.

# 11

# PRIMACY OF THE INTELLECT
# OR THE WILL

[208] Opinions have always been divided about the priority of the intellect or the will, both among people generally and especially among psychologists and philosophers. This disparity can be explained to a remarkable degree by the difference in nature and character, in gender and age, in experience and environment. From the beginning one person is more rational, another more emotional, and a third more willful. The intellect is generally more developed in a man and emotions more in a woman. Also, in his early years a person is more sanguine, in his youth more melancholy, in adulthood more choleric, and in old age more phlegmatic. Thus age and experience exert their influence in the appreciation of the intellect, the heart, and the will; in the first half of life there is high expectation, and one usually cherishes the power of thought and the exertion of the will, but in the second half there often is disappointment, doubt, or quiet resignation.

Philosophers therefore also differ considerably in their thoughts about the primacy of the intellect or of the will. From the beginning, Eastern philosophy had a different character from Western philosophy in Greece. The former is mystical and theosophical, the latter is characterized from the beginning by intellectualism. Socrates even considered virtue to be knowledge; Pythagoras, Plato, and others assigned priority to thought, also above sensory perception, and tried to construct the world of being from the world of ideas. The

Ed. note: Originally published as "Primaat van verstand of wil?" in *Paedogogisch tijdschrift* 13 (1921): 15–21.

intellect was the foundation of the soul and the creative, shaping power of the world.

Christianity brought another perspective; it appeared antithetically against worldly wisdom and placed it over against the foolishness of the cross. [209] It placed the emphasis on spiritual renewal (regeneration), on faith and conversion, and on good deeds, which no doubt arise more from the heart than from the head, because with the heart we believe unto righteousness and with the mouth confession is made unto salvation (Rom. 10:10). It was especially the church father Augustine who (although his philosophy otherwise was strongly Platonic) took into account this significance of heart and will. At times he emphasized the will so strongly that in modern times many have counted him among the voluntarists.

Whatever the case, medieval Scholasticism, with Thomas Aquinas as its principal representative, was predominantly intellectual; the intellect was considered to be the most precious gift to humanity—higher and nobler than the will. It was the same with the newer philosophy introduced by Bacon and Descartes. Both branches set great store by the intellect, although the first attached greater value to sensory perception and induction and the second more to thought and the deductive method. This philosophy resulted in the Enlightenment of the eighteenth century, which was thoroughly rationalistic and idolized reason. Kant also continued in this direction. He gave priority to practical reason over theoretical reason, because it established the supersensory (which could not be known or proved) as reality by faith; nevertheless, according to Kant, it was reason that promulgated the moral law and built theological postulates on that. And this elevation of reason led further to the idealistic philosophy and panlogism of Hegel.

However, this development of intellectualism and rationalism always evokes a reaction about the heart and the will. During the Middle Ages, mysticism arose next to Scholasticism, and Rousseau opposed the rationalism of the eighteenth century. This was followed by Romanticism and later by the voluntaristic philosophy of Schelling, Schopenhauer, and von Hartmann, by Nietzsche's teaching about the power of the will and the *Übermensch*, and the pragmatism of James and others. This voluntarism sees the most prominent factor of the life of the soul not in the intellect but in the will and conceives of the will as a force, which is either still connected to some consciousness or precedes it as a blind, illogical will and in due time produces consciousness.

And as the life of the soul is perceived, so another metaphysical building is erected on it. If a person lacks an objective norm in his thought, for example, in the Holy Scriptures, then he constructs the world and God according to his own image. [210] If the intellect is the real essence of the soul, then the world is seen as embodied thought, world events as a psychic process, and God as Reason. If, however, the will is considered to be the basic force of the soul, then it naturally follows that people will imagine the world and God as will. The will is then the original being; the will is substantial and primary in all creatures, plants, animals, and people; imagination and consciousness are secondary. God himself is will, the force in all things. Psychological intellectualism and voluntarism lead to analogical conceptions in metaphysics; as one takes a position in psychology and metaphysics, one is forced into a specific position in pedagogy. Thus one has to choose, for example, between [Johann Friedrich] Herbart and [Wilhelm] Wundt, between an academic and a trade school.

If one wishes to form a somewhat independent judgment about the important question posed regarding the primacy of the intellect or the will, one must give a careful account of the meaning of intellect and will and the primacy of one of those terms. And then one must note that the intellect certainly is not total consciousness, not even the most important part of it, but only a certain function of cognition. In cognition we distinguish, for example, sensory perception, memory, imagination, conscience, reason, and then also the intellect. In our consciousness we encounter not only conceptions (with judgments and decisions), but also awareness, memory, images, ideas, ideals. It is therefore very one-sided, even a total misunderstanding of reality, if one identifies consciousness or even thought itself with the intellect. In earlier times, when one normally had a broader conception of the intellect [*intellectus*], one could somewhat justify it, but today, when the intellect is usually described as the capacity for ideas, such identification is completely unjustified.

The same holds true for the will. The so-called capacity for desire or striving is certainly not identical with the will or willing; instead, it covers a much wider area. Besides the actual willing, one also encounters terms such as feelings, moods, affections, passions, inclinations, striving, desires. Among all these phenomena that we notice in the capacity of knowing and striving, the intellect and the will assume a much smaller place in life than we normally think. In everyday life a person experiences many more ideas, images, sensations, and desires than conceptions, logical reasons, and intentional decisions of the will. [211] Therefore, when we discuss the primacy of the intellect or the will, we must know what we mean. Are we considering the intellect or the will only in a narrow and limited sense, or are we considering consciousness and striving in their broadest meaning? If the latter, then we encounter not one question but many—or rather, the question then comes to us in various stages. For the sake of brevity, we will here distinguish three issues: Is it a primacy of instinct or striving? of ideas or desire? and then, more narrowly, of the intellect or of the will?

However, before we make a brief remark about each of these three questions, we must know what we mean by "primacy." Does one wish to state only that the intellect or the will assumes first place? Or does one wish to relate this purely chronological order to the idea that one or the other has priority, is the most outstanding, excels above the other capacity? And finally, is it also necessary to answer a question: Does this primogeniture of the intellect or of the will perhaps also carry a certain power or dominion of the one capacity over the other? Is the intellect the master of the will, or does the will govern the intellect? If one bears in intellect the significance attributed to the word "primacy" (for example, when speaking about the primacy of Saint Peter or of the pope), then no one will consider these questions superfluous.

All these questions will benefit us in our attempt to determine our position regarding the problem posed earlier. Let us first look at instinct or striving. Instinct is usually described as an unconscious but purposeful action (an infant seeking the mother's breast, birds building their nest, their migration in the spring and fall). This description is not totally wrong, but it is open to misunderstanding. The instinct is based on a feeling, a notion, an awareness of desire or aversion, and thus is not completely unconscious. And that consciousness, no matter how weak, undoubtedly precedes the action. The action appears to be unconscious, but it behooves us to speak with great modesty, because we really do not know much about the activity. We can penetrate into the animal soul of the newborn child only so far as we see an analogy in ourselves, but we actually remain outside of it, especially if the conscious comes closer to the unconscious and seems to arise slowly from it.

[212] But without going into this any further, it is certain that the action (for example, the movement to the mother's breast) presumes the feeling of desire or aversion mentioned above but does not arise from it. It points back to an inborn striving, to an original force in the organism. When the infant feels hungry, then it seeks, gropes for, and takes the mother's breast. There is no indication here of priority or dominance, but there is harmony and cooperation between the two factors. That harmony seems self-evident and totally natural, but as we consider it carefully, we are here faced with an inexplicable fact, a divine ordering. The animal psychologist Lloyd Morgan states that the harmony between the biologically valuable and individual fulfillment is an original given that we must accept if we want to understand life at all. Soul and body, spirit and matter, subject and object, man and world—these are made and meant for each other.

What else is involved in the relationship between idea and desire? On the one hand it is difficult to deny that there are no desires without ideas, nor can there be. One cannot desire the unknown; *ignoti nulla cupido* [there is no desire for what is unknown]: unknown is unloved. There is no desire or aversion, no love or hate, no affection or repugnance, without our having some consciousness of it. But again, one must understand this carefully. Desire itself as *act* presupposes consciousness, a realization, an idea of that which one desires, but the realization does not arise from or is not generated by that consciousness; rather, the idea points back to another, original capacity or power of the soul. And that desire as *capacity*, as potential, is present in the soul from the beginning. The capacities for knowing, desiring, and striving are equally as original as *capacity* so that one cannot speak of primacy or even of priority. As mentioned above, the idea of desiring as *action* precedes the desire, but this priority is not the same as primacy, priority, or dominance. After all, even though there are no actual desires without ideas, there are ideas without desires. The awareness of beauty occurs apart from desire; many ideas are recognized and accepted as true by many people, without desire playing a role. It is true that as soon as our self-interest comes into play, we are able to call white black and truth a lie, but that actually proves that desire often dominates the idea. That is to say that the idea certainly has influence on desire but that, speaking relatively, the power of desire over the idea is often much greater. [213] Idea and desire respond to each other; they continually act on each other.

This will become even more clear when we finally focus on the primacy of intellect or will. However, we still must briefly address the distinction between intellect and reason. The distinction is not easy to formulate and earlier was determined quite differently than today. Here it will suffice to indicate the usual distinction that the intellect is the capacity for concepts and reason the capacity for ideas. The eighteenth century was rationalistic, the nineteenth intellectualistic. Reason has content; it contains a series of norms, maxims, and a prioris and in the light of those sees reality and strives for a logical, a logos-constructed, world. The intellect, on the other hand, is a formal capacity: it does not contain content, it wants to set aside all prejudices and preconceptions, it idolizes thought without presuppositions [*Voraussetzunglosigkeit*], and it imagines the ideal of a completely comprehensible, mechanical world. As we noted above, both conceptions were attacked by voluntarism, which allowed that it was perhaps true that the whole world is logically constructed and in its essence rests on reason, but this *essence* is different from *existence*. The being, the existence, of the world is derived not from pure thought but only from act of will (will-deed). Schelling and others therefore said that the will is primal essence.

However, if the will is thus separated from all consciousness, then it is no longer the will in the true sense. Instead, it is joined either with blind impulse and fate, or with complete arbitrariness and happenstance. But that notion misuses the word "will" and leads to all kinds of error. In the true sense of the word, and according to an old definition, the will can be described as rational self-determination. Thus it can be clearly distinguished from striving, desiring, and so forth. Then it naturally follows that consciousness and specifically also reason (not just the idea) precede the will. More exactly, this is theoretical or practical reason: reason with norms of true and untrue, good and evil, beautiful and ugly; it is not reason as a formal capacity, but reason filled and enriched with knowledge.

But even here priority is certainly not the same as primacy, privilege, and dominance. Certainly, intellect and reason offer the will ideas (thoughts), introduce choices, and offer advice; however, intellect and reason have no other power than that of reasonable and moral persuasion, because the freedom of the will (which is a fact) excludes force.

On the other hand, the will certainly [214] has great power over consciousness, the intellect, and reason. First of all, it is the will that puts observation and thought to work and keeps them working. Attention is therefore as much the work of the will as of the intellect, and the will (rooted in desiring and frequently in desire) often pushes attention and thought into a certain direction. If this were not so, then there would not be a sinful darkening of the intellect. From the heart come the issues of life and the life of the intellect. The kind of philosophy one has depends on the kind of person one is. The intellect and the will are therefore in reciprocity: the head enriches the heart, but the heart directs and leads the head.

Let us add a final comment here that also has pedagogical value. The intellect may and must precede the will, but sometimes the will does not come along, and then the intellect must let the will go its own way. People usually *know* better, but they do not *want* to do right. In every person there is a duel. But this is different from the one experienced by Paul in Romans 7. Paul did not only *know* better, but he also *wanted* to do better; he had a devout, heartfelt desire to do God's will, but he *could not* do better because of the power of the flesh. The natural man, however, *knows* better, but he does not *will* to do better. In the core of his personality, Paul is on the side of God's law; but the natural, unregenerate person is, in the core of his personality, outside and over against God's law, even though he must agree with his intellect (his conscience) that the law is good. Knowledge alone does not convert a person, does not turn around the heart and the will. The will, on the other hand, often exerts great power over the intellect, on reason, and even on conscience and leads these in a certain direction, be it right or wrong.

Let us therefore not disagree about the priority of the intellect or of the will. Both are outstanding gifts, placed by God in human nature. Each has its own terrain and exercises dominance there. The intellect (the capacity for knowing) is necessary for the acquiring of knowledge; the will (the capacity for striving) is indispensable for determining our stance over against the known world. Both must be formed and developed in the child. Education and nurture, development of the intellect and character formation always belong together. They relate to each other every moment—the intellect to the will and the will to the intellect. Sin has broken the oneness, the harmony between these two and replaced friendship with enmity. But Christian nurture again seeks agreement and cooperation; it again restores honor that belongs to both; it strives for perfection of the whole person.

# 12
# TRENDS IN PEDAGOGY

[215] Pedagogy is a philosophic subject and is closely related to theology or philosophy. It is true that recently there have been various attempts to loosen this bond and to make pedagogy a completely independent subject. These attempts, however, will not succeed because education always assumes an answer to questions about human origin, essence, and purpose; and this answer (if ever possible) cannot be supplied by any exact science, but only by religion or philosophy.

The history of education and its theory confirms this in all nations and all times. Everywhere they are governed by worldviews and also by the cultural situation and social milieu. This is true for undeveloped and developed people, for people from East and West. Theologians and philosophers have therefore been especially occupied with the problem of education.

One can thus understand that Christianity brought about a great change in the theory and practice of education. Christianity is not pedagogy as such, no more than it is a social or political system or some kind of special science. Through regeneration, Christianity has made the person a citizen of the kingdom of heaven and has put him in a new, childlike relationship with God. At the same time, it had a most powerful influence on all of life in society and state, in science and art, and also on education and nurture. This influence is also shown in the fact that when Christianity through the ages split into various churches and confessions, each of these groups brought about its special and unique changes in the common educational ideal.

Ed. note: Originally published as "Richtingen in de psychologie," *Paedogogisch tijdschrift* 1 (1909): 172–82.

[216] In addition, especially since the Renaissance, various other educational ideals have found acceptance, all of which had a more-or-less philosophical origin and attained widespread supremacy, especially through the Enlightenment and the more recent philosophy. Hegel's speculative rationalism particularly exercised a powerful influence on schools and education in the nineteenth century: it forced both in a one-sided intellectualistic direction, which was also fostered through the flowering of natural science and [Johann Friedrich] Herbart's psychology.

However, since about 1870 a strong reaction has, for various reasons, developed against this intellectualism. The promise that the money given to schools would be provided through less cost for prisons did not come true. The misery in the lowest classes increased dramatically. With further research, science proved unable to solve the deepest problems. The better they became known, the soul and life and even nature proved to contain more mysteries. Russian and Norwegian novels brought to light unexpected depths of humanity and the world. And the outcome of the French-German War [1870–71] proved that the Romance peoples were far behind the German and Anglo-Saxon race.

Thus the praise and jubilation about schools and education, also for a long time in our country, gradually gave way to pessimistic complaints and unmerciful judgments. At times the criticism hardly left anything intact. Following Rousseau and Tolstoy, all of our culture was condemned and regarded as the cause of all our miseries. Our modern education was particularly considered to be an impenetrable thicket of foolishness, prejudices, and blunders. Education, it was said, destroyed all that was good in a child: desire for knowledge, capability of observation, independence and personality. Instead, education filled children with fear and fright, brought about anemia and nervous breakdown, and often caused suicide. It would be desirable if a flood would come and obliterate education from the earth. Even though the criticism was fortunately not always this shrill, nearly everyone became convinced that our system of schooling and education, which for years had been regarded as nearly perfect, was terribly deficient. Thus reformation had to come, not just here and there, on some issues, but completely and radically, in head and members.

And thus the designers and builders of all civilized nations got to work. They can generally be divided into four groups. The first group is formed by those who know no other firm foundation either for all of our culture or for our school system than what Christianity offers in its ecclesiastical confessions. [217] Even though it would certainly be worth the effort to review this group, because of time constraints, it can be omitted in this place and for this group until another opportunity. Just permit this observation: this group forms a broader phalanx, assumes a firmer position, and is more strongly armed than its opponents imagine. Moreover, this group inspires us with courage in the struggle in our country, encourages us to persevere, and even more than they have till now, can provide us with weapons and equip us for both offense and defense.

A second group is formed by those who want to place pedagogy on one of the idealistically tinted philosophies, such as the moralism (independent morality) of [William] Salter, the pragmatism of [William] James, the voluntarism of [Wilhelm] Wundt, the philosophy of spirit of [Rudolf] Eucken, the creative evolution of Henri Bergson, and others who have made their entrée into the modern world. They differ in many ways among themselves, but they all agree in connecting with the doctrine of evolution and making it serve teleology. In nature everything proceeds mechanically and according to fixed laws, but finally in humanity, nature produced a being that is equipped with understanding or spirit or intuition, with moral consciousness or self-consciousness or will. This being is therefore able to turn itself around and to turn against nature, to break its mechanism and inevitability, and to rule and lead nature according to its will. Humanity is therefore open to education, and this education serves especially to strengthen body and soul, to exercise the will, to form the character, to enrich the emotions, and to develop personality. This process will be served not only by education and physical training but also by art and religion and morality. Superficial and one-sided intellectualism has disdained these pedagogical strengths and banished them from the schools, but they must be brought back because they are indispensable means for human perfection.

In a third group one can include all those who want to make pedagogy independent from all metaphysics and instead build pedagogy on modern society or modern learning. The first group can again be divided into the pedagogues who make society subject to the individual, and others who subordinate the individual to society. [218] The founders of individualistic pedagogy were Max Stirner and F[riedrich] Nietzsche, and the builders were Ellen Key with H. Pudor, A. Bonus, L. Gurlitt, and others. While they hurled their anathemas at all of modern society and culture, in the schools they were busy with tremendous passion for the rights, freedom, independence, and even the majesty of the child. And in their coat of arms they all carried, with muted or glaring colors, the slogan, "Who trains the least trains the best."

Others, however, were diametrically opposed to them and were deeply impressed with current social life: they thought that above all they should educate the individual as a member of society. This approach generally works very well and moderately in the social pedagogy of [Paul] Natorp. It is already much more one-sided in the national education of Doctor [George] Kerschensteiner in Munich, who in the modern democratic, industrial state wants to achieve general education through vocational training and to create the ideal person as a useful person.

This educational ideal is still more radical in the pedagogy of Paul Berge-mann, who completely disallows the rights of the individual and grossly exaggerates the importance of society. This idea is lauded in the most radical and consequential manner in the Social-Democratic Party [in the Netherlands]. In its program, this party mostly limits itself to what can be achieved in the foreseeable future, but from there it advances to [August] Bebel's explanation, which intends the socialization of all of education. Thus, no matter how many important differences there are in social pedagogy, as a whole the movement is characterized by the idea that it sees in schooling and education a *means* [to reach the place] where only society (the state) is in control and where it can maintain itself and reach perfection.

Among those who wish to make pedagogy independent, we mentioned the pedagogues who look for a foundation in modern science. In general they can be called positivists, although they differ among themselves. They either look for positive ideas that can serve as a foundation for the philosophy of education, in a certain hierarchy of sciences (along with the older positivists such as [Auguste] Comte and [Herbert] Spencer), or they try to find them in empirical psychology (especially child psychology) and experimental peda-gogy (along with the more recent proponents). However, the latter view leads imperceptibly to the most modern, biological interpretation of pedagogy that Stanley Hall promotes in America, regarding schooling and education as only one of the many means for improving the human race.

[219] Many of the attempts we have mentioned are not only proposed on paper, but have also been put into practice. We will not discuss those because of time constraints. Let us in conclusion merely summarize this brief overview of the trends in pedagogy: (1) Negatively and formally, there is great agreement, because all these reformers consider the existing situation insufficient, and they press for transforming the whole school system, such as improvement in the training and position of teachers, better divisions and connections among the schools, sifting and selection of pupils, smaller classes, fewer subjects, and so forth. (2) As soon as principles enter the discussion, there are all kinds of differences and strife—about the relationship of Chris-tianity and culture, family and school, the individual and society, body and soul, mind and will, and so forth. (3) With a completely secular idea of the task of education, these differences are irreconcilable, because the purpose of the creature is never found in the creature itself, but from the nature of things, only in God, the Creator.

# 13

# Classical Education

[220] The word *Classicus* in itself means no more than belonging to a class, but in ancient Rome it was the name of the citizen who belonged to the wealthiest and most heavily taxed class. According to tradition, King Servius Tullius divided the whole Roman population by property into five classes: those in the first class, who paid the highest taxes, were the *classici* par excellence. Classified apart from them and from proprietors in general were the *proletarii*, who could not serve the state with their money but only with their offspring; according to Servius Tullius's division, they constituted the sixth and poorest class.

It is easy to understand that the word *classicus* was soon transferred to people who excelled above others in other areas. It was used, for example, for a witness who was completely reliable, of a writer of the first rank, of a student who excelled others with his gifts, and so forth. This distinction continued as long as Latin was spoken, but it disappeared in the Middle Ages [only] to reappear in the time of the Renaissance. The term then assumes the general meaning of excellent and exemplary, and it becomes the designation for whatever is authoritative and serves as a model. And while humanism assigned authority mainly or exclusively to Greek and Latin writers, *classicus* became limited to authors of "classical" antiquity.

The study and imitation of the writers during the flowering of Greek literature goes back to well before our Christian calendar. In general, one can say that as soon as literature and art have reached their highest development

Ed. note: Originally published as "Klassieke opvoeding, I, II," in *Stemmen des tijds* 7/1 (1918): 46–65, 113–47.

with a certain group of people, then a different direction arises among the epigoni. Some, already called "moderns" in ancient times, want to press forward and go their own way, but others look with adoration to the past and seek their goal in imitation of the masters. [221] Originality and imitation, Romanticism and classicism, freedom and authority change continually, also in the arts. Authority gained the upper hand when the high-mindedness of Ptolemy's followers gained lofty heights in the scholarship of Alexandria, and the library there acquired many manuscripts. At that time the Greek writers from previous centuries were studied diligently and interpreted and explained in many different ways; grammar, criticism, and the history of literature were practiced carefully. The foundations of philological scholarship were established there, but originality was replaced more and more by imitation.

This imitation became true especially in the third century before Christ, when the so-called Asiatic outlook arose in Asia Minor, which took delight in an artificial, puffed-up style. At that time many orators and writers took the Attic writers of the fifth and fourth centuries before Christ as their model; they were designated as proponents of Atticism. An identical movement occurred later in Rome, when the verbose rhetoric of Sulpicius and especially of Hortensius (114–50 BC) elicited a reaction from Cicero, the student of Molon in Rhodes (hence, the School of Rhodes); an even stronger reaction came from the followers of the old Attici, such as Pollio, Caesar, and others.

However, Greek language and culture continually declined from that time on, both in the West and in the East. This tradition deteriorated into empty declamations of rhetoricians, such as Libanius; exhausted itself in attempts to attack Christianity, [attacks] as practiced by Celsus and Porphyry; or tried to restore itself by renewing the systems of Pythagoras and Plato. In 529, Emperor Justinian forbade education in philosophy in Athens. Then the schools of the Syrian Christians in Edessa, Nisibis, Damascus, and others became the seats of Greek learning. There the Arabs became acquainted with this learning, and in an unbelievably short time they were able to make this learning their own and to elevate it to its highest flowering. Centuries later Greek literature became known again in Christian Europe, via a detour through Syria and Arabia and through Arabian and Jewish writers in Spain.

When Christianity gained entrance into the Greco-Roman world through the preaching of the apostles, it soon faced the serious question about its posture toward the existing richly developed culture. This question had to be faced practically even before it had been considered theoretically. [222] The admonition of Christ and the apostles that one must not be conformed to the world, but must bear all persecution and violence patiently, resounded very seriously. In their teaching, critical and passive qualities were so obvious that there was virtually no room for active participation in the life of the culture. Still, Christians were in the world and were not able to leave the world. Such might be possible for a few ascetically inclined people, but the majority could not live that way. They got married and were given in marriage; they had children and had to educate them for some kind of occupation. They themselves were involved in various jobs and had to work for their daily bread. Thus they participated in manual labor and industry, in commerce and shipping, and even in the service of army and state. The same happened in relation to the ideal elements in the Greco-Roman culture, such as literature and art, science and philosophy. Here again, the practical question arose before the theoretical, because they had children who had to be educated and the Christians themselves desired a learned profession. Where could one obtain such training apart from the pagan schools? After all, in the beginning the Christians themselves did not have their own institutions of education, except for the catechumenate, and for a long time in many places lacked such institutions.

As soon as the question was posed in theory, there was difference of opinion. Tatian and Tertullian stood on one side and wanted nothing to do (at least in theory) with pagan philosophy. "What does Jerusalem have to do with Athens, the academy with the church? We no longer need philosophy since Jesus, and no scientific research since the gospel. The whole culture of the Roman Empire is a *pompa diaboli* [the devil's parade], because whatever is not from God is of the devil."[1] Directly opposed to this view stood the Alexandrian school of Clement and Origen, which loved literature and sought a union of philosophy and theology, of culture and Christianity. Many Christians continued to cling to the ancient culture with deep affection, and such were saddened when it was ruined, as ancient history eventually turned into the Middle Ages. In the East, toward the end of the fourth century, Nemesius, bishop of Emesa in Phoenicia, and Synesius, bishop of Ptolemy, are typical examples of such affection; both continued to retain their Neoplatonic systems. In the fourth and fifth centuries in the West, Ausonius and Sidonius proved that interest in Latin literature continued in Gaul as well, and [for them] even surpassed their interest in Christianity. [223] Actually, the "great unknown," who received the name [Pseudo-]Dionysius the Areopagite, took over the philosophy and expressions of Neoplatonism and gave them a legitimate place in Christian mysticism in the beginning of the sixth century.

1. Ed. note: The quotation marks are added; Bavinck is actually paraphrasing here and does not cite the actual passage from Tertullian. Here is the full citation:
What indeed has Athens to do with Jerusalem? What concord is there between the Academy and the Church? What between heretics and Christians? Our instruction comes from "the porch of Solomon" [Acts 3:11], who had himself taught that "the Lord should be sought in simplicity of heart" [Wis. 1:1]. Away with all attempts to produce a mottled Christianity of Stoic, Platonic, and dialectic composition! We want no curious disputation after possessing Christ Jesus, no inquisition after enjoying the gospel! With our faith, we desire no further belief. For this is our palmary faith, that there is nothing which we ought to believe besides. ("On Prescription against Heretics" 7; in *Ante-Nicene Fathers* 3:246)

The church sought to avoid the one extreme as well as the other and took a middle road. On the one hand, the church could not deny asceticism because it had already sunk its roots much too deeply into the life of piety, was supported everywhere by the dualistic thought of the age, and from the second century was encouraged and promoted by the church itself. However, the church did force asceticism into narrower boundaries, assigned it an important but not an exclusive place, and was able to absorb it and make it serve its own ends. In the meantime the church steadily assumed a more positive attitude with regard to the world, especially since the days of Constantine. It absorbed as much culture as was necessary to subject and guide it, and the church raised itself to be an empire of culture, which soon governed all areas of secular life. Thus, on the one hand, the church acknowledged marriage, family, occupations, science, art, and so forth as natural gifts that could be appreciated and enjoyed (as Augustine said, *magna haec et omnino humana* [this is great and wholly human]). On the other hand, all these gifts were of a lower rank, inferior to and in the service of the supernatural order, which had descended to earth in the church and in its hierarchy, mysteries, and sacraments.

Christians could thus make free use of the treasures that the Greco-Roman culture possessed. They were like the people of Israel, who in their departure from Egypt had taken the gold and silver of their oppressors and decorated the tabernacle with it. Christians performed a God-pleasing work when they dedicated all human gifts and energies that had been revealed in ancient culture to its highest purpose. Thus the paintings in the catacombs already resembled the style of antiquity, the architecture of the churches was arranged according to the models of the basilica, and philosophy was used for the defense of the Christian faith. In all these cases practice preceded theory, but the theory soon received its recommendation and justification from men such as Gregory and Basil in the East and Lactantius, Ambrose, and Augustine in the West.

[224] In the same way, the church accepted Latin as the church language. Until the beginning of the third century, Greek had been the church language in Rome—not Attic Greek, but the Hellenistic common language [Koine Greek] that came into use after Alexander in the then-known world. But this Greek was slowly replaced by Latin, first in the African church, and after that in Rome. The division of the Roman Empire into an Eastern and a Western part lent a hand to this disappearance of Greek from the western part of Europe; around the seventh century it was virtually unknown here. However, the Latin that took its place was generally not classical Latin but the common written and spoken language of the era of the emperors; besides, all kinds of foreign elements and newly formed words became an accepted part of the language. Jerome especially exerted great influence on this church Latin, first through his translation of the Vulgate and second through his editing of the

prayers of the church of Rome. Later, this church Latin was further developed, changed, and enriched through Scholasticism and the Renaissance.

In still another way the church gave opportunity to the ancient culture. In the violent times experienced by Europe during and after the mass migrations, an incredible amount of art and literature of antiquity disappeared. Thus one must appreciate even more the boon that a great number of manuscripts were collected, saved, read, and copied in the monasteries. The first monastery library was founded by Cassiodorus around 540 in the monastery Vivarium in Bruttium. When he withdrew from public life at this time, he devoted himself completely to literary work and made this work compulsory for all the monks in his monastery. For this task he supplied all the available tools known at the time and presented his own work as a model. His monastery was destroyed in 580, but the Benedictine monks of Nursia continued this work in his spirit and made the monasteries foci of civilization and asylums of scholarship.

This striving for learning, which found its center in the monasteries with the transition to the Middle Ages, was promoted by the fact that various learned men did their utmost to collect the knowledge and wisdom gained in antiquity and to provide brief summaries. Boethius had already made a beginning with this effort. (He was connected with the court of Theodore the Great for a long time, but in 524 he fell into disfavor and two years later he was executed.) [225] Boethius laid the foundation for medieval scholarship. He made many writings of Aristotle available to the West through translation and commentary. His translation of the *Isagoge* of Porphyry became the handbook for logic, his writings in mathematics and music provided the building blocks for these disciplines, and his theological treatises adjusted Aristotelian philosophy to theology and thus prepared the medieval method for the practice of all scholarship. Other men continued this work: Martianus Capella (ca. 430), Cassiodorus (ca. 540), and Isidore of Seville (ca. 636) prepared textbooks about the so-called seven liberal arts [*artes liberales*], divided into trivium and quadrivium, and thus handed down the knowledge of antiquity to the Middle Ages.

Moreover, the ancient rhetorical schools continued in the Frankish Empire under the Merovingians (481–752). These schools devoted great care to the practice of received art forms and styles, and they promoted a one-sided formalism. However, they also provided opportunity for a cultured education and imparted all kinds of knowledge. Several Frankish kings were friends of Latin poetry, and women from that time were often praised for their education and knowledge. Later these studies found a strong protector in Charlemagne. For the elevation of the Christian life, he needed an educated clergy; he therefore founded a school at his court, with the leadership assigned to Alcuin [from 782], and here education was provided in all seven liberal arts as preparation for theology. Of even more importance were the cathedral and monastery schools founded in the south, but with the Christianizing of people all over Europe, the most important bearers of this development came from Christian-Germanic culture.

This culture, that began during the Frankish reign and achieved its greatest flowering under Charlemagne, deteriorated during the ninth through the eleventh centuries but was regenerated in the eleventh and twelfth centuries through so-called Scholasticism. In a certain sense one can already see the beginning of Scholasticism with the method of scholarship by Alcuin, Rabanus Maurus, Paschasius Radbertus, Ratramnus, [John] Scotus Erigena, and others, but then one must distinguish between the preparatory period and the time of flowering that began only in the twelfth century. The first period, from about 800 to 1200, is marked more by its Platonic, Neoplatonic, and Augustinian character; the second period is much more influenced by Aristotle and Boethius. [226] It was introduced to this influence because Christian Europe—through the Arabs, Jews, and after 1453 the Greeks— gained knowledge of the many writings of Aristotle and the most significant works of Arab and Jewish scholars. Thus the West gained two things—first, better knowledge and stricter application of the dialectic method; and second, much richer scholarly material in the areas of physics and metaphysics, of psychology and ethics, of jurisprudence and theology. As soon as Christian scholars began to use these methods, Scholasticism achieved its highest flowering and gave the university its existence.

In this period Scholasticism went back to antiquity (especially to Aristotle and his commentator Boethius) in much greater degree than during Charlemagne's time. In the Middle Ages it was exactly this scholarly direction—the method and ideas of Aristotle's philosophy—that influenced theology, philosophy, and all disciplines known at that time. Aristotle became *praecursor Christi in naturalibus* [precursor of Jesus in natural matters] just as John the Baptist was *praecursor in gratuitis* [precursor in matters of grace].

However, although Scholasticism was very occupied with the works of antiquity and with those of Arab and Jewish scholars, one cannot actually speak of classical education and classical study. After all, Greek was completely unknown; people read the Greek authors, including Aristotle, only in translations and commentaries. Neither did people read these works to be nurtured mentally or morally to true humanity, because there never is any indication of an aesthetic or cultural-historical appreciation of antiquity. The word "humanity" does occur in the Middle Ages but simply indicates (for example, in Thomas) a virtue among other virtues, such as friendship, piety, religion, and so forth, and the word "classical" is completely absent at this time. One learned Latin because it was the language of the church and of scholarship—certainly not to speak or write pure Ciceronian Latin. People did not consider it a dead but a living language; they handled it arbitrarily and formed the most barbaric words: from *a* and *se* they formed *aseitas*, from *per* and *se* came *perseitas*, and [they coined] words such as *entitas, ubeitas, quidditas,* and so forth. Thus people did not strive to be formed by classical Latin but instead to transform Latin to current demands, and to make it as serviceable as possible for practical purposes. In wealth of vocabulary and sentence structure, one became more and more separated from original Latin.

[227] The same held true for the content of the literature. People still read Latin prose writers and poets, such as Caesar, Cicero, Ovid, Virgil, Horace, and so on, but especially philosophical works, notably Aristotle. People did not read literary works to be shaped by them but to obtain the knowledge that was found in them; Scholasticism had no other sources of learning than books. In theology, Scholasticism derived its life from Scripture and even more from the tradition of the church fathers. In scholarship and philosophy, one did not consult nature and history but the works that had been written about those fields in antiquity. And often people did not even consult these works but were satisfied with handbooks and textbooks; they quarried their information mainly from Capella, Cassiodorus, Donatus, and others. Classical literature was thus pushed to the background and had to give way to the study of art, grammar, rhetoric, dialectics, and so forth. Moreover, dialectics often became a means to make distinctions, pose questions, and open disputations that occurred completely outside of everyday life, and at the most [such discussions] had some academic worth.

It goes without saying that eventually there would be a reaction against such an academic system.[2] The reaction came in that peculiar cultural movement known as the Renaissance. If conceived broadly, this movement already began in the thirteenth century with Francis of Assisi and Dante. The Renaissance is nothing other than the birth of that new spirit that, over against the authority and objectivity of the medieval outlook, again emphasized the subject, the individual, and gradually revived the thirst for freedom. Since that time, one finds in Christian Europe an ever stronger desire for freedom—freedom from church, hierarchy, and tradition, from priest and sacrament, Scholastic theology and philosophy, from ingenious dialectic and barbaric Latin, from "Gothic" and barbaric art, from the unnatural and poor taste. Personality escapes from repressive power.

In this Renaissance, humanism assumed its own place, because it defined the spiritual direction that began in Italy with Petrarch in the fourteenth century; [228] humanism wanted to nurture and form the personality awakened to self-consciousness by putting it in touch immediately and directly with

2. For the following section, see especially the important work of Fr[iedrich] Paulsen, *Geschichte des gelehrten Unterrichts auf den deutschen Schulen und Universitäten vom Ausgang des Mittelalters bis zur Gegenwart: Mit besonderer Rücksicht auf den klassischen Unterricht* (Leipzig: Veit, 1885); idem, 2nd ed., 2 vols. (1896–97). On the Renaissance also see Doctor [N. B.] Tenhaeff, *Handelingen van het achtste Nederlands Philologen Congres, 26/27 Apr. 1916* (Leiden: Sythoff, 1916), 206ff.

ancient literature, the *humaniora*. It is true that in the arts department of the universities one also studied the liberal arts, but usually this knowledge was obtained only from textbooks. Humanists, however, wanted to return to the sources themselves, first to the Latin and later to the Greek writers. Petrarch was not yet acquainted with Greek, but Boccaccio could already read Homer in the original. Manuel Chrysoloras (d. ca. 1415, from Constantinople) from 1397 was the first teacher of Greek in Florence and other Italian cities [in the Middle Ages].

This study of the classics had a totally different goal in mind from that intended by Scholasticism. Humanism was very interested in nurture and education, and thought that the purpose of education was to be sought in *humanitas*. Originally this word meant only "humanness, friendliness, love of people" ("philanthropy," from Greek), but gradually it came to mean a humane culture that supersedes nationality and that must be acquired through education. It is curious that humanism sought this culture especially in reason, in *oratio*, as proof and expression of *ratio*. Joh[annes] Sturm and others usually described the purpose of education as *sapiens atque eloquens pietas* [wise and eloquent piety], and here the emphasis was just as strongly on *eloquens* as on *sapiens*. Humanism idolized *rhetorica*; it preferred to translate John 1:1 as *eloquentiai* or *sermo*: *in principia erat sermo*. In antiquity *humanitas* was also often related to *doctrina* or to *sermo* because knowledge and culture, that is, *ratio*, finds its most important expression in *oratio*, and the humanists liked the *ratio-oratio* wordplay very much.

The high estimate of the word was related to their opposition to Scholasticism. On the value of general concepts, the Scholastics were divided among themselves into realists and nominalists. The humanists, however, did not see the importance of this question and regarded it as a contrived argument that had to be discarded with all of Scholasticism. They also felt themselves, through a certain unconscious sympathy, most closely linked to the nominalists, because in their ideology, they valued the word higher than the realists. However, the humanists disapproved of both groups because they did not study Aristotle in his own, original writings but in translations and commentaries, and because they repeated his thoughts in an artificial, unnatural form, that did not do full justice to him. [229] But when they themselves began to study Aristotle, they were disappointed in his philosophy. They gradually reached the point of pulling down Aristotle from his lofty heights, where he had been placed by Scholasticism, and they also turned their backs on his dialectic and logic. Aristotle and Aristotelian philosophy had been elevated in the Middle Ages, but humanism regarded them as the great spoilers of reason, of healthy human understanding (*ratio*), of language, of style, of the natural expression of thoughts into words (*oratio*). Logic therefore had to give way to rhetoric, Aristotle to Cicero, and Quintilianic, barbaric Latin of the Middle Ages to pure, classical Latin.

When the humanists thus returned to the sources and became absorbed in the writings of the ancients, their eyes were opened to the beauty that was revealed in literature and the arts. It was as if they, like Columbus, had discovered a new world. Antiquity appeared to them as a period of ideal humanity, which one must now try to relive or at least to which one must try to lead all those who value human, real culture. With many humanists this revering of the classics turned into enmity against the church, Christianity, and even against all religion, although this was not always the case. Many strove for a reconciliation between humanism and Christianity, and with Joh[annes] Sturm described the purpose of education as *sapiens atque eloquens pietas*—as true piety linked organically with thorough knowledge and genuine culture. This description is not incorrect as such, but the humanists used it one-sidedly in the sense that knowledge of all things and noble formation could be acquired only through the study of the classics.

Nevertheless, humanism had commendable merits. One could mention many issues, but let us briefly point out a few. First, one must remember humanism for its significance in the Reformation. In the beginning there was great agreement and a strong relationship between the two movements. The return to Holy Scripture in the Reformation had its analogue in the humanist revival of classical antiquity. Luther was second to none in his scorn for Aristotle and Scholasticism; Melanchthon and Zwingli were humanists, and humanists like Erasmus, although they often pulled back later, promoted the Reformation strongly. [230] Second, humanism is to be thanked for the rich development it gave to the study of languages and related subjects. The interest in Greek and Latin literature led to the discovery of a multitude of manuscripts, from unknown to famous authors, which had to be critically sifted, published, and provided with commentaries. And many disciplines— poetics, rhetoric, philosophy, and history—benefited from these publications. From the classics, a literary-aesthetic appreciation came to expression that differed to a considerable degree from the philosophical use that Scholasticism had made of the classics. Universities appointed scholars in classical literature, who were characteristically called *poetae, oratores, rhetores*, professors in *eloquentia*. Classical philology achieved the rank of a significant and extensive discipline, especially through men such as J. J. Scaliger, [Claudius] Salmasius, J. G. Vossius, and others. One must notice, third, that classical education in the true sense owes its origin to humanism.

This classical education gradually received its own institutional place in the Latin school, the *gymnasium*. One must note here that at first there was no sharp distinction between the Latin school and the university. The school often included higher subjects in its education, and the university frequently included preparatory classes. As a result, mature men sometimes sat in the school desks, and lads of fifteen were enrolled as students in the university. There was great diversity among the curricula; nearly every school had its own curriculum. But gradually a division occurred. Melanchthon, the *praeceptor Germanae*, had especially great influence here. He organized the complete school system, wrote textbooks for various subjects, developed a plan for the universities and professional schools, and strongly emphasized preparation for theology through literary and philosophical study, because knowledge of the three languages of the cross was indispensable for the servant of the gospel.

Thus many schools came into existence in Germany, in our country, and elsewhere where Latin was learned to such a degree that one could speak and write it, and sometimes the fundamentals of Greek and Hebrew were taught as well. Actually, the teaching of Greek did not amount to much. When humanism arose in Italy, it showed great affection for Hellas; in the church a union between East and West was attempted (1439); [231] Greek scholars received an enthusiastic welcome in Italy after the [Ottoman Muslim] conquest of Constantinople [in 1453]; and Greek language and literature were practiced diligently. From Italy this love for Greek was transplanted to Germany; in 1485 Alexander Hegius, friend of Agricola and teacher of Erasmus, already adopted it in the curriculum of the school in Deventer; Melanchthon introduced it in Wittenberg in 1518; Joh[annes] Sturm made spacious room for it in the gymnasium in Strassburg in 1538, and the Jesuits followed this example in 1548. However, even though Greek appears in the curricula of many Latin schools since those early times, one must not form an exaggerated notion of this practice. Greek was often only a matter of memorization; Latin continued to be the chief subject, and the speaking and writing of Latin continued to be the main purpose of education.

There was also substantial disagreement about the writers to be read in these schools. Some, such as [Jacob] Wimpheling, wanted to exclude immoral writers such as Ovid and substitute Christian authors such as Lactantius, Ambrose, and the like. Others, for example Erasmus, limited the subject to classical authors but then differed over the question of whether Plautus could be admitted to the schools. There also were many names in use for these schools. People spoke of "Latin schools" in distinction from the old parochial and later the people's and city schools. But they also transferred the names "gymnasium," "academia," and "lyceum" to these preparatory schools, even though those designations were also used for the university, and they spoke of "gymnasium *illustre*" if the teaching of philosophy, theology, or other disciplines took place there. The name "gymnasium" was most in vogue; in Greek it was the name of the building for gymnastics; later it was used in Latin for a school of rhetoric. In the Middle Ages it became the general designation for a scholarly institution of education, and since the sixteenth century it gradually became the name for a school with a complete humanistic curriculum: with education in the three ancient languages, or at least the two classical languages.

The study of the classics, and in that connection classical education, already began to deteriorate in Germany in the seventeenth century and in other countries in the next century. There were several reasons for this deterioration. On the one hand, culture moved more and more in the direction of realism, which turned its back on verbalism. On the other hand, rationalism gained dominance; it trusted in the force of its own reason, and it looked down with disdain on the past, with its prejudices and superstitions. [232] The result was that interest in classical literature was lost and [that literature] was valued only for its historical value.

Philology, just as other disciplines, deteriorated into polyhistory, poly-mathematics, pansophism—into erudition that expressed itself in research-notes scholarship, scholarly citations, and encyclopedic tomes. Under the influence of this direction in scholarship, classical education increasingly took on a formal character; there was no longer any aesthetic or cultural or historical appreciation of the classics. The highest aim was the imitation, the replication of the ancients in language and style, prose and poetry. Latin and Greek really became dead languages—just a *Fundgrube* [mine] for citations and examples.

In the second half of the eighteenth century, Romanticism and neohuman-ism began to oppose this development. Both movements reacted against the Enlightenment, with its arid knowledge and abstract rational concepts; both also sought to go behind this cold system, to seize life itself in its im-mediacy and originality, in order to restore ardor and richness to one's own heart. Romanticism, however, turned to the Middle Ages and saw the most original and richest of such a life in Roman culture; meanwhile neohuman-ism looked to classical culture, found the highest and noblest expression of human life there, and tried to honor again the idea of humanness. [Johann Joachim] Winckelmann introduced this period of neohumanism. Already in his youth he was irresistibly attracted to the Greek writers. Later, when he went to Italy, he found in the works of antiquity what he had long sought— freedom, simplicity, truth, beauty, life. In his history of the art of antiquity, he uncovered this beauty to his contemporaries and placed it in opposition to the popular and insipid art and style of his age.

Winckelmann was the pioneer, and many others followed him. Lessing wrote his book about Laokoon, Goethe his poem about Iphigenie, Schiller sang of the Greek gods. Voss published his translation of the *Odyssey*. Herder listened to the voices of the nations in their songs and deeds, and there he heard the triumphal song of humanity. All these songs and works of art were expressions of one and the same soul that lived in the human bosom and then, according to place and time, expressed itself in various ways and forms by the people in the East and in the West, in the past and in the present, only in different ways and different forms. They altogether form one organic whole, are inspired by one thought, propelled by one divine force, and striving after one goal—the forming of the human race into genuine, free humanity. [233] According to Lessing, what appears to be education from our perspective is from God's perspective the revelation that he grants successively to mankind, thus leading them to the realm of the true, the good, and the beautiful, the human kingdom fused with God's kingdom.

This new perception of humanity for the first time awakened the historical sensibility and gave birth to the philosophy of history, of religion, and of language. But above all it became significant for classical study and classical education. Gesner and Heyne in Gottingen, F. A. Wolf in Halle, W. von Humboldt in Berlin, and others introduced neohumanism to the study of antiquity. This study differentiated itself very prominently from the Scholastic and old-humanistic conception.

First, the study of classical antiquity was elevated to an independent and organic discipline, especially by Wolf. He was the first to call it *Altertumswissenschaft*. It was to be a discipline that must get to know ancient humanity in all the expressions of its life—language, history, knowledge, art, philosophy, religion, morals, social and political relations, and so forth. It was to know these people not only in their words, but also in their deeds and works. This study must therefore be practiced for itself. It was not for the practical use that could be derived from it, nor just as preparation for theology and jurisprudence, but in the first place because of its own interest and worth. Classical study is an end in itself.

Second, the Greeks must be in the foreground in this study of antiquity. In the Middle Ages and also (although with different intent) with old humanism, Latin continued to be the main subject and usually nothing much came from the study of Greek. But neohumanism reversed these roles and gave priority to Greek language and literature. According to W. von Humboldt, no other people combined so much simplicity and nature with so much culture. People especially admired the expressive rest, the beautiful simplicity, the harmonious forms, the ideal completeness in the Greeks and all the expressions of their lives. The true, the good, and the beautiful were united in a unique and exemplary manner. With some neohumanists the revering of the Greeks took on a religious character; for them the highest ideal was to live as a Greek.

[234] Third, there was therefore, according to the neohumanists, no better means to educate a person to humanity and to produce harmonious development of all his gifts and powers than the study of Greek antiquity. After all, rationalism considers only the development of the mind and expects all benefits from reason. Supernaturalism is just as one-sided, and it educates only for eternity. The study of antiquity, however, develops both spirit and emotions, mind and heart, soul and body; it provides harmonious formation, an ethical-human education. Moreover, do the Greeks and Romans not far surpass the Jews in knowledge and civilization? According to Wolf,

Christianity was "through an addition of Greek thought Judaism improved, or if you will, through an addition of Judaism debased Greek thought." According to his student [August] Boeckh, Christianity was destined to be dissolved into purer humanity.

Fourth, in that case classical education itself must undergo a great change. With old humanism, *imitatio* was the goal of education. One had to learn Latin in such a way that one could speak and write like Cicero and think and express oneself in the same way as Latin speakers. Thus it became especially important to compile *res et verba* from the Latin—*verba* even more than *res* because the form was more important than the content. But here also neohumanism turned the order around. In classical education the main intent was not following and imitating the ancients. Instead, the significance was that through the reading of classical authors, one tried to enter into their spirit, to make their observation and thinking one's own, and then, being formed in this way, one could then begin to move freely and independently in this milieu. Thus the main purpose of formal formation from the texts was shifted; acquiring issues and words was replaced by the forming of self to a noble humanity through the ancients. Not the grammar with all its details but the literature itself came to the foreground. Education was no longer to be just memorization but had to have a philosophical-historical, an ethical-human, character.

In the nineteenth century these principles governed classical philology for a long time. In our country Professor Ph[ilip] W[illem] van Heusde was the inspired interpreter of these views. The institutions of preparatory secondary education (which came to be called "gymnasia") were transformed accordingly. But this neohumanistic direction also came to an end; the nineteenth century brought even greater changes in classical studies and education than those to which they were subjected in previous centuries.

[235] The changes that the nineteenth century brought about in the ideas about classical studies and education exceed in importance those caused by humanism and neohumanism. The changes were of two kinds. They were partly the result of the development in philology itself, and they can be explained partly by the priority granted gradually to natural science in our society.

The development that came to philology in the previous century can be attributed especially to all kinds of discoveries that occurred in the area of history. The nineteenth century was especially rich in this regard, and it appears that the twentieth century will not be behind its preceding one. Archaeological excavations already began during the Renaissance in the uncovering of a section of the catacombs in 1578. But systematic and strictly methodological excavations were first begun in the nineteenth century. In Egypt they were prepared through Napoleon's expedition in 1798; in Assyria they began with the discovery of Nineveh by Botta and Layard in 1842 and the following years; in Babylonia they date from the year 1851, when J. Oppert accompanied the French expedition to Mesopotamia; and the excavations in Palestine were begun by the Palestine Exploration Fund, which was founded in 1865. Since those years, archaeological explorations in all those countries have been continued diligently, until they were restricted or even discontinued when the [First] World War broke out in 1914. England and America, Germany and Austria, France, Russia, and Italy are competing against each other to raise again the old Eastern civilization from the grave, and these explorations have been crowned with extraordinary success. Ancient cities have arisen from the ashes: palaces, castles, towers, libraries, and graves have been exposed; inscriptions, art objects, murals, coins, and so forth have been brought to light in great numbers. Knowledge of the ancient civilization in the East increased, and the field of history acquired a great number of items and data that enabled it to climb much higher than before and to go back to the times before Moses and Abraham.

[236] These explorations were also important for the knowledge of the Scriptures of the Old Testament and of Israel's history. At one time the idea was prominent that Israel was an oasis in the desert, an island in the sea of nations, completely separated from the world. There is certainly some truth in this view, because Abraham was called to leave Chaldea and go to a land that God would show him and [because] the people that would come from his loins must be a holy people, who were not allowed to mingle with the nations around them. On the other hand, the Old Testament itself teaches that Abraham was an Aramite, that his descendants were enslaved in Egypt for hundreds of years, that the people of Israel, after their entry into Canaan, lived in a land continually populated by all kinds of people. It was also situated between the empires of Assyria and Babylon on the one side, and Egypt on the other. Throughout the ages Israel continued to be touched by and interacted with the nations by whom it was enclosed on all sides, and frequently it endured the influence of these nations, often at the expense of its own character and calling, until it was later dispersed among the nations and in the Diaspora fulfilled its mission to the world.

All of this is now revealed, confirmed, and expanded through the new data that archaeological and historical explorations have brought to life. The excavations enable us, much better than before, to know the milieu in which Israel lived, and they make it possible to give a clear account of the political relationships of Israel to Assyria and Babel, Media and Persia, Egypt and Phoenicia. They also throw light on the social situations, religious and moral life, learning and art among those ancient nations, and contribute to a better understanding of much of what we encounter in Israel. In some ways we can say that the old nation of Israel has been released from the isolation in which it was rather one-sidedly enclosed before. In spite of special revelation that was given to Israel, one finds fibers and threads everywhere that connect it with the surrounding nations.

What happened to Israel also occurred to classical antiquity in the past fifty years, but to much greater degree.[3] The discoveries made in this area have delivered it from seclusion and have cast a totally new light over its origin and development. [237] The excavations here were first conducted by Heinrich Schliemann, who had become wealthy in business but who also had great love for archaeological studies. On one of his many journeys, he came to Greece and Troas in 1868 and started excavations at his own expense in Hissarlik; he surmised that ancient Ilium, or Troy, had been situated there. He was richly rewarded for his labors here, but the later results of his excavation were even more brilliant: in Mycenae, the old city of Agamemnon, in the plain of Argos (1876); in Orchomenos, an old city in Boeotia (1880–81); in Tiryns, an ancient royal castle, also in the plain of Argos (1884–85). After Schliemann's death in 1890, these excavations were continued by others and also extended to other parts of Greece, to the islands in the Aegean Sea, especially Crete. All these explorations have led to better insight into the history of Greece's most ancient period.

At one time it was generally assumed that Greek culture began approximately in Homer's time and was indigenous. However, excavations have now shown that another civilization preceded the culture of Homer's time, usually called Mycenean or Achaean-Cretan. This Mycenean culture blossomed especially in the years 1500 to 1000 before Christ, and it also had a predecessor in the so-called pre-Mycenean culture of 2500 to 1500 BC, and was followed by the actual Greek culture. The latter began when the Dorians settled in Greece around 1000 BC and gradually took over the existing culture. With this discovery the dogma of the origin of Greek culture collapsed. Not only that, but Mycenean culture—which became known by the ruins of the astonishing palaces and castles in Mycenea, Tiryns, Orchomenos, and Crete—showed remarkable relationship with those found in Asia Minor and thus pointed to an Eastern origin. Moreover, all kinds of facts proved that already in ancient times there was busy traffic among nations and countries situated around the Mediterranean—Egypt, Palestine, Phoenicia, Asia Minor, Crete, and Greece—and that this contact increased continually through the centuries, especially after 1500 BC. Thus there was no isolation for Greece either; from ancient times all kinds of relationships existed between East and West. The culture of the West originated under the influence of the East.

[238] Many scholars thought they had to maintain the originality of Greek culture and called the influence of the East a fable. Professor Ed[uard] Zeller of Berlin, the author of the famous *Die Philosophie der Griechen*, wanted to have nothing to do with such an influence; he was a diligent defender of the

---

3. For the following discussion, see Doctor R[obert] H[erman] Woltjer, *De beteekenis van het Oosten voor de klassieke oudheid* (Utrecht: Ruys, 1912); idem, *Het Woord Gods en het woord der menschen* (Utrecht: Ruys, 1913); Paul Wendland, *Die hellenistisch-römische Kultur in ihren Beziehungen zu Judentum und Christentum* (Tübingen: Mohr, 1907).

independence of Greek philosophy. These so-called classicists were no doubt correct to a great extent, since they emphasized the originality and uniqueness of the Greek spirit over against the extreme Orientalists. After all, the Orientalists went much too far in asserting that the Greeks had taken over everything from their predecessors and had added nothing new to it. These Orientalists followed in the footsteps of church writers of the first century who taught, for example, about Plato that all the true and good that one finds in him had been derived from the Scriptures of the old covenant. However, scholars begin to see more and more that the one does not exclude the other. One certainly does not minimize Greek culture when one accepts that the Greeks built on the foundations laid by others. This is true for material as well as spiritual culture; in agriculture, industry, and commerce as well as in art, learning, and religion.

The Greeks used and adapted the inherited forms and norms in an independent and original manner. They put the stamp of their own spirit on their culture, and through their brilliant ability they lifted it high above what existed in the East. For example, the philosophy in the East, which was more and more joined with all kinds of theosophical and mythological elements, was gradually cleansed of these elements in Greece and conceived as learning that was to be exercised not for usefulness or advantage but because of its own worth. The East may have had great influence on philosophical thought in Greece, but the philosophical systems here exhibit a totally different character from those we meet in Egypt and Babylon, in Persia or India. The same also goes for all features of culture, religion, morality, art, literature, and so forth.

Acknowledging this development reduces the objections that were raised against the acceptance of Eastern influence on Greek culture. The number of scholars who continue to maintain their old, classical point of view is slowly becoming smaller; most of the younger scholars of the study of Greek civilization accept, to a smaller or greater degree, such an Eastern influence. [239] The facts that are adduced for such evidence are irrefutable and continually increase the more one becomes acquainted with the history of Greece. For example, Orphic mysticism—with its teachings of preexistence and immortality, guilt and redemption, cleansing and reunion with god—runs like a subterranean stream through the history of Greek religion; it has its greatest following among the lowest levels of the people but also exerts strong influence on philosophers and poets, such as Pindar, Pythagoras, Plato, and others; it retained its significance still later in the period of Hellenistic-Roman civilization.

Naturally, all these remarkable findings and discoveries brought about a great change in the ideas about the origin and development of Greek culture and also in the related issue of classical education.

In the first place, as already briefly mentioned above, the isolation in which Greek civilization was formerly imprisoned was totally broken. Classicism considered Greek antiquity in the same manner that theologians at one time judged Israel: as a piece of history by itself, completely shut off from its surroundings by a wall of separation, without contact with the neighboring nations and cultures. But this view has had its day. The discoveries in Assyria and Babylon, Egypt and Asia Minor, Greece and the islands have broadened the horizon of world history tremendously and have shed new light on the contacts and dealings of ancient people. Artificial walls have been leveled, and the brief, unrelated chronicles of separate nations have made room for the universalistic view of the history of antiquity.

To supplement and strengthen this view, let us mention the noteworthy fact that the language of the New Testament lost its generally accepted uniqueness in the same way. The hundreds and thousands of papyri, inscriptions, and shards with writing (*ostraka* [ostraca]), as found in Egypt in recent years, have acquainted scholars with the everyday Greek language, the common spoken and written language that came into use in the Hellenistic era after Alexander the Great. This language, commonly called "Koine [Greek]," proved to be largely the same as the language of the New Testament. Words that at one time were seen only in the New Testament were found in the papyri of Egypt; sentence structures earlier considered Hebraic were found to be very common; [240] the meaning of many words that seemed strange in the New Testament were clarified by the use of the same words in Greek, as it was spoken and written daily. Of course, the New Testament retains its originality and uniqueness in the thoughts that are communicated; however, to express those thoughts, it uses the language of its time. And thus here also, in place of isolation we discover a connection, a bond, a relationship. One finds this relationship between the Greek in the Septuagint, in the New Testament, in the ordinary spoken and written language of the Hellenistic period, and in the Greek church fathers. According to Professor [Dirk Christiaan] Hesseling, modern Greek is actually closer to the language of the New Testament than to Homer.[4] For this reason the language that the so-called Atticists used for their literary works at this same time (in order to revive old Attic) cannot be the criterion for determining what constituted genuine Greek at that time; the language of Isocrates and Demosthenes was an artistic language that never was spoken by a Greek.

In the same way, ancient Greece no longer existed on its own. From its beginning and throughout its history, it lived in very close contact with the neighboring as well as Eastern countries. Actually the Greeks themselves were aware of this; through their own writers they acknowledged that they were much indebted to other nations. Thus Herodotus already points to the Egyptian origin of the names of Greek gods and oracles, and he judges that the sun clock, the sundial, and the division of days were taken over from the Babylonians. Only later, especially because of the Persian wars,

4. D. C. Hesseling, "De afstamming van het Griekse volk," *De gids* (October 1917): 148.

there arose a strong national consciousness among the Greeks so that they looked down from their pinnacle and considered other nations to be barbarians. But even this disdain was temporary, and in the Hellenistic period there was a growing appreciation for non-Greek nations. Alexander the Great's campaign to *found* a world empire, in which he wanted to unite all nations into a political unity and a common culture, promoted a cosmopolitan mood. The contrasts between Greeks and barbarians decreased. The conventional boundaries drawn by languages, religions, and morals were continually erased. Geographically and historically, the horizon expanded in all directions. [241] The West learned to know the East, and the feeling of spiritual superiority was replaced by dependence. The Greeks began to glorify whatever came from the East. Eastern philosophical and religious concepts, astrology, and magic were eagerly accepted. Greeks and Romans themselves began increasingly to regard the East as the land of their origin and the source of their culture.[5]

Second, classical antiquity in itself is [now] regarded differently from earlier days. Before the universalistic view of history arrived, which placed classical antiquity in relationship to the culture of surrounding nations, classical antiquity was not regarded as a whole but was studied piecemeal. It was divided into many areas and studied by various scholars in various departments, with no organic treatment and no mutual cooperation at all. The historian of antiquity paid no attention to the area of law; the jurist was preoccupied only with laws and scrupulously avoided the area that belonged to philology; the philologist was little concerned with the area of religion; and so forth. But this atomistic view of antiquity is also disappearing and is being replaced by an organic treatment. Not only is the culture of classical antiquity connected with surrounding nations, but the culture itself also is a unity in which all parts are very closely connected. Laws, political science, social relationships, history, art, philosophy, religion, morals, customs, and so forth are not separate from each other, neither in antiquity nor in any other nation at any time. Rather, they are as though members of one organism, whose nature is determined by the character of the whole. They all bear the same stamp, which demonstrates that they belong together, date from the same era, and are developed in the same milieu.

The old philology has thus expanded significantly and even changed its shape; it has become (in the sense that J. J. Scaliger and F. A. Wolf already wanted) an *Altertumswissenschaft*, a subject of Greek antiquity as a whole, in which many scholars work together. The scholars of law, history, religion, philosophy, language and literature, art, and so forth have come much closer to each other. Jurists, theologians, literary scholars, philologists, and

5. Woltjer, *De beteekenis van het Oosten*, 9ff.; Wendland, *Die hellenistisch-römische Kultur* 13ff.

philosophers work together and enlighten each other. [242] The knowledge of antiquity has become much more important than it was earlier, when it was limited to a small, isolated area.

This increase and importance of knowledge has especially come to the fore in a specific area of Greek antiquity. In theological studies the period between Malachi and the New Testament was nearly completely rejected; it was an era that did not count and was at the most mentioned in passing with a few words. In the same way, the old philology remained silent about the period from Alexander to Augustus. Its interest was focused solely on the so-called Attic period; what came after that was considered to be retrogression and decay, and it could be neglected without harm. Just as classical antiquity, according to earlier philologists, was not in any way related to the culture of other nations, so at its demise it was by itself, separated by a chasm from the period of decay that followed. The Attic culture formed an oasis in the desert.

New research has led to a totally different view here also, especially since the work of [Johann Gustav] Droysen. The Hellenistic period began more and more to arouse attention and interest in the circle of classical philologists, even to such a degree that one can say that the study of antiquity is dominated by Hellenism. There are good reasons for such a development. When Alexander united his Greek Empire with the East, he created opportunity for the Greek language and culture to spread out to all regions and to create a unity among the nations, which formerly had been separated by all kinds of walls. He formed a cultural unity that was later secured and strengthened by the political unity of the Roman Empire. The earlier independent states and cities were all [being] taken up into one community, the world as it was then known, and all nations began to think of themselves as citizens of one empire and subjects of one monarch. This development had many consequences: a cosmopolitan mood, a leveling of former differences and distinctions, a widening of the horizon, an elevation of natural law above whatever had been founded by civil laws, customs, and morals, opposition to slavery, greater appreciation for women, popularizing of learning, syncretism in religion. Cosmopolitanism and individualism also went hand in hand at this time, just as later in the era of the *Aufklärung* [Enlightenment].

[243] Because of all these changes, the Hellenistic period was of unusual significance—in itself and no less in the consequences for the future. It had significance in itself because a new view of the world and of life appeared. All of culture took on a different character: religion, morality, philosophy, art, and so forth were liberated from their national bonds and regarded as possessions of all of humanity. As far as its importance for the future, it is sufficient to note that Hellenism prepared people for Christianity and laid the foundation for our modern culture, because this culture is the product of the coming together of East and West, of the Semitic and the Aryan races.

The third change that the more recent concept of classical antiquity brought about concerns the motives that compel its study. The older and the more recent humanism regarded classical antiquity as a unique, elevated, unsurpassable example, which must be followed by all who value true civilization. Humanists considered the study of antiquity as the only true means for nurturing people toward humanity. Here neohumanism thought especially about Attic antiquity, which reached its highest flowering in the fifth and fourth centuries before Christ, notably in Athens. It considered this small Greek world as the lost paradise, as an ideal of untainted purity and beauty, as a model of true humanity, to be admired and followed continually. According to [Paul] Wendland, they ascribed the same canonical and normative worth to Atticism as they did to the Old Testament.

However, this classicist dogma of the Greek ideal of culture also succumbed to criticism and was generally abandoned. In passing we must also note that the ideal of the old humanists, the pure speaking and writing of Ciceronian Latin, is no longer valid for us. One can lament that Latin is no longer the language of learning, of scholars, and of their schools, because the absence of a common language in this area is a great loss. But it is impossible to restore Latin to the position in scholarship that it had at one time. One would have to restore the current gymnasium to a Latin school, as it was at one time, where most of the hours were devoted to Latin and all the other subjects were shortchanged, and one would have to educate young men to become complete strangers to their own era.[6]

But the ideal of neohumanism has also lost its appeal for us. [244] After all, this ideal rested more on fantasy than reality. Historical research has demonstrated that Greek culture, also in the Attic period, did not nearly have the unity and harmony that, for example, Schiller assigned to it; Greek life also knew its doubt and struggle, its suffering and misery. But above all, we live in a different time. Classical antiquity is so far removed from modern culture: because the latter rests in so many ways on different foundations and contains other elements, we hardly feel the relationship of our culture with the ancient. It lies so far in the past that we can no longer use it as a model. It is not so much the Middle Ages, but rather the modern period, which began in the fifteenth century, that has created such a deep chasm between antiquity and us.

Thus at present we have a remarkable situation. At the same time that classical *study* has gained expansion and significance as never before, the motives for classical *education* have weakened and become old. Still, the one is closely related to the other. The classicist conception of the study of

6. On February 7, 1911, Mr. de Marez Oyens pleaded in the First Chamber for such an old Latin school, with twenty hours a week for Latin and beyond that only Dutch language and history, without modern languages (*Acts of the First Chamber*, 372).

Greco-Roman antiquity has proved untenable and has been replaced by the universalistic, cultural-historical view, which uses the psychological and comparative method. The significance of classical antiquity for our civilization has never been realized as clearly as today; next to Christianity, that is where the roots of our culture are to be found. Classical antiquity thus does not have only historical value [for us], such as the history of China or Japan, but it also has cultural-historical significance [for us], and in that regard the study of antiquity today is even more necessary and significant than ever. But this modern view entails that the earlier motives for its study, while obsolete, must be replaced by other motives. Even the whole study of classical antiquity at the university, the education of future teachers for the gymnasium, and the classical instruction at the gymnasium—these must all undergo great change.[7]

[245] The reforming of the gymnasium was, however, not compelled only by the development and expansion of classical philology; it was even more forced by modern culture, which arose in the fifteenth century and began increasingly to dominate life. There are three factors in particular in the creation of this new culture that need to be considered.

The most important of these is the awakening of the love for nature in the Middle Ages. As remarked above, the Renaissance was, broadly conceived, a reaction of man's personality, which again became conscious of the power that oppressed it from the outside. When this personality awakened and opened its eyes, it saw a different world everywhere—different from what it had so far come to know through church and tradition. It saw a different world open up in classical antiquity, in Scripture, and also in nature. In the Middle Ages nature was scorned; it was regarded as something unholy, as the domain of the evil one, as the home and workshop of demonic powers. One was most secure if he or she fled from, suppressed, castigated, and killed it. But now the human subject experienced an awakening; it came to realize its inner life; it regained its own soul and therewith the soul in nature. And when man saw nature in this manner, face-to-face, freed from the spectacles of asceticism, he was seized by deep emotion. This nature was rather different from the workshop of demons; it was a revelation of divine glory, a theater of God's creating and permeating power. And the soul experienced an awakening of deep longing for nature, an ardent desire to know and fathom it.

---

7. *De klassieke oudheid in het gymnasiaal onderwijs: Rapport in opdracht van het Genootschap van Leeraren aan Nederlandsche Gymnasiën* (*A Report Commissioned by the Organization of Secondary School Teachers*), composed by Jan Watzes Bierma, H. Bolkesteyn, E. H. Renkema, J. Van Ijzeren (Leiden: Sythoff, 1916). Cf. the discussion of this report by C. R. de Klerk in *Algemeen handelsblad* (August 4, 1916, evening edition); and also the opening address by Professor Vogelsang to the Eighth Netherlands Philology Congress [see n. 2 above], and the address by Professor H. Cannegieter, "Taalwetenschap in het taalonderwijs," in that same congress held in Utrecht, April 26–27, 1916 (*Handelingen van het achtste Nederlands Philologen Congres*, 1–12, 249–66).

But in the beginning this love for nature had a peculiar character. As it is revealed, for example, to Francis of Assisi, it is religious through and through. In Francis's praise of creatures, he feels himself related to all of creation; he speaks of brother son and sister moon, of brother fire and sister water, and summons all of them to praise the Most High with him. This peculiarity continues to characterize the awakened love of nature for a long time. People wanted to learn to know and penetrate the secrets of nature; yet they thought that nature could not be known from books, as Scholasticism taught, but only through immediate empathy, through ardent sympathy. After all, the world and man were related to each other. One was the macrocosmos, the other the microcosmos; the same divine force lived and worked in both. God's immanence, which was enjoyed in the soul, led to the profession of God's immanence in the world. [246] God is not far away but nearby: this is the slogan that resounds from that era in mysticism, in the philosophy of nature, and in medical science. And thus men like Mirandola, Reuchlin, Cusanus, Cardanus, Nettesheim, Paracelsus, and others summoned assistance from neo-Pythagorian number symbolism, Neoplatonic mysticism, the philosophy of Averroes, the Kabbalah, astrology, magic, and alchemy in order to solve the secrets of nature. Only divine enlightenment can uncover the mysteries of nature.

This mystical philosophy of nature was of great significance for the rise of modern culture, and for a long time there was no thought of opposition and conflict between natural science and theology. Moreover, natural science in the modern era came from the mysticism of the Middle Ages, just as the natural science of the Ionic philosophers came from Orphic mysticism. Natural science tried to understand the world according to an analogy with man himself, as a spiritual unity, as a living organism. The thinkers listed above did not want to explain the world mechanically and materialistically but dynamically, as a continuing development of the life of nature, which at times was pantheistically identified with divine life. However, the desire for knowledge of nature did impel people to research and experiment, no matter how naively and clumsily, and these attempts benefited later natural sciences. Alchemy prepared the way for chemistry, astrology came before astronomy, number symbolism promoted the mathematical method, just as painting and sculpture in turn created the need for anatomy and mechanics. It is thus remarkable that most of the scholars mentioned above combined all kinds of strange fantasies with profound and sound judgments. Cusanus, for example, was a Scholastic and mystic, but he was also involved in mathematical and scientific work. And Leonardo da Vinci was an artist but also one of the founders of the newer natural science.

A second factor of significance for the development of modern culture was finding and applying a more precise method, and in that connection, a different conception of worth and purpose in scholarship. Scholasticism was completely familiar with the idea that all knowledge of the mind begins with sensory perception; however, this truth remained only a theory and was not put into practice, since people thought that all knowledge was contained in books, and other scholarly aids were lacking. [247] Still, already in the thirteenth century, Roger Bacon had indicated that observation and experience are the true route to learning, and others later followed in his footsteps. But of special significance was the surprising number of discoveries and inventions that occurred from the fifteenth century onward. One need to think only of the discovery of America by Columbus, of the sea route to India by Vasco de Gama, of the first journey around the world by Magellan. Then there were the discoveries of the revolution of the earth on its axis by Copernicus, the elliptical path of the planets around the sun by Kepler, the four satellites of Jupiter and the ring of Saturn by Galileo, the law of gravity by Newton. And then followed the inventions of movable print, gunpowder, the compass, optic glass, thermometer, barometer, burning mirror, air pump, and so forth. Through all of these things, man's horizon was broadened, his relationship to the world changed, and learning was recognized as a force that could perform great service in the struggle for existence.

It was especially the philosopher Francis Bacon [d. 1626], of Verulam in Saint Albans, who realized this significance of learning and tried to determine its method accordingly. According to Bacon, learning up to that time was in a lamentable state and urgently needed a renewal, an *instauratio magna* [great restoration]. Negatively, this renewal meant that whoever wanted to achieve knowledge must first discard all preconceived notions. Among these Bacon included not simply unfounded and incidental views but all learning that mankind assumed to have accumulated up to that time. From his pinnacle he looked down on the ancients, all of whom were ready to talk and were rich in words but were poor in deeds. The ancients, whose antiquity gained them authority with many, bear that name incorrectly; they are not the ancients because they lived at a time when the world was much younger and learning was just developing. The true ancients are those living now, who have the experience of many ages behind them and who stand on the shoulders of their ancestors.

When a person has thus laid aside all prejudgments, then he himself must observe and experiment: in other words, he must apply the inductive method. He must not study things from books, nor let himself be led by theology or other speculations, because theology does not belong in scholarship and is purely a matter of faith. [248] A person must look at things himself and ask them what they are. We will not derive any benefit from those who are in their element with words, who amuse themselves with dialectic subtleties, who derive all their wisdom from books. We can come to firm and certain knowledge only by way of pure experience [*mera experientia*], by way of impartial observation and careful experiment. We must sit obediently at the feet of nature and become like children in our receptivity.

The knowledge that we obtain by this method will be not only certain and trustworthy but also useful and fruitful. Bacon lived in a period of many discoveries and was excited about the inventions of his time. Under the impression of these victories of learning, he proposed a completely different conception from what had been valid up to that time. For Bacon, knowledge does not have purpose in itself and is not practiced for itself; it has purpose for life. For him learning is the most certain and the strongest means of obtaining power: knowledge is power. A person can do as much as he knows. We can conquer things only when we know them. Former learning was as unfruitful as nuns because it stood outside of life and was practiced in a monk's cell. But genuine learning, which would be practiced from now on, takes its place in the reality of life and is therefore fruitful for life. This happens not in a coarse, egotistic sense, as if it would put all kinds of advantages in one's lap, but in another and higher sense, in that it enriches all of human life through inventions and advances the well-being of mankind.

In this way Bacon called people from books to reality, from words to deeds, from verbalism to realism. He thus brought about a major revolution in the thinking and striving of the people of Europe. Until then people had looked backward. Christian Europe turned its eyes to the past, to apostles and prophets, to church fathers and Scholastics. Even the humanists, no matter how convinced of their own worth, looked up admiringly to the classics as their models. The sixteenth century was the era of the Reformation and of humanism.

However, with Bacon and in a different way with Descartes, a change came about. They looked for paradise, the state of happiness of humankind, not in the past but in the future. The ancients might have been the pioneers of learning, but they were not the finishers; they must therefore not be followed but rather outpaced and surpassed. [249] A new learning had to arise that would be practiced according to a strictly empirical and experimental method that would achieve power through knowledge and grant man dominion over nature. Thus natural science came to the foreground through men such as Copernicus, Kepler, Galileo, Descartes, and especially Newton. Natural science (at least of inorganic nature) developed into a mechanical, causal conception of nature that put aside all metaphysics and teleology and sought to explain all phenomena from action and reaction and finally from the all-controlling law of gravity. In the beginning of this movement, Deism still accepted the working of a Creator and tried to maintain man's independence and the immortality of the soul. However, materialism tried to understand man himself as a machine and expanded its dominance ever further, until a reaction occurred toward the end of the previous [nineteenth] century and the dynamic worldview again found acceptance with many scholars.

As the third factor we must mention the development of society. Just as various academic subjects gradually separated themselves from theology and philosophy in the more recent era, in the same way society withdrew itself ever more from the custody of church and state. Society developed its own existence and began to lead a life of its own. Through commerce, industry, worldwide contacts, machines, and factories, various occupations and companies increased continually, but the requirements for practicing these occupations became ever higher. The more society developed, the more it needed instruction and training. Famous pedagogues—such as Ratichius, Comenius, Locke, and Rousseau—saw these needs and proposed another theory of learning. The old method of nurture and education had as its main purpose to have the student acquire a knowledge of the past and to induct him into one of the existing guilds for learning, art, or craft. This method worked well in its time but is not suitable today. It overloaded the memory, but critical thinking was underdeveloped; it created people learned but not wise, obedient but not independent; it prepared for school but not for life. Today we need a different education, one that is derived from nature and that takes its position not in antiquity but in the present. Its purpose is to form a person to be an independent being, with his or her own thoughts and judgments, to be a useful, helpful member of society.

[250] This realistic idea in education firmly put itself in the present. It assumed that the material offered by the present was sufficient for education and nurture, and it took seriously the needs of modern society. These needs focused on the fact that there had to be schools that (in distinction from the humanistic institutions for the learned professions) would provide knowledge and skill for real life and would train young people for various occupations in society. Such a school was first founded in Pietist circles. Driven by compassion for neglected youth, in 1705 Christoph Semler of Halle published his *Nützliche Vorschläge von Auffrichtung einer mathematischen Handwerk-Schule* [Useful Proposals on Establishment of a Mathematical Trade School]; he demonstrated that the skilled labor class forms the foundation that supports both other classes (church and state) and that in the future this group needs particular training in a (as he called it) *mathematische und mechanische Realschule* [mathematical and mechanical trade school]. Semler found much sympathy for his idea, and he founded such a school himself in 1707 (and another in 1708), where children were taught one hour a week by studying replicas for the design of timepieces, warships, compasses, and so forth. This school was not very successful, but until the end of his life, Semler remained true to his principle that next to (or even in place of) academic schools, there also should be vocational schools that taught children *Realiteiten* [real-life things], and these would make schooltime not torture but pleasure.

The same spirit moved the minister Johann Julius Hecker, who had first been a teacher in the *Pädagogium* [secondary school] of Francke in Halle. In 1747 he founded an *ökonomisch-mathematische Realschule* [economic-mathematical trade school] in Berlin, which was intended for lads and young men who were to be trained *not* for the learned class but for an occupation in society. This example was followed in many cities. The *Realschulen* founded at this time were all actual vocational schools, but under the influence of Resewitz, Gedike, and Spilleke they gradually assumed a different character. They no longer were vocational schools but became educational institutions that aimed for general spiritual formation, intellectual strength, and a sense of freedom, and for promoting the education of the citizen. Thus three schools of preparatory secondary education came into existence in Germany in the nineteenth century: the gymnasium, with both classical languages as main subjects; the *Ober-Realschule*, chiefly for mathematics and natural science as well as modern languages, but without Latin and Greek; between these two schools was another institution, officially called *Realgymnasium* since 1882, with Latin and modern subjects. When the last two schools developed so completely [251] that they had as many subjects as the gymnasium and could be considered equal, the struggle developed about equal rights, which lasted a long time, and not without rancor. However, following a government decision on December 7, 1870, the graduates of a first-class *Realschule* received the right to study in a university philosophy department and to take examinations in mathematics, natural sciences, and modern languages. An imperial decision on November 26, 1900, granted the three institutions equal rights. The humanistic gymnasium lost all its privileges except for theology, and this last privilege was also recently nullified by the government.[8]

The education law of 1857 in our country [Netherlands] already contained a recognition and regulation of extended elementary education; however, this law was certainly not sufficient for the rising needs of society. These needs were felt especially in the circles of the so-called industrial-technical citizenry; this group, on the one hand, did not belong to the working class and could not be satisfied with just elementary education, but on the other hand, was not destined for a learned profession. This segment of the population needed not only vocational skills, which at that time could still be obtained partially in the workshop [via apprenticeship], but also felt a need for broader theoretical development than could be supplied by elementary and extended elementary education. Prime Minister Thorbecke tried to fill this gap with the Statute for Secondary Education of May 2, 1863. But the *hoogere burgerscholen* ["higher-citizens schools," between the vocational schools and the gymnasiums] that were founded in the most important cities according to this law, either by the central government or municipalities, have more and more departed from the purpose for which they were intended. Thorbecke described secondary education as [involved in] forming the numerous citi-

8. For further discussion about this development of preparatory education in Germany, see Professor H[endrik] Burger, *Klassiek en modern opgeleiden voor de poort de hoogeschool* (Amsterdam: van Rossen, 1910), 340, and for other countries, 42ff.

zens who had finished elementary education but especially wanted to prepare for the various positions in industrial society. The elementary school had to form the civilized, the university the learned, and the secondary school the industrial people. The *hoogere burgerscholen* did not or did very little to answer this purpose. Instead of providing terminal education for the industrial class in society, they have more and more become institutions for preparatory secondary education that prepares students for [252] study at the university to be doctors, dentists, pharmacists, and especially for study at the Technical University in Delft, the Royal Military Academy in Breda, the National Veterinarian School in Utrecht, the National University for Agriculture in Wageningen, and the Netherlands Commerce University in Rotterdam.

When the *hoogere burgerscholen* gradually and without notice developed in a direction totally different from what was originally intended, they became competitors with the gymnasiums, and a struggle for equal rights between these two institutions could not be avoided. This struggle began in 1877 and has continued for the past forty years. From time to time appeals were directed to the government. For example, the university departments of mathematics and natural science and the Medical Society proposed that the *hoogere burgerschool* be assigned the same rights as the gymnasium, at least in admission to academic examinations and graduation from the departments of mathematics, natural science, and medicine. In dealing with the change and amendment of the law about the regulation of higher education when Kuyper was prime minister, Mister De Savornin Lohman took the opportunity to propose an amendment that granted the rights just mentioned to the graduates of the *hoogere burgerschool.* Prime Minister Kuyper answered that he could not accept such an amendment at that time because the crucial issue of classical education should not be decided in such an incidental manner. But he also declared that he was not an absolute proponent of a classical education for all future students, and he would certainly not make it mandatory for all who desired to attend a university.[9]

Since then the attempt to have equality between the *hoogere burgerscholen* and the gymnasiums has increased. In 1916 a movement started in Groningen to establish a National Society for obtaining legal equality for classical and nonclassical education in gaining admission to study in all university departments. The plan immediately found much support, and the society was established and appointed Mister J. Limburg as chairman. As a member of parliament, Limburg—along with Misters Albarda, Bongaerts, De Savornin Lohman, Van de Velde, Visser van Ijzendoorn, and Ijzerman—presented a proposal to the Second Chamber on February 16, 1917. The proposal recommended that a student should have the right to take the admission examinations for the university departments of medicine, mathematics, and natural

9. *Acts of the Second Chamber of the States-General,* March 8, 1904, 1490ff.

science after the student had received a certificate of successfully passing the final examination of the *hoogere burgerscholen* [253] with a five-year program and equal examinations as established by the law. The proposal immediately received favorable acceptance. The Minister of Internal Affairs, according to the Report of the Response on the Tentative Conclusion regarding the National Budget of 1917, changed his earlier opinion and agreed with it. Outside of the Chamber the proposal was recommended in a large number of declarations, which were presented by both divisions of the Royal Academy of Science; the Curators and the Senate of the University of Amsterdam; the senates of the National Universities of Leiden, Utrecht, and Groningen; the Technical University in Delft; and so forth. On May 4, 1917, the proposal was accepted in the Second Chamber 49 to 17, and on August 3, 1917, in the First Chamber on a voice vote.

The arguments for the proposal were indeed very weighty. First, they concerned the unfairness to the graduates of the *hoogere burgerscholen*. Even though they had been admitted to the university, had taken the same courses, and passed the same difficult examinations as the graduates of the gymnasium, they were not admitted to the academic examinations and commencement. It is true that they have the opportunity to study Latin and Greek for two years, to undergo a national examination, and thus to receive the same rights as the graduates from the gymnasium, but this in-between classical study is expensive, time consuming, and of little value. Mister Lohman calls it a senseless stumbling block.

Second, the arguments concerned the interest of academic learning. Many students of the *hoogere burgerscholen*, robbed of the privileges of the gymnasium graduates, go to other countries or to the Technical University of Delft. By this action they are deprived of the opportunity "to write a dissertation, to be in regular contact with learned scholars, to learn to compose a well-written thesis under continuing evaluation and encouragement, to weigh and order the data and opinions in their significance for the solution, and to develop in an extensive treatment the answers obtained in one's own research—in a word, to learn how to conduct research oneself."

Third, the arguments for the proposal concerned the interests of Dutch industry in general, and the chemical industry especially. Particularly since 1914, [254] the demand for well-trained chemists has increased in exceptional degree, both here and in other countries. Since these cannot be obtained in the next few years from the warring countries, it is highly urgent that the Netherlands fill the deficit, not only in this field, but also in botany, zoology, geology, and others.

However, no matter how important all these arguments might be, with many proponents there was another, more principled issue. This came to the fore already in that the Limburg proposal was only a first step on the road that would lead to complete equality between the *hoogere burgerscholen* and the gymnasium. When the Transitional Commission drew up its report, it appeared that several members of the advisory committee wanted to equalize classical and nonclassical study for all departments, and in the Transitional Commission a minority (Misters Drucker, Hebrecht, and Symons) agreed with that position.[10] When the national budget for 1916 was discussed in the Second Chamber, Mister Visser van Ijzendoorn expressed the wish that the graduates of the *hoogere burgerscholen* also would be admitted to the academic examinations and commencement in the department of jurisprudence. The National Society founded in 1916 strives for the legal equality of classical and nonclassical preparation for all university departments and subjects. Professor Hamburger from Groningen expressed the same sentiment and rejoiced when the Limburg proposal breached the wall that separates the *hoogere burgerscholen* from the university.

It is also remarkable that many proponents of the Limburg proposal who complained about the discrimination against graduates of the *hoogere burgerscholen* had little feeling for the unfairness that this proposal inflicted on the students of the gymnasium. This unfairness is certainly not a minor issue. With the acceptance of this proposal, the *hoogere burgerscholen* are not put on a par with the gymnasium, but placed above it. The graduates of a *hoogere burgerschool* immediately gain one year of study time, since the *hoogere burgerschool* takes five years, and the gymnasium six. Moreover, the students who earn a diploma from the *hoogere burgerschool* and want to be admitted to the academic examinations and commencement in the departments of mathematics, natural science, and medicine up to now had to study Latin and Greek and take a national examination. [255] Now, however, they are completely and suddenly excused from this additional study. Finally, as students in medicine they have the advantage that they have been better prepared; they are usually ready for the first examination in natural science in one year, while the graduates of the gymnasium often need two years. In many ways the gymnasium will thus be disadvantaged by the Limburg proposal, and the fear is not unfounded that the gymnasium will eventually lose all its students in the natural science division.

Third, it is generally known that many scholars today would like to see classical studies abolished as soon as possible. Among mathematicians and natural scientists, as well as among physicians, there are still many today who enjoyed and appreciated their classical studies. However, that number decreases every year, and the number of those who judge that classical study is outdated is increasing; at least they judge that classical study cannot be preferred in any way to nonclassical, realistic study.

10. *De klassieke oudheid in het gymnasiaal onderwijs: Rapport,* I:825ff. Ed. note: Bavinck simply identifies this as *Rapport* I:825ff., which is problematic because the bibliographic information from WorldCat indicates it is a volume of 206 pages. It is possible that Bavinck was working with an earlier, prepublication draft of the report.

In all fairness, we must admit that both sides have been guilty of exaggeration. Just as many scientific scholars have looked disdainfully at classical study, in the same way many classicists have looked (and still look) down on the study of reality. While Barthélemy Saint-Hilaire said that the loss of Aristotle would do more harm than that of all newer philosophers, Cobden declared that one issue of the *Times* would teach more than all of Thucydides. There are those who hold that modern culture is completely sufficient in itself and who expect more from an introduction to that culture than from antiquity. This idea is closely related to the change sketched above that has taken place in scholarship. Formerly the idea was dominant that scholarship was to be engaged in for its own sake, or rather, for the sake of truth; knowledge concerns intelligible (things) by means of known causes (*per causas scire; scientia est intelligibilium*); however, since [Francis] Bacon, and then further since Kant's criticism, Comte's positivism, and Spencer's agnosticism, the idea has been that usefulness is the foundation of all knowledge, knowledge is power, and learning is from and for life.[11] The idealistic conception gave place to the biological, the pragmatic, the realistic.

[256] We must do complete justice to this last idea. In general it is true that learning in its present state was born from the needs of life and carries that stamp in all its aspects: medical, juridical, and so forth. This character becomes especially obvious since the more-recent natural sciences have developed, and man has been granted dominion over the powers of nature, [to an extent] that continues to surprise us and expands every day. In the past century, the study of nature has had such an influence on science and society that no one can consider it a negligible quantity; the most passionate devotee of antiquity must reckon with this influence. Modern culture, in which natural science occupies first place, contains so many elements that can lead to learning that no one can deny its foundational value. There are many scholars, both in our country and elsewhere, who never enjoyed a classical education, and who still must be reckoned among the stars of scholarship;[12] through its long history the *hoogere burgerschool* has also earned its right of existence as preparation for many academic disciplines. One cannot argue much against what the Society for the Promotion of Natural Science and Medicine said in its statement to the Second Chamber. The exercise in mod-

11. Cf. the lecture of Professor Zwaardemaker about the most recent shape of physiology, as cited by Doctor J. W. Moll, *De idee der universiteit in haar toekomstige ontwikkeling* (Groningen: Wolters, 1910), 11. See also Professor H[endrik] Burger, *Middelbaar onderwijs en universiteit* (Amsterdam, 1913).

12. Professor [Hendrik] Burger figured that of the 105 professors and lecturers in the departments of medicine, mathematics, and natural science at the four national universities, 26 had received a classical and 73 a modern education; of the latter, 49 had received a diploma from a *hoogere burgerschool*. See his *Middelbaar onderwijs en universiteit*, 18; and also see his *Klassiek en modern opgeleiden voor de poort der hoogeschool* (Amsterdam: Van Rossen, 1910), 29ff.

ern languages, the study of nature and life in its countless diversity—both can render excellent culture and taste, just as can be given by the study of classical languages; and a preparation along this route can also guarantee suitability for scholarly learning and independent study. Neither is there opposition from a Christian point of view to modern learning. After all, those who teach the humanities can be as one-sided as those who teach [present] reality, and more recent natural science has more and more escaped from materialism. Also, the *hoogere burgerschool* has, in recent years, continually gained more sympathy in Christian circles.

Nevertheless there continues to be a difference between the two educational views. There is difference in appreciation of the past and the present, difference about the idea of scholarship, and up to a point, difference in worldview. [257] But if the difference runs so deep, then the government cannot decide the issue; then the only solution is that the two views must contend with each other in society, and the future will decide which preparation is the best for the practice of scholarship: the one provided by the gymnasium, or the one by the *hoogere burgerschool*. The proponents of classical education have therefore shown liberality when they not only did not resist the Limburg proposal but even recommended and supported it.

But if the proponents of classical education are serious about this and consider classical study to be the best foundation for mathematics, natural science, and medicine, then they cannot sit still; they must watch that equality of the *hoogere burgerschool* and the gymnasium does not more and more become a legal advantage for the *hoogere burgerschool*. One can join Doctor Bonebakker when he declaims to the friends of antiquity: Let them go—the ordinary ones, the spirits with earflaps, those who think only about usefulness and their own advantage. Let them go—those spiritual dullards, in whom there is no passionate spirit that makes them desire to grow up in the gentle air of antiquity. For the most noble in many generations, among many nations, antiquity has always been what the South is every autumn for the migrating bird—"the sunny fatherland." However, it is difficult to demand from the pupils who come to the gymnasium that they already should feel love and enthusiasm for what they do not know. They and their parents need correct information to find out which education is to be preferred. What happened in Germany? After the *Ober-Realschule*, the gymnasium, and the *Realgymnasium* had for some time become equal in the graduates' admission to the theological department in the universities, many professors (65) in theology, juridical and political disciplines, philosophy, philology, history, and art published a declaration in the *Wochenschrift für klassische Philologie* of February 5, 1917. They emphatically declared that, according to their opinion, the humanistic gymnasium (apart from its great and general educational importance) in all respects remained the best preparatory school for the study of the spiritual disciplines.

But "doctrines stir us, examples pull us" [a Dutch proverb: *Leeringen wekken, voorbeelden trekken*]. The best information is supplied not by such a declaration but through the school itself, the distinction of its education, the devotion of the teachers, the nurturing strength that proceeds from the school. The acceptance of the Limburg proposal has made reforming the gymnasium urgent, though it has been necessary for a long time, as well as reforming the [258] *hoogere burgerschool*, which was originally not intended as a foundation and thus must be changed accordingly. Both institutions need reforming, especially in their connection to elementary education; they need a better regulation of the qualifications of the teachers, so that, especially in the lower classes, the subject teachers will be replaced by general teachers;[13] they certainly also need the simplification of subjects and examinations.[14] One need not learn everything needed in life at school, and one need not know everything in an examination. Life itself is an excellent school, and one can certainly leave something for that "school." A little that is good is better than much that is poor.

Let us focus on reforming the gymnasium: this has been delayed because there has been a lack of unanimity among the experts for years. The differences of ideas were many: the complete elimination or the simplification of Greek; which authors to read;[15] the elimination of mathematics for the A-students,[16] at least after the fourth year; a more or less radical separation of A- and B-students in the fourth year or after the fourth year, or only in the sixth year; a five-year gymnasium or a six-year *hoogere burgerschool*; and the desirability of separate classes for archaeology and geography. Other controversies concerned the usefulness of teaching natural history in the first and second year, and then again to the B-students in the fifth and sixth year; teaching chemistry for one hour to the B-students in the two final years; the simplification of the final examination; and the presence of government officials at the examination.

However slowly in coming, some points of more agreement have appeared. First, many agree with the advisability of offering exactly the same education to the students of the gymnasium and of the *hoogere burgerschool* in the first and second year; only after this year (that is, at age fourteen or fifteen) would the students have to choose whether they will go to the gymnasium or the

---

13. At one time this was also the wish of Professors Naber, Spruyt, Boot, Speijer, van der Meij, and others.

14. The final examinations at the *hoogere burgerschool* cover seventeen subjects!

15. For example, should one read only Attic authors or also authors from the Hellenistic and Christian eras, such as the New Testament, the church fathers, Lucianus, Plotinus, Thomas à Kempis? Cf. D. Plooy, "De litteratuur uit de Romeinsche keizertijd op onze gymnasia," *Stemmen des tijds* 2 (May 1913): 716–41; *C. R. de Klerk in *Van onzen tijd*, April 1916.

16. Ed. note: The gymnasium was divided into two tracks: Division A corresponded approximately to today's humanities and social sciences, and Division B corresponded to the natural and physical sciences and mathematics.

*hoogere burgerschool*. Second, there also is more agreement about the simplification of teaching the classical languages (limiting the number of hours
and the number of authors) and the expansion of teaching mathematics and
natural science. [259] Third, there is some agreement about the advisability
of postponing the separation of the students into various divisions until the
sixth year and of dropping the ancient languages for the B-students and
natural science for the A-students. These ideas were advocated with warm
conviction and strong arguments by the rector of the public gymnasium in
Arnhem, Doctor B. I. Hooykaas and his supporters. They were also accepted
with general concurrence in a meeting of rectors and associate rectors in
Utrecht on November 3 of last year [1917], so that now we can speak of a
*communis opinio* [common opinion]. Moreover, as the government representative said at the close of the meeting, in this way the coupling of the
gymnasium and the university can take place in a simple manner, without
having to change the law. And now one can hope that the government will
soon take up this important issue.

Although much would be gained for the gymnasium with this change,
it is not the main issue in the reform. That issue is the nature, the method,
the goal of classical education. One can say without fear of contradiction
that the one-sided grammatical-critical method that has long reigned in
our country and other countries has done much damage to the love for
classical antiquity. If at the gymnasium or university one spends weeks and
months reading Homer, Plato, Sophocles, and others without any serious
attempt to introduce the student to the person and the time of the authors,
and the content and the philosophical, aesthetic, cultural, historical value
of their works, then one cannot expect that the student will feel interest
or love for classical antiquity. At that age [the student] can perhaps not
fully explain why, but he feels the emptiness of such education, and later
he realizes how much more fruitful all these hours could have been for the
development of his insight and taste. Fortunately, that time is past and the
new development in classical philology sketched above not only presents
the opportunity but also firmly demands, both for the education of the
teacher at the university and for the student at the gymnasium, that we go
in a different direction.

[260] Classical antiquity is no longer the ideal of education for us, and
it will never again be that. [Tadeusz] Zieliński said, "Antiquity shall not be
the norm, but a living force of today's culture."[17] But the great cultural and
historical value of that antiquity has never been realized as well as today.
The influence of Israel and also of Hellas and Latium on our culture is

17. [Tadeusz Zieliński,] *Die Antike und wir* (Leipzig: Dieterich, 1905), 66; cf. also A[dolf] Harnack,
*Die Notwendigkeit der Erhaltung des alten Gymnasiums* (Berlin: Weidmann, 1905); also printed in
A. Harnack, *Aus Wissenschaft und Leben*, 2 vols. (Giessen: Topelmann, 1911), I:67–92.

much more clear to us now than in previous centuries; these are and will remain our spiritual forebears. The study of antiquity is therefore not only of formal and practical value: for the development of thinking, understanding Greek and Latin terms in our scholarship, understanding citations and allusions in our literature, and so forth. Its lasting value also lies in the fact that the foundations of modern culture were laid in antiquity. The roots of all our arts and learning—and also, though in lesser degree, the sciences that study nature—are to be found in the soil of antiquity. It is amazing how the Greeks created all those forms of beauty in which our aesthetic feeling still finds expression and satisfaction today; in their learning they realized and posited all the problems of the world and of life with which we still wrestle in our heads and hearts. They were able to achieve that, on the one hand, because they rose above folk religion and struggled for the independence of art and learning; but on the other hand, they did not loosen art and learning from those religious and ethical factors that belong to man's essence. In the midst of distressing reality, they kept the faith in a world of ideas and norms. And that idealism is also indispensable for us today; it cannot be replaced or compensated for by the history of civilization or new literature.[18]

But maintaining classical education is also related to a national and international concern. Professor Hatman once said that our country must devote itself to the study of classical antiquity because of its famous past; the maintaining of Latin is a national concern because with it we maintain something that has always been our honor and our fame. There certainly is truth in that assertion, but international concerns weigh even more heavily; Viscount Bryce recently called attention to this.[19] [261] The current world war estranges nations from each other—nations that belong to each other according to history, religion, and culture, but it appears that all unity and cooperation will be submerged under enmity and hate for a long, long time, perhaps forever. As nationalism and chauvinism increase, Germany, France, and England are busy with their own, national culture, and whatever was held in common up till now is pushed into the background. That is why it is an international concern to maintain and build on the foundations on which modern culture rests. If there is one thing that is essential in these grave times, it is that Christian nations be reconciled to each other, close ranks, and take to heart the call to conserve the treasure that has been entrusted to them in religion and culture. This is also true for religion, for the Christian religion. Recently Professor [Rudolf]

18. Cf. also the appreciation of classical antiquity from a Christian point of view: [August Friedrich Christian] Vilmar, *Über den evangelischen Religionsunterricht in den Gymnasien* (Marburg: Elwert, 1888); [Joseph] Kleutgen, *Über die alten und die neuen Schulen* (Münster: Theissing, 1869).

19. Viscount Bryce, "The Worth of Ancient Literature to the Modern World," *Fortnightly Review* DCIV (new series) (April 1917): 551–66.

Eucken from Jena pointed out correctly that the Bible—which until now has formed a common foundation for religion and art—is increasingly discarded by both.[20] How will these nations ever again become a power for mankind if they do not possess an inner unity in Scripture and do not draw from one communal well?

20. R[udolf] Eucken, *Die geistesgeschichtliche Bedeutung der Bibel* (Leipzig: Kröner, 1917).

# 14

# OF BEAUTY AND AESTHETICS

[262] Today the term "aesthetics" is commonly used for the philosophy of beauty. This term began to be used when Alexander Gottlieb Baumgarten, who was born in Berlin in 1714, accepted the position of professor of philosophy in Frankfurt on the Oder and died there in 1762. Baumgarten was a student of Christiaan Wolff, who tried to make the philosophical ideas of Leibniz more practical and useful for the happiness of humanity. Baumgarten tried to complete the teachings of Leibniz about the higher knowledge acquired through reason by positing knowledge attained through the senses. He therefore wrote *Aesthetica acroamatica* [in Latin], published in two volumes in Frankfurt in 1750–58. He took the [first word] of this work's title from a Greek adjective that means "observing, feeling" and that is derived from a verb translated as "to perceive, to observe with the senses," primarily with the ear, but also with the eye, smell, taste, and touch. The word was therefore very appropriate to indicate what Baumgarten intended with his work: to elucidate the philosophy of sensory knowledge. But this knowledge, attained through the senses, now culminated as though in the observing of beauty, which according to Wolff is none other than the harmony and completeness of an observed thing [*perfectio phaenomenon*]. Aesthetics, as philosophy of sensory knowledge, naturally had to result in a theory of beauty, in an *ars pulchre cogitandi* [the art of thinking beautifully] or *ars formandi gustum* [the art of forming taste]. And thus the name "aesthetics" gradually came in use for the philosophy of beauty.

Ed. note: Originally published as "Van schoonheid en schoonheidsleer," in *Almanak* of the Free University of Amsterdam Student Body (NDDD), 1914, 262–80.

However, even though the term "aesthetics" is of rather recent vintage, the idea indicated by it is much older and dates from the time of Greek philosophy. In the classical nation of poets and thinkers, the need soon arose to give an account of the essence and laws of beauty. [263] At first no one clearly discerned the distinction between beauty and the good, or between the good and the useful. Plato, however, penetrated ever deeper and examined not only the concept of beauty but also the special meanings of the comic and the tragic, the elevated and the absurd, and so forth, and can therefore be called the father of aesthetics. He especially tried to give a metaphysical foundation to beauty and to derive it from the world of ideas. Even though we see many beautiful things on earth, we do not behold beauty itself; this has a unique, perfect existence in the world of intelligible things. The ideas that belong there are more-or-less imprinted on the material world by the demiurge and shine through the visible, and we therefore behold the beauty also in nature around us. And since art essentially exists in the imitation of nature, it also in turn displays beauty. But art is really an image of an image, an imprint of an imprint, and thus of secondary value; in the ideal world there is actually no place for works of art without a moral intent.

In this way Plato provided the basic concepts for a doctrine of beauty from which later generations would benefit for centuries. Plato originated the metaphysical and normative aesthetics that was then supplemented by Aristotle at some points and conceived much more broadly by Plotinus. Later it had its strongest influence on the church fathers, such as Clement and Origen, Gregory of Nyssa and Augustine, Pseudo-Dionysius, Thomas [Aquinas], and Bonaventura, as well as Roman Catholic and Protestant philosophers and theologians. And in the idealistic philosophy of Schelling and Hegel and others, it once more regained its spiritual preeminence.

According to this more-or-less dogmatic aesthetics, beauty is originally supersensory, as spirit; it has objective existence and belongs to the worlds of invisible things as an independent reality or in God's consciousness or as an idea. The visible world, however, is to a greater or lesser degree part of this spiritual nature and reveals it insofar as it displays in itself or in its various creatures harmony, proportion, order, diversity in unity, and unity in diversity. Beauty thus lies first of all in the content, in the idea, but harmony characterizes its appearance. Wherever in the world it in its various forms shows a finite expression of the infinite, beauty is absolute idea.

[264] Since the appearance in nature never fully corresponds to the idea, one can go in two directions in the consideration of art. If one is committed, with Plato, to the perspective that all art must be imitation of nature, and we see in art a weaker reflection of the beauty in nature, then art is naturally relegated to the third and last rank, and then has only subordinate value. However, in contrast to that position, one can start from the same principle and assign a much higher calling and meaning to art

If nature, because of the strength of its materialism, is only an inadequate reflection of the idea, then one can assign to art the purpose of overcoming this imperfection in the beauty of nature; it does so by corresponding to the idea and thus seeming to destroy the material completely through absolute perfection of the form. Then art, as with Schelling in his first period, assumes the highest position, even above religion and philosophy, because it is the complete revelation of the absolute, finally the perfect manifestation of the divine idea, the total reconciliation of the antithesis between the real and the ideal.

Finally, the uniqueness of this metaphysical aesthetics comes to expression in that beauty affects human emotions in a special manner. Because beauty is related to the true and the good and is one with them in the absolute idea, it may not evoke any sensations that are opposed to them. According to Plato, art even has to be in the service of moral purposes, and in later philosophy the true, the good, and the beautiful were often joined in an unbreakable triad. However, beauty can still be distinguished from the good and the true. Beauty even evokes peculiar sensations and moods in human beings; it purifies our affections, reconciles the opposites in our life, brings harmony to the soul, and bestows peace and rest.

In the new era a strong reaction has arisen against this "dogmatism" in aesthetics (as it actually has against all scholarship). This began in England where, under the influence of empirical philosophy, Shaftesbury tried to explain aesthetic enjoyment psychologically. Others—such as Hume, Burke, Erasmus, Darwin—tried to explain beauty sensually as a sensory quality of things that affects the human soul and relaxes the nerves and has its greatest significance socially through the arousing of love and sexual lust.

[265] Then came the philosophy of Kant: as in science, religion, and morality, he sought to find a middle road between dogmatism and empiricism. Kant saw very clearly that beauty was something other than the useful and the pleasant, and that it was more than just a question of taste. According to Kant, observation and enjoyment rest on an a priori synthetic judgment, on the aesthetic *Urtheilskraft* [power of judgment], an innate feeling of desire and distaste that is different from sensory knowledge (as Baum thought) and from sensory desire (according to the utilitarianism of his day). Because of this feeling, we are able to value and enjoy a thing aesthetically, to observe it in such a way that we completely forgo an object's content and material, its usefulness and purpose, and admire it solely for its form while remaining completely disinterested. As Schiller wrote, "One does not desire the star, but one delights in its beauty." But Kant did err in that he separated beauty from all content. He saw beauty only as form and also wanted to explain it completely from an innate feeling of the subject. For him, beauty has no foundation in objective reality but is really a lovely illusion necessarily arising from the organization of the human spirit.

A third reason for the shift in method in aesthetics is the empirical and positivistic trend into which scholarship in the nineteenth century began to move, after the disillusionment with idealistic philosophy. Gradually the conviction also arose that in the philosophy of beauty one could no longer proceed from some kind of a priori dogma or try speculatively to understand the essence of beauty but that here also one had to use empirical knowledge as a guide, or at least to begin with the study of aesthetic phenomena or facts. We probably will never know what the essence of beauty is; let us therefore examine what happens inside of us when we feel something beautiful and search as much as possible how this feeling starts and develops in one person and in humanity. The first scholar who led aesthetics into these new channels was a professor of philosophy in Leipzig, Gustav Theodore Fechner. In a short work, *Zur experimentellen Aesthetik* (1871), and later in a two-volume work, *Vorschule der Aesthetik* (1876), Fechner showed the necessity of replacing an aesthetic from above with an aesthetic from below. [266] He himself began this work by questioning a large number of people to establish which lines and figures were most pleasing to them. Thus experience became the foundation of the newer aesthetics, and searching for the laws that govern aesthetic phenomena became its purpose.

Of course, in itself this empirical and experimental method cannot be rejected. Just as in philosophy in general, aesthetics may not neglect the objective data, the facts, and phenomena in its domain. The philosopher may not close his eyes to reality and may not construct the world from his own brain, and the aesthetician must form and perfect his taste, his judgment, his knowledge from the works of nature and art. Just as in all scholarship, so also in the theory of beauty observation and thought, inductive and deductive methods must go together. Actually, the great philosophers have always combined these methods, and it is always very one-sided if men such as Plato in antiquity and Schelling and Hegel in recent times are always accused of ignoring empirical methods and just reasoning at random. Their works testify to the opposite. Or to turn it around, the proponents of the empirical and experimental method demonstrate all the time that their observation is accompanied and led by reason.

However, as soon as aesthetics turns in the direction of empiricism, it will see boundless areas of investigation spread out before it: wherever its eyes turn, there are people who have enjoyed something beautiful or have made something beautiful. Scholars in aesthetics can investigate all of that. They can try to improve and extend the experimental method first applied by Fechner. For example, they can try to find out which lines, figures, colors, shapes, changes in sound and tone, and so forth give the most pleasure to the greatest number of people. They can also try subjectively to penetrate these same people to discover what is going on in them when they see and enjoy something beautiful; what must be ascribed to the object and what to the subject; which aesthetic and nonaesthetic factors are at work; how the pleasure from beauty affects facial expression, bodily posture, increase in pulse rate; and so forth. Everyone knows that when aesthetics enters these areas, it will encounter all kinds of complicated processes, make a beginning, but not see the end of its labors. [267] For example, just consider all the various circumstances and considerations that can make a painting pleasing to someone. There are certainly not only aesthetic elements that play a role here, but frequently other factors that have little to do with aesthetics count just as much. These include the relationship to the artist, the fashion that frequently sets the tone also in art, the high price that one pays for the art object, the thought about the adulation of the people that one will receive as buyer and owner, and so forth.

All of these factors deal only with the method, as experiments can be conducted by us or others in our environment. And then all kinds of questions and problems come to the fore. Should one try to approach these observations about beauty subjectively (through introspection) or more objectively? More psychologically or more physiologically? Can these experimental methods be used only with elementary aesthetic impressions? Or can they be expanded to higher, more complicated phenomena of aesthetic enjoyment? By this route can one hope to reach a determination of certain characteristics of beauty? In short, all the questions that occur with empirical psychology repeat themselves here, and all the trends that one finds there also appear in aesthetics.

Even then, we have pointed only to a comparatively small area in which empirical aesthetics can move. The field of investigation becomes much broader, even endless, if it takes into account the objective aesthetic phenomena that the history of humanity discloses and [if it] seeks to discover the reasons, the development, the laws.

First, scholars can begin an investigation into the sense of beauty that is inherent in man. They can try to discern in what ways, from which factors, under what influences this sense came to be; how it developed through time in various peoples; and if there is unity among the motley, infinite diversity, what this unity is. Second, they can focus their attention on the artists who have created this beauty and determine what uniqueness separates them from other people, from what milieu they come, how they have developed themselves, what their special gift was, and in what direction they have cultivated this gift. Third, they can survey the art objects that have been created throughout the ages by various peoples and by all humanity and survey their origin, development, influence, similarity, diversity, and so forth. [268] Even without any further direction, it is clear to everyone that investigation into aesthetics in each of these three areas can be extended infinitely, and also go into the most minute details. Only this needs to be added, that in all this investigation, aesthetics can use the most varied methods and find recourse in the most divergent explanations. The scholar will understand humanity's sense of beauty, the artists' creative urge, and the value of works of art according to his own worldview; he will take into account factors psychological or physical, ethnological or cultural-historical, biological or evolutionary, climatological or social. Here also there are nearly as many directions as there are scholars.

There is not a moment of doubt that empirical aesthetics has a right of existence and that it has conclusively proved this right by its striking results. What a light on the artist and the work of art when both are placed in the context of their time and place, of the people and social circumstances! And it has been proved through investigation, especially of the art of so-called primitive people, that the elements of culture, also aesthetic culture, are the same for all humanity and that the art of the simplest people is essentially formed according to the same laws as the highest creations of art!

However, this does not take away the fact that empirical aesthetics is without doubt one-sided and cannot produce what it intends.[1]

This lack becomes immediately obvious when the beauty of nature does not receive the attention it deserves, because here it is not possible to conduct psychological, physical, or cultural-historical investigation. Still, the beauty of nature is there and it expands before our eyes in wonderful diversity. There are entire periods in history when this is not noticed and valued. But when the culture has made people (especially city dwellers) feel fed up with disturbances and unrest, then the desire for the beauty of nature returns, and one sees a return from the city to the country. The theory that art always follows nature is but a half-truth, even when one remembers that imitation is not copying or mimicking and that nature must be broadly understood, because with the artist originality plays as important a role in his work as what he observes from the outside. The beauty of nature may therefore not be put in second place behind the beauty of art. [269] Both are revelations, each in its own way, of true beauty, which is not sensory but spiritual—according to Plato [it is] found in the ideal, and according to Holy Scripture [it is] found in God's splendor and displayed in all the works of his hands. The acknowledgment of this spiritual beauty is even the prerequisite for maintaining beauty in its supersensory reality and for doing justice to the truth that both natural and artistic beauty are independent revelations of beauty.

Moreover, empirical aesthetics is not sufficient in the search for the human sense of beauty. After all, it is certain that man is affected by the world that surrounds him, not only religiously and ethically, intellectually and practically, but also aesthetically. However, the more we think about this phenomenon the more strange and mysterious it becomes. What is the nature of this aesthetic affection, and what is its origin? Is it a function of the lower or higher

---

1. Ed. note: This may be the shortest paragraph of H. Bavinck on record.

cognition, of observation or feeling? Is this feeling, or whatever one may call it, innate, or has it developed slowly through selection or heredity in the struggle for existence? All kinds of theories about these problems have been proposed in the history of aesthetics, and still there certainly is no unanimity, in spite of all the empirical and experimental investigations. Scholars speak of mimicking and aesthetic appearance, of conscious self-deception (illusion) and disinterested pleasure, and so forth. Lately an explanation has become popular that was prepared by others and has been especially developed by Professor [Theodor] Lipps of Munich, called empathy [*Einfühling*]. In general this refers to the habit of people to ascribe and to transfer their own observations, feelings, moods, and the condition of one's soul to things outside themselves. We consider beautiful that in which we see an expression or a symbol of our own inner life, so that we feel ourselves as though one with the observed object.

Such an empathy undoubtedly exists and is even applied by us every moment, because we understand other people, animals, plants, and the whole outside world in no way other than according to an analogy of our own soul. A child already begins that way when it plays with its doll, and an adult person does the same when he makes nature like himself and elicits tones from nature based on his own feeling. However, this empathy is not restricted to the aesthetic domain but is operative everywhere, even in exact sciences. [270] And the question thus becomes specifically, "How does aesthetic empathy differ from all others?" But then all the other problems that arose about the human sense of beauty come back at once: From where comes this aesthetic humanizing of all things outside of us? Is it innate or acquired, psychological or physical, an operation of consciousness or feeling? Is the subject of this humanizing inspiration totally independent of the object, or does the object also make a contribution? And does it have to fulfill certain conditions in order to elicit human aesthetic responses? All these questions can be answered in very different ways, and one can add many more. All the questions—just as with investigation into the origin of religion, morality, culture, and so forth—finally lead to the conclusion that with the sense of beauty, we are dealing with a phenomenon that is part of human nature: a predisposition and susceptibility of the soul to find pleasure and to enjoy oneself in things that fulfill certain conditions.

Empirical aesthetics also comes to the same conclusion if it investigates the creative gift of the artist. Knowledge about psychological, physical, historical, and social conditions can be of great service. If one studies the origin, disposition, development, and milieu of the artist, one can better understand and appreciate not only his person and character but also his art. And through this psychological and historical investigation, one can also be cured of all kinds of foolish theories about artists and art that are making the rounds. Thus the slogan of "art for art's sake" in history has virtually no ground to stand on.

Even though the creative gift and the creative urge in the artist are essential, these can become operative through all kinds of ways and means—for example, through finances—without the art suffering because of that. Genius itself does not even know the circumstances by which it is inspired.

But even if we finally know everything about the artist's circumstances that has been brought to light by careful investigation, at the end we finally face a mystery, the secret of personality, the inscrutability of genius. It is true that in recent years much work and effort has been expended on the study of personality and genius. This was done partly with the hope that if one knew how nature had generated genius in the past, then nature could be guided by human acumen to produce an ever-increasing number of *Übermenschen* [supermen] artificially. [271] To explain the origin and essence of genius, scholars explored not just heredity but also neurasthenia and pathology. Even though one does not want at all to minimize all these investigations, finally one cannot say much else than what the ancients confessed. Art is a gift, the poet is not made but born, and an artist is an artist by the grace of God: [as Ovid said,] "Est deus in nobis, agitante calescimus illo [there is a deity in us, and by that power we are inspired]." It might be true that being a genius does not exclude effort and labor, that genius (according to Edison's exaggerated expression) consists of only one-tenth inspiration and nine-tenths perspiration. We can also admit that genius does not come completely from special gifts but is an unusual strengthening of ordinary gifts found in all people. Nevertheless, we still are faced with an original power that is not explained by any law of nature, and it points back to a divine, creating Almighty.

Finally, empirical aesthetics does not reach its goal by studying the works of art in their origin, development, and history. One does not need to argue that prehistoric, ethnological, comparative, social, cultural-historical investigation can perform a good service here. No works of art, no more than artists, fall from the sky; instead, they are closely connected to the culture of a people and country and era. They are determined by the purpose that they are to serve, by the material from which they are formed, by the milieu in which they originated, by the level of technology with which they are constructed. Whoever knows nothing about all these factors will not be able to judge the works according to their value or appreciate and enjoy them. Even history teaches that the desire for art was at first connected with all kinds of practical, religious, social, and political interests and that the desire for art released itself from those other interests only gradually to become independent.

However, all these investigations have not been able to lift the veil that hangs over the origin and essence of art and works of art. This is shown in that today there are just as many divergent ideas as there were in earlier days: one person explains art from play, another from sexual desire, a third from rhythm, a fourth from feelings and actions that also occur with animals, and so forth. But more and more the conviction is gaining ground that with art just as with religion, we must accept an original human impulse and an urge that we cannot explain from other inclinations or activities. Some have even proposed that each art has an independent origin and that an archetype has never existed. And thus there remains, in spite of all exact study, the greatest possible difference about the essence of art.

[272] History reveals two ideas specifically that have alternated with each other and have kept each other in balance: the classic and the romantic. But since these views have lost their supremacy, there now is a situation in the arts that Mister Berland recently called "anarchy," and which is the same as one finds in religion and philosophy, in jurisdiction and morality. According to this scholar, great art (meaning general art) is not possible today because of the lack of a reigning worldview. The subjectivization of thought, which led to complete spiritual confusion with the French Revolution, has necessarily brought about an eclectic direction in architecture. A walk in Amsterdam, from the Dam to the train station, will convince any thoughtful observer of that eclecticism. And a person will then not find the characterization of an *anarchistic* situation in the arts too extreme when he regards the present diverse trends: realism and naturalism have been replaced by symbolism and mysticism, and these in turn have been pushed aside by cubism and futurism. The futurists may appear as prophets of a new and better future and announce that after the art of silence and slumber the art of motion, speed, clamor, and noise will come, but their word finds acceptance in only a very small circle. And it is doubtful whether, according to [Hendrick Petrus] Berlage's expectation, a new and great art will be born from the democratic idea.

After all the excursions in the world of aesthetic phenomena, aesthetics is therefore forced to return to the ancient principled problems that were already proposed at the initial consideration about the essence of beauty. Let me say once more that aesthetics, no more than any science, can do without a firm empirical foundation. Psychological and historical studies are indispensable for the proper understanding of the essence of beauty, the gift of the artist, and the works of art. An aesthetics from below must precede an aesthetics from above.

The aesthetic from above, however, continues to maintain its right of existence. The father of empirical aesthetics, Fechner, even reserved a place for aesthetics from above, and many aestheticians follow his example to this day. [273] Even though philosophy and metaphysics have been greatly dishonored for a time, the unsatisfying results of empirical research have finally made it necessary to go from the sensory to the suprasensory and to find there a solution for the problems about the origin, essence, and purpose of things that arise in the human spirit. Aesthetics also rises immediately above the empirical if it wants to know what beauty is, why some things affect us aesthetically, and what the foundation of aesthetic appreciation is. When empirical aesthetics investigated these three questions in recent years, it reached (as mentioned above) a negative conclusion insofar that at the end of its labor it always came to the mysterious phenomenon of the aesthetic relationship between man and his environment. As long as this is the case, the human spirit cannot rest. Neither will man be constrained by the gloomy assurance of positivism and agnosticism that the essence of things cannot be known; instead, he strives for an answer to the questions that have vexed him throughout the ages. And only in this way will aesthetics become a true, philosophical field of study, because study is never satisfied with the *that* but seeks for the *why*; [with Virgil] it wants "rerum dignoscere causas [to discern the causes of things]."[2]

Our human aesthetic relationship to our environment is not the only relationship, or the first. It is preceded by the intellectual, or rather, in general, the relationship of consciousness. We are so disposed from birth that we receive impressions not only from ourselves but also from the outside world and can transform these impressions into concepts. We have the wonderful capacity to absorb the world outside ourselves into our consciousness and thus to enrich our spirits. Besides, at the same time and in relation to it we have also received the power to penetrate into the world through our wills, to shape it according to our ideas, and to make it serviceable to our freely chosen purposes. The practical relationship is paired with the intellectual one from the beginning. Both relationships can be varied endlessly according to the sphere in which the person operates; they change in religion, morality, in family and society, in agriculture, industry, commerce, and so forth. But these two original relationships of humanity and our environment always return. As conscious, thinking, knowing beings, we draw the world to ourselves and absorb it spiritually; and as striving, acting beings, we approach the world and influence it.

In addition to these relationships, however, comes a third: the aesthetic. Some have denied it a class of its own and have tried to reduce it to one of the two others. [274] The rationalism of the eighteenth century regarded the sense of beauty as only a characteristic and operation of lower, sensory cognition. Opposed to those who regard consciousness of beauty as a totally disinterested pleasure, [Jean-Marie] Guyau asserts that beauty is indeed a matter of desire and will and represents a practical interest. In his judgment, beauty cannot be essentially distinguished from the pleasant and useful, or the creation of artists from other practical labor.

Here again we see the truth that in this world nothing exists by itself: everything is interrelated. In human beings themselves, there are not two or three capabilities that work apart from each other; the works that we produce have this in common: they are the revelation of our ability and to that extent are

2. Ed. note: The reference, not given by Bavinck, is to Virgil, *Georgics* 2.490. A variant read "rerum cognoscere causas (to understand the causes of things)."

all "art." Nevertheless, there is an unmistakable distinction between science and art on the one hand, and between art and technology (and all practical labor) on the other. The scholar is interested in something quite different from the person who enjoys or produces art. They walk different paths, they use other means, and they aim for a different purpose. The scholar wants to know, understand, and judge the world; the aesthetic person wants to enjoy it and revel in its beauty.

In the same way, art and technology can be distinguished. There is a close connection between them, even more so in earlier times than today, now that the elevation of crafts can be called a pressing demand of our time. But the difference between the two is not thereby erased. With technology and even with a craft, the purpose always lies outside the product, which for some reason must be practical and useful. But a real work of art contains the purpose in itself, apart from the service that it may prove to have. There is so much difference between science and technology on the one hand, and art on the other, that it is often said that the incredible development enjoyed today by science and technology has in no small measure damaged art.

The connection and the differences among science, technology, and art can also, in a somewhat different way, be expressed with the idea that the true, the good, and the beautiful are one but also three. The Greeks spoke only of a duality—the good and the beautiful—and often melded these into one concept; they sought wisdom but did not have truth. Yet Christianity made known the content and the value of truth; it awakened in people's hearts a love for truth that was stronger than death. [275] Augustine gave expression to this when he said, "We are seized [caught up] by the love of searching out the truth [*rapimur amore indagandae veritatis*]," and he found this truth—this eternal, absolute truth—in God alone, who was at the same time the highest good [*summum bonum*] and the highest beauty [*summum pulchrum*]. Thus in Christian theology, God was often described as the highest truth, the highest good, and also the highest beauty. However, since this last designation had been touched by Neoplatonic influences already in Augustine, many others, especially Protestant theologians, exchanged it for the more Scriptural terms of majesty and glory. But all three existed originally in God, were one with his essence, and thus actually were one. Only later were these three ideas separated from the theistic foundation and marked as metaphysical realities; or elevated to the rank of gods, whose cult, according to Haeckel, constitutes the core of the new, monistic religion.

If truth, goodness, and beauty (glory) are originally ascribed to God, then they of course and above all bear a supersensory, spiritual character and cannot be opposed to each other in their inner nature. None of the three coincides with sensory, sense-perceptible, empirical reality; they are elevated as norms above the laws of nature, as ideas above sensible reality. Neither are they perceptible by sensory cognition such as animals possess but only through the higher cognition of man, through the spirit that lives in man. Just as truth is high above reality, so goodness is elevated above the useful and beauty above the pleasant. All three belong to the world of intelligent things, even though objectively the sense-perceptible things and subjectively the senses of rational man in his observation and acquisition provide essential services.

Their unity, however, does not exclude diversity. They may be one objectively and real, but they differ from each other formally with regard to *ratione ratiocinata* [understanding rationally determined] and *ratione ratiocinante* [understanding legitimately inferred]. Neither the good (see Wollaston) nor beauty (see Boileau) can be reduced to truth; neither does beauty coincide with the good (as the Greeks taught), nor is the good to be grouped together with beauty under the wider rubric of aesthetics (see Herbart). Neither does the difference lie in the fact that beauty, in distinction from truth and goodness, provides rest, peace, and pleasure, because truth and goodness do the same. After all, if we increase in knowledge, make a discovery, or a new truth comes to us, then we enjoy ourselves greatly, and doing a good deed brings as its first reward peace and self-satisfaction. [276] The cross of Christ teaches us before and above all that truth and goodness are not always one in a formal sense. The eye of faith may see glory in this, but the Greek mocks this foolishness and it is an offense to the Jew. Whoever sees Christ only with the physical eye sees in him no form, beauty, or appearance that would make us desire him.

However, beauty corresponds to thought and being, complies with logical law, and is such that our knowledge of it pleases us. Goodness agrees with "ought to [*zullen, sollen*]" and "to be"; it corresponds to the moral law and is of such a nature that only the possession of that goodness satisfies us. Beauty is different from either of those in that it does not have its own content, and thus it is not coordinated with or on a par with the true and the good; beauty always derives its content from the true and the good, and it is their revelation and appearance. Beauty thus consists in the agreement with content and form, with essence (idea) and appearance; it exists in harmony, proportion, unity in diversity, organization, glow, glory, shining, fullness, perfection revealed [*perfectio phaenomenon*] or whatever one wants to name it. But beauty always is in relation to form, revelation, and appearance.

One should not object here that beauty, as just described, always would require sensory appearance and thus would not have room for spiritual beauty, for God's glory. It is true that pantheism has deduced this from the nature of beauty, but that is completely unjustified. God is distinct from the world and is the Blessed One and the Glorified One in himself. When Scripture speaks of God's glory it is always in reference to his revelation, either in his works (Ps. 8) or for the angels (Isa. 6) or in and for himself (John 17:5). Beauty is always a matter of purely spiritual or spiritual-sensory perception. And while the truth is something in which *knowledge* delights, the good is something whose *possession* satisfies us: beauty is that of which the *perception* pleases us. [As Thomas Aquinas said,] *Pulchra sunt, quae visa [audita] placent* [things are beautiful that please when seen (heard)].

However, with this vision all those questions and difficulties that we met before now return. One can easily say that beauty always involves appearance and is a matter of perception. But what is that perception? Is it an operation of the lower, the sensory or of the higher cognition, of mind and reason? [277] Is it an action of the lower or higher capacity for striving, of desire or of the will? Or is it perhaps something totally special, an affect of a separate capability, which we call "feeling"? Moreover, becoming aware of beauty is an attribute of the subject, but is the object, the perceived item, not at all involved? Must this object "obey" certain conditions and laws in order to elicit appreciation of beauty in people? Or does the awareness of beauty rest solely in an inborn or gradually acquired organization of the human spirit in the struggle for existence? Or is the perception completely dependent on empathy, on a subjective humanizing of the perceived object so that the whole world, according to some philosophers, is human perception (with the exception or inclusion of the *Ding an sich* [thing in itself])? Or if this phenomenalism is untenable and if the object in aesthetics (as in any other science) cannot be eliminated, wherein does the beauty of the object then exist? Is it only the form that counts, so that the artist is totally free in his choice of material and may display the most intimate and scandalous, as long as it is done in a beautiful manner? Or is beauty essentially bound to content, as well as to truth and goodness, and even if it were possible, is it really permissible to break this triad? In short, is Satan beautiful if he appears as an angel of light?

These are all questions that cannot be answered here but that serve to stimulate thoughts and to demonstrate that we face the same problems in aesthetics as in epistemology, problems that deal with the relationship between subject and object, between the "I" and the "non-I," between man and the world. It therefore is also self-evident that in answering these questions, every aesthetician comes from the perspective that he generally assumes in philosophy, and this fact proves again that thinking is always governed by a worldview.

Let us conclude with just a few comments. Perception (as we saw above) as the means whereby beauty is observed points back to a sense of beauty that is by nature peculiar to man, just as in religion, morality, cognition, and so forth. Man cannot be understood as a monistic and evolutionary unit; he is and was, as far as we can go back into history, a being that forms a unity, although imbued with different gifts and capabilities. Among these gifts is the sense of beauty, the delight in appearance, the joy of observation. [278] But this innate discernment is, just as all other so-called innate ideas, no more than a capacity and an urge that becomes action under the influence of the outside world and that takes a very different form with various nations and peoples in sundry places and times. However, there is a common foundation to all this variety and contradiction: there always is an aesthetic relationship between man and the environment in which he lives. There are no people without some sense of beauty, even if very primitive; neither are there any people without some native art. All art forms are already present in simple forms with the so-called nature people, and they are all developed from elements and constructed according to laws that we also observe in a higher development.

This sense of beauty is not rooted in sensory observation or in lower cognition. Naturally, these contribute to the origin of awareness of beauty, just as in science "nihil est in intellectu, quod non prius fuerit in sensu [there is nothing in the intellect that was not earlier in the senses]" [John Locke]. Still, beauty as such becomes known only through the human spirit, and not through sensory eye or ear or through lower cognition; after all, it is first of all just like every idea and norm, of a spiritual nature, and only things that are related know each other. However, the sense of beauty is not merely a quality or activity of higher cognition, of mind and reason: knowing that something is beautiful is one thing; seeing, feeling, and enjoying it is something different. Often there is an enormous difference between a real pedagogue and a practitioner of pedagogy, between a person who knows people and a scientific psychologist. The same holds true for a person who enjoys beauty and an aesthetician. Living and knowing are different. And that is not all. On the one hand, there is not one normal person who is deprived of all sense of beauty, and on the other hand, there is no one whose sense of beauty is developed strongly in all areas. There are many people who have a feeling for poetry but not for music, or for music and not for painting, and the gifts of artists are no less diverse.

But no matter how different the sense of beauty may be, it is always related to the awareness and enjoyment of beauty. As human beings we are not unaffected observers of the world stage; whatever we observe through our senses we also appreciate and evaluate—on a lower level according to the standard of functionality, usefulness, and satisfaction; and on a higher level according to the norms of true and untrue, good and evil, beautiful and ugly. [279] And then, often without any further thought, as soon as we experience the awareness, we form a judgment of worth; this resonates in our heart and awakens a feeling of desire or dislike, of appreciation or rejection. At that point we are no longer in the sphere of consciousness, but we have entered the sphere of feeling, emotion, affections. At this moment it does not matter if this is a peculiar human capacity, distinct from reason and will. But there is no difference of opinion that the awareness or the observation of beauty, especially with sensitive natures produces an instant and immediate enjoyment of beauty.

This enjoyment can be very different, according to the strength of the impression and the sensitivity of the person who receives it. At times beauty gives us no more than a quiet, pleasant, peaceful feeling. At other times it moves us so deeply that we become silent and can only whisper to ourselves, "How beautiful! How beautiful!" At still another time the beauty captures us so strongly and brings us such ecstasy that we must give expression in shouts of joy and wonder. And the beauty always awakens in us images, moods, and affections that otherwise would have remained dormant and not even known to us. Beauty thus discloses us to ourselves and also grants us another, new glimpse into nature and humanity. It deepens, broadens, enriches our inner life, and it lifts us for a moment above the dreary, sinful, sad reality; beauty also brings cleansing, liberation, revival to our burdened and dejected hearts.

We cannot express in words what a valuable gift the Creator of all things has granted to his children. He is the Lord of glory and spreads his beauty lavishly before our eyes in all his works. His name is precious in the whole earth, and while he did not leave us without a witness, he also fills our hearts with happiness when we observe that glory. Beauty and the sense of beauty respond to each other, as the knowable object and the knowing subject, the *religio objectiva* [responding] to the *religio subjectiva*. Truly, awareness of beauty cannot be fully explained as "empathy"; when observing and enjoying true beauty, it is not man who bestows his affections and moods on the observed object, but it is God's glory that meets and enlightens us in our perceptive spirits through the works of nature and art. [280] Humanity and the world are related because they are both related to God. The same reason, the same spirit, the same order lives in both. Beauty is the harmony that still shines through the chaos in the world; by God's grace, beauty is observed, felt, translated by artists; it is prophecy and guarantee that this world is not destined for ruin but for glory—a glory for which there is a longing deep in every human heart.

Because beauty is such a rich, divine gift, it also must be loved by us. It does not, however, have the same compelling force for us as the true and the good. Because beauty does not have its own content, and because it deals with appearance and observation, it is tied more closely to the luxury of life than the true and the good, and it reached freedom and independence much later. The theistic worldview therefore remains a religious-ethical one as opposed to the aesthetic view of pantheism. Art cannot replace worship, nor can the theater replace the church, nor can Lessing's *Nathan* replace the Bible. Beauty can prophesy about the promised land and can give us a glimpse from a distance, as from Mount Nebo, but it is only religion, reconciliation, and peace with God that ushers us into the Canaan of peace.

Nevertheless, beauty also has its right and value. We should be truly sympathetic (even though there are harmful exaggerations) if, as a reaction to intellectualism in education and nurture, "aesthetic culture" again has a modest place and if vocational training is again used for the renewal of artful crafts. The same holds true when aesthetic demands are made in home building and urban design as protection against the defacement of our landscape and when many attempts are made to educate our people aesthetically.

This latter education especially deserves our support. Whatever virtues our people may have, we lack the grace of the French and the well-mannered behavior of the English. Our country is often characterized on the one hand by coarseness that mocks all dignity, and on the other hand by a stiffness that is without any charm. We will not judge here whether Calvinism is to blame for that and has ruined our national song and art and left behind (as is sometimes and still recently declared) "a totally uncouth (putrid?) people." In any case, such a serious accusation must goad us to deny that with our deeds. Along with truth and goodness, beauty also needs to be honored.

# 15

# ETHICS AND POLITICS

[281] The subject of this lecture is, I admit, chosen under the influence of current events, and could therefore stir up the fear that I would bring the war [World War I] into this peaceful meeting and provoke a passionate debate. But even though the topic is very current, it always has been and remains timely. We can therefore discuss it objectively and pertinently, so that it will promote concurrence of insight rather than deep disagreement.

However, there are particular difficulties associated with the discussion of this topic. These difficulties arise, first of all, from ethics. The expectation expressed so frequently—that with the demise of a religious foundation, moral principles would remain unaffected—has certainly not been fulfilled in all respects. Rather, the differences have increased to the point that there is no agreement about any moral commandment, be it authority, life, marriage, or property; and opinions are very far apart about the origin and foundation, the method and criterion, of moral goodness. Even if we leave amoralism aside, the division remains wide. Does morality have its origin in needs and inclinations that are not moral in themselves, or is it an original characteristic of human nature? Is its value determined by its usefulness or by its own inner standard? Who is right—Plato or Darwin, Kant or Comte?

These questions are extremely important; if they had to be answered before we could proceed to the discussion about the relationship between ethics and

Ed. note: Originally published as "Ethiek en politiek," in *Stemmen des tijds* 5, no. 2 (1916): 32–96; also in *Verslagen en mededeelingen der koninklijke Academie van Wetenschappen, afdeeling letterkunde,* series 5, vol. II (Amsterdam: Joh. Muller, 1917), 99–128. This speech was delivered in the meeting of the Literary Division of the Dutch Royal Academy of Science in 1915.

politics, we would not reach that point for hours or days. [282] Fortunately we can assume a practical standpoint and proceed from the indisputable fact that whatever the origin and foundation of morality, it now constitutes an indestructible element of human nature. The categories may at one time have originated differently, but now they are constant. In agreement with Virchow and Ammon, Professor Hugo de Vries declared, "Man is a permanent type; he remains what he is." And we can add that he is and remains a reasoning and moral being.

We may even go a step further. The moral dimension that now is an essential aspect of human nature does not exist only in form and without content (in the imperative category of "You must—and that's it!"). From birth, morality takes a certain direction and includes a certain content, although it is not rigid and unmovable. Last year [1914] Victor Cathrein published a three-volume work with Herder publishers in Freiburg, *Die Einheit des sittlichen Bewusstseins der Menschheit*—a book that was the fruit of many years and extensive study.[1] In the book Cathrein tries to prove that moral thinking and acting everywhere rest on the same matrix of moral thoughts and principles and that there is an eternal and unchangeable moral law that governs the whole world. This issue is also of the greatest importance for the unity and completeness of the moral law, for its truth and value.

However, for our present purpose those theories can remain outside of our discussion, and I can base myself again on fixed and immovable ideas. No matter which factors have caused this situation and whatever route was taken to come to this end result—among all cultured people (and for simplification we will leave the so-called nature people out of the discussion), there now is indeed a rather strong agreement on moral principles. In the application to certain persons and actions, the moral judgments will often differ, but these judgments will be determined among civilized people according to rather similar norms. In somewhat the same manner, we all make similar distinctions in the area of what is morally good and morally evil, between right and wrong, virtue and vice. Even those who greatly differ on the foundation of morality do produce a list of virtues and vices that demonstrate an unexpected and therefore even more remarkable similarity. According to Professor Heymans, it is the same with ethics as with logic. [283] Today, because of all kinds of reasons, the practitioners of science arrive at very different results, but they all begin with the same convictions about the distinction between truth and falsehood, and they all feel bound to the same laws. In the same way, there are certain general moral norms in human consciousness by which we judge ourselves (and especially others). We thus prove that the law is written in our hearts.

---

1. Ed. note: Victor Cathrein, *Die Einheit des sittlichen Bewusstseins der Menschheit: Eine ethnographische Untersuchung* (Freiburg and St. Louis: Herder, 1914).

If in this manner we have been able to push aside the difficulties that face us in the treatment of this subject from an ethical perspective, we immediately hear equally severe objections from the side of politics. After all, politics has had a long history, has been defined very differently throughout time, and is still used with various meanings. Modesty requires that we leave to jurists the task to come to more unity and clarity about this issue. For a practical and clear discussion of the subject of this lecture, permit me to make the following distinctions.

With the Greeks, "politics" first of all meant the rights of the citizen and then the practice of these rights by participation in city or state government; it also meant state government, with the principles and the forms (monarchy, republic, democracy, and so forth) in which it was practiced. Works in which this city government was described and developed had such titles [in Greek] as *Politeia, Politikē, Politikos, Nomoi*; and in Latin *De republica, De civitate, De legibus*. Because the philosophy, or scholarship, of that time was divided by Aristotle into theoretical and practical, with the latter being divided into *ethica, oeconomica,* and *politica,* the last term [*politica*] came to be used for the philosophy or theory of the state.

The position of politics in the practical branch of philosophy, however, proved that it was not regarded as a pure academic field, as for example was physics or metaphysics. From ancient times there was a difference of opinion about whether the adjective *politica* had to be combined with *scientia* or with *ars*. History has moved the meaning of the word more and more from the theoretical to the practical side. In any case, politics is no longer *the* academic discipline about the state but only *one* of such disciplines, and it includes at least two subjects. As the general *theory* or philosophy or science of the state, it examines the origin, essence, purpose, task, authority, and forms of the state. But this general theory is to be distinguished in many ways from the *art* of politics that applies the theory to certain circumstances and relationships and takes into account the interests of the state as a condition for the welfare of the state. [284] The theory indicates the essence and calling, the rights and boundaries of the state; the art of politics provides the insight into what the state must do in certain circumstances to fulfill its task and reach its goal. The first rests primarily on philosophical studies, the latter on historical; the first is primarily theoretical, the second practical, meaning *prudentia.*

Both of these subjects, however, must still be distinguished from politics as *praxis*. Here we are dealing neither with the theory nor with the art of politics, but rather with the tact, or skill, of the statesman to speak or to do what is required at a given moment for the welfare of the state. A scholar of theoretical politics or the philosophy of the state can, in a certain sense, ignore the present and still have profound insights centuries ahead of or centuries before his time. The student of practical politics must be located in the midst of history, must interpret the present with the past, and see the past in the light of the present; he can then offer solutions that are of great importance and rich understanding for the direction of the state. But both of these still remain outside the immediate reality of life. The statesman, however, must not only understand the past and the present; he must above all have the skill, the capability, the proficiency, the political genius to use the circumstances of a concrete event to hit the right mark. Bismarck therefore compared the able statesman to a hunter or fisherman; with fishing and hunting, nearly everything depends on patient waiting, the correct observation, and then the sudden use of the right moment: that is how it goes in praxis politics. In that sense, every statesman must be a *Realpolitiker*. It is not a matter of words but of deeds—although the word can also be a deed.

In all three ways that the word "politics" is used here [theory, art, praxis], one may regard politics as a high, noble, nearly sacred matter. If it is true that it can degenerate so horribly, especially in practice, then this is confirmation that "the best is corrupted the worst." As theory, as an art, as praxis— politics is concerned with that form of community among people that is the indispensable condition and essential foundation for the well-being of a nation, for safeguarding its independence and freedom, for developing its gifts and talents, and also for fulfilling its calling in the history of humanity. Although the three meanings of the word "politics" are different, the one cannot do without the others. [285] Without insight into the essence and calling of the state, politics falls victim to opportunism without principles, utilitarianism, and egoism. Without knowledge of the past and present, of the obligations now demanded of the state, and of the rules according to which these obligations must be carried out, politics soon deteriorates into politics of pedantry or politics of feeling. And without the wise tact of the statesman in the practice of politics, it will remain barren in spite of all its knowledge, will bungle good chances, and will allow favorable opportunities to slide by.

If, however, politics as theory, as art, and as praxis forms a threefold strand that may not be broken, then this idea of its own accord leads to the connection that exists between ethics and politics, which it already assumes. But not everyone is convinced of this connection. It has been denied by many at one time or other, especially in the previous century.

In ancient times it was the Sophists who maintained the right of the strongest as the only natural right and who let other rights and morality rest on capricious regulations that the mighty ones had determined to their own advantage. In more recent philosophy, similar ideas were proposed by Machiavelli, Spinoza, and Hobbes; politicians who elevate might above right, in theory or in practice, have been present in all times and all nations. There is truth, however, in the argument of [Alfred] Fouillée that the English spirit is more inclined to sacrifice right to expediency and the German to sacrifice right to might. The English show a greater affinity for the trend of the eighteenth century and the Germans for the nineteenth century, and the difference between them is great. The eighteenth century declared that the state existed by contract, from the free will of the parties, and thus by chance and caprice. As a reaction against this individualism, the nineteenth century, under Hegel's influence, took its stance in the Absolute and saw in the whole world a continuous process of the absolute idea. In that process the state also had its place, even the highest place, because it was the union of family and society, the completed reality of freedom, the reality of the moral idea, the moral spirit, as the public, distinct, substantial will. Whether people want to acknowledge it or not, in the process in which the essence of self-consciousness comes to the state, individuals are only moments: "It is the way of God with the world, that the state has come into being. Its foundation is the power of reason which is realized in the will." However, Hegel notes especially that with this idea of the state, one may not have specific states in mind but rather "must consider the idea of the real God." [286] This idea of the state also runs its course throughout history and realizes itself gradually through wars and judgments, because world history is world judgment, until it reaches true reconciliation, in which the state is fully unfolded as the image and reality of reason.

Hegel's philosophy expresses the beautiful thought that the state, with its right and might, does not rest on chance and caprice but in the final analysis rests on reason. One cannot deny, however, that Hegel erases the distinction between what should be and what is too much and thus has promoted restoration and conservatism in a dubious way. If the Absolute realizes itself and takes care that everything in its place and its time is reasonable and moral, what else remains of right and freedom for the citizen but to fall in with whatever is, to subject himself unwillingly to the deified state, and at most try to understand reality with his mind?

Moreover, when Hegel speaks of nature and of development of nature, this concept is totally different from what came after him. For Hegel as for Goethe, nature did not stand in opposition to spirit. Rather, spirit had logical priority and came to higher and fuller revelation in nature, in the whole world with its various domains. Here German idealism agreed with the philosophers of the rights of nature; their use of this term recalls the time when nature included the whole world, not only the physical but also the spiritual.

However, after Hegel the meaning of the word "nature" underwent a significant change. This change came about through Feuerbach turning Hegel's philosophy upside down, through the historical materialism of Marx and Engels, through the influence of the more recent natural science, through Comte's positivism, through Darwin's theory of selection, with its struggle for life and survival of the fittest. Now the word "nature" has become the designation of the material world, with its material atoms and mechanical-chemical operations, from which people have tried to understand the phenomena of life, soul, and spirit. Thus the relationship was completely turned around: matter did not come from the spirit, but the spirit from the material, thought from brains, all ideology from economic relationships, and, further back, from material atoms and mechanical forces.

When in this framework the state is called a product of nature, it has a totally different meaning than it did at one time. [287] Now the materialistic and sociological school means that the state is to be regarded as a physical entity that at one time inevitably came from the economic structure of society, just as the latter in the same manner came from the biological and the biological in its turn came from the mechanical processes. The same laws, operations, and forces rule everywhere. Everything in man, society, and state run with the same inevitability as do the stars in the firmament; the gravity of nature is like the mutual interdependence in society. There is no need for a priori theories, for metaphysical speculations, for abstract ideas and value judgments. Instead, only facts are to be the foundation of all sciences, as well as those of the state and rights; these also must become positivistic and use sociology as their foundation. Then at some time they will become exact sciences, just like astronomy—the natural sciences of the state and of rights, that is, social physics.

Just as in nature the struggle for existence is the strongest force for development and progression and therefore rules and must rule, the same force is equally indispensable and essential between social classes in society and in humanity between nations. According to [Walter] Bagehot, war is the most important force for the perfection of people and the art of war the most brilliant phenomenon in the history of humanity. The only thing that counts in that struggle is might and power. Morality does not play a role. The state is really power, and it stands above and outside of rights and is itself the highest right. For its continuation it may demand and do everything, and dedication to the state is the citizen's highest duty. And this power of the state is also the mother of rights. There is no such thing as natural or innate right. Rights are always born from the struggle between dissimilar groups, tribes, and peoples and come into being only in a union of such groups through a power organization; all rights contain a segment of the state and the power of the state. There are no rights outside of the state; justice always follows the police. Through these rights the state in turn creates morality, but this morality is totally different from what was formerly created in a group by custom or convention. This [state] morality is much higher than that formed by custom or convention and the two are continually at war. But in this way there is further development of rights, and in such wars between groups classes, and nations, might always prevails.

Politics and ethics thus form the greatest imaginable opposites. Politics is the philosophy of the *power* of the state and in practice can never be anything else than realpolitik. [288] This position was assumed with full awareness in the anonymously published *Grundsätze der Realpolitik* [*Fundamentals o*

*Political Realism*], in which the author, Gustav Diezel, called the close connection between power and rule the fundamental truth of all politics and the key to all of history.[2] Since that time, many statesmen of word and deed have held up before people this "gospel" of power as the highest wisdom.

In this theory of power there is (as we will see later) an element of truth; taken as a whole, however, it suffers from very serious defects. There is the immediate objection that it was developed too much under the influence of current spiritual trends, although the movement protests against all a priori arguments. With the Sophists, the theory arose out of skepticism that undermined all truth and certainty and thus also all scholarship. With Machiavelli and Hobbes, the theory served to use the absolute power of the monarch to end the division in the country. Today it is closely related to the materialistic spirit and the theory of mechanical evolution. However, this theory is already passé; in many prominent circles realism has taken the place of idealism. Besides selection, the struggle for existence, the inheriting of acquired characteristics, and the survival of the fittest, many other factors are accepted in the process of development today, such as mutation, regenerative powers, and psychological and ideal operations. As Prince Kropotkin remarked several years ago and has repeated many times since, Darwinism—according to which life is always a struggle in which the weak succumb and only the strong survive—is a very one-sided theory.

Besides struggle in the animal and human world, we also see signs of sympathy, love, and mutual support that creatures of the same species show each other when they protect the weak against the strong and thus form a strong factor in the evolutionary process. This factor existed and operated from the beginning in social instincts, especially in maternal love, by which the members of a family, generation, and tribe were very closely bonded to each other.

To go beyond this time and to assume with Rousseau or Hobbes a prehistoric, idyllic, or barbaric natural situation is arbitrary (as Professor Doctor S. Bril of Breslau remarks) "as long as we have no certain knowledge about the origin of man." This much is certain, that as far as we can go back into the past through history, we find a community that is in some way regulated externally by morals, customs, conventions, and tradition and not by the state. [289] With [Rudolf] Stammler we can therefore make a distinction between a purely physical [community] and a social community, between the law of nature and external rule, and also, in that connection, between natural and historical scholarship. Humanity, with its own reasoning and moral nature, stands between those two. Thus, as soon as there are people, their communities display another, a *human,* character, notwithstanding all similarity that

2. Ed. note: Gustav Diezel, *Grundsätze der Realpolitik angewendet auf die staatlichen Zustände Deutschlands* (Stuttgart, 1853).

we may see with certain animals, and in spite of their sometimes primitive forms; it is not purely physical, but from the beginning also psychic, religious, ritualistic, ethical, and judicial. Mister [M. W. F.] Treub (just as Stammler) is therefore correct when he protests against historic materialism, that the economic structure of society was never completely material but always and from the beginning included all kinds of other relationships: psychological, religious, philanthropic, ethical, judicial. In society there is no judicial superstructure over an economical foundation; the economic foundation is already largely judicial.

In such a primitive society the community has an even stronger religious, ritualistic, ethical character than the people that have a rich culture. Everything is still undifferentiated in customs; only later a clear distinction develops gradually among religion, morality, justice, art, and education. But even then, when the community has developed this far, there continues to be a deep bond and a mutual influence among all these expressions of their lives.

In the Ten Commandments of the moral law, the service of God constitutes the content of the first table. In Christian theology, "religion" was for a long time treated under moral virtues, that is, under justice. The Hebrew word for justice includes both morality as well as justice; the relationship between the two words was felt so deeply that sometimes all justice was reduced to morality, while at other times all morality was reduced to justice. Moral good is a just demand that the moral order of the world applies unconditionally in a categorical imperative to every person and to the whole person; and justice (*jus*) is an application of the *justum* to certain forms of society. Both develop or deteriorate together; even in the most modern state there continues to exist an indispensable and unbreakable reciprocity between these two concepts, just as there is between all elements of culture. This is true because they both have their origin and root in the one indivisible human nature, with its multifaceted gifts and strengths.

[290] If we look at history, not from the vantage of one century or one-half century but of all centuries, then we will see that this connection between morality and justice, between ethics and politics, has been recognized at all times by all important people.

With the Greeks, politics was a part of ethics. Plato and Aristotle did not deduce the state from accident or caprice but from ethical necessity. In a logical sense the state comes before the individual, because the whole precedes the parts and the goal precedes the means. Man is by nature a social being and cannot reach his social destiny except in and through the state; he can only be perfect and happy in community. The state is the essential condition for the origin and existence of knowledge, art, education, and mental and moral nurture—in short, for the triumph of good over evil. The task and purpose of the state is therefore the healing of the soul, a happy and virtuous life, and politics is therefore a component of practical philosophy, the application of ethics to the free citizen.

This thought about the relation between ethics and politics soon took on a fixed form in the theory of so-called natural law. To understand this properly, one has to go back to ancient peoples. As [Chantepie de la] Saussaye says, they did not know the difference between the moral and the natural order. The law of the universe is at the same time natural, religious, ritual, moral, and political. One term serves to indicate it in all its various applications: Tao in China, Rta in India, Asha in Persia, Ma'at in Egypt. Heaven, earth, family, people, kingdom are all ruled by the same law. The order for the state is grounded in natural, cosmic, divine order. The same principle was held in ancient times by the Greeks; before the appearance of the Sophists, the people and the sages were generally convinced that what happened in the polis [city-state] was good, reasonable, natural, and divine. Man and philosopher, religion and philosophy, mysticism and physics—all were one, it seemed. The soul of man felt related to the soul of the world.

However, when they later came into contact with other nations and came to know other customs and morals, rights and laws, then doubt and uncertainty arose, and the Sophists drew the conclusion that all rights and morals were historic, positive, conventional. To avoid this skepticism, Plato and Aristotle found an escape in the distinction between the essential and the accidental, concept and image, thought and observation, idea and reality. In his *Ethica,* Aristotle also applied this distinction to justice; besides justice that rests on legal conclusions, he also accepted justice that applies by nature to all, and he thus became the father of natural law.

[291] Later this theory was greatly expanded. The Stoa determined a relationship of natural law to cosmic reason and to human reason, meaning right reason, in which natural law was contained as general and innate concepts. Cicero deduced it from a created, inborn *lex naturae*, which, according to general consensus, was common to all people. Posidonius, Seneca, and others saw it as an inheritance that humanity had preserved from the golden age. Philosophers introduced all kinds of distinctions in natural law. They spoke not only of an eternal law that, according to Cicero, was born simultaneously with the divine spirit but also about a natural law, natural rights, and human rights and finally about civil, existing, and positive rights.

All these terms about natural law were gradually taken over by Christians and associated with Bible texts such as Matthew 7:21; Romans 2:14–15; 13:1, and according to their content were identified with the Ten Commandments. However, the large number of expressions became the cause of much misunderstanding. It is similar to those who identify Augustine's *civitas terrena* [earthly city] with our state and do great injustice to the church father. Whoever does not clearly distinguish the terms of church fathers and Scholastics, of Roman Catholic and Protestant scholars, runs great danger of assigning a meaning to the origin and rights of the state, government, private property, and slavery that was never intended.

At any rate, it becomes very clear that Hugo Grotius is not the father of natural law; he only made some changes in the theory, and it soon became clear that these were not improvements. First, he continued what the Spanish theologian Gabriel Vasquez had in some way already done before him. Grotius made natural law, at least hypothetically, independent from God. Second, through a one-sided deduction from reason, he changed natural law into rational law. As a result, natural law came to be regarded more and more as a system of laws and rules, that was fixed outside of history and could be established in an explanation of the rights of man. Grotius's theory also brought along a worse evil than if reason and free will really were the foundation of justice: one had to hold to a hypothesis of a prehistoric state, either idyllic or barbaric, but at least a natural state without justice. In this way, natural law was considered as so hypostatized and mechanized that it lost all life and soon succumbed under the sharp criticism of the historical and sociological school. For many years, natural law was considered an antique concept that could be safely stored in a historical museum or was like a weed sprouting here and there that could be pulled out, roots and all.

[292] It is therefore very remarkable that in recent times the theory has come back to life vigorously—not in the historical, rationalistic form that it had assumed since Grotius, but in its ideal shape and indestructible principle. We owe this revival in general to the reaction of idealism that arose against materialism, but it has its special origin in neo-Kantianism, which went in a new direction in theology, philosophy, and jurisprudence. We owe the revival also to the restoration of a priori principles: the settled conviction from historical investigation that religion, morality, justice, and aesthetics cannot be explained from extraneous factors but are constants and grounded in an original essence of human nature. Finally, we are indebted to the psychology of the subconscious, which has demonstrated that the human soul reaches back much further and is richer than mind and reason and will.

The profound thought that is at the foundation of natural law is, according to Emil Lack, none other than the question about the absolute meaning of right and justice. It has therefore become a universal historical principle, which cannot be struck down by any criticism. Its immortal value consists in the fact that it has believed in and has held on to suprahistorical, timeless norms. Indeed, with justice we cannot do without such norms, with neither religion, nor morality, nor aesthetics. There is, after all, an indisputable distinction between being and belonging, reality and value, fact and norm, between justice that matters positively according to law and justice, that *sein soll* [must be], that *richtige Recht* [correct justice], as Stammler calls it. This distinction does not minimize in the least the great contributions of the historical and sociological school, which have opened our eyes to the development o justice and the powerful influence that they have exerted on social groups and relationships. But the necessity to make the above-mentioned distinction is forced on us from all sides.

It is important to note that the law is always incomplete and faulty; it never covers the richness of life. This comes to expression especially in a court of law, when the judge is not sufficiently served by the law and in most cases does not find its interpretation and application sufficient; then he consciously or subconsciously makes use of values and norms that are not expressed in the law but that are derived from his own conscience and experience.

[293] From of old, next to the law of guilt and punishment of the perpetrator, there also was room for reasonableness, for the realization that no matter how precise and complete the law, it can never completely fulfill the demands of justice.

Of even more importance is the fact that much justice operates in society that is not recorded in laws or that there are many laws on the books that no longer count in practical life. Even more serious, there are always positive, operating laws that are unjust according to higher standards or that can become unjust in different times and circumstances. There also is ideal justice that ought to be recognized as justice, which struggles upward out of daily life and strives for recognition. All development of justice, after all, comes about because people or groups of people have gained the conviction about another, better justice and have begun a battle against existing law in the name of this higher justice.

But this points out further that the idea of justice has a teleological character. As soon as we have a sense of justice about something, we demand that it should govern. "What must be" is inherent in justice, but this "must be" is a purely ethical phenomenon; it is thoroughly moral. It does not become justice from the outside; it cannot be explained from usefulness or interest; it is not related to the demand of society or the power of the state. This urge is in man since birth, roots justice in morality, and creates an unbreakable bond between politics and ethics. Just order is grounded in moral order and possesses its strong, unshakable permanence.

Having arrived at this point, we can take one more step. If this moral order in which justice is rooted is not a human imagination, a dream, an illusion—beautiful but deceitful—then it must exist in objective reality. If it is not just a subjective appreciation and an aesthetic feeling, then its assessment must be based on reality. And then that profound concept naturally returns that we saw in all peoples, in all religions, and in all philosophical systems: the order of justice is based on the moral order, and this is related to the cosmic order and the divine order that governs all things. Civil right has human right as its background: it points back to a law of nature, it is rooted in natural law, and it is revelation of the eternal law that originated simultaneously with the divine spirit. Emil Lack therefore gave this definition of philosophy of law:

"It is the search for a transcendental order, or the characteristic value connection of law, the question of a frame of being in a worldview."

[294] If morality and justice are so closely related, then it is very difficult to point out the distinction between the two. Maintaining the relationship is (and also was historically) considered more significant than pointing out the distinction. Apart from the Stoma's distinction between complete and incomplete duty, the question was first posed when Grotius increasingly separated natural law from ethics and based it on the foundation of a social contract. The result was that coercion had to be incorporated into the idea of law, because a contract among people offers little certainty if it is not maintained by coercion. Thus morality and justice came to stand apart from each other. Justice had nothing to do with morality, meaning the inner disposition, but only with the deed (and a deed can be coerced by the strong arm of the government) and morality obtained its own sphere, totally separated from the sphere of justice.

With Pufendorf and Thomasius, who developed this theory, some connection remained between the two spheres, because the right of the state and the coercion for the well-being of the people became subordinated and at the same time morality was built on a eudaemonistic foundation. But this connection was also broken when Kant appeared and banished eudaemonism completely from ethics. For Kant, morality is present only when good is performed only for itself, out of regard for duty; only the goodwill constitutes true and unconditional good. Morality is thus related only to disposition, to character; its commandment comes from inside the person, in the categorical imperative, and has only the inner urge at its disposal. Legalism, on the other hand, pays no attention to and is not concerned about internal motivation; it is satisfied with the deed, with the external action; its imperative comes from outside the person; and it is maintained by outside force. Morality intends to safeguard the inner peace in the soul, and legalism the external peace among people.

This distinction exerted a strong influence. It not only became part of (in altered form) the philosophy of Fichte, Schelling, and Hegel, but it was also frequently presented as an irreconcilable contrast. On the one side appeared a man like Nietzsche, who turned accepted morality upside down and recognized only the right of the strongest; on the other side was someone like Tolstoy, who on the basis of the Sermon on the Mount declared accursed the whole state with its jurisdiction, police, and military. [295] Much greater however, is the number of those who avoided these extremes and made a distinction between the morality of the individual and the morality of the state, and thus they posed a most serious problem.

The fact cannot be denied that today we have, although not a complete separation, certainly a distinction between ethics and politics, between morality and justice. But it is doubtful if it can pass muster. The boundary between the two can hardly be drawn as the difference between internal inclination and external deed, because morality does involve not only the will and character but also acts and deeds. A good tree may expectedly and naturally produce good fruit, but the good remains a quality of both the fruit and the tree. Conversely, justice is not satisfied with only the mere external obedience to the law but is certainly also interested in motives. When Stammler declares that the economist examines the content of social relationships and the jurist is concerned only with its form, then Mister Treub observes correctly that legal regulations are certainly not only concerned with form; a society without, for example, property or marriage laws would be completely different from one in which these laws were acknowledged and maintained. But apart from this issue, for the judge to pronounce a just verdict, he must consider both the deed and the character of the perpetrator; in the same way all justice, to be sound and strong, must satisfy the ideas of righteousness that reside in the people and that are rooted in their conscience. Whoever detaches justice from those ideas and seeks its stability in power and coercion does not make justice stronger but weaker, and undermines its foundations.

If one objects that in a perfect society where everyone does his duty there would be no place for justice, we would answer that the same could be said, in the same degree and in the same way, for the moral law. In both cases, however, people forget that love is not the abolishing but the fulfilling of the law, and for that reason it is so sacred and wonderful, since it fully satisfies the demands of the law.

Furthermore, the distinction of justice does not lie in coercion. Justice certainly is power, one of the strongest powers in the world—I nearly said, stronger than religion and morality. But that is not a contrast, because the power of religion and morality lies in the fact that in our conscience they are experienced as the justice of a Higher Power for the benefit of our whole personality. [296] However, all this power is of a moral nature, *pouvoir moral* [moral power], which differs enormously from the physical, coercive power that acts in maintaining justice in the state. Of course, this coercive power is also of the greatest importance and absolutely necessary in a society such as ours. It is a concomitant, a security and guarantee of justice, but it is not inherent in justice and is not an essential aspect of it.

After all, there are communities of justice without the *state*, such as the community of the family, generations, and tribes, and even the organization of a band of robbers. There is justice without coercion because the church has justice that, at least in Protestant Christianity, excludes coercion. There is justice without coercion because the moral law includes the virtue of righteousness, which commands that we give each person his due. There is justice without coercion because there is much justice in society that is not at all—or only very generally—regulated by law, and such justice is based on custom and fairness, on good faith and good morals. There is justice without coercion because in many cases coercion to comply with legal duties (for example, to royalty) is impossible; here we count on other factors, such as sense of duty and honor and the awareness that society was, in the first place, maintained through such moral influences. There is (to mention no more but still the most important) justice without coercion because one must obey God more than men.

The distinction between morality and justice and thus also between ethics and politics must be found in a different way. According to custom, justice [recht] points first of all to the subjective ability that gives a person the right to something. This meaning appears frequently in our everyday speaking: the right to speak, to stand on one's rights; the right to one's wages; the right will win. More generally and related to the same adjective, "right" is the term for the inner, moral rule used for anything that is not crooked or askew or slanted, but straight, honest, good, true, and beautiful.[3] All these qualities have a value that we do not assign arbitrarily, a value that belongs to it by nature and that we, sometimes in spite of ourselves, acknowledge and praise. Truth, virtue, and beauty never are in the service of violence; they cannot even find escape there without denying themselves. They are powerless, defenseless as a lamb over against brute power and cruel coercion. But these virtues have one thing that places them above all their enemies: the white robe of innocence. And therefore they possess that wonderful, secret power that is called justice.

[297] Justice is not derived from the outside, but rests in and flows from nature. It is a spiritual power that belongs to everything insofar as it is true and good and beautiful. [It is] the mighty self-defense with which nature (that Calvin even is willing to call "God-fearing") has been especially endowed by God with holiness. Seen in this broad sense and from this point of view, one can call justice and morality two sides of the same task. What is true, good, and beautiful can be as weak and helpless as a child in a crib, but it has the right to be and to be honored. Whatever is false, evil, and shameful does exist and often assumes violence in order to rule, but it has no right to exist and is itself so convinced of this that it clothes itself in a robe of light and thereby brings honor to the true and the good.

On earth all these moral qualities are concentrated in man. Justice is therefore a privilege that is especially granted to reasoning, to moral human nature, to the personhood—not in opposition to, but in concord with, community. When this community and each of its members is exposed to all kinds of violation and oppression in this world, then a part of that justice is put into law and placed under the protection of the government. Some scholars, such

3. Ed. note: Bavinck plays here with the Dutch word *recht*, which means, inter alia, law, right, claim, title; it also serves as an adjective, meaning "straight" (as in a line) and "appropriate" (e.g., word). The second usage is found, though less frequently, in English.

as the late Professor [H. J.] Hamaker, accordingly try to make a distinction between morality and justice, as follows: Justice is the term for that part of morality in a society that the government has apparently taken over, solemnly sanctioned, and maintains in a more solemn and official manner than society can do through public opinion, jurisdiction, and penalties. The whole distinction is thus based on something incidental and changeable, on the attitude that the government assumes in regard to regulation of conduct. If the government puts out its protecting hand, then it is justice; if it does not concern itself with it, then it continues to be morality. And this stance of the government is very different and changing in different times and places.

There is some good in this concept in that justice and morality are very closely related and considered to have existed long before government. However, it is a very one-sided concept insofar as it counts morality and justice as having the same content and it calls justice the part of morality that rather incidentally and arbitrarily is sanctioned by the government. It is true that the task of the government cannot always be determined with clear boundaries, since it changes with time and circumstances. [298] But Hamaker lauds an absolutism of the state that does not have to honor any boundary in family or property, in religion or morality; and if it would promote the interest of the state, it could mark all morality as justice. But even if the state would be allowed to do so, it would never be able to, because morality and justice do not at all have the same content, since they look at the same issue from different points of view. Justice in the objective sense, and even more precisely in the positive sense, is not in itself morality even though it is grounded in morality. Rather, it is a certain side of morality. It is that aspect of morality that can be taken under the protection of the government, and the government is even capable and suitable for this, as upholder of righteousness. Positive justice is thus rightly called that ethical minimum that the government can and must maintain within the sphere of its capability so that real morality and also all of human life can develop in all its depth and breadth and so that all the people can develop the fullness of their strengths and gifts.

Justice therefore, insofar as the government places it under its protection, always has a serving capacity. The people are not there for the government, but rather the government for the people, the state for the community.

From this distinction between morality and justice flows the notion that, up to a point, one can speak of an individual and a state morality. There is truth in the description that the state is *power*. Even when [Fritz] Berolzheimer calls politics the theory of state's power, then that definition is not in itself wrong, although easily open to misunderstanding. The error begins when the power of the state is put forth as purpose and that power is no longer the means for maintaining righteousness. Actually, we see this happen all the time in national and world politics, in major and minor politics, in the politics of parties and states. Whoever turns in this direction and unfortunately sees his attempts crowned with success—that person will go from bad to worse and finally will not fear any lie or deceit. Plato already complained about the ordinary politicians who want to make the state serve their interest; their generation has not yet died. But no transgression will undo the right of law. The power of the state is and remains in its essence at the service of righteousness.

This calling of the state brings with it peculiar obligations, yet obligations that are inside the boundaries of ethics, not outside of ethics. There is great difference of opinion about this calling, but whether one regards the state as a justice state or a culture state or a combination of both, in every instance the state has an eminently moral task. [299] The state is certainly not morality, as Hegel proposed. However, the state does fulfill such a noble and elevated task, both within the country and outside it, that the state must be counted as a moral task and must be considered as the fulfillment of one of morality's most outstanding precepts. Is the state not bound to justice and to moral principles in national politics in its legal, executive, and judicial powers? Is it not considered a great advance that colonial politics are moving more and more in an ethical direction? And would anyone dare to contend that the state does not have to concern itself with morality in its foreign policies, in the regulation of international personal rights, in its making of treaties, trade agreements, and all such?

One could hesitate to answer this last question affirmatively when considering a country at war. Then, from beginning to end, the most fundamental principles of ethics are denied and the simplest stipulations of justice are trampled underfoot. But here it also becomes clear that, as always, justice and reality are two, without justice ceasing to be justice. Only this—there is a law of peace and also a law of war: both exist until and in and after the war. It is less than true to propose that during a war justice always and everywhere ceases to exist. Grotius saw it differently and better. In his introduction to his book *De jure belli ac pacis*, he rejects the proposition that nothing is unjust as long as it is useful; he strongly rejects the opinion that justice and war exclude each other; during and in war justice does not cease, and neither does morality. Just as the government has to restrain crime with coercion and penalties in the nation in the cause of righteousness, in the same way the state does not bear the sword in vain in regard to other nations. Acting in this way, the state fulfills a thoroughly moral calling because it maintains righteousness, and with love this is an eminently ethical virtue.

These two virtues are not the same, but even less do they exclude each other as Marcion and many others declared, because love without righteousness deteriorates into anarchy, and righteousness without love degenerates into despotism. Love can be reduced to righteousness because righteousness does not demand only "to each his own" but also "to each yours—your involvement, your care, your love." And righteousness can be reduced to love because love is the content of a commandment that begins with "thou shalt." Still, the two virtues are distinctive, as are all virtues, and these various duties, no matter how different, flow from one moral law. [300] It is the same moral law that comes to parents and children, employer and worker, industrialist and businessman—but it assigns to each very different duties. Similarly, it is the same law that holds for government and citizens. However, in agreement with the very special task that the government has to fulfill in the world, the law calls the government to duties that no citizen can or may carry out. The state is not the vehicle for love and mercy but of righteousness; it is the sovereign dominion of justice. The state has opportunity, with the power at its disposal, to maintain the rule of law, both nationally and internationally. If it does so, it places itself, according to its essence and calling, in the service of the moral law; it makes politics subordinate to ethics; it encloses and protects a domain in which human personhood can come to its richest development and reach its highest goal.

Let me conclude this summary discussion with a brief remark about international justice, which can perhaps best serve as a test case for our arguments. Whether there is a *jus intra gentes* [justice among the nations] depends completely on the definition one gives to justice. If there is no justice without coercion, then it is impossible to even speak of international justice, and one perhaps derives some malicious pleasure from seeing the documents of agreement go up in flames in the current war. In fact, we all are profoundly impressed that international justice is virtually without power and yields at the first attack so that there are attempts from all sides to support this weak justice with the power of an international army. One can respect these efforts, even though one expects little good from its outcome.

However, even if none of these attempts is successful, then human rights are still not without value or power. First, human justice was not devised by Grotius; it was developed long before him and goes back to ancient times. International justice ultimately rests (and must rest), either implicitly or explicitly, on two pillars: the Christian principle of the oneness of the human race in origin and essence, and the principle of the catholicity of God's kingdom. These principles have not been totally unproductive in history; they have worked as a yeast and continue to do so. Recently Franz von Liszt made the notable remark that human justice certainly has a future: history teaches that after every great war justice comes forward with power and makes a step forward. This was true after the Thirty Years' War, the Napoleonic wars, the Crimean War, the [Franco-German] War of 1870–71, and this will certainly happen again after the current World War [I]. One cannot believe that a crisis such as we are currently experiencing (no matter how apparently useless and without purpose) will not bear some fruit and will not at all benefit the principle of peace. It is true that people and nations learn slowly, extremely lowly, and every lesson must be repeated countless times. But history also teaches that many ideas, such as humanitarianism, philanthropy, freedom of religion, emancipation of the lower classes, constitutional government, and so forth have slowly and with much struggle found a place in the consciousness of nations.

Of course, ideas do not offer a conclusive guarantee against state absolutism and despotism on one hand, and revolution and anarchism on the other, and the power of ideas is often exaggerated. Still, principles are not without value. Even though they have no coercive power, they are rooted in natural law, which is founded on the order of the world and which points back to eternal law; these principles are also intended for development. International justice is founded on this moral order. It is not ready made and for immediate use; it is even susceptible to be violated at any moment. But it does exist; we all judge accordingly and test the actions of world powers by it. International justice shall proceed and become stronger to the degree that it penetrates into the consciences of monarchs and nations and is increasingly founded on an ethical basis.

Will the outcome ever be that we will reach a kingdom of love and peace? Science has no answer for this. But with his *Critique of Pure Reason*, Kant intended to curb science so that a place for faith and hope would remain.

# Appendix A

## Foreword by C. B. Bavinck

This is the last publication of my beloved and respected eldest brother, his final work. His hand has now laid down his pen; he was not even able to write the preface to this volume.

Shortly before his illness, in consultation with the publisher, he planned a volume that would gather together a number of essays that had been published in various journals. He was still able to make the choice himself. Later, when I visited him during his illness, he told me that he believed that the collection of essays he had assembled would continue to be of interest to future generations because they dealt with important subjects that remain the order of the day. The plans were completed; nonetheless, "man proposes, but God disposes."

Not knowing what would befall him, he requested that the publisher hold the presses until the conclusion of the General Synod [of the Gereformeerde Kerken, Nederland]. However, as we now know, even before the Synod was dissolved, while it was still in session, he was struck by the final illness that in God's own purposes brought him to the grave.[1]

In the meantime, there were several weeks of temporary respite after this onset. The old characteristic passion for work resumed. Not only was he able to receive several proofs of this volume from the publisher but [the publisher]

Ed. note: Coenraad Bernardus Bavinck (1866–1941) was the younger brother of Herman Bavinck and the father of renowned missiologist Johan Herman Bavinck (1895–1964). Ordained as a minister in the Christelijke Gereformeerde Kerk in 1890, he served the Gereformeerde Kerken, Nederland congregation of Rotterdam from 1894 until his death.

1. Herman Bavinck went home to his Savior on July 29, 1921.

also discussed with him an additional project, a brochure addressed to the Reformed community of the Netherlands, pointing out to them the incredible seriousness of the times and calling them to unity and faithfulness.[2] Sadly, it was not to be. And, even with respect to the proofs of this volume, he had to be content with reviewing only the initial draft. Shortly after his momentary respite, he again declined to the point of not being able to work.

To ensure that his project, now begun, would come to satisfactory fruition, he approved the publisher's suggestion that the undersigned review the succeeding proofs. Thus, the labor was able to proceed and now, after his departure, it sees the light of day.

May all those who read this final fruit of his richly gifted spirit find in it reasons to gratefully acknowledge this gift and with God's blessing use it for the same purpose for which he labored so many years, namely to value, to further, and to establish the faith that overcomes the world, the faith in which he died and from which a world and a life view have been built.

Rotterdam
August 6, 1921

---

2. Ed. note: Hints of the contents of such a brochure are now available with the publication of G Harinck, C. Van der Kooi, and J. Vree, eds., *Als Bavinck nu maar eens kleur bekende: Aantekeningen van H. Bavinck over de zaak netelenbos, het schriftgezag van de Gereformeerde Kerken (November 1919)* (Amsterdam: VU Uitgeverij, 1994). These notes by Bavinck about the deposition of the Rev J. B. Netelenbos by the Synod of the GKN in 1920 are important for understanding the climate o discussion about the authority of Scripture and for considerations about Bavinck's alleged "change c heart" on these matters. Netelenbos was a former student of Bavinck's and appealed to his teacher' authority for some of his own questioning of the traditional Reformed view on Scripture. Bavinck notes indicate how keenly he followed the discussion.

# Appendix B

## Theology and Religious Studies in Nineteenth-Century Netherlands

For the purposes of this essay, it is important to trace how and to what degree the religious studies approach has thrust aside theology in the state universities in our country. Already in 1848 Professor Opzoomer, before he was appointed as a member of the Government Commission for proposing a bill for higher education, had advised removing the theological faculty[1] from the university. [40] He persisted in his effort on the bill, which he submitted as a minority report of the Government Commission. However, in 1849 the Commission itself advised retaining the theological faculty. On the other hand, in 1868 the bill of Prime Minister Heemskerk mentioned only four faculties. He judged that because of the separation of church and state, the Netherlands Reformed Church itself was responsible for the training of its ministers. In the 1869 bill of Prime Minister Fock, there were no academic departments as such and he committed all final examinations to government commissions, but he did judge that theology as an academic discipline could not be absent from higher education and he established a doctoral degree for theological subjects. The 1874 bill of Prime Minister Geertsema did not wish to retain the theological faculty and was the first that established a department of religious studies. When this bill appeared for a vote in the departmental sections, it was supported by a minority, but another minority wanted to

---

This appendix is the full text of 39 (bottom)–48 in the Dutch text, pages that were abridged and rewritten in the text of chap. 3. See chap. 3, note 3.

    1. Cf., the source note to chap. 3.

maintain the old theological faculty with some changes. However, the *large majority* judged that the theology faculty should be abolished and that the subject of religious studies belonged in the literary department.

This position was in complete agreement with the ideas of Heemskerk, who had in the meantime replaced Prime Minister Geertsema. Heemskerk did not overturn the bill of his predecessor, but on December 11, 1874, he presented a Reply Memorandum about the discussions in the departmental sections, accompanied by a revised bill of the law. Completely in accord with his own ideas of 1868 and with the large majority of the Chamber, Prime Minister Heemskerk proposed terminating the theological department and absorbing the religious studies subjects into the literary department. One would think that this revised bill would receive a favorable reception from the large majority. But what happened? The bill came to the departmental sections and on April 16, 1875, an extensive report appeared. Again, there were three groups. Some wanted to retain the theology faculty, others wanted to replace it with religious studies, and still others wanted, along with the prime minister, to terminate it and to absorb the subjects of religious studies into the literary department. However, this latter group was no longer the large majority; they had become the minority. The majority now wanted to replace the theological faculty with a religious studies department.

Of course, Prime Minister Heemskerk did not understand this change and he expressed surprise about this sudden shift of the majority. [41] What could be the reason that so many members of the Chamber had turned around and now desired a department of religious studies? That reason was not hard to find. Several documents had been presented, especially from the synod of the Netherlands Reformed Church and from the senates of the universities, notably the University of Leiden. The synod was unable or unwilling to create its own institution for the training of its ministers. The theology faculty of Leiden strongly insisted on a department of religious studies. And especially, many members of the Chamber began to fear that the state, by agreeing with the prime minister, would lose all influence in the training of ministers. The state must continue to maintain its influence on the church through the education in the universities! Because of these deliberations the majority of the Chamber had turned around.

The prime minister again proposed a revised bill. He was willing to let go of the idea to include the subjects of religious studies in the literary department. He was also willing to postpone the main decision and to retain the faculties of theology without change until the Netherlands Reformed Church was ready with its own training program. But he was not willing to concede one point: he did not want a department of religious studies in the university. However, the Commission of Reporters (Misters Jonckbloet, Moens, and De Bruijn Kops) proposed an amendment for the establishing of a religious studies department; this proposal was adopted by the Chamber.

However, the Chamber, as proposed by Mister [A.] van Naamen van Ee-mnes, placed the religious studies department under the heading "Faculty of Theology"—a name that did not fit at all anymore. Soon the intrinsic false-hood of this name was revealed conclusively. Since the faculty of theology was intact, the government and some members of the Chamber wanted to place pedagogical and practical theology in the theological faculty, but these proposals were voted down. The Chamber had retained the faculty of theology in name but had in effect introduced a department of religious studies. In this way a strange department came into existence in the state universities: a faculty that is *called* theology but is actually a department of religious studies. In this way theology is maimed and robbed of its heart and life.[2]

The subjects incorporated in this marvelous department are a motley jum-ble. [42] One cannot discern a unity of conception; it would be impossible to construct an encyclopedic overview. The strange mixture betrays the curious history of the manner in which this law was born. Some subjects remind one of the old theology, while others belong undoubtedly to religious studies. Others are of such a nature that one does not rightly know what is intended. Nearly everyone is therefore forced to admit that this is an anomalous situation, since the facts speak loudly.[3] Nevertheless, there are some, also academicians, who are conservative enough first to acquiesce easily in the current situation, then to excuse it, and finally even to praise and defend it. Professor Doctor S. Cramer went so far as to call the law a masterful stroke.[4]

However, this unfortunate development of theological study at our state universities places the professors who must lecture there in a very difficult situation. This is shown most clearly in the case of Professor J. H. Gunning, successor of Professor [L. W. E.] Rauwenhoff at the University of Leiden. When he accepted his position on September 21, 1889, he believed that he could, in good conscience, not just be a member of the department of religious studies but that he also could retain his Christian convictions in his teaching of the philosophy of religion. In his inaugural oration he even professed that the faith of the church must and can be the basic principle and starting point of the philosophy of religion. After all, that faith alone would fully uphold the freedom of research in religion: it alone could explain its origin and develop-ment and thus could also make this learning fruitful for the church.[5]

2. Cf. Mr. B. J. L. de Geer van Jutphaas, *De wet op het hooger onderwijs* (Utrecht: Bijleveld, 1877), 147ff.; A[braham] Kuyper, *"Onnauwkeurig"?* (Amsterdam: J. A. Wormser, 1889), 9ff.

3. See, e.g., [L. W. E.] Rauwenhoff, *Theologische tijdschrift* 12 (1878): 206–12; [G. H.] Lamers, *De wetenschap van den godsdienst: Inleiding* (Utrecht: Breijer, 1891), 57.

4. See S[amuel] Cramer, *Beschrijvende en toegepaste godgeleerdheid* (Amsterdam: Van Kampen, 1890), 14.

5. J[ohannes] H[ermanus] Gunning [Jr.], *De wijsbegeerte van den godsdienst uit het beginsel van het geloof der gemeente* (Utrecht: Breijer, 1889). Further explained in idem, *Het geloof der gemeente als theologische maatstaf des oordeels in de wijsbegeerte van den godsdienst*, parts I–II (Utrecht: Breijer, 1890).

After some time, however, Professor Gunning came to a completely different conviction. He slowly concluded that philosophy of religion is in principle a modern subject that could not and should not be taught by him as a believing theology professor. There was no other solution than to discuss the issue with the other professors. Professor Tiele graciously took over philosophy of religion in exchange for Professor Gunning teaching the history of the doctrine of God. Many times Professor Gunning has explained the principled objection that he gradually developed about the philosophy of religion, and it has recently been clarified in detail and in the same vein by Doctor [H. H.] Meulenbelt.[6] [43] Briefly, the argument goes as follows: Religious studies does not proceed from faith but from unbiased research and impartial love of truth. It does assume in the researcher a general religious inclination but not a positive Christian faith conviction. Rather, it is impartial and unbiased over against all religions, including the Christian religion. It puts all religions on the same level, recognizes no essential differences, and rejects the opposites between true and false. It also judges that the Israelite and Christian religions developed along historical and psychological paths, just as the heathen religions did.

Religious studies tries to find the true, pure religion by impartial, comparative research of all the religions of the world; this pure religion, as the basis of all historical religions, gradually emerges and comes to light. Actually, with this method Christianity is subjected to the abstract understanding of religion as conceived by the practitioner of religious studies. All of this is in direct opposition to the Christian faith. In our faith, Christianity is not one religion among many, not even the highest among many, but the only true religion, and all heathen religions are idolatry. Thus the Christian who practices religious studies forsakes his confession and crosses over into the territory of his opponents.

No one will be able to deny the seriousness and weight of these objections. Neither can Professor [G. H.] Lamers, who in his work on the Science of Religion (*De wetenschap van den godsdienst*) attempts to show that religious studies can and may be practiced from a Christian point of view.[7] But his arguments are not so strong that they cannot be subjected to serious criticism by Doctor Meulenbelt in his "*Medias in res*" [see n. 6 above]. Professor Lamers himself has felt this criticism and has tried to ward off this "rash attack" of Doctor Meulenbelt.[8] Perhaps Professor Lamers has reason

6. J[ohannes] H[ermanus] Gunning, *Werkelijkheid van den godsdienst* (Nijmegen: H. ten Hoet, 1891); idem, *Nog eens: Werkelijkheid van den godsdienst* (Nijmegen: H. ten Hoet, 1891); idem, *Godgeleerdheid en godsdienstwetenschap* (Utrecht: Breijer, 1892); H[endrik] H[uibrecht] Meulenbelt, "*Media in res*": *Een woord over de verhouding van godsdienstwetenschap en theologie en over het Christendom in de inrichting der encyclopaedie van godgeleerdheid* (Nijmegen: H. ten Hoet, 1891), 7–59.

7. Lamers, *De wetenschap van de godsdienst: Inleiding*, 7–20.

8. G. H. Lamers, *Ter zelfverdediging en terechtwijzing: Een onberaden aanval afgeslagen* (Utrecht: Breijer, 1892).

to complain about the tone of Doctor Meulenbelt's writing and to be sad, surprised, and irritated about the manner of his attack.[9] [44] Professor Lamers also rightly points out several weak points in the argument of his attacker. Thus he correctly notes that if Christianity is the object of theology, then the Jewish religion can hardly be included in that category.[10] Equally correct is the objection that Doctor Meulenbelt in his encyclopedia of theology [see n. 6 above] cannot assign an appropriate place to the study of religions.[11] And I also consider the criticism irrefutable that a theology that wants to speak in God's name cannot be consistent with a denial of inspiration.[12] But even though these and other remarks about Doctor Meulenbelt cannot easily be refuted, it is still to be lamented that Professor Lamers did not go more deeply into the real objection of his attacker and that of Professor Gunning against religious studies. Certainly the issue is important enough and fully worth principled treatment.

Apart from the question of whether religious studies can and may be carried out from a Christian point of view, one point becomes more and more obvious: theology and religious studies are incompatible and cannot be contained in one faculty or department. On the one hand, no one has been able to assign a suitable place for religious studies in the encyclopedic system of theology. Theologians have tried to find such a place, and the history of religions has in turn been placed in introduction to theology (Clarisse), historical theology (Doedes, Hagenbach), systematic theology (Raebiger), and throughout the field of theology; it has also been placed in church history and the history of missions (Meulenbelt). But this searching already proves that theologians do not know what to do with religious studies. All have discerned the importance of the study of religions and for better or worse have found a place for it here or there.[13] However, this benefits neither theology nor religious studies. Theology is always theology of a certain religion, and even, if we want to speak accurately, of the Christian religion. But this restriction naturally excludes other religions.

Moreover, religious studies is much too large and important a subject to be satisfied with such a modest place somewhere in theology. [45] This does not mean, of course, that a professor of theology, for the benefit of his disciples, cannot present an overview of the history of religions, a subject of which every theologian today must have some knowledge. Giving such an overview may be a practical requirement but it is not a matter of principle. The history of religions claims a larger space than theologians, for the sake of propriety, are

9. Ibid., 12ff.
10. Ibid., 25–29.
11. Ibid., 31–32.
12. Ibid., 37–39.
13. [Jacob Izak] Doedes, *Encyclopedie der christelijke theologie* (Utrecht: Kemink en Zoon, 1876), 3–94.

willing or able to give in their encyclopedia of theology. In addition, even if the history of religions could in this way be absorbed somewhere into theology, then the philosophy of religion still would not have a place. And that subject certainly is not the least important part of religious studies.

On the other hand, it is equally impossible to absorb theology into religious studies. Professor Lamers[14] favors this arrangement, and Professor Chantepie de la Saussaye calls it formally correct.[15] However, with this arrangement Christian theology is robbed of its character. It is considered on a par with the theology of other religions: it ceases to be positive and, just like other religions, has only historical value. The professor of religious studies might personally consider Christianity to be the highest or even the only true religion, but that view is incidental and not necessary. If his research leads him to value Muhammadanism or Buddhism more highly, he certainly has the right to do so. Then it speaks for itself that there is no longer a place for dogmatic and practical theology; for that reason the law of 1876 eliminated them, and biblical and church historical subjects assume, comparatively, too large a place in this law. A department of religious studies can, according to its principles, not allow a right to exist for any explicit theology. The positive result of comparative research in all religions is taken up in the philosophy of religion. That subject is in effect the dogmatics of religious studies. It does not matter if this philosophy of religion has come in the place of dogmatics or of natural theology; it has, in fact, assumed the status and significance of dogmatics.

Professor Gunning has therefore clearly seen the incompatibility of theology and religious studies. In this respect, his reservations are irrefutable. The problem is that he has put the issue too personally by claiming that as a Christian theologian he cannot teach the philosophy of religions, and he is satisfied that from now on his subject will be taught again by a modernistic colleague. [46] This issue, however, is not subjective and personal but objective and theological. Theology and religious studies exclude each other if they both strive for the rank of a departmental discipline. In the one there is no place for the other. If religious studies has its own department, then theology must disappear, and vice versa. This seems so clear that it really is strange that many attempts are still made to absorb the one into the other.

If this is the situation, then the choice about which of the two has a right to the rank of a department is not in doubt. One reason would be sufficient: a department of religious studies would not tolerate a place for theology anywhere in the university, while a department of theology can fully recognize and honor religious studies. A religious studies department is naturally

14. Lamers, *De wetenschap van den godsdienst: Inleiding*, 22.
15. Ch[antepie] de la Saussaye, *Lehrbuch der Religionsgeschichte*, 2 vols. (Freiburg: Mohr, 1887–89). I:7 [ed. note: cf. 2nd ed., 1897; 3rd ed., 1905].

intolerant and does not permit theology in the realm of university disciplines. But a theology department certainly does not desire that the history and philosophy of religion be excluded from the university.

One must also add that the indispensability of good theology is felt more and more. For years people shouted, "No doctrine but life; religion is not a matter of the mind but of feeling, a matter of the emotions." But the one-sidedness of this theory becomes more and more obvious. Everywhere one sees the awakening of the need for explicit doctrine, for a certain content of faith. Religion is also serving God with the mind, and it therefore must be the truth and must provide knowledge (John 17:3). Religion cannot be found in unconscious, dark, emotional sensations. The significance of doctrine for life is recognized more and more and the scorn for dogma seems to be near an end. Now and then there are also voices in our country that speak differently and that want a clear answer to the question about the only comfort in life and in death. And the great objection that has been lodged against the existence of theology finally seems to be losing force. Since Kant, some have, with all kinds of feelings and in all kinds of ways, repeated [the watchword] that no knowledge of God and of the supernatural is possible; they claimed that natural theology is not scientific, that the proofs for the existence of God have no value, and that God is unknowable. But this agnosticism seems to be disputed more and more. [47] The proofs for the existence of God are again being honored. Doctor A. Bruining has recently revived the study of those proofs in our country.[16] Some signs of the times indicate a reaction that will be good for theology.

On the other hand, the objections against a department of religious studies are certainly not to be considered minor. First, if it maintains the right and worth of its object of study—religion—it is hampered by the same objection that denies the right of existence to theology. After all, religion assumes two facts: the existence and knowability of God. His right and worth can be maintained only if God exists and reveals himself to humanity in some way or other. Professor Lamers therefore says rightly that the philosophy of religion must finally end in objective reality as the ground for subjective phenomena.[17] Whoever denies God's existence and revelation completely can discern only a pathological phenomenon of the human spirit in religion.

Second, it is not clear why religion must be the subject of its own academic discipline while other psychic phenomena—such as moral life, intellectual life, and aesthetic life—are researched and discussed in the department of literature and philosophy. One can, at the most, find a practical reason for this, but there is no argument from principle unless one again finds the right of existence for religious studies in theology, in the existence and knowability of God.

16. A[lbert] Bruining, *Het bestaan van God* (Leiden: Van Doesburgh, 1891).
17. Lamers, *De wetenschap van den godsdienst: Inleiding*, 52.

Third, the establishment of a department of religious studies in our [Dutch] universities is not in agreement with the scientific demand that is required for the study of religions. Although the study of the Christian religion is assigned to several professors, only one professor is appointed for the study of all the other religions (with the exception of Judaism and Christianity). With that in mind, Professor A. Pierson rightly said, "The description of many religions appears to me to be an interesting compilation, but without scientific worth."[18] His colleague Professor de la Saussaye answered that this objection could be refuted only by a truly scientific study.[19] But the question is exactly whether a truly scientific study of the material is possible in this case and whether the study of sources (a first requirement of science) is not virtually impossible. [48] Without wanting to diminish the value of the handbooks of the history of religion, some doubt seems to be justified here.

Finally, a department of religious studies is hampered by yet another objection. If it were established true to its ideal, and not because of practical obligations, it would not prepare [a student] for any profession and thus would not appeal to any student. Students in the university not only seek knowledge, but most of them also want, primarily, a preparation and training for a profession in church or society. A department of religious studies, however, is completely outside everyday life and does not prepare for anything. And even in our country, where theology has in various ways compromised with the "real world," one often hears complaints that theological study does not sufficiently take into account the office and ministry for which students are to be trained.

For all these reasons one must disapprove of our country's 1876 law that changed the [university] departments of theology into departments of religious studies.

18. A[llard] Pierson, *Studiën over Johannes Kalvijn*, part 2, *Nieuwe studiën over Johannes Kalvijn (1536–1541)* (Amsterdam: Van Kampen, 1883), vii.
19. De la Saussaye, *Lehrbuch der Religionsgeschichte*, I:5.

# Scripture Index

# Name Index

Agricola, Johann, 218
Albarda, J. W., 235
Albert the Great, 95n29
Alcuin, 213, 214
Alembert, Jean d', 159n36, 160n38
Ambrose, 212, 218
Ammon, C. F. von, 262
Anaxagoras, 106
Aristotle, 94, 96, 106, 180, 213, 214, 215, 216, 217, 238, 246, 268, 269
Athanasius, 96
Augustine, 73, 96, 176, 186, 200, 212, 246, 255, 269
Ausonius, 211
Averroes, 230

Bacon, Francis, 98, 200, 231, 232, 238
Bacon, Roger, 95n29, 231
Baer, Ernst von, 101
Bagehot, Walter, 266
Balfour, A. J., 193
Barrett, W. F., 193, 193n51
Barth, Karl, 9
Basil the Great, 212
Baum, 247
Baumgarten, Alexander Gottlieb, 245
Bavinck, Coenraad Bernardus, 7n2, 10, 279
Bavinck, Herman, 7, 7n1, 7n2, 8, 8n5, 9, 10, 11, 13, 14, 15, 16, 17, 18, 19, 21, 22, 23, 24, 24n2, 25, 29n2, 49, 49n1, 50n2, 53n3, 53n4, 55n5, 55n6, 63n2, 64n2, 66n3, 68n4, 70n5, 78n7, 81, 81n1, 86n11, 89, 96n34, 105n1, 108n2, 155n30, 156n31, 178n10, 182n19,

183n24, 194n54, 195n57, 211n1, 237n10, 250n1, 254n2, 274n3, 279, 279n1, 280n2
Bavinck, Jan, 14
Bavinck, Johan Herman, 279
Bebel, August, 208
Becker, Julius, 194n52, 195n56
Bekker, Balthasar, 88
Bennett, Edward T., 193, 193n51
Bergemann, Paul, 208
Bergson, Henri, 196n58, 207
Berlage, Hendrick Petrus, 253
Berland, 253
Berolzheimer, Fritz, 275
Bierma, Jan Watzes, 229n7
Biesterveld, Petrus, 21
Binet, Alfred, 192n49
Bioleau, N., 256
Bismarck, O. E. L., 264
Boccaccio, Giovanni, 216
Boeckh, August, 221
Boethius, 213, 214
Bois-Reymond, Emil Heinrich du, 102n44, 114, 175, 175n1, 175n2, 183
Bois-Reymond, Paul David Gustav du, 83–84, 84n5, 85, 86, 87, 89, 101
Bolkesteyn, H., 229n7
Bolt, J., 8n5
Bon, Gustave le, 187n31, 187n33
Bonaventura, 246
Bonebakker, 239
Bongaerts, M. C. E., 235
Bonnot, Jules, 147, 147n3
Bonus, A., 207

292

# Subject Index

Absolute, 265
absolutism, 278
adolescence, 64
adulthood, 199
aesthetics, 10, 245–60
affections, 258
age, 199
agnosticism, 103, 197, 254, 287
agriculture, 153
alchemy, 230
Alexander the Great, 225–26, 227
Alexandria, 210, 211
Alliance of Reformed
    Churches holding the
    Presbyterian System, 7
*Altertumswissenschaft*, 220, 226
Anabaptists, 17, 38, 133
anarchism, 142, 276, 278
    in art, 253
Anaxagoras, 92
animism, 86–87, 179n11, 194
anthropology, 58
antiquity, 209, 241–42
Anti-Revolutionary Party, 81n1, 82, 143
Apostles' Creed, 33, 97
apperception, 171, 181, 189
Arabs, 93–94, 95
Arab scholars, 214
archaeological explorations, 221–23

Aristotle, 93, 94, 96, 106, 118, 180, 214, 216, 246
    on politics, 263, 268–69
arithmetic, 92
art, 249, 252–53
    and culture, 250
    and nature, 246–47
    and science, 255
    and technology, 255
    "art for art's sake," 251
artist, gifts of, 251–52
asceticism, 129, 133, 194, 212, 229
associated conscience, 177
assurance, 26
Assyrians, 92
Assyriology, 56
astrology, 230
astronomy, 92, 230
Athanasius, 96
atheism, 103
Atomism, 106, 111–12
atonement, 43
Attic Greek, 210, 212, 225, 227, 228
Augustine, 96, 97, 200, 212, 255, 269
authority, 210
autonomy, 52
awakening, 70–74, 77
awareness, 176

Babylonians, 92
Bacon, Francis, 26, 98, 231–32, 238
Bacon, Roger, 231
Baghdad, 94
Baumgarten, Alexander Gottlieb, 245
Bavinck, C. B., 279
Bavinck, Herman
    death of, 21, 24, 279
    first visit to North America, 7
    modesty, 21
    public career, 10
beauty, 10, 245–60, 274
    in diversity, 145
    of nature, 250
Bebart, Johann Friedrich, 206
becoming, 106, 118, 143
being, 105–6, 118, 143, 172
    and mechanical worldview, 110–11
Belgic Confession, 99
Bergemann, Paul, 208
Bible
    and archaeology, 222–23
    diversity and organic unity, 23
    on nature, 96
biology, 112
body and soul, 166, 179, 181, 202
Boethius, 213, 214